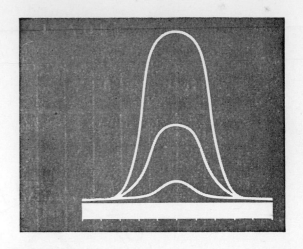

STANFORD-BINET

Manual for the Third Revision

LEWIS M. TERMAN

Late Professor   Stanford University

WITH REVISED IQ TABLES BY SAMUEL R. PINNEAU CHILD STUDY CENTER
SAN FERNANDO VALLEY STATE COLLEGE

INTELLIGENCE SCALE

Form L—M

MAUD A. MERRILL

Professor Emeritus   Stanford University

HOUGHTON MIFFLIN COMPANY • *Boston* • The Riverside Press

ACKNOWLEDGEMENTS

Grateful acknowledgement is made to authors, publishers, and other copyright holders for permission to reprint from the copyright material listed below.

Anastasi, A. *Psychological Testing.* New York: Macmillan, 1954.
Bradway, K. P., et al., "Preschool IQs after Twenty-five Years," *J. Educ. Psychol.,* 49, 1958.
Cronbach, L. J. *Essentials of Psychological Testing.* New York: Harper, 1949.
Hebb, D. O. *Organization of Behavior.* New York: Wiley, 1949.
McNemar, Q. *The Revision of the Stanford-Binet Scale.* Boston: Houghton Mifflin, 1942.
Sontag, L. W., Baker, C. T., and Nelson, V. L. "Mental Growth and Personality Development: A Longitudinal Study," *Monogr. Soc. Res. in Child Developm.,* 23, 68, No. 2, 1958.
Terman, L. M. *The Measurement of Intelligence.* Boston: Houghton Mifflin, 1916.
Terman, L. M. and Merrill, M. A. *Measuring Intelligence.* Boston: Houghton Mifflin, 1937.

The Riverside Press

CAMBRIDGE, MASSACHUSETTS
PRINTED IN THE U.S.A.

P r e f a c e The present revision of the Stanford-Binet Tests aims at providing test users with a single scale that, while preserving the characteristic features of previous revisions, eliminates out-of-date content and improves general structure. Items making up the new L–M Form have been chosen from those of the 1937 scales. The retained items were selected because they have continued to meet the requirements of validity and reliability and have been shown to be suitable in form and content as a result of testings of between four and five thousand subjects. The assessment of these tests provides reasonable assurance to test users that the third Revision of the Stanford-Binet Scales can be relied upon to perform even more dependably the functions that have come to be expected of them.

It has not been either feasible or expedient to repeat the ten-year research program of the 1930's upon which the 1937 standardization was based. Some sources of error in test construction may remain, but it is hoped that this revision will provide its users with an instrument whose value has been enhanced by the wealth of important information that has been accumulated concerning its use in the years since 1916 when the first Stanford revision was published.

The Stanford revision has lost its senior author. Dr. Terman, to whom the development of mental testing owes more than to any one of his generation, died on December 21, 1956. He was the last of the pioneers. Before his death, plans for the third Revision had been formulated and were well on their way toward completion.

It is a pleasant task to acknowledge the indebtedness of both Dr. Terman and me to colleagues and to former students who have contributed so generously of their time and counsel; to school people for their hearty cooperation; to our highly competent and devoted research staff; and to our publishers whose backing and support have facilitated our project since its inception. Specific acknowledgment to our project assistants and to the research people who have made available their test records for our use has been made in appropriate places in the text. In addition to her contribution of pre-school test records, Dr. Nancy Bayley offered many valuable suggestions. I am grateful to Dr. Hal Robinson and to Dr. C. L. Winder for their critical reading of the text. My most special debt in completing this revision is to Dr. Nancy Robinson for her devoted and highly skilled assistance in the arduous task of checking innumerable details of test procedure and standardization and her discerning reading of the entire text. Finally I wish to express my particular indebtedness to Dr. Quinn McNemar for countless aids, suggestions, ideas, and criticisms. Through two revisions of the Stanford-Binet he has contributed expert statistical advice and has helped divert us from error. I am grateful to him now for his continuing friendly counsel.

Maud A. Merrill

Stanford, California

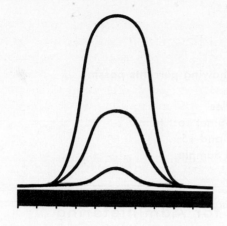

Contents

PART ONE · Essential Features of the Stanford Revisions

	PAGE
1. THE FIRST REVISION, 1916	5
2. THE SECOND REVISION, 1937	7
The 1937 Revision a Binet type test	7
Item selection	9
Selection of subjects	9
Reliability and validity	10
3. THE THIRD REVISION, 1960	12
Preliminary Considerations	12
Criteria for the selection of items	13
Locating items in the scale	14
Factors affecting IQ variability	14
IQ variability in relation to age	15
Correlations between retests	16
A frame of reference for classifying IQs	17
Problems involved in test revision	19
Essential Features of the 1960 Scale	20
Sources of material for scale revision	21
Determining the difficulty of items	23
Procedures employed in the analysis of test records	24
Clarification of scoring principles and test administration	25

Changes in the 1960 Scale   25
   Content   25
   Structural changes   26
   Revised IQ tables   27
Shifts in Item Difficulty   28
   Characteristics of curves showing percents passing   29
Validity and Reliability   32
Abilities Sampled by the Scales   33
Factor Analyses of Stanford-Binet Test Items   34
Stratified Samples at Ages 6 and 15   35
The Two-and-a-half-year-old Sample   37
Summary   39

PART TWO · Guide for Administering and Scoring - Form L-M

TESTING PROCEDURE   45

1. GENERAL DIRECTIONS   46

Adherence to Standard Procedure   47
   Working within a frame   47
   Order of giving the tests   48
General Principles of Procedure   49
   When may a question be repeated?   49
   Ambiguous responses   49
The Importance of Rapport   50
The Testing of Preschool Children   53
The Appraisal of Responses   55
   Mastery of the scoring rules   55
   Avoidance of the "halo" effect   55
   Scoring not purely mechanical   56
Administering the Tests   56
   The surroundings   56
   The presence of others   57
   Manipulating the test material   57
   Duration of examination   58
   To maintain standard conditions of testing   58
   Where to begin testing   59
   Scattering of successes   59
   Determining the basal age and ceiling (maximal) level   60
   Abbreviated tests   61
   Alternative tests   62
Computation of MA Scores   62
Finding the IQ   64

2. SPECIFIC INSTRUCTIONS FOR ADMINISTERING FORM L–M

YEAR	PAGE	YEAR	PAGE
II	67	IX	92
II–6	69	X	94
III	71	XI	97
III–6	74	XII	99
IV	76	XIII	102
IV–6	79	XIV	105
V	81	Average Adult	109
VI	83	Superior Adult I	113
VII	86	Superior Adult II	115
VIII	88	Superior Adult III	119

3. SCORING STANDARDS FOR FORM L–M

SCORING PROCEDURE   125

YEAR	PAGE	YEAR	PAGE
II	126	IX	168
II–6	129	X	181
III	130	XI	187
III–6	132	XII	196
IV	135	XIII	200
IV–6	138	XIV	204
V	140	Average Adult	208
VI	145	Superior Adult I	218
VII	151	Superior Adult II	222
VIII	160	Superior Adult III	227
		Vocabulary	232

PART THREE · Revised Intelligence Quotient Tables

PINNEAU REVISED IQ TABLES   257

APPENDIX A Conversion Tables   339

APPENDIX B Tests of the L–M Scale in 1937 and in 1960   342

APPENDIX C Corrected CA Divisors for Ages beyond 13–00   348

REFERENCES   351

INDEX   355

List of Tables

PAGE

1. Distribution of IQs of the 1937 Standardization Group . . . 18

2. The Assessment Group Tabulated by Areas 21

3. Distribution of Successes on the Reading and Report Test . . 31

4. Average Percent Passing 1937 Revision and the 1960 Stratified
   Samples 32

5. Percentage Distribution of Occupations of Fathers 37

6. Distribution by Grade of 100 Fifteen-year-olds 37

7. Stratified Samples Compared with Equivalent Age Groups in 38
   1937 . . . .

8. Means and Standard Deviations for Two-and-a-half-year-olds 38

List of Figures

                                                                            PAGE

Fig. 1.   Scattergram of Correlation Between L and M IQs
               at CA7 11

Fig. 2, 3.   Distributions of Percents Passing Two Tests of
               the 1937 Scale 15

Fig. 4.   Distribution of Composite IQs of the 1937
               Standardization Group 18

Fig. 5-10   Typical Curves 30

Fig. 11.   Distribution of IQs of 850 Two-and-a-half-
               year-olds 39

Copying a Circle (III, 5) 131

Drawing a Vertical Line (III, 6) 132

Picture Completion: Man (V, 1) 141

Copying a Square (V, 4) 144

Copying a Diamond (VII, 3) 156

Paper Cutting (IX, 1) 170

Memory for Designs I (IX, 3) 175

Memory for Designs II (XII, A) 199

Plan of Search (XIII, 1) 200

STANFORD-BINET INTELLIGENCE SCALE

PART ONE ▶

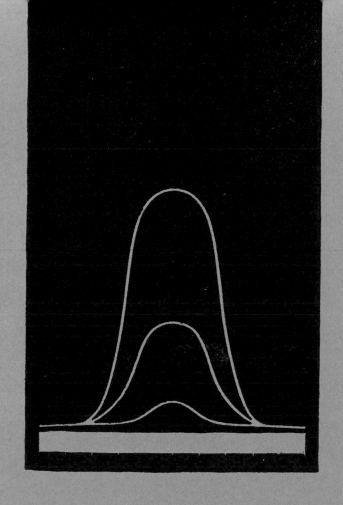

Essential Features of the
Stanford Revisions

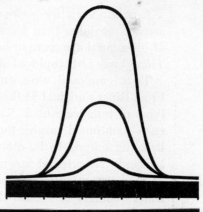

ESSENTIAL FEATURES OF THE STANFORD REVISIONS

1. THE FIRST REVISION, 1916

Terman's first revision of the scale originally devised by Binet and Simon was published in 1916 and constituted a pioneering effort to apply the methods of precision which were being developed in the new science of psychology to the measurement of intellectual abilities. *The Measurement of Intelligence* offered, as its subtitle indicated, "An explanation of and complete guide for the use of the Stanford Revision and Extension of the Binet-Simon Intelligence Scale" (20). This revision of the Binet-Simon scale incorporated the features that characterize scales of the Binet type, that is, the use of age standards, the kinds of mental functions brought into play, and the concept of measurement of a "general intelligence" which functions as mental adaptability to new problems.

The 1916 Scale attempted to provide standards of intellectual performance for average American-born children from age three to young adulthood, which was assumed, on the basis of available information for purposes of the scale, to be age 16. Tests were arranged in order of difficulty by age levels. The intellectual ability of an individual, determined by his performance on the scale, was judged by comparison with the standards of performance for normal children of different ages.

Intelligence ratings were expressed as mental age scores. One of Binet's basic assumptions of the original scale was that a person is thought of as normal if he can do the things persons of his age normally do, retarded if his test performance corresponds to the performance of persons younger than himself, and accelerated if his performance level exceeds that of persons his own age.

A person's relative position in his own age group (average, brighter than average, or duller than average) Terman indicated by computing the ratio of his mental age score to his chronological age, the conventional ratio IQ. The IQ was first employed in the 1916 scale.

Tests employed were varied and heterogeneous, as Binet's had been. From Binet's original 54 the number of tests was increased to 90. The same types of tests were used. Tests involving the "more complex mental processes" continued to give the best results in differentiating persons judged by other criteria to be more intelligent from those judged to be less intelligent. No attempt was made to measure separate mental faculties such as memory, attention, sensory discrimination, etc. It had been one of Binet's sources of success that he had abandoned the old laboratory approaches to the measurement of "mental faculties or functions" for the more dynamic method of measuring intelligence at work. This consisted of testing a combined functional activity which conceived intelligence to be the sum of the thought processes which are involved in mental adaptation. His best known description emphasizes direction, adaptation, and self-criticism as the aspects characterizing intelligence in action.

The 1916 Stanford scale increased the number of the old Binet items by about a third. Tests that were found to have inadequate discriminative value were dropped. The scale was standardized on a sample of approximately a thousand children and four hundred adults. Careful attention was given to the selection of these cases in an effort to obtain a representative sample of the general American population. This constituted a pioneering step in the all-important development of sampling practices to be further refined in the construction of later scales.

Of equal importance for the development of testing techniques was the provision, for the first time, of detailed instructions for administering and scoring each test. Each test constituted "an abbreviated experiment" in which behavior was observed under controlled conditions and interpreted with a degree of objectivity heretofore unsought in the field of measurement of mental ability.

During the twenties and early thirties the use of this scale both for research and for clinical diagnostic purposes formed the broad experimental basis for later revisions. Although affording a satisfactorily valid and reliable measure over a fairly wide intermediate range, abilities below the mental age of four and at the adult levels were very inadequately sampled. Certain tests of the scale were found to have low validity, instructions for administering and scoring were still lacking in the precision necessary to insure objectivity and comparability of results, and no alternative form was available.

It was to correct these recognized faults of the scale and to afford a more adequate sampling, both of subjects and of their abilities, that the second revision of the Stanford scale was undertaken.

2. THE SECOND REVISION, 1937

In 1937, *Measuring Intelligence,* the most extensive and comprehensive of the Stanford Revisions, was published by Terman and Merrill (21). This second revision of the scale, following upon years of experience in the practical use of intelligence tests, incorporated the results of a ten-year research and standardization project.

During the years intervening between the publication of the 1916 scale and the beginning of work on the second revision, a large amount of information had been accumulated on the behavior of various types of mental tests, the interrelationships of tested abilities, and the relative merits of specific tests as measures of intelligence. Certain types of tests had generally proved to have higher correlations with the various independent estimates of the trait than others. And whether the test maker defined the trait he proposed to measure as "general mental adaptability," as "capacity to learn," or as "simply a working hypothesis," there was considerable amount of agreement on which types of tests yielded the highest correlations with acceptable criteria of intelligence.

The main features of the 1937 revision are too well known to need extensive review here. However, a brief résumé of standardization procedures and re-examination of the rationale underlying their use seems to be indicated for two reasons: 1) some of the current criticisms still reflect misunderstandings concerning the technical procedures employed in the development of the scale and 2) because in current popular usage IQ is so often used as a synonym for intelligence, unrealistic expectations have come to be attached to intelligence tests. So, while it is not our purpose to review the techniques employed in the construction procedures of the two forms which make up the 1937 scale,[1] certain construction procedures do need re-emphasis because of their importance for understanding the essential characteristics of the scale and the selection of materials from the 1937 scale to be included in the 1960 scale.

The 1937 revision a Binet-type test

The scale, as revised in 1937, retained the distinguishing characteristics of Binet-type tests, utilizing the same assumptions, methods, and principles. It made use of age standards of performance and the assumption that general intelligence is a trait which develops with age. It provided a wider sampling of the same kinds of mental activities and it remained a measure of general ability rather than of specific or related groups of abilities.

---

[1] A detailed account of the standardization procedures will be found in the authors' *Measuring Intelligence* (21) and an analysis of procedures essential to the standardization in McNemar's *The Revision of the Stanford-Binet Scale* (16).

The 1937 revision remained an age scale. In spite of the difficulties involved in the construction of an age scale, it seemed important to retain the mental age concept because it is so essentially identified with Binet tests, especially the Stanford-Binet, and with the clinical thinking that has developed in connection with its use. The expression of a test result in terms of age norms is simple and unambiguous and assumes no statistical sophistication on the part of the layman. It is the least pretentious of units for the estimation of mental level. Clinicians have found that this is an easily accepted and non-threatening way of helping parents understand the needs and limitations of the retarded and the capabilities of the gifted.

The same kinds of test situations that had proved useful in the 1916 scale continued to prove useful in the second revision. So the 1937 scale continued to sample the same kinds of mental activities that Binet had found to be useful in distinguishing differences in intelligence. Prominent among subtests that have proved their worth are analogies, opposites, comprehension, vocabulary, similarities and differences, verbal and pictorial completions, absurdities, drawing designs, and memory for meaningful material and for digits. Though the 1937 scale provided a wider sampling of abilities than did the earlier scale, including more pictorial and manipulative items, it was still heavily weighted with test situations in which verbal ability was an essential element. Many of the so-called performance test items tried out for inclusion in the scale were eliminated because they contributed little or nothing to the total score. They were not valid items for this scale.

The 1937 scale, with its two comparable forms of 129 subtests each, remained, like the 1916 scale and like Binet's original scale, an instrument for the measurement of "general intelligence." Like them it included a great variety of heterogeneous test items. Some of the items contributed more to the total than did others, but all made sufficient contribution to the total to justify their inclusion in the scale; that is, they had to be demonstrably suited to the measurement of "general mental ability" as that term was understood by the test makers and users.

The primary criterion to be satisfied, characteristic of tests of the Binet type, was to secure such an arrangement of subtests constituting the scale that the mean mental age of unselected subjects should agree closely with mean chronological age. Perfect agreement would be indicated by a mean IQ of 100 at each successive age level. In order to accomplish this it was necessary (a) to select a representative population at each age, and (b) to allocate the subtests to the proper age levels.

This posed a two-fold sampling problem: first, the selection of test items that could be shown to be fairly representative samples of intelligent behavior at the various age levels, and second, the selection of persons whose responses were to provide standards or norms for such behavior.

Item selection

The search for suitable test material yielded hundreds of test items which were sifted for their merit in providing standard situations in which intelligent behavior could be observed. Trial items for the final scale were selected first, because they would probably correlate well with acceptable criteria of intelligence; second, because experimental try-out had shown a rapid increase in per cent passing of children of known mental age (or CA for preschool children); and third, because an acceptable index of correspondence between item and criterion had been obtained for each item in the critical ratio of the difference between the mean mental ages of subjects passing the item and those failing it.

The items thus selected, 209 making up the provisional Form L and 199 the provisional Form M, were further analyzed after the two forms had been administered to a carefully chosen sample of 3184 subjects. Practical considerations were taken into account as well as statistical factors in determining the suitability of items for inclusion in the final scales. Factors that contributed to greater objectivity in scoring, made for ease of administration, and enhanced interest, as well as variety of content were important considerations in the choice of materials for the scale.

In the final statistical analysis two procedures contributed further data on validity: (a) again, each item had to show an increase in per cent passing for the successive age levels; and (b) the biserial correlation of each subtest with the total score had to be high enough to indicate that each contributed to what the scale as a whole was measuring.

Selection of subjects

The importance of securing a representative group of children to serve as subjects for the standardization of the tests cannot be overestimated. Because of its importance in the establishment of norms for the scale elaborate precautions were taken to insure that at each age level a representative group of children was tested. The final 1937 standardization group consisted of 3184 native-born white subjects, including approximately 100 subjects at each half-year interval from 1½ to 5½ years, 200 at each age from 6 to 14, and 100 at each age from 15 to 18. Every age group was equally divided between the sexes. Limitation of the group to subjects who were within one month of a birthday (or half-year birthday) gave homogeneous groups. Age samplings below 7 and above 14 gave the most trouble.

Details of the sampling procedure have been fully described in *Measuring Intelligence* (21, pp. 12–21). They included such considerations as efforts to secure an adequate geographical distribution, testing in 17 communities in 11 widely separated states, choice of urban, suburban, and rural communities, the selection of schools within a community and the use of methods obtaining random age sampling wherever testing was done. Despite such precautions, the sample proved to be slightly higher in socioeconomic level than the census figures indicated for the general population and to include a disproportionate number of urban as contrasted to rural subjects. Adjustments were made in mean IQs to allow for these sampling inadequacies (21, p. 36).

Reliability and validity

Evidence concerning the reliability of the 1937 scale was derived from comparisons afforded by scores obtained on Form L with those obtained on Form M for the standardization group. Tests on the two forms were given less than a week apart. Equivalence of the two forms and stability of the obtained IQs were indicated by the generally high degree of relationship found.

Important especially because of their clinical implications are certain characteristics of the relationship that was found between (a) reliability and age, and (b) between reliability and IQ level of subjects. McNemar's analysis of the standardization data (16, pp. 55–70) indicated that the 1937 scale was more reliable for older than for younger children and more reliable for lower than for higher IQs. The scale was most reliable at the point where the clinician was most likely to need to make differentiations of greatest diagnostic importance.

Since reliability is a function of both age and magnitude of IQ it was necessary to compute reliability coefficients for the ages separately. At ages 2½ to 5½, the reliability coefficients range from .83 (for IQs 140–149) to .91 (for IQs 60–69); at ages 6 to 13, the range is from .91 (for IQs 140–149) to .97 (for IQs 60–69); and at ages 14 to 18, the range is from .95 (for IQs 140–149) to .98 (for IQs 60–69).

A graphic illustration of the relationship between level of IQ and scale reliability is afforded by the scattergram shown in Figure 1. The plot shows the distribution of IQs obtained by seven-year-old children of the 1937 standardization group on Form L and Form M. Examination of the figure reveals that there is a closer relationship between L and M IQs at the lower IQ levels than at the higher. This characteristic "fan-shaped" distribution was found to be typical of all age levels.

This relationship between scale reliability and magnitude of IQ is an essential feature of the IQ technique employed in an age scale. It must exist if IQs are to have constant meaning from one age level to another. As we shall see, the variability of mental age scores increases as age increases. It should be expected that a subject's fluctuation in mental age

FIGURE 1

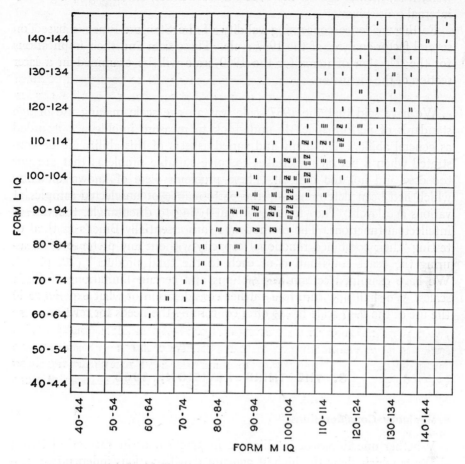

Scattergram of Correlation between L and M IQs at CA7 (1937) (21, p. 45)

score will be proportional, not to the variability of his chronological age group, but to the variability of his mental age group. Seven-year-olds who have IQs in the 140–149 range will have mental ages in the neighborhood of 10 and show greater variability than seven-year-olds who have IQs in the 60–69 range and mental ages between 4 and 5.

The item selection procedures employed in the development of the 1937 scale also offer the chief evidence of the validity of the scale. As we have already pointed out, the preliminary selection of items was based on evidence that the items were testing the same kinds of mental functions that had proved useful in the 1916 scale. Next, each item must show an increase in per cent passing from one age to the next, and finally, each item must correlate with the scale as a whole. The various criteria were, thus, mental age on the 1916 Stanford-Binet, chronological age, and internal consistency.

Further evidence concerning validity of the Stanford-Binet is based on several factor analyses of the 1937 scale. These data and their implications for the selection of items for the 1960 scale will be examined in a later section of the discussion.

We have said that the 1937 scale was an age scale making use of age standards of performance. It undertook to measure intelligence regarded as general ability. The many and varied aspects of this ability are demonstrated when a person undertakes to solve suitable problems that are not too easy and not too difficult. These problems were of known difficulty which had been determined by the performance of unselected samples at various age levels. They tested, without trying to disentangle, the various intellectual functions. The method was thus essentially Binet's method of testing "their combined functional capacity without any pretense of measuring the exact contribution of each to the total product" (20, p. 43). We have examined certain implications and certain limitations of Binet scales. We shall now turn to a further consideration of what experience in the use of the 1937 scale has to offer concerning the needs for revision.

3. THE THIRD REVISION, 1960

Preliminary Considerations

Whether one thinks of intelligence in practical or in theoretical terms, the tests which show the highest agreement with various independent estimates of the trait tend to be highly intercorrelated. In general there has been a fair amount of agreement among test makers concerning the types of situations which best discriminate differences in intelligence. Studies of internal consistency, whether employing factorial methods or correlation of items with total score, agree closely in showing tests such as abstract words, vocabulary, analogies, verbal absurdities and the like to have higher efficiency in differentiating degrees of *general intellectual ability* than do the manipulative items in the scale (7, 16).

The aim of the 1937 scale to provide a measure of general intelligence has been fairly successfully realized, but it should be clear that the very factors that contribute to its success as a measure of general intelligence must interfere with its usefulness as a measure of the various separate aspects of mentality which many test users expect of an intelligence test. Items were included in the scale because they contributed to the total score. For example, vocabulary at the VI-year level correlated with the total score .65, finding missing parts in a picture .46, tracing a maze .60. Each contributed to the total score, but each involves several special aspects of intellectual ability. The maze test, for instance, involves motor coordination, depends upon comprehension of verbal instructions, upon remembering, perceiving, the ability to reason, and many other behaviors. Grouping tests together according to some logical classification scheme on the basis of some special ability which they appear to have in common has little psychological justification. *Too, such classifications as have been proposed have little in common, varying from one test user to another, and have often been proposed with no attempt at validation.* One scheme, for instance, classifies the maze test as a "reasoning test"; according to a second classification scheme the same item is in the performance category.

Attempts to construct profiles that are psychologically meaningful on tests designed to yield a single measure of general mental ability have been very discouraging. Profile analysis, as Cronbach points out, "tempts the psychologist to make more definite diagnoses than its validity warrants" (8, p. 150).

But if a test is not suited to the measurement of differential aptitudes, that is not to say that it offers meager opportunities for observation. The skillful and experienced clinician may make meaningful, even if unquantified, observations on the qualitative aspects of a subject's performance, his methods of work, his approach to problems, and many other clinically significant areas of his behavior in the standard situations presented by the test. Many important personality characteristics are revealed and may be observed in the course of testing. The Stanford-Binet presents a rich field for such observations. *And, of course, the problem of the validity of the clinician is as pertinent to the effectiveness of testing as the validity of the tests.* Recognizing the limitations of a test is an element of strength in its usefulness.

Criteria for the selection of items

In the development of an age scale the test maker is concerned with the selection of tests that show an increase in per cent passing at successive age levels. In the measurement of a developing function like intelligence this requirement is of major importance. Such data supply information concerning validity and help determine the difficulty of the item and its location in the scale. An item for an age scale "cannot be regarded as valid unless it yields a larger per cent passing for successive age levels through childhood" (16, p. 83). It will be, of course, equally obvious that increase in per cent passing with age does not *insure* validity. Height increases with age, so to a point does strength of grip, and yet, of course, measures of such physical traits are uncorrelated with total score on the test, hence are not coherent with the scale as a whole. Nor would they correlate significantly with other criteria of intelligence.

Locating items in the scale

In addition to data on validity, important information concerning the difficulty of the specific items for their location in the scale is contributed by the per cents passing at successive ages. If the test score is to be expressed in terms of mental age units, then at each successive age level the mean mental age that the test gives must equal mean chronological age. And in order to appoximate this result, tests must be properly allocated to the various age levels.

This is an empirical procedure. No single per cent passing can be *the correct* percentage for all age levels because no single per cent passing for all age levels will give a scale in which average mental age will equal average chronological age at all age levels. In general, at the younger ages the percentages are somewhat higher than are those at the upper ages where mental age units are smaller. There is less difference between a twelve-year-old and a thirteen-year-old in terms of measureable mental age than there is between a six-year-old and a seven-year-old, and the differences between mental age levels become still more striking when a two-year-old is compared with a three-year-old. Thus, with the 1937 scale, Form L, at the III-year level a correctly located item (Fig. 2), building a bridge with blocks, was passed by 73 per cent of three-year-olds, whereas the vocabulary test at the X-year level (Fig. 3) was passed by only 59 per cent of ten-year-olds. And because no items in our scales are perfect or ideal items for measuring intelligence, and no sample is ever entirely free from the influence of selective factors, the percentage will not be exactly the same for each test at each age level.

Factors affecting IQ variability

Curves of per cent passing by age affect the variability of IQs. If at a given age level some of the items are too hard, that is, they are passed by a lower percentage of the subjects at that age, and the rest of the items, to offset the hard ones, are a little too easy, then the variability of the IQs for subjects of this age will be restricted in comparison with those for subjects of other age levels where there is a better distribution of per cents passing. The opposite effect will be achieved where there is too great a concentration of items of medium difficulty; the resulting IQs will have greater variability (16, p. 85). In the 1937 scale at age six the standard deviations were low because there were too few items of medium

FIGURE 2

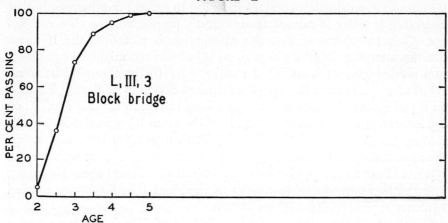

FIGURE 3

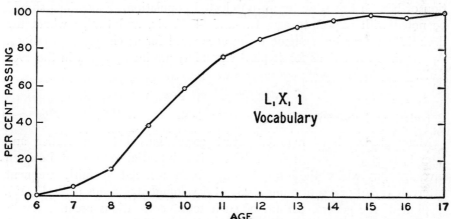

Distribution of Per Cents Passing Two Tests of the 1937 Scale

difficulty; at ages two-and-half and twelve they were high, as compared with the standard deviations for other age groups, because here were included too many items of medium difficulty. That the extent of variability is partly a function of item difficulty is now well-known, but was empirically demonstrated in McNemar's statistical analysis of the 1937 scale.

IQ variability in relation to age

If the scale is to yield comparable IQs at all age levels, it is essential that the standard deviations at the various age levels shall be approximately equal. The use of IQs rests on the assumption that variability in terms of IQ remains approximately constant from age to age, or, in other words, that variability in terms of mental age is directly proportional to chronological age. Only to the extent that this assumption is true does the IQ have constant meaning, as otherwise a given IQ at one age might be equivalent to a much higher or lower IQ at another age. If, for example, the mean IQ at seven years were 100, and the standard deviation of the IQ 20, then an IQ of 120 would fall plus one sigma from the mean for that age. If, on the same scale, at the next higher age level the mean IQ were also 100, but at that age the standard deviation of the IQ 10, then an IQ of 110 would occupy the same scale position as 120 IQ at age seven. Obviously, for such a scale, IQs would not be comparable between subjects of different ages. Numerous investigations have shown that scales of the Binet type do show a marked tendency to yield constant IQ variability.

On the 1937 scale the standard deviations of IQs fluctuate around a median value slightly in excess of sixteen points. Sixteen has therefore been generally accepted as the representative value for the standard deviation of IQs on this scale for an unselected population. Exceptions should be noted with respect to ages two-and-a-half, six, and twelve where the deviations appear too extreme to be accounted for as chance fluctuations. Appropriate corrections for atypical variability are incorporated in the 1960 scale.

Correlations between retests

Many studies have reported retest correlations between earlier and later tests of the same subjects. There is substantial agreement between investigations where the subjects have been retested at fairly frequent intervals as part of a continuing study of developmental trends (2, 3, 13, 19). Typical of the general pattern of such retest correlations are the results reported by the Fels Research Institute (19) covering a ten-year period. At the earlier age levels Form M was given and thereafter L and M were alternated on successive years. In general, the correlations decrease as the interval between two tests is lengthened, and the correlations increase as the child grows older if the interval between two tests is held constant (19, p. 29). The Fels data show that the correlation between tests given at age 3 with retests of the same subjects at age 4 is .83, and that at successive age levels the correlations with the 3 year tests regularly decrease until at age 12 the coefficient has dropped to .46. Correlations between adjacent age levels in the 8 to 12-year period are the highest. In evaluating the Fels test-retest correlations we should note that, though the mean IQ of the Fels sample is considerably above the average (approximately 120 at all ages), the authors point out that, since their cases fall within a range of 80 to 180 points, the range of abilities is not narrow.

Somewhat more stable relationships between earlier and later test scores are indicated by the results currently reported by Bradway, Thompson, and Cravens (6). Subjects originally tested as part of our 1937 standardization, who were at that time between age 2 and age 5½, were retested after a ten-year interval and again twenty-five years after the original testing. These investigators point out that "The degree of relationship between the initial composite IQ (Forms L and M) of these subjects when they were in the age range from 2.0 to 5.5 (mean age 4.0) and Form L IQ when they were in the age range from 26.5 to 32.2 (mean age 29.5) is expressed by a Pearsonian r of .59. This compares favorably with the r of .65 found for the same group in the first follow-up after only ten years. The correlation between the 1941 and the 1956 testings is .85." For these subjects the mean IQs were approximately the same at the first and second testings (112.8 as compared with 112.3), but there were significant increases in IQs between early adolescence and adulthood. The mean IQ increase from 1941 to 1956 was 11.3 points. The length of the interval between testings is an important factor in the significance of these findings. After such long intervals between testings there is no memory carry-over from earlier to later tests, nor are the responses of the subjects or the subjects themselves modified in any way by being part of an experimental group.

Many important considerations are involved in these retest studies, especially those continuing over a period of years like the Fels study, the Berkeley Growth study, the Macfarlane Guidance study, and others. Results of such studies have a bearing on issues relevant to the patterns of mental growth, the shape of the growth curve, terminal point, and the nature of intelligence as the tests measure it over the period of continued development. The bearing of some of these points on changes in the scale will be considered in a later section.

A frame of reference for classifying IQs

The distribution of the 1937 standardization sample, given in Figure 4, has provided a "common frame of reference" for results of testing various other population samples since its publication. It provides, too, a basis for statistical classification of IQs. Common meanings have come to be attached to categories defined by certain IQ limits. For example, between IQs 90 and 110 will be found approximately 46 per cent of the cases making up this sample. This corresponds in a general way to our concept of average ability. The distribution of IQs of the standardization group is shown in Table 1. As Merrill pointed out in 1938 (17), the classificatory terms used carry no implications of diagnostic significance for IQ categories. "Average or normal" has statistical meaning as designating the middle range of IQs. So, too, IQs 60 and below indicate "mental deficiency" with respect to average mentality on the scale and carry no necessary diagnostic implications

FIGURE 4

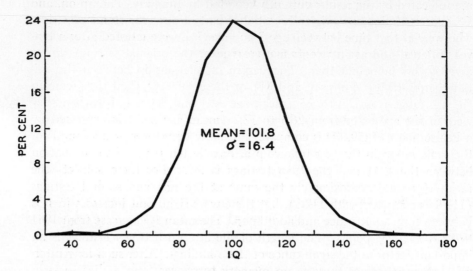

Distribution of Composite IQs of 1937 Standardization Group

TABLE 1

DISTRIBUTION OF THE 1937 STANDARDIZATION GROUP

IQ	Per Cent	Classification
160–169	0.03	
150–159	0.2	Very superior
140–149	1.1	
130–139	3.1	Superior
120–129	8.2	
110–119	18.1	High average
100–109	23.5	Normal or average
90–99	23.0	
80–89	14.5	Low average
70–79	5.6	Borderline defective
60–69	2.0	
50–59	0.4	Mentally defective
40–49	0.2	
30–39	0.03	

such as are usually attached to the term "feeblemindedness." "Very superior" is applied to subjects whose IQs fall well within the top 1.5 per cent of the group. Many other behaviors contribute to diagnostic categories. The table serves as a "frame of reference" to indicate how high or how low any specific score is in relation to the general population.

Problems involved in test revision

The immediate problem pertinent to a decision concerning the extent and character of desirable modifications to be incorporated in any revision of the 1937 scale hinges upon balancing advantages to be gained by bringing test content up to date, making use of more adequate methods of test construction, and benefiting by experience gained in the use of the tests against the disadvantages that may result from the introduction of changes in a body of material that has acquired such a wealth of significance. Anastasi has put the dilemma understandingly. Against the desirability of frequent revisions one must consider the fact that "revision may render much of the accumulated data inapplicable to the new form. Tests which have been widely used for many years have acquired a rich body of interpretive material which should be carefully weighed against the need for revision" (1, p. 200).

Practical considerations must weigh heavily here, too. McNemar in his statistical analysis of the standardization procedures employed in the ten-year research project points out that "only those who have been through the mill are in a position fully to appreciate the difficulties involved in constructing such an age scale" (16, pp. 83–84). Hebb in discussing the problem of setting up adequate control groups refers feelingly to "the tremendous task" of obtaining (intelligence) "test data for a good sample of the general population even if only a sample of 50 or 60 subjects . . ." (11, p. 280).

In setting our course for the 1960 scale we have tried to miss the rock of too rigid adherence to outgrown techniques and at the same time to avoid being drawn into the whirlpool of conflicting theories. We have asked ourselves what users of the Stanford-Binet could reasonably expect of the scale in 1960.

We have been at some pains to review the well-established characteristics of Binet type tests. The scale in 1960 retains these major characteristics. Because of practical considerations we have not undertaken to restandardize the scales, but have undertaken to check existing standards against current empirical data. In the 1930's, for example, 69 per cent of the three-year-olds of the standardization group recognized and could name 5 out of 6 items consisting of miniature object reproductions of *shoe, watch, telephone, flag, jack-knife,* and *stove.* In the 1950's only 11 per cent of children whose mental age on the scale was three years were able to do so. The presence of obsolete material, such as the old-model telephone and out-of-style stove in this naming objects list, does, of course, change the difficulty of particular tests. Again at the XIV-year level it is not so obvious why the picture absurdity test, The Shadow, should be so much easier for subjects whose mental age is 14 than it was for fourteen-year-olds in the 30's. Eighty per cent of the 1950's group pass this test at the XIV-year level as against 63 per cent in 1937.

The above illustrations serve to indicate some of the issues involved. Shall substitute material be used to replace material that is obsolete? How, without repeating the whole original standardization project, shall the present difficulty of test items be determined? How can the irreplaceable original standardization population be made use of in 1960?

Several considerations, both practical and theoretical, determined the choice of the plan which finally worked out.

Essential Features of the 1960 Scale

It was decided to incorporate in a *single scale* the best subtests from the L and M Forms of the 1937 scale. Accordingly, the 1960 revision is the L–M Form. This procedure avoids the duplication of items (which was necessary in 1937) to secure the required number of satisfactory subtests at each level. This makes it possible to include an alternate subtest at each level whereas before alternatives were available at the preschool levels only.

Chiefly, of course, limiting the number of subtests in this way made possible the selection of only the most discriminative items. A better scale could thus be constructed without sacrificing the basic soundness of the original selection procedures.

There is, in 1960, less need for alternative forms of equivalent difficulty than there was in 1937 when no other well constructed individual tests were available for the clinician. That the use of Form L has so far exceeded the use of the M Form as to make the continued publication of an alternative form of chiefly academic value is indicated by the publisher's figure on the extent to which users of the test buy L as against M materials and test blanks and by the published accounts of investigations reporting test results. It would be safe to say that Form L is used five times as frequently as Form M. The importance, however, of continuing to make avaliable the two equivalent forms for research purposes is indicated in the published results of such continuing long-term investigations as the Fels studies, the Berkeley Growth and Guidance studies, and others which have contributed so outstandingly to our understanding of mental growth and development.

Sources of material for scale revision

The *selection of subtests* to be included in the 1960 scale was based on the records of tests administered during the five-year-period from 1950 to 1954. These test records were compared with the tests given in the early 1930's upon which the 1937 revision standardization was based. Subjects from various types of communities in different parts of the country were included in the 1950's assessment group. While all ages between 2½ and 18 were represented in the group of 4498 subjects upon whom the 1960 scale item selections were based, they were not proportionally distributed among the various age or mental age groups.

Though the subjects whose test records were used as a basis to determine the *present difficulty* of items in the 1937 scale were not chosen to constitute a representative sampling of American school children, great care was taken to make sure that special selective factors were avoided. The individual testing program in most schools is set up, not according to a design for research, but, very properly, to meet the practical needs of pupils and teachers in a learning situation. Few "school tests" could be used, however adequately given, because of the bias introduced by the fact that children who are referred for individual testing consist mainly of those who present some special adjustment problem.

TABLE 2

THE ASSESSMENT GROUP TABULATED BY AREAS

	Form L Item Analysis	Form M Item Analysis	L-M Stratified Samples	Pretesting Modified or Substitute Items	Total Number of Subjects
New Jersey	892				892
Minnesota	850	208			1058
Iowa [1]	102				(636)
New York and California				96 + 588	684
Massachusetts	91				91
California	1258	897	200		2355
Totals	3193	1105	200	684	5716
Main Sample		4498			

[1] The Iowa total includes 336 cases, tested in 1940–44, for comparison with a similar sample similarly obtained tested ten years later in 1950–54. Both CA and MA breakdowns were made in an attempt to make a study of comparable populations, but the numbers of cases in each CA or MA class were too small to make comparisons meaningful. The number of cases that could actually be used is further reduced by the small numbers at the higher MA categories.

Accordingly, it was only when the testing program had been so set up that all children at a given school or all pupils in a given grade had been tested that the results of school testing could be used and then only when complete tests had been given by competent examiners, school psychologists or psychometricians who meet the requirements for certification.

Tests given by graduate students in training in the clinical training program at Stanford University were also included. Close contacts with student trainees over the years since the first Binet scale was translated have convinced the authors that after 50 hours of training in testing, student trainees who have survived the rigorous selective processes of a graduate clinical training program can be expected to give correctly administered tests. All such tests given by carefully supervised student examiners have been checked by a staff assistant and by the director of the clinical training program (Merrill) and have been used for detailed study of specific items as well as for general inter-test comparisons.

In no case, of course, have tests given to children referred to a psychological clinic been included. Children in the public schools in the vicinity of Stanford University represent a somewhat highly selected group, but within recent years, including the five-year-period represented by our study, the character of the local community has changed very radically due to the rapid increase in population and infiltration of industries, large factories, and assembly plants into a formerly residential area. Schools of both low and high status have been included in the California sample, as well as in the samples from other parts of the country, and within each school group random methods of selection have been used to determine the choice of subjects to be tested.

The scale in use in the 1950's could also be checked from the results of testing done at research centers. The Minnesota and California Institutes of Child Welfare, and the Iowa Child Welfare Research Station contributed test data of great value for inter-test comparisons at the preschool levels.[2]

At the *preschool levels*, subjects making up the assessment group were drawn from California, Minnesota, Iowa, and New York. A group of 850 two-and-a-half-year-olds was included, even though the testing had been done slightly earlier (in 1946–48), because it represented the entire child population of that age in a small middle Western city located in the midst of an agricultural area.[3] Supplementary data for evaluating inter-test com-

[2] Many of the records for our preschool level tests were obtained through the generous cooperation of staff members of child research institutes. To Dr. Nancy Bayley, formerly of the California *Institute of Child Welfare*, to Dr. Dale Harris of the Minnesota *Institute of Child Welfare*, and Dr. Boyd McCandless, director of the Iowa *Child Welfare Research Station*, we express our grateful appreciation.

[3] The authors are indebted to Dr. Katherine E. Roberts and her associates formerly of the Rochester *Child Health Institute* for making these records available to us.

parisons at the preschool level were obtained from tests given at public child care centers where the sampling of cases was less restricted at the lower socioeconomic levels.[4]

Records for *school age subjects* were obtained from California, Massachusetts, and New Jersey.[5]

In addition to the above groups of subjects whose test results may be said to represent the test in use in the 1950's, we set up two stratified samples, a group of 100 six-year-olds and a group of 100 fifteen-year-olds, drawn from two California communities, which we selected because they had been just at the mean age of the 1937 standardization group. These subjects were selected and tested by our three project examiners who were all experienced clinical psychologists. Mrs. Elizabeth Mecia and Dr. Frances Benvenista organized the sample and did the testing of the fifteen-year-olds; Dr. John Schummers of Palo Alto did the selection and the examination of the comparable sample of six-year-olds. Dr. Schummers also did pretesting of modified items for inclusion in the L–M scale. Since these two groups were given both Form L and Form M, these tests could be later re-scored to furnish some of our most valuable data on Form L–M for purposes of evaluation and comparison.

Choice of the stratified samples was determined by occupational grouping of fathers and, in the case of the fifteen-year-olds, by grade placement also. Percentage representation in occupational categories was determined by 1950 Census figures. Six groupings were made: I, Professional and technical workers, 8.2 per cent; II, Managers, officials, proprietors, farm managers and farm owners, 21.2 per cent; III, Clerical and sales workers, 12.5 per cent; IV, Craftsmen, foremen and operatives, 40.2 per cent; V, Private household and service workers, 6.6 per cent; VI, Laborers — farm and non-farm, 11.2 per cent. Grade distribution of fifteen-year-olds in the United States (9) furnished the data for determining the per cent of our group to be chosen from each grade from V to XII.[6] Six-year-olds from both kindergarten and first grade were included.

Determining the difficulty of items

Since comparisons were to be made among the subtests of the L and M Forms of the 1937 scale the difficulty of items was determined by comput-

[4] We are deeply indebted to Dr. Shirley Thomas of Brockport, New York, for giving highly skilled assistance in testing items for the preschool levels.

[5] Miss Louise Crozier, school psychologist, of Elizabeth, New Jersey, gave unstintingly of her time in making item tabulations of over 950 Stanford-Binet tests given by herself in the course of recent school surveys. Additional material from school files was tabulated for us by Mrs. Augusta Sisk, of Lincoln, Massachusetts.

[6] Grade	V	VI	VII	VIII	IX	X	XI	XII
Census percentages	1.4	2.9	6.2	13.6	29.5	36.1	4.9	1.0
1956 Sample	1	3	7	15	30	37	6	1

ing the percentages of children passing at successive *mental ages*. This procedure predetermines that a scale based upon this criterion will measure the same functions that were used in selecting the mental age group, in this case, mental age determined by the scale. It was thus possible to minimize the effect of sampling biases in the absence of a standardization group. This characteristic of mental age curves must be taken account of in evaluating the criteria for selection of subtests.

Procedures employed in the analysis of test records

Curves showing per cents passing were constructed for each subtest making up the L and M Forms for purposes of comparison with the 1937 results. Chi square probabilities were computed for all subtest comparisons between the 1937 and 1960 percentages. Internal consistency was checked by computing the biserial correlation of each subtest with total score on the test. It was necessary to make many individual item analyses to determine the difficulty of recombinations of subtest items drawn from other age levels in the other form. There is practically no new material, but in the few instances where drawings have been modified in the picture vocabulary, items have been pretested before inclusion in the scale.

Original tabulations were made separately for the various communities thus enabling us to check for possible regional differences. Social and economic differences between the various schools could not be avoided, but could be used to evaluate differential effects on subtest difficulty. Especially valuable in this respect were comparisons between low and high status socioeconomic groups making up our two stratified samples. Test situations reported by experienced examiners to favor children from more favored home environments over the underprivileged child have been tested to reveal any differences that may be significant.

"The Birthday Party" (L, III, 4), for example, was thought by some psychologists to present a situation which discriminated against the low socioeconomic class children. This was checked by computing the percentages of successes and failures for occupational group VI against groups I–IV separately for each item of the test and found to be failed no oftener than the other items at that level by the low status group as compared with the high status group.

Similarly regional differences were checked in the case of items like "snow" and "coal" which presumably might be passed with greater frequency by children from the east and middle west.

One frequently criticized item is the "Late to School" Comprehension item (L, VII, 4) because it presents an unfamiliar school situation to children who are taken to school by bus. Our data indicate that in schools where bus transportation is used this item presents a comprehensible problem in the same category with the "Lost baby" item and, at a higher level of difficulty, with the problem of "What makes a sailboat move." In the L–M Form the six comprehension items are now combined and credited (with different scoring requirements) at the two age levels.

Clarification of scoring principles and test administration

Greater precision and objectivity have been sought in efforts to further clarify ambiguities of scoring principles and test administration. Improvements in record booklet design and arrangement of the *Manual* should help eliminate some common types of errors and facilitate scoring and test recording. Experience in training students in the use of the scale, the published accounts of the experiences of others with scoring and administering the tests, and the questions and comments of users available through correspondence with the authors and publishers, have furnished the background and have been the main sources of information concerning faults of this sort.

Of course, we have not been able to anticipate and provide for all contingencies that plague the conscientious tester and that contribute to lowered objectivity and precision. Many a user of the scale will doubtless find some (to him) particularly objectionable item or unwelcome practice still retained in the L–M Form. To the possibility that this may have been an oversight of the test makers another alternative may be suggested. The statistical-minded Galton used to admonish himself, "Whenever you can, count!" It is easy to remember the misses and forget the hits — how many times the objectionable test has *not* been refused by negativistic two-and-a-half-year-olds as well as the times they just said "No" or remained obstinately silent. We counted, whenever we could!

The essential features of the scale remain the same. The 1960 scale is an age scale. The guiding principle has been to secure an arrangement of tests that makes the average mental age that the scale gives agree closely with chronological age. Difficulty and location of subtests has been determined by percentages passing at successive mental age levels checked against the 1937 scale values. Internal consistency has been determined by correlation of each subtest with the total score.

Changes in the 1960 Scale

Content

Changes in the scale have been of two sorts, content and structure. Changes in content have been in the direction of elimination of the less satisfactory subtests or of items that duplicate retained items, relocation of items otherwise satisfactory, and rescoring where a change in scoring requirement effected the indicated change in difficulty. Modification of retained items has been held to a minimum. Other content changes have consisted in efforts further to clarify directions for test administration and scoring and to improve the arrangement and suitability of scoring illustrations.

Structural changes

The more radical changes have been directed toward the correction of long recognized structural inadequacies of the 1937 scale. It will be recalled that the mean IQs that the scale yields at the various age levels are somewhat above 100 (21, p. 35, Table 5). The per cents passing the various subtests of the scale provide the necessary data for locating the items of the scale. These percentages indicate the difficulty of subtests for subjects of the several age levels and show the position of each subtest in relation to other subtests. One way of adjusting the mean IQ at the various age levels would be to increase the difficulty of the subtests at the various age levels. The easier a test is, the more subjects of a given age level are able to pass it. If, then, in choosing subtests for the 1960 scale the test maker is guided by this selective principle he should be able to modify the scale accordingly. This was not done by guess or just personal judgment. The per cents passing items by age (Table 26 in McNemar's *The Revision of the Stanford-Binet Scale*) were corrected by the amount the mean IQ at each chronological age level exceeds 100.[7] These corrected values served as a rough guide to the selection of suitable subtests for location at the various age levels in the L–M scale. Of course, in an age scale it is never possible to make an exact determination of the percentages that should pass at any given level. As we have seen, the percentages are variable, somewhat higher at the lower age levels and lower at the higher age levels. No set of values empirically determined will ever quite meet the requirements of an ideal scale.

Two important built-in corrections have been incorporated in the 1960 scale. The first achieves an *adjustment of IQs for atypical* variability. The second extends the IQ tables to include ages 17 and 18 on the assumption, based on recent retest findings, that mental growth, as measured by the Stanford-Binet, extends beyond age 16. It was pointed out earlier in our discussion that due to certain artifacts of the scale at some age levels the standard deviations of obtained IQs were either greater or less than the value

[7] Mean MA $=$ Basal $+ \Sigma p_i$ (proportion of passes beyond the basal). Illus. CA 3 Form L Values from McNemar's Table 26 (4)

$$\frac{IQ}{36(1.048)} - \frac{B}{24} = \frac{\Sigma p_i}{13.73} \quad \frac{12}{13.73} = .874 \ (p_1 + p_2 + p_3 \cdots p_n)$$

obtained at the majority of age levels. Notable exceptions occur at ages 2½, 6, and 12. At age 6 the SD is too low and at ages 2½ and 12 somewhat too high in comparison with the representative value of 16 IQ points around which the standard deviations at other age levels seem to fluctuate by amounts not exceeding chance expectations. New IQ tables have been constructed for the 1960 scale which give IQs that are comparable from one age level to another. This is done by taking into account differences in variability at the various age levels. The resultant values deviate only slightly (at most age levels) from the simple ratio of age to mental age which was used in the previous IQ tables. These 1960 IQs also take into account the fact that the mean IQs for the standardization population of 1937 were slightly above 100 and are computed on the basis of the adjusted values (21, p. 36, Table 6). The IQs included in the new table have been corrected by an amount that compensates for differences in variability of standard deviations at the various age levels. For example, a child of 12 years of age with a mental age of 16 years 6 months obtains an IQ of 132 by this "deviation method" as compared with an IQ of 138 by the simple ratio of age to mental age, and a two-and-a-half-year old with a mental age of three-and-a-half years obtains an IQ of 132 as compared with a ratio IQ of 140.

The most important direct evidence that *mental growth as measured by the Stanford-Binet extends beyond age 16* is that furnished by the Bradway, Thompson, Cravens study (6) based on retests of subjects in our original standardization group discussed previously. (See page 17.) These authors point out that the highly significant increase in IQ which they report (all but 19 of their 110 subjects obtained a higher IQ in 1956 than in 1931) occurred between the early adolescent years and adulthood. The average gain in IQ for these subjects from preschool age to adolescence was zero, but from adolescence to adulthood IQs computed in the conventional way, using CA 16 as the divisor, showed a mean increase of 11.3 points. These data are consistent with the findings reported by other investigators. Evidence that mental growth continues beyond 16 has been shown in many studies. The indication that Stanford-Binet scores of the same subjects continue to increase beyond 16 is supported by Bayley's findings reporting the results of continued testings in the course of her Berkeley Growth Study (2, 3).

Revised IQ tables

The revised IQ tables present *deviation*, or standard score, IQs for ages 2 through 18. These revised IQs avoid the inadequacies of the conventional ratio IQs $\left(\dfrac{MA}{CA} \times 100\right)$ in that (a) a given IQ now indicates the same relative ability at different ages, (b) a subject's IQ score, ignoring errors of measurement, remains the same from one age to another unless there is a change in ability level, and (c) a given change in IQ indicates the same amount of change in relative standing regardless of the ability level of the subject.

Basically the revised IQ is a standard score with a mean of 100 and a standard deviation of 16. These values approximate the values obtained on the total 1937 standardization sample. In computing these standard scores the means used were the adjusted means for the 1937 standardization sample (21, p. 36); the standard deviations were smoothed values for the combined L and M standard deviations for the various age levels (21, p. 40, Table 7). This is equivalent to the deviation method of computing IQs.

Shifts in Item Difficulty

For the purpose of establishing the present difficulty of the 1937 scales, studies were made using the results of more than five thousand tests administered during a five-year period in the 1950's to compare with those obtained for the original standardization population. Successes and failures on the separate tests were computed for each mental age level, validity of the separate tests determined, and present suitability of items taken into account in determining the choice of subtests for the L–M Form.

The main comparisons are between the 1937 percentages for successive age levels and the percentages obtained for the 4498 subjects tested in 1950–54 and tabulated by successive mental age levels. Additional data on L-tests at the preschool levels were furnished by the sample of 850 cases who represent the entire two-and-a-half year old population of one city.

The two stratified samples tested in 1956 and 1957 furnished valuable supplementary data on age levels above IV. For the six-year-olds, who were given both the L and M Forms, per cents passing could be computed for tests at age levels IV to X. For the fifteen-year-olds, who also were tested on both forms of the 1937 scale, per cents passing could be computed for items located at age levels X through SA III.

Further supplementary information was gained by tabulating separately the percentages of successes at chronological ages 6 to 12 for subjects whose IQs fell between 90–110.

More data were available for Form L than for Form M tests. Form M analyses were based on tests of 1305 subjects whereas for Form L, 3393 subjects were available. The two stratified samples of 200 subjects, of course, contributed to the tabulations for the tests of both forms.

When re-combinations of items were used or an evaluation of specific items of a given subtest was needed, it was necessary, of course, to make separate tabulations and separate item analyses. Considerable pre-testing was done to determine the difficulty of modified or substitute items. Three of the picture-vocabulary items were redrawn (*telephone, ship, and airplane*). Substitutions were kept to a minimum and were used chiefly to replace items in tests which were otherwise too valuable to discard.

Characteristics of curves showing per cents passing

The main purpose of our curves showing per cents passing was to afford direct comparisons with the standardization group. Such curves characteristically (a) show regular increase from younger to older age levels; (b) are sharper and steeper at the lower age levels becoming progessively flattened as the upper levels are reached; and (c) show a decrease in the percentage of passes for at-age tests, i.e., the percentage of two-year-olds who pass II-year level tests on the average is greater than the percentage of fourteen-year-olds who pass ,XIV-year level tests. Curves for the tests comprising the two forms generally followed these characteristic patterns.

Typical curves are shown in Figures 5 to 10. Figure 5 shows the percentages of subjects in successive age groups who passed the Sorting Buttons test at the III–6 year level in Form M. At the lower age levels both MA and CA curves are characteristically steeper than the curves for the higher age level tests, such as the Vocabulary (L, XII, 1) Figure 10.

Puzzling, at first, was a characteristic difference that appeared between MA and CA curves. Both showed increases in number of successes (per cents passing) with increasing mental and chronological age, but the MA curves were more sharply inflected. This caused the items to appear to be harder for the younger ages and easier for the ages beyond the at-age point where the curves crossed. This effect could, of course, have been predicted. An *unselected* group of subjects at a specific mental age includes the brightest and the dullest. It includes chronologically younger cases with above average IQs and chronologically older cases with below average IQs. On the other hand, an unselected group at a certain chronological age, while it includes the brightest and dullest *at such an age*, has no chronologically younger or older cases, nor does it possess a common mental age. If we examine the upper and lower ends of the MA and CA curves for the Vocabulary test at the VIII-year level we shall be able to see what is happening. Suppose, for illustration, we assume that there are 100 cases at each MA and CA level between ages 5 and 14. Referring to the curve (Figure 9) we note that no child who has a mental age of 5 passes the test whereas 4 of the brightest five-year-olds pass this VIII-year level test. Seventeen of the bright six-year-olds pass it, but only 5 whose mental age

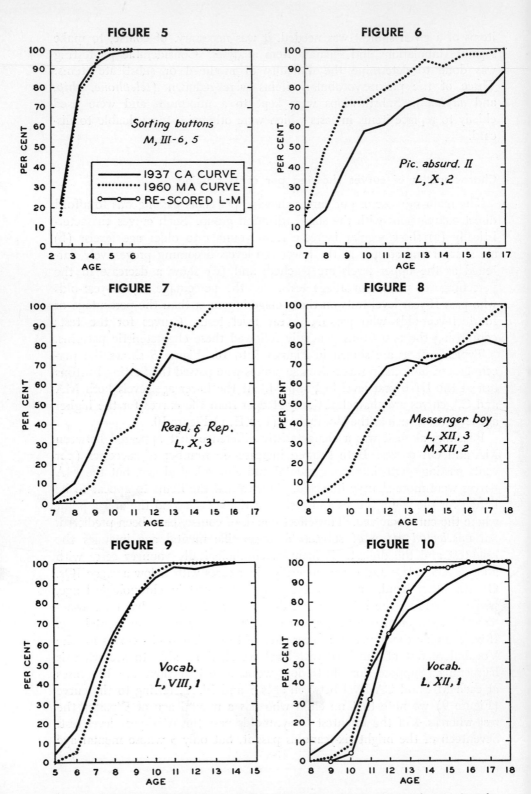

FIGURE 5

Sorting buttons
M, III-6, 5

—— 1937 C A CURVE
········ 1960 M A CURVE
o—o—o RE-SCORED L-M

FIGURE 6

Pic. absurd. II
L, X, 2

FIGURE 7

Read. & Rep.
L, X, 3

FIGURE 8

Messenger boy
L, XII, 3
M, XII, 2

FIGURE 9

Vocab.
L, VIII, 1

FIGURE 10

Vocab.
L, XII, 1

Curves Showing Distribution of Per Cents Passing at Several Age Levels

is 6 succeed. The mental age group fails to include those brighter five and six-year-olds who pass this test, but who, because they have higher mental age scores, do not fall into the V and VI-year mental age groups. In the case of subjects at the higher age and mental age groups the situation is reversed. Subjects with a mental age of 12 all pass the test, but the group of subjects whose chronological age is 12 includes 3 of the duller ones who do not pass it. The fact that these two curves are significantly different at the .01 level does not mean that in 1960 the Vocabulary test at this level is failing to maintain the 1937 level of difficulty. No single figure gives an adequate basis for assessing the difficulty of the subtests of the scale.

Changing the requirement for passing the Vocabulary test at the XII-year level (Figure 10) brings the 1960 figures at that age level into agreement with the 1937 percentages. A score of 15+, instead of 14 as the requirement for passing, increases the difficulty of the test at all age levels and brings into sharp contrast the characteristic differences between mental age curves and curves based on increase in per cent passing from one chronological age to the next.

An unequivocal answer to the problem of determining subtest difficulty is illustrated in Figure 6 showing that the Picture Absurdity test, Frontier Days (L,X,2,), is in 1960 easier than it was in 1937. Less easy to evaluate are the situations presented in Figures 7 and 8. Both items were eliminated for reasons that concern the adequacy of their contribution to the scale as a whole. Figure 7 shows present status of the Reading and Report test at the ten-year-old level. The curves are so sharply divergent that it is at once revealed, with no indicated reason(s), that this test is not adequate to be included in the scale for the new form. Table 3 analyzes data derived

TABLE 3

DISTRIBUTION OF SUCCESSES OF MENTAL TEN-YEAR-OLDS ON THE READING AND REPORT TEST

Grade	N	Mean IQ	% +	Per Cent Passing		
				Mem.	Time	Errors *
III	40	114	12	27	30	22
IV	34	104	32	73	44	29
V	17	96	65	76	88	82
VI	10	86	30	80	50	100
VII	1	82	-	-	-	-

The MA 10 sample included 11 subjects in second grade in the same school system who were omitted from the tabulation. Since these children had not attended school "the equivalent of two or three years" the test was omitted on the assumption that their school experience had been inadequate to enable them to acquire the basic reading skills. The mean IQ of these 11 cases was 118.

* The 51-word passage is to be read aloud in 35 seconds or less with not more than 2 errors in reading. The subject must then report what he read, earning 10 or more memories.

from a representative sample of 102 mental ten-year-olds. This analysis causes no obvious reasons to emerge, but supports the accuracy of our data for rejection of the Reading and Report test. Figure 8, referring to the Messenger Boy test, may reflect changes in difficulty explainable, in part at least, by cultural changes which have occurred in this country within the twenty-odd year period since the old norms were established. A German adaptation of the Stanford-Binet makes use of a redrawn picture centering on the broken bicycle situation, an approaching Volkswagen, and the signaling German youth "telegramm" in hand. In continental Europe, apparently, messenger boys on bicycles are still common enough sights to be assumed to be a part of their subjects' everyday experiences.

Additional information concerning the relative difficulty of the L and M Forms in 1937 and 1960 may be gained from Table 4 showing the average per cent passing tests at the successive age levels from IV to IX and from XI to SA III for the two stratified samples. Averaging the percentages in this way for the various age levels masks the deviations of individual subtests which may be either easier or harder in 1960, but does bring out the rather remarkable stability of the two original forms in general level of difficulty.

Validity and Reliability

Evidence for validity of the 1960 scale stems from three chief sources. The choice of items according to mental age on the 1937 scale assures that the new scale is measuring the same thing that was measured by the

TABLE 4

AVERAGE PER CENT PASSING
1937 REVISION AND 1960 STRATIFIED SAMPLES

	Form L						
Age Level	IV	IV–6	V	VI	VII	VIII	IX
CA 6 in 1937	96	91	90	72	30	13	3
CA 6 in 1960	98	93	90	84	35	25	7
	Form M						
CA 6 in 1937	99	94	87	76	29	15	4
CA 6 in 1960	98	96	91	79	41	21	7

	Form L							
Age Level	XI	XII	XIII	XIV	AA	SAI	SAII	SAIII
CA 15 in 1937	83	79	71	70	46	33	20	10
CA 15 in 1960	91	85	81	82	51	37	19	10
	Form M							
CA 15 in 1937	84	79	70	68	47	32	22	8
CA 15 in 1960	91	84	75	76	52	44	28	7

original scale. Secondly, regular increase in mental age from one age to the next checked with increase in per cent passing from one chronological age to the next in both forms of the 1937 scale. And thirdly, the choice of items was determined by their correlation with total score on each form. The first two criteria have already been discussed; our third criterion of internal consistency remains.

Biserial correlations were computed for each of the subtests of the L and M Forms of the 1937 scale. The retention of a test for the 1960 scale depended in part on its correlation with the total score based upon all the tests in the form. Correlations were computed in all cases for the age corresponding to the age placement of the test, and, in most cases, for ages adjacent to the age placement level. Tests with low biserial correlations with the total score were not included in the L–M scale.

In Appendix B will be found the biserial correlations for the tests included in the L–M Form. The mean correlation for the 1960 scale is .66 as compared with a mean of .61 for all tests in both Forms in the 1937 revision. At the preschool levels, 2–6 through 5, the 1960 mean is .61, the 1937 mean .62.[8] For year levels 6–0 through 14–0 the 1960 mean is .67, the 1937 mean .60. The adult levels, AA through SA III, have the highest correlations, the 1960 mean is .73, the 1937 mean is .61. Comparing mean correlations in 1937 and 1960 of only those subtests used to make up Form L–M, relatively the same variation appears. The mean 1937 correlation for comparable subtests was .62. Since the correlation with total score constituted one of the criteria for test selection it is reasonable to expect the L–M Form to have somewhat higher validity in this respect. However, the fact that a test had a high biserial did not insure its being included if it failed to prove satisfactory in other respects, whereas tests that had low correlations with the total were dropped even though they were satisfactory in other respects.

Additional evidence that the Stanford-Binet continues to maintain its high reliability is afforded by the fact that for both Form L and Form M the biserial correlations remain high. Reliability of the L–M Form is increased by reason of its high level of biserial correlations between individual subtests and the total.

Abilities Sampled by the Scales

Further analysis of the biserial correlation throws some light on the abilities sampled by the scales. Verbal tests continue to indicate higher

---

[8] A study by Bradway (5) reporting the "predictive value" of Stanford-Binet preschool items affords a further check on those preschool tests included in the L–M scale. The "predictive value" of an item is its biserial correlation with Stanford-Binet retest IQ obtained ten years later. The average predictive value of L–M preschool items was .52. She found verbal and memory items to have higher predictive value than nonverbal items.

validity than non-verbal.[9] Verbal average for the L–M Scale is .65. The 1937 average for the L–M verbal tests was .63. Non-verbal tests of the L–M scale correlate with the total .58 whereas in 1937 they had an average biserial correlation of .51. Selection of the best of the performance items may account for the higher correlation. An item analysis of the tests of Form L, reported by Cole (7) for a sample of English school children, gave an average validity coefficient of .53 for verbal tests of that form. Cole gives figures for a group of items which he classifies as manipulative (average correlation .43) and pictorial (average correlation .35). Manipulative tests for Form L given in the 1950's average .56 and the same items in 1937 averaged .54. Pictorial tests in Form L averaged .61 and .60 respectively in 1937 and 1960. Since the tests were standardized on American children the averages for the two groups are not directly comparable.

The English study reports, also, results for the "Eight Best Tests" in order of their efficiency. They are Vocabulary, Abstract Words, Sentence Building, Similarities and Differences, Analogies, Sentence Completion, Verbal Absurdities, and Reasoning, the same types of items which have been found to be the most valid tests of intelligence, the types of tests which best predict the subject's level of problem solving ability. In 1960 in the L–M scale these "Eight Best Tests" had an average correlation of .73 with the total scale, whereas in 1937 they correlated .68 with the total. Omission from the L–M scale of the less valid items, those contributing little to the scale, accounts for the higher validity coefficients.

Memory items in the 1960 scale are better distributed and better selected, though they constitute about the same percentage of the total (14 per cent of the 1937 items and 13.9 per cent of the 1960 items). *The 1960 scale is less heavily weighted with memory items at the adult levels.* They make up 12.5 per cent of the adult tests (AA through SA III) as against 23 per cent in the 1937 scales. The average correlation with total score is about the same for the L–M scale as for these same tests in 1937 (.60 in 1960 and .61 in 1937).

Factor Analyses of Stanford-Binet Test Items

Several important issues are raised by the results obtained in the various factor analyses of Stanford-Binet items. An adequate consideration of those findings and of the conflicting interpretations of the results is beyond the scope of the present discussion. Evidence for a single common factor would, of course, support the view that the scales measure general intelligence as that term has been used in connection with the development of methods of measuring it. McNemar's factorial analyses (16) of the items making

[9] Classifications into verbal and non-verbal tests were made by Merrill in 1942 for McNemar's arrangement of special scales described in *The Revision of the Stanford-Binet Scale* (16, Chapter X).

up the L and M scales has furnished the most comprehensive study of the intellective functions which the scales measure. His findings support the view that a single common factor would explain performance on the Stanford-Binet. This does not exclude the possibility that group factors may be present at some of the age levels. The presence of group factors is pointed out by Jones (15) in factorial analyses of the items at four separate age levels of the Stanford-Binet. Jones' interpretation of these findings differs from McNemar's earlier study which comprised the entire scale. Hofstaetter's (12) factor analyses of the inter-age correlations of Bayley's eighteen-year growth study supports the view that after the age of 4 years the tests (Stanford-Binet was used from age 2 to age 14) measure a general intellectual factor which he calls "Manipulation of Symbols." Hofstaetter obtained three factors to account for a child's achievement in "intelligence tests." The first factor, which he calls "Sensori-motor Alertness," accounts for the variance of mental age scores for the first two years. Between 2 and 4 years a second factor "Persistence" is operative and after 4 years "Manipulation of Symbols."

The interpretations of these and other statistical investigations of Stanford-Binet test data indicate that the "organization of intelligence" that is measured by the tests can be described in terms of general, group, and specific factors. "The relative weight," as Anastasi points out, "given to general and group factors varies with the theoretical framework of the investigator, the statistical methodology employed, the type of tests selected and the nature of the subjects tested" (1, p. 125).

In selecting tests for the L–M Form, the factor loadings of McNemar's analyses for the various age levels were taken into account. Though items with low first factor loadings were not entirely eliminated, all items which are highly saturated with the general factor were included. Reducing the number of memory tests at the adult levels was done in order to make these levels factorially consistent with the rest of the scale.

Our biserial correlations correspond very closely to the first factor loadings of McNemar's analyses. Thus the assumption that the L–M scale has a high factorial validity, also, is justifiable from analysis of the biserial correlations.

Evidence that this Form measures the same intellective functions at all parts of the scale is better for the intermediate and upper age levels than for the preschool levels where few changes have been made and our population samples are less good.

Stratified Samples at Ages 6 and 15

Comparisons between Forms L and M of the 1937 revision and the 1960 scale, Form L–M, were made for our two stratified samples. Other partial comparisons were possible for our large unselected sample of two-and-a-half-year-olds.

The fifteen-year-old sample was drawn in 1955–56. Tests were given during the school year. The second sample, consisting of six-year-olds, was drawn from the same communities and tested during the school year 1956–57. There were 100 subjects in each sample, 50 boys and 50 girls, and both Forms L and M were given to each subject. The interval between tests was about a week and, in half the cases, L was given first and M second, the other half had M first and L second. At the 6-year level, 67 per cent of the subjects were within 2 months of a birthday, and of the fifteen-year-olds 80 per cent were within 4 months of a birthday. Testing was done at school by three research examiners. Two of these examiners were clinical psychologists holding the Ph.D. degree, the third had been trained for the original research project and had participated in the testing of the standardization group for the 1937 revision.

Occupations of fathers for the two samples tested were defined by the *Dictionary of Occupational Titles*. The classifications used were the Census categories and each of our samples was chosen so that representation in each category was proportional to the 1950 Census figures. School placement of fifteen-year-olds was proportional to the 1950 Census figures for the United States (9). Six-year-olds were either in first grade or public school kindergarten. School entrance requirements determine the age at which children are accepted in first grade. The two communities were located in fast-growing industrial areas in California where, in spite of the utmost care in making our selections, the samples chosen are probably somewhat biased in the direction of superior social and economic status. In an area where the population has doubled in the past 8 years and the economy has changed rapidly from a predominantly rural and agricultural status to industrial developments and manufacturing, there is undoubtedly a tendency for the more vigorous and skillful to predominate in all occupational categories.

The two stratified samples were closely comparable. Table 5 shows the percentage distribution of occupations of fathers for the two groups in comparison with the 1950 census figures.

To use grade placement as a guide to the selection of our hundred fifteen-year-olds presented difficulties in schools where social promotions are practiced rather than the use of actual achievement. Accordingly, our distribution of fifteen-year-olds above and below the average grade for their age was guided by achievement test records. The distribution of fifteen-year-olds is shown in Table 6.

The six-year-olds were about equally divided between first grade and kindergarten. As testing continued during the school year and the children who were chosen were within 2 to 3 months of a birthday, there were no indications that selective factors were operating here.

TABLE 5

PERCENTAGE DISTRIBUTION OF OCCUPATIONS OF FATHERS

	Occupational Group	Employed Males in U.S. 1950 Census.	Fathers of 1956–57 Groups	
			CA 6	CA 15
I	Professional & Technical	8.2	8	8
II	Managers, officials, proprietors, farm managers and farm owners.	21.2	21	21
III	Clerical & Sales Workers	12.5	13	13
IV	Craftsmen, foremen and opera-tives	40.2	40	39
V	Service worker — public and pri-vate	6.6	7	7
VI	Laborers — farm & non-farm	11.2	11	12

TABLE 6

DISTRIBUTION BY GRADE OF 100 FIFTEEN-YEAR-OLDS

Grade Level	V	VI	VII	VIII	IX	X	XI	XII	Total
1950 Census	1.4	2.9	6.2	13.6	29.5	36.1	4.9	1.0	
1957 Sample	1	3	7	15	30	37	6	1	100
1937 Revision		3	6	25	40	28	5		107
Mean L-M$_{IQ}$	82	75	86	92	107	111	115	144	

There were no significant differences found for either group on either the L and M Forms or IQs on Form L–M.

Comparisons between Form L and Form M for these two stratified samples indicate that whatever shifts in difficulty have occurred among the individual subtests, they have not affected to any marked extent the total score on the test. It has, of course, been possible to analyze the difficulty of all test items within the total range of successes and failures for both age levels. The analyses have afforded a valuable check on the results obtained by comparing the various mental age levels. Table 7 summarizes the main comparisons between IQs obtained for the L and M Forms, for Form L–M, and the results for the original standardization group.

The two-and-a-half-year-old Sample

The two-and-a-half-year-old group was given only the L Form. The mean MA on Form L was 2–10, σ 4.4 and mean IQ 113.6, σ 14.4. The comparable

TABLE 7

STRATIFIED SAMPLES COMPARED WITH EQUIVALENT AGE GROUPS
IN 1937

| | | Age 6 | | | Age 15 | | |
		N	Mean IQ	σ	N	Mean IQ	σ
Form L	1957	100	106.3	15.1	100	106.2	17.1
Form M	1957	100	106.1	14.5	100	106.6	17.6
Form L-M	1957	100	104.5	16.2	100	104.7	16.4
Form L	1937	203	101.0	12.5	105	102.8	19.0
Form M	1937	203	102.1	13.2	105	102.6	19.3

The difference between the 1937 mean IQ on Form L and the 1957 mean IQ on Form L–M is not significant at age 6 and not significant at age 15.

mean IQ for the original standardization group was 109.9, σ 20.6. It will be recalled that age 2½ was one of the age levels at which atypical variability occurred in the standardization group. The standard deviation of IQs over the entire age range was 16.4. A possible explanation of the high variability at this point was suggested by McNemar's finding at this age level a sex difference that approaches statistical significance (C.R. 2.6), (16, p. 45). Our sample offered ample evidence on this point to serve as a check on the earlier finding. The mean IQ of 412 boys was found to be 112.9 compared with 105.7 for the 1937 revision group which consisted of 49 cases. The mean IQ for 438 girls in the group tested in 1947–48 was 114.8 as compared with a mean of 115.5 for the 53 girls of the 1937 group. The critical ratio of the difference between means for the 1947 groups was 1.92 (p = .055). Standard deviations for the latter group were respectively 14.44 for males and 14.47 for females.

TABLE 8

MEANS AND STANDARD DEVIATIONS FOR
TWO-AND-A-HALF-YEAR-OLDS

	N	Mean IQ	σ
Form L_{IQ} boys	412	112.9	14.4
Form L_{IQ} girls	438	114.8	14.5
Form L_{IQ} total	850	113.8	14.5
Form L-M_{IQ} total	850	109.0	12.6
Form L_{IQ} (stand. group) 1937	102	109.9	20.6

FIGURE 11

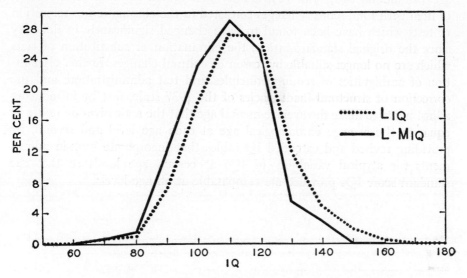

Distribution of IQs of 850 Two-and-a-half-year-olds

Revised IQs (incorporating the correction for atypical variability at age 2½) were computed for our sample of 850 cases. This (deviation method) IQ gives us the nearest approximation to the L–M mean IQ for the sample tested in 1947–48. To differentiate it from the L_{IQ} we shall designate it the $L–M_{IQ}$. A comparison of the findings summarized in Table 8 indicates that the present sample is considerably more homogeneous in ability than was the original sample. The difference between L and L–M mean IQs is highly significant ($p = < .0001$); that between the mean for the standardization group and the L–M mean is not.

Summary

The Stanford Revision in 1960 retains the main characteristics of scales of the Binet type. It is an age scale making use of age standards of performance. It undertakes to measure intelligence regarded as general mental adaptability. The 1960 scale incorporates in a single form, designated as the L–M Form, the best subtests from the 1937 scales. The selection of subtests to be included in the 1960 scale was based on records of tests administered during the five-year period from 1950 to 1954. The main assessment group for evaluating the subtests consisted of 4498 subjects aged 2½ to 18 years. Changes in difficulty of subtests were determined by comparing the per cents passing the individual tests in the 1950's with the per cents passing in the 1930's constituting the original standardization group. Criteria for selection of test items were: (1) increase in per cent passing with age (or mental age); and (2) validity determined by biserial correlation of item with total score. Changes consisted in the elimination or relocation of tests which have been found to have changed significantly in difficulty since the original standardization; the elimination or substitution of tests which are no longer suitable by reason of cultural changes; further clarification of ambiguities of scoring principles and test administration; and the correction of structural inadequacies of the 1937 scale, first by introducing adjustments to make the average mental age that the scale gives more nearly equal to the average chronological age at each age level and second, by providing revised and extended IQ tables that incorporate built-in adjustments for atypical variability of IQs at certain age levels so that the standard score IQs provided are comparable at all age levels.

PART TWO ▶

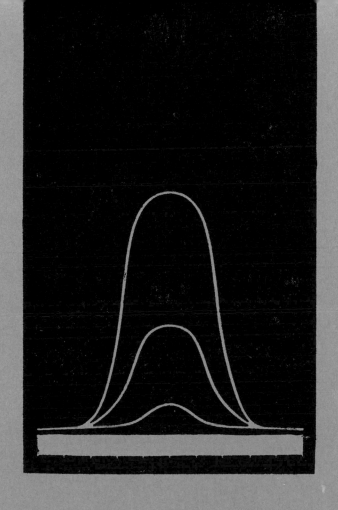

Guide for Administering and
Scoring, Form L-M

GUIDE FOR ADMINISTERING
AND SCORING, FORM L–M

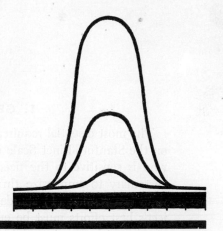

TESTING PROCEDURES

In indicating the procedures to be used in administering the individual tests of the L–M scale, we have sought to provide for the examiner specific guidance in setting up the same testing situations that were used in the establishment of the scale norms. The task of the examiner is to determine *what a given subject does under these conditions.*

For each subtest specific instructions have been given in the exact words to be used. Where alternative choices in the form of a question are permitted the choices have been indicated, for example, varying the form of the question in the Vocabulary test. Appropriate follow-up questions to clarify ambiguous responses on such tests as Verbal Absurdities and Abstract Words have been specified. Though it has been obviously impossible to anticipate all of the special situations that may arise during the administration of a test, instructions for handling those most likely to occur have been provided, e.g., administering Three Commissions (IV–6,5) or Word Naming (X,5).

Careful study of the general instructions for administering the scale should provide the examiner with an understanding of the principles upon which the test procedures were worked out. Questions not covered by the specific instructions given for each individual test should be settled in accordance with these principles and practices.

1. GENERAL DIRECTIONS

The most essential requirement for determining a valid mental test score on the Stanford-Binet Scale is an examiner who knows his instrument and who is sensitive to the needs of the subject whom he is testing.[1] It is customary to emphasize three conditions which are essential to securing valid test results: (1) standard procedures must be followed; (2) the subject's best efforts must be enlisted by the establishment and maintenance of adequate rapport; and (3) the responses must be correctly scored. Unless the tests are given in strict accordance with the procedures by which they were standardized, the examiner can never be sure what his results mean. Yet, as any experienced clinician knows, an examiner can be letter perfect in following directions for administering the tests and still not succeed in giving a valid test. Procedure ought to be familiar to the extent that the examiner's entire attention can be directed to the subject, to putting him at ease and enabling him to exert optimum efforts in the testing situation. If an examiner has failed to elicit the subject's best efforts the only certain thing is that the resulting score will be too low to some unknown degree. So, too, unless the examiner is thoroughly familiar with the scoring standards he is liable to omit some essential condition necessary for scoring, such as failure to follow up responses not recognized as ambiguous or failing to give the required number of trials because the quality of a response has been misjudged, in either case leaving the test protocol incomplete.

[1] Our training procedures and scoring standards have been in close agreement with those described by Pintner and his associates in the *Supplementary Guide for the Revised Stanford-Binet Scale*, (18). Since many students have found the Pintner Guide with its more comprehensive cataloguing of responses a useful supplement to *Measuring Intelligence* we have included in the present revision a more extended list of classified responses and a more detailed account of administration procedures.

Adherence to Standard Procedure

It cannot be too strongly emphasized that unless standard procedures are followed the tests lose their significance. Each individual subtest is an abbreviated experiment in which the conditions have been carefully set up. The subject's behavior under these controlled conditions is observed for purposes of evaluation by means of established norms. *Results are valid for the specific established normative conditions and not otherwise.* The discipline of the laboratory has furnished the training ground for instilling respect for standard procedures. Clinical training sensitizes the examiner to the needs of the subject. In the testing situation these attitudes should reinforce each other and not conflict, as sometimes happens.

The special procedures for giving the tests have been carefully worked out for each test situation. Procedures have been so planned as to provide the basis for an easy and natural approach to each of the presented problem situations. The directions have been made simple and natural so that they may serve as an apparently spontaneous and informal presentation of the tasks. Following a standard procedure does not restrict the examiner to a stilted or formal manner. Indeed, the acquisition of testing skill consists initially in learning to work effectively within a specific frame of reference.

Working within a frame

The examiner who has not acquired an ingrained respect for scientific method is apt to fail to appreciate how seriously slight changes in the test procedure, such as altering a phrase, omitting some part of the instructions or adding further explanation may influence the response. No less serious is the perfunctory or rote repetition of instructions which were devised to invite interested participation in a task of suitable difficulty. Whereas the beginner is apt to feel uncomfortably restricted by the standard instructions, the skilled examiner is able to accept a structured situation in which to evaluate his case. He can make use of the conditions of testing to support his subject. Neither a conscientious desire to see a child perform to the limit of his abilities nor a blind faith in a kind of clinical omniscience leads him to alter the standard conditions of the test to suit the requirements of the individual case. If he has reason to believe that a particular examination has not yielded an adequate measure of the subject's ability, he specifies his reasons for so thinking and notes incidents that substantiate his points.

Standard conditions of testing are best maintained by following as nearly as possible the conventions established in the course of test standardization.

The order of giving the tests in each year group should be followed as it is presented in the manual and the record booklet. The L–M Form, in order to avoid unnecessary confusion in designating subtests by number, has followed the L sequence and L test numbers. So, while the order at any year level is not always that of the original series it follows closely, and attention was given to the effect of one test on another that followed or preceded and to the avoidance of monotony in an effort to maintain interest. The order in which items appear within a given subtest is based upon the relative difficulty of the items, and it is, therefore, advisable not to alter the order of presentation. For example, the level of difficulty of the second and third items of the Ingenuity Test hinges upon the use that the subject is able to make of the experience he has gained in the solution of the first and simplest problem.

Serial testing — that is, giving all of the tests of one type consecutively (e.g. digits, sentences, etc.) — has been a much discussed practice. Its advocates point out the time saving value of such a procedure, and the possible advantage to the subject in the establishment of a "mental set" for repeating digits, giving similarities, or the like. Several experiments (10, 14, et al.) have been designed to test various hypotheses concerning the relative advantages and disadvantages of changing the order of giving tests from the standard sequence. There is some evidence that the difficulty of the items is not significantly affected by presenting the same types of items consecutively. However, the arguments for disrupting the present order, which helps maintain the subject's interest by varying the character of the tasks at the several age levels, seem to us to be inadequate to justify such radical changes in procedure as are involved in serial testing. Keeping children too long at a monotonous task usually makes it difficult to maintain rapport.

It probably could be demonstrated that the order of giving the tests could be adapted in various ways to the needs of some particular subject or group of subjects, to secure maximal motivation or to avoid frustration, and obtain higher IQ ratings. The *adaptive method* of alternating hard and easy tests suggested by Hutt (14) seems to us to offer inadequately demonstrated advantages to offset the complications introduced by so many individual variations. The method imposes upon the examiner many additional subjective judgments involved in decisions concerning choices and suitability of test sequences to be used. IQ gains were found for a poorly adjusted group, but no advantage was demonstrated for the method when adaptive testing was tried with public school children.

The accepted practice is to limit changes in test order to *practical* requirements of testing. Thus, it is sometimes advisable, in order to secure the child's effort when a certain type of test (such as repeating digits or drawing) is found to arouse resistance, to shift temporarily to a more agreeable task. When the subject is at his ease again, it is usually possible to return to the troublesome tests with better success. Such difficulties are particularly likely to be encountered with preschool children.

So, too, the examiner may misjudge the subject's intelligence level so seriously that the point at which he begins testing proves to be too easy or too hard. Chances of securing valid results may be jeopardized unless change is made at once to a level just hard enough that the subject needs to deliberate in order to solve the problem presented by the test, and yet the problem is not so hard that he feels that no one can do it.[2]

General Principles of Procedure

Specific instructions are given for administering each test, but some general principles governing procedure should be noted.

When may a question be repeated?

If the subject does not understand the question, or asks what is meant, it is permissible to explain only by *repeating the pertinent part of the formula,* unless an alternative form of instruction is given in the manual to meet such an emergency. The examiner may even repeat the test question more than once if the child remains silent. However, except in the case of young children repetition is not often called for and in general should be avoided.

It will, of course, be understood that under no circumstances may the items of any of the *memory tests* be repeated, such as digits, sentences, stories, and the like.

It is never permissible to repeat the question after an unsatisfactory response has been given, however sure the examiner may be that the subject is capable of answering correctly. The rule has, however, one exception: if the subject's response indicates that a part of the formula has been misunderstood because of the examiner's faulty enunciation or the subject's imperfect hearing, the entire formula is repeated. When in the Vocabulary test, for example, a subject sometimes defines *tap* as "something you wear on your head", it is obvious that he has understood the examiner to say *cap.*

Ambiguous responses

A frequent source of error in testing occurs when the examiner fails to follow up ambiguous responses. Responses which are unscorable by reason of

[2] See also section on test administration, pages 59ff.

ambiguity, or because the meaning the subject has intended to convey is not clear, have to be omitted unless the examiner has asked for further clarification by appropriate questioning. This situation is particularly likely to arise in giving the Vocabulary test, Verbal Absurdities, and Abstract Words. A scorable response can usually be elicited by such requests as *"Tell me what you mean"* or *"Explain what you mean"*. *"Tell me more about it"*, usually evokes further elaboration by the addition of irrelevant details which are of no help in scoring, and the easiest answer to *"Can you tell me more about it?"* is "No".

To be asked for further explanation of what seems obvious to the child sometimes elicits only a puzzled repetition of what he has already said. Often just a repetition of the original formula emphasizing the crucial word, *"Yes, but what does pity mean?"* or *"Yes, but what is pity?"* will bring results.

A special problem sometimes arises in connection with the scoring of a word or situation that has acquired a new connotation by reason of some local or current happening. For example, *Mars* in the Vocabulary test may be defined quite correctly as *"a candy bar"*, but acceptance of this response as fulfilling the requirements of a plus credit may change the difficulty of the item. In such cases we have made it a practice to ask the subject whether he can give another meaning. Say, *"Yes, and can you tell me what else it means?"*. Only if the standard meaning of the word can be given is the item scored plus.

Unnecessary questioning should always be avoided. There is always in a follow-up question an implication that in some way the examiner is dissatisfied with the subject's response. Some children are so sensitive to this implied lack of approval that they change their previous response. Others may be discouraged from further efforts to express what they mean in different terms. Acceptance of the first response while asking for further clarification tends to dispel this implication of disapproval. In making the necessary on-the-spot evaluation of ambiguous responses the advantage of thorough familiarity with the scoring standards is obvious. Just which follow-up question to use depends on the context and what kind of clarification is needed. Just how many follow-up questions to use has to be more or less a matter of judgment on the part of the examiner. If one follow-up question does not suffice the examiner must continue his efforts to determine to his satisfaction whether his subject knows or does not know the correct response.

The Importance of Rapport

To elicit the subject's best efforts and maintain both high motivation and optimal performance level throughout the testing session are the *sine qua non* of good testing, but the means by which these ends are accomplished are so varied as to defy specific formulation. The address which puts one child at ease with a strange adult may belittle or even antagonize another. The competent examiner, like the good clinician, must be able to sense the needs of the subject so that he can help him to accept and adjust to the testing situation. Sympathetic, understanding relationships with children are achieved in the most diverse ways and no armory of technical skills is a satisfactory substitute for this kind of interpersonal know-how.

Children usually accept the test without much question or explanation, particularly if they are tested at school and in familiar school surroundings. Elaborate or painstaking explanations are usually not necessary and should not be offered unless asked for. Questions about why he is being tested should be discussed with the child who is concerned about the situation. Questions can usually be handled quite matter-of-factly without going into involved or embarrassing explanations. Children are accustomed to accepting the decisions of adult authority figures. The confident assumption on the part of the examiner that the child will come willingly to the testing room is usually enough. Raising the question as to whether or not the child wants to come with the examiner invites explanations or indecision if not refusal. Of course, the problems presented in a clinical situation where it is necessary to handle emotionally disturbed children are much more complicated. But it is surprisingly easy for most people to adjust to a structured situation where specific things are required and the tasks are within the capacities of the subject.

Keeping the subject encouraged contributes much to the maintenance of satisfactory rapport. This can be accomplished in many subtle, friendly ways; by an understanding smile, a spontaneous exclamation of approval, an appreciative comment, or just the quiet understanding between equals that carries assurance and appreciation. Any stereotyped comment following each test becomes perfunctory and serves no purpose other than to punctuate the tests. In general it is effective to praise frequently and generously, but if this is done in too lavish and stilted a fashion it is likely to defeat its own purpose. Expressions of commendation should be varied and should fit naturally into the conversation. The examiner should remember that he is giving approval for effort rather than for success on a particular response. To praise only the successful responses may influence effort in the succeeding tests. Thus, praise should seldom be given between the items which are part of a particular subtest, but should be withheld until all of the items have been given in order not to encourage persistence in an inferior type of response. One exception to this rule is the Vocabulary test which is itself a sort of scale within the Scale.

Under no circumstances should the examiner permit himself to show dissatisfaction with a response, though he may smilingly refuse to accept a flippant answer obviously intended to "test the limits". With younger children, especially, praise should not be limited to tests on which the child has done well. Young children are characteristically uncritical and are often enormously pleased with very inferior responses. In praising poor responses of older subjects, the examiner should remember that the purpose of commendation is to insure confidence and not to reconcile the subject to an inferior level of response. In the case of a failure that is embarrassingly evident to the subject himself, the examiner may take occasion to point out that he doesn't expect the subject to be able to do all of these things, or he may interject, *"That was a good try!"*. The difficulty of the items may be commented upon especially as a subject is nearing his ceiling level. Such comments as *"That was a hard one!"*, *"You haven't had that one yet in school, have you?"*, or *"I don't expect you to know all of them, but I do want to see how many of them you can do"*, and the like, serve to keep children and older subjects from getting discouraged and help sustain effort. Commendation should always be alive and appropriate, not the perfunctory repetition of a set phrase. People in a testing situation are more comfortable if the examiner is free to let them know that their efforts are appreciated.

Handling questions about successes and failures becomes a problem with some subjects, especially those insecure children who are always asking, *"Is that right?"* Often such a reply as "That was very good" fails to satisfy. In this situation a friendly grin softens a refusal, such as *"I'm asking you. I'm not telling the answers!"*. Sometimes *"I can't tell you, that's against the rules"*, is enough to satisfy the child. And, of course, examiners must not give the correct responses even after the subject's response has been completed and recorded. The comment *"All right"* after a response is sometimes taken to indicate teacher's acceptance of the right answer. In that case, omission of the stamp of approval would imply that the response was not all right. In any case it is better to avoid the usually perfunctory *"All right"* for more spontaneous comments such as *"Good!"* and *"Fine!"*.

Although the examiner should always encourage the child to believe that he can answer correctly if he will only try, he must avoid the practice of dragging out responses by too much urging and cross-questioning. To do so robs the response of significance and discourages spontaneous effort. While the examiner must be on his guard against mistaking exceptional timidity for inability to respond, he must also be able to recognize the silence of incapacity or the genuineness of an *"I don't know"* from the child who knows when he knows not!

The competent examiner must possess in a high degree judgment, intelligence, sensitivity to the reactions of others, and penetration, as well as knowledge of and regard for scientific methods and experience in the use of psychometric techniques. No degree of mechanical perfection of the tests themselves can ever take the place of good judgment and psychological insight of the examiner.

The Testing of Preschool Children

Because of the special problems involved in dealing with young children in a test situation, preschool testing requires its own technique. Young children do not easily become absorbed in an externally imposed task; their attention is easily distracted and they are quickly fatigued. Their responses are likely to be influenced by hunger, restlessness, desire to please the examiner, timidity, and a hundred other motives and circumstances. They are much less motivated than older children by competition or the desire to measure up to a standard. Such personality traits as shyness, dependence, and negativism are apt to determine the behavior patterns to a more marked extent than is the case with older children whose social experience has accustomed them to conform to a more stereotyped pattern.

Particular care should be taken to see that a young child is physically comfortable. He should never be tested when he is hungry, or tired, or in need of a nap. If he begins to show fatigue, the test should be discontinued. Where possible, a low table and child's chair should be used.

In general it will be found desirable to exclude observers, particularly parents, teachers, or siblings. In the case of a very young child, or even an older one who is timid or dependent, it may be desirable to have one parent present, but never both, and never another child. In such cases the parent should be instructed to keep in the background, allowing the examiner to manage the situation and the child in his own way. The parent must be warned never to reword a question or to say anything which would suggest the answer.

The initial approach to the child is of the greatest importance in securing the best test results. How to meet this situation is something the examiner will have to determine in each case for himself. No one technique is suitable for all subjects. It is generally wise to allow the child time to accustom himself to the new situation before beginning the examination. With a shy or timid child it is advantageous to direct his attention away from himself either by ignoring him or by interesting him in other things.

The examiner will find it an aid to equip himself with some toys for use in getting acquainted with the child. A box of small toys is easy to carry and interesting to a child.[3] Needless to say, these should never be the same as any of the test material, nor should the child ever be entertained with any of the object material from the tests. Apart from the risk of invalidating a test which has not yet been given, the material is likely to be damaged. The examiner should at all times be in control of the situation and not allow the child to dominate the proceedings.

Great care must be exercised to keep the child motivated. His desire for approval and his natural curiosity are among the most potent aids the

[3] Extra space is provided in the Form L–M examiner's kit for an "extra" toy supply.

examiner has. Thus it becomes the examiner's task to keep the child encouraged and confident by liberal praise and by taking advantage of every bit of curiosity shown. When attention lags, it is often possible to stimulate curiosity by the promise of interesting material to come. When the usual methods to secure motivation are ineffective it is sometimes helpful to promise a reward, such as the privilege of playing with specified toys, or returning to his home.

In the drawing tests, the examiner will find the use of a crayon or thick pencil desirable for young children, both because it evokes greater interest and is easier for them to manipulate than the ordinary pencil.

The tests have been made as interesting and varied as possible, but certain of those which have proved to be the best measures of intelligence are not among the most interesting to the child. It often requires great ingenuity and resourcefulness on the part of the examiner to keep the child's attention on the task long enough for him to become interested in it. On the other hand, some of the testing material is so interesting that it may divert the child's attention from the task of the test. Of course, the examiner must never give the directions for the use of any of the object material while the child is handling it, since it may then be impossible to know whether the response is purposeful or just a random activity. Also, the items of a test should never be presented until the examiner is sure he has the child's attention. Without first securing attention there is considerable danger of wasting a test because of the rule against repeating it once a response, however perfunctory, has been given. There is also danger of failing to get a response for a test in which an item cannot be repeated under any circumstances, such as Memory for Digits.

In preschool testing it is the examiner, even more than the child, who must constantly be adapting himself to new situations and meeting emergencies. It is impossible to give hard and fast rules for the conduct of the examination, but it cannot be emphasized too strongly that it must be a standardized, controlled experiment with the procedure as rigidly adhered to as possible. It is not always possible with young children to preserve the order of giving tests. The examiner must be skilled in stopping short of the point at which urging will tend to arouse or intensify negativism; in sensing when it is desirable to go to a more pleasing test with the idea of returning to the troublesome one at a more favorable moment. He may find a time when the child is less negativistic, or he may be able later to present the material in a more attractive way. He should make it his goal to leave no test which the child has not attempted. On the other hand, the examiner must not be deceived by the child who is eager to proceed to something more to his liking and gives an offhand answer rather than one which is representative of his best effort.

The Appraisal of Responses

Mastery of the scoring rules

Instructions for scoring follow each test of Form L-M. It is, of course, very necessary for the examiner to acquaint himself thoroughly with the scoring rules, standards, and sample responses in the scoring standards, pages 123–253. It is as important to know what constitutes a satisfactory response as it is to use the correct procedure in presenting the problem to the subject. We have aimed to secure objectivity of scoring by indicating as clearly as possible the guiding principles involved, and by giving numerous examples of satisfactory and unsatisfactory responses.

The examples given are verbatim responses copied from our case records, and they accordingly resemble closely the types of responses any examiner may expect to secure. They are not, however, a random sampling of such responses. In general we have given only a few examples of responses which were so obviously either satisfactory or unsatisfactory that no one would fail to score them correctly. A majority of the illustrations have been selected from responses which are nearer the borderline. The difficult task of the examiner is to learn to distinguish the barely plus responses from those which are barely minus. Among the samples are also illustrations of ambiguous responses which call for further questioning.

It will be found that the responses have been scored from a common sense point of view, making the differentiation between plus and minus as free from arbitrary, artificial, and academic distinctions as possible. In the same spirit, the examiner must free himself from purist prejudices regarding ungrammatical speech and be as willing to credit a correct response awkwardly expressed as one that is given in the best literary form. It is necessary to be very alert in order to judge whether the poorly formulated answer really carries the correct meaning.

Avoidance of the "halo" effect

Scoring must be kept free from the "halo" effect. Each response must be judged on its own merits without regard to other successes or failures. The examiner must guard against allowing his scoring to be influenced by any general impression he has formed of the subject's ability. There is a natural tendency to overestimate the ability of a sprightly, self-confident, talkative child, and an examiner has to be very careful to avoid scoring the responses of such a subject too leniently. Scoring must not be tempered by any conviction that the subject could have answered correctly if he had really tried; the task is to score the response which has actually been given. The "halo" effect will be reduced by making a full record of the responses.

Scoring not purely mechanical

Although it would be impossible to overemphasize the importance of mastering thoroughly the scoring rules which have been laid down, the fact remains that the scoring of Binet tests can never be made as objective as the stencil scoring of some of the pencil and paper tests. Even the veteran examiner now and then encounters a novel type of response which he finds difficult to classify as a plus or minus. A good many of the tests occasionally bring a response so near the borderline that the most competent examiners would not unanimously agree in scoring it. The task of those who use the Stanford-Binet scales is to learn to score each test as nearly as possible the way it was scored in the process of standardizing it. Only in the degree to which they accomplish this task will their results be comparable with the established norms. Considerable practice as well as careful study of the instructions is necessary in order to acquire a ready skill. At best, however, the instructions are far short of being "fool-proof". Formulas are not adequate substitutes for scientific judgment or for common sense.

While one could wish that the Binet scales were entirely free from subjectivity of scoring, this limitation is the price that is paid for its great flexibility and richness as compared with tests which are stencil-scored. The price is not excessive in view of the greater psychological insight that the Binet-type of test affords.

Administering the Tests

The surroundings

The most desirable testing-room is one to which the child is accustomed and where he feels at ease, but which is free from distracting stimuli. An unused schoolroom is particularly good even with such attention-compelling elements in the total situation as the clumping of small feet through the adjacent halls, slamming doors, and distant voices. These things are all familiar aspects of the usual working situation. They are reassuring to a child who is inclined to be a bit timid and are to be preferred to the bare clinic room without even the comforting presence of ordinary furnishings. It is our experience that excellent testing may be done under very inadequate physical conditions. If children are easily distracted, it must be remembered that the undivided attention of the examiner and the ever-varied test situations are powerful counter-attractions. Each new task is short and interesting. The sequence of tasks within each age level has been arranged with a view to sustaining interest.

The clever examiner avoids hampering too much the freedom of the wriggly youngster between tasks. It is easier to command undivided attention for the few moments of a given task if the atmosphere is easy and informal and there is not too great insistence on sitting still. The importance of making the child comfortable, physically as well as mentally, is obvious. He should have a comfortable position and proper light for working.

The presence of others

Of all the distracting influences the presence of another person is one of the most objectionable, especially if that person is the child's mother or teacher. Contrary to what one might expect, the presence of a stranger is a much less disturbing influence. It is often easier to test the child in a classroom full of student observers than in a clinic room with the mother present. If the child is alone with the examiner, he is more at ease from the mere fact that he does not feel that he has a reputation to sustain. Parents and teachers have for so long been centers of reference and authority in the child's world that in their presence he cannot free himself from the psychological "field forces" which they exert upon him. Even if they betray no sign of approval or disapproval of the responses given, their presence tends to inhibit spontaneity and to act as a distracting influence that interferes with the establishment of rapport between the child and the examiner. In the case of a shy child it is sometimes advisable to have the mother come into the examining room with the subject and then withdraw as soon as he has become adapted to the situation. However, with very young children it is often necessary to have the mother present during the entire test.[4]

When the testing is done at school, especially when a classroom is used during a vacant period, interruptions are apt to occur even over a Please-Do-Not-Disturb sign on the door. Testing should not be continued during the interruption. If discontinuing testing procedures does not achieve its purpose of hastening the departure of the intruder, the examiner may inquire of a too-interested teacher whether the room is free at this period and offer to move to another room if she has to use her desk. A child who comes bursting in to get a book or pencil can be asked to leave if he lingers to watch what the other child is doing. In any case the exercise of tactful consideration on the part of the examiner usually terminates interruption promptly.

Manipulating the testing material

The examiner must have his material arranged in such an orderly fashion that he loses no time fumbling around to find the needed card, watch, or pencil. Such delays both jeopardize rapport and needlessly prolong the test. It is particularly important that the material be systematically arranged when much object material is to be used, as in the testing of young

[4] See discussion of testing preschool children, page 53.

GENERAL

children. Material not in use should be kept inconspicuous. We have found it convenient to use an extra chair, placed beside the examiner out of sight and reach of the child, to accommodate the box of testing material. Especially in the case of exuberant young children, the miniature dogs, cats, scissors, and thimbles used in the tests are much too tempting for tiny hands and should be kept out of sight as well as out of reach if the examiner is to maintain control of the testing situation.[5] Even with older subjects care should be taken to keep card material which is to be used for the next test face down on the table, or return it to its compartment in the carrying-case cover, to avoid distraction or over-timed exposure.

Duration of examination

About the only danger of fatigue lies in making the examination too long. The fact that the required tasks are novel and interesting to a high degree insures that under ordinary conditions fatigue is not likely to interfere to any appreciable extent. An hour is ordinarily not too long for an administration, except in the case of the younger children. Testing time may even extend to an hour and a half without noticeable loss of interest or signs of weariness. Children vary so markedly in their test reactions that it is impossible to predict time requirements. It is sometimes desirable to introduce a few minutes' intermission. In exceptional cases a test requires so much time that it is necessary to break it into two sittings. The examination of a young child can usually be completed in half an hour to forty minutes, that of an older child frequently requires an hour and a half. The experienced examiner requires considerably less time than the novice.

To maintain standard conditions of testing

Have the instructions always at hand. Do not try to memorize the whole scale before attempting to practice a test. Memory slips occur; the beginner improvises, practices errors without immediate check, and then has to re-learn. As practice continues a glance at the instructions is sufficient for adequate recall, but even experienced examiners need to re-read the procedure occasionally to prevent small deviations creeping in.

Screening the record booklet from the subject's view should be done inconspicuously. Using a blotter to screen the digits is both convenient and natural. Interposing the *Manual* as a barrier between examiner and subject is an affront to some children and usually causes embarrassment.

Responses should be *recorded* as nearly *verbatim* as possible in the record booklet, scored at the time provisionally, and *always re-scored* later as a double check on accuracy. The record booklet should always show a clear

[5] See also discussion of testing preschool children, page 53.

record of the subject's successes and failures. For each part of each subtest the examiner should record either + or −. This is important, both in providing additional checks on accuracy and indicating the marginal character of success or failure on the subtest. More inaccuracies in test scores result from carelessness in checking clerical errors than in failure to apply correct scoring principles.

Examiners find that occasionally a subject is distracted by watching the recording of his responses, especially the record of his successes and failures as + or −. It is a good plan to recognize the subject's interest in the writing down of his responses, but to discontinue the use of the + and − symbols. We substitute check marks. Plus is √ and minus √°.

Where to begin testing

The test should be begun at the point where the child is likely to succeed, but not without some effort. If the tasks at the starting point are too difficult, the child may become discouraged and refuse to try; if they are too easy, he is not sufficiently challenged and becomes over-confident. In determining where to begin one must take into account the chronological age, grade placement, general behavior in the test situation, and any other pertinent information that may be available. In the case of children who are presumably somewhere near average in ability, it is usually good practice to begin with the age level just below a child's chronological age. If the subject's ability level has been very much over-estimated the examiner must, of course, go back to a more appropriate level. Sometimes it is necessary to change at once to avoid too much initial discouragement on tasks that are too difficult.

Scattering of successes

Examiners who are familiar with the Stanford-Binet scales are accustomed to the fact that successes and failures in an individual test record normally scatter over a wide range of age levels, the scatter usually being greater at the higher age levels than at the lower ages. The reason for this is that the magnitude of the intervals between successive age levels is greater in that early period of mental growth measured by the lower age tests than at any later stage of development; the difference between mental ages 2 and 3 is many times greater than the measurable difference between mental ages 13 and 14.

Though many attempts have been made to attach diagnostic significance to "scatter", we have never found evidence that seemed to justify its use as a diagnostic sign. However, the fact that the pattern of abilities differs from one individual to another would lead one to expect characteristic differences between individuals in the distribution of their success and failures on the test.

Whatever the nature of intelligence may be, its manifestations in the individual are uneven. One individual will do better with one kind of material than he does with another. Thus, he may succeed well on tasks involving immediate recall, whereas in drawing designs he may function at a lower level. Abilities are always manifested and measured in relation to experiences and training, and the behavioral composite which we call intelligence is of necessity modified and molded by these factors. No cross section view of the performance characteristic of children in general at particular age levels will ever be found to be perfectly characteristic of a specific individual.

Determining the basal age and ceiling (maximal) level

In computing mental age, all successes and failures are taken account of, including any failures that may have occurred below the highest age level where all tests have been passed and successes beyond the first age level at which all tests have been failed. For convenience in computing test scores, we designated as the basal age that level at which all tests are passed which just precedes the level where the first failure occurs. It sometimes happens that a subject passes all of the tests at a higher age level than the one in which his first failure occurs. For purposes of scoring, of course, this does not change the base from which we determine the score, nor does the fact that he may pass tests beyond the first age group at which he has failed all of the tests justify ignoring these successes. In effect the subject undertakes every test of the scales, although *actually* he is given only that portion of them which is appropriate to measure his abilities. The range of these abilities is roughly demarcated by the basal and ceiling (maximal) levels. The normal scattering of successes and failures spreads over several age levels as illustrated in the samples.

No problem exists concerning allowance for credits. All successes and all failures are taken into account whenever they occur. There has, however, been much discussion concerning the proper procedure for the examiner to follow when he finds that an item which is scored at more than one level has been failed at an age level below that which he thought was going to be the basal. For example, suppose in testing an eleven-year-old child the examiner begins with the X-year level at which all tests are passed. He proceeds to the XI-year tests and finds that Memory for Designs is failed at the XI-year level and also at year IX. Is it necessary for him to go back to the previous age levels until he finds a point at which all tests at a given age level are passed? The answer depends, in part, on practical considerations concerning the degree of reliability of the intelligence rating and its importance in contributing to diagnostic assessment. At this point (all 6 tests of year X passed, one given and failed at year XI which is also failed at year IX) the examiner should continue to complete the testing at the XI-year level. Then, depending on whether his subject is mostly failing or mostly succeeding, decide whether to return at this point to the IX-year level or proceed to find his ceiling level. Suppose he finds that there are only two successes at the XI-year level. He then has very little assurance that he can assume that all of the tests below that provisional basal would be passed if he were to give them. Going on to give the XII-year level will afford further evidence. He finds one success here and at year XIII all failures. The experienced examiner will recognize that testing has been near the upper limits of the subject's range of abilities, and will have no question that he must return to the age levels below year X to obtain a reliable estimate of the subject's intelligence. If, however, the subject's scattering of successes and failures followed a more normal pattern — extending over several age levels, six or more, and he found no behavioral problems — he might reasonably decide against the longer range testing on the assumption that the chances that those tests would be passed were consistent with those of the scales concerning allotment of credits assumed to be plus below the basal.

Abbreviated tests

The use of the starred tests of the L-M scales makes it possible to obtain in about three quarters of the usual testing time a somewhat less reliable estimate of a subject's intelligence. The abbreviated scale is scored by re-distributing the allotment of credits so that each of the four tests at an age level is more heavily weighted than each of the single tests when all six tests are given. Thus, four tests at year VIII would receive 3 months credit each instead of 2; at Average Adult level four tests instead of the usual eight would increase the credit for each test from 2 months to 4 months.

An alternative method of securing an abbreviated test score which cuts down the time about 20 per cent and yields a somewhat more reliable rating has been suggested by Wright (23). Wright's method differs from the Terman-Merrill method only in that the basal and ceiling levels are determined on the basis of all six tests (at each) rather than on the starred tests only. That is, when a provisional basal age is found at which all four starred tests are passed the examiner gives the other two tests at that age level and, if either is failed, continues testing until an age level is found at which all six tests are passed. The ceiling level is determined in the same way by finding the age level where all six tests are failed. The final rating, then, is computed for a scale of four tests at each age level, except at basal and ceiling levels, where the number of tests is increased to the full scale basis. This latter method seems to offer increased reliability at a cost of very little greater investment of time. Both methods of abbreviating the test have been found to yield somewhat lower IQs on the average, the Terman-Merrill method slightly lower than the Wright method. However, Watson's survey (22, pp. 259–263) of studies reporting the results of the use of the abbreviated scales indicates that the difference between means for full scale IQs as compared with the abbreviated scale IQs is in no case statistically significant.

Alternative tests

At each age level in the L–M scale an extra test has been included for use as a substitute when a test has been spoiled in giving, as occasionally happens. This permits a more reliable appraisal of ability than is the case when a spoiled test has to be discarded and the total credits for the age level pro-rated among the remaining tests passed at that level. *Under no circumstances, however, may an alternative test be substituted for a test which has been failed.*

Computation of MA Scores

Mental age (MA) on the scales is found by crediting the subject with his basal age plus all additional credits earned beyond his basal. At the lower end of the scales tests are grouped at half-yearly intervals: II, II-6, III, III-6, IV, IV-6, and V and each test passed in this age range earns a credit of 1 month towards a mental age score. From year VI through year XIV each year-group represents an interval of twelve months and we therefore count 2 months towards mental age for each of the six tests at these levels. Above year XIV the tests have been given heavier weighting in order to make IQs for the upper age levels comparable to IQs for the lower age levels. At the Average Adult level the number of tests is eight and each test is given 2 months' credit making a total of 16 months' credit for this level. At Superior Adult level I, each of six tests receives 4 months' credit, Superior Adult level II has six tests at 5 months' each, and Superior Adult level III six tests at 6 months' each. The samples on pages 63 and 64 of mental age computation illustrate the procedure.

In Sample 1 tests below the basal age level are assumed to be passed and above the ceiling age level assumed to be failed. Score is then computed by adding to the basal age (3), credits for successes beyond: one month's credit for each test at the half-year levels and 2 months' credit for the one test passed at the VI-year level.

Sample 2 illustrates the correct procedure for computing scores at the upper end of the scale where weighted credits are assigned and also the assignment of credits where there is a failure at an age level below a level where all six tests have been passed.

COMPUTATION OF MA SCORE FOR A FOUR-YEAR-OLD CHILD

Year Level	Number of Tests Passed	Months' Credit Per Test	Total Credits Years	Months
III	6 (Basal age)	–	3	–
III–6	5	1	–	5
IV	3	1	–	3
IV–6	2	1	–	2
V	2	1	–	2
VI	1	2	–	2
VII	0 (Ceiling age)			0
			3	14

Mental Age Score, 4–2

COMPUTATION OF MA SCORE FOR AN ADULT

Year Level	Number of Tests Passed	Months' Credit Per Test	Total Credits Years	Months
II — XIV	(not given)	(Credit pre-supposed)	14	—
AA	8	2	—	16
SAI	5	4		20
SAII	6	5		30
SAIII	3	6		18
			14	84

Mental Age Score, 21–0

Sample 3 illustrates the situation posed by the problem of scoring failures below a level where all six tests are passed and scoring successes beyond a level where all tests have been failed. The examination was begun at the X-year-level and the subject's first failure occurred at the XI-year level. The test failed was one that is scored at two levels and was also a failure at the IX-year level. At age XII the examiner failed to follow-up an ambiguous response on the Verbal Absurdities test which he later found to be unscorable. That test had to be omitted and credits assigned on the basis of five tests in the age group instead of six. At the Average Adult level one of the tests also earns credit at SAII.

COMPUTATION OF MA SCORE FOR A TEN-YEAR-OLD CHILD

Year Level	Number of Tests Passed	Months' Credit Per Test	Total Credits Years	Months
VIII	6 (Basal age)	–	8	–
IX	5	2		10
X	6	2		12
XI	5	2		10
XII	3 (out of 5 given)	2.4 (pro-rated)		7.2
XIII	2	2		4
XIV	1	2		2
AA	1	2		2
SAI	0			0
SAII	1	5		5
SAIII	0 (Ceiling age)			
			8	52.2

Mental Age Score, 12-4

Finding the IQ

IQs for the L-M Form will be found by referring to the Pinneau Revised IQ Tables, Part Three. These tables are comparable in make up to those constructed for the 1937 revision and are to be used in the same way; that is, one finds the MA in years and months for a given test record and opposite the appropriate CA reads the IQ score. *It is not necessary for the examiner to make any adjustments or corrections.* All adjustments for the revised IQs have been "built-in" to the tables as set up.

MA score is computed as shown in the above samples. CA is recorded in years and months in the conventional way, e.g., 10-2 designates 10 years, 1 month and 16 days. (One month and 15 days would be 10-1.)

Revised IQs may also be computed by the use of a formula by means of which conventional ratio IQs can be transformed into the standard score or deviation IQs of the revised tables. The formula (which was used for making up the revised IQ tables) and tables for converting conventional into deviation IQs are furnished in Appendix A and Appendix C.

2. SPECIFIC INSTRUCTIONS FOR ADMINISTERING FORM L–M

2. SPECIFIC INSTRUCTIONS FOR ADMINISTERING
   FORM L–M

YEAR II

1. *THREE-HOLE FORM BOARD (Must precede Three-Hole Form Board: Rotated, Year II–6, A)

MATERIAL: Form board 5″ × 8″ with three insets for circle, square, and triangle.

PROCEDURE: Present the board with the blocks in place. Place the board so that the base of the triangle will be towards the subject. Say, *"Watch what I do."* Remove the blocks, placing each on the table before its appropriate recess on the side toward S. Then say, *"Now put them back into their holes."* Allow two trials. Return the blocks to the board for a second trial and repeat the procedure.

Count it a trial when the child has arranged the pieces to his satisfaction as indicated by pushing back the board or looking up at the examiner.

SCORE: 1 plus. All three blocks must be placed correctly in one of the two trials.

2. DELAYED RESPONSE

MATERIAL: Three small pasteboard boxes and a small toy cat.

PROCEDURE: Place the boxes in a row about two inches apart. Say, *"Look, I'm going to hide the kitty and then see if you can find it again."* Make sure that the child is watching and then hide the cat first (a) under the *middle box,* then (b) under the box at E's *right,* and then (c) under the box at E's *left.* Screen the boxes each time and count aloud from 1 to 10 at the rate of 1 per second. Remove the screen, and say, *"Now find the kitty!"* The child's *first* choice in each trial must be the correct one.

SCORE: 2 plus. If in any trial E has been unable to prevent two boxes from being turned over simultaneously, that trial is scored minus.

3. *IDENTIFYING PARTS OF THE BODY (Same as II–6, 2)

MATERIAL: Large paper doll.

PROCEDURE: Show the paper doll and say, *"Show me the dolly's hair."* Same for *mouth, feet, ear, nose, hands,* and *eyes.*
(a) Hair, (b) mouth, (c) feet, (d) ear, (e) nose, (f) hands, (g) eyes.

SCORE: 4 plus. The child must clearly indicate the parts on the paper doll.

4. BLOCK BUILDING: TOWER

MATERIAL: Twelve 1-inch cubes.

PROCEDURE: Place the blocks in confusion before the child and then build a four-block tower out of his reach, saying, *"See what I'm making!"*
Then, pushing the rest of the blocks toward the child, say, *"You make one like this." "Make yours* (pointing) *right here."* E's tower is left standing while the child is attempting to build another. If E's tower is knocked over it should be rebuilt. Illustrate several times if necessary.

SCORE: The child must build a tower of four or more blocks in imitation of E's tower and in response to E's request, not spontaneously either before or later. It is purposive behavior in which we are interested rather than the spontaneous play activities involving manipulation of material. The tower must stand by itself at the four-block stage.

5. *PICTURE VOCABULARY (Same as II–6, 4; III, 2; IV, 1)

MATERIAL: Eighteen 2″ × 4″ cards with pictures of common objects.

PROCEDURE: Show the cards one at a time. Say, *"What's this? What do you call it?"*

SCORE: 3 plus. See scoring standards, page 126.

6. * WORD COMBINATIONS

PROCEDURE: Note the child's spontaneous word combinations at any time during the interview.

SCORE: Combinations of at least 2 words. See scoring standards, page 129.

ALTERNATE

A. IDENTIFYING OBJECTS BY NAME

MATERIAL: Card with dog, ball, engine, bed, doll, and scissors attached.

PROCEDURE: Show the card with the six small objects attached and say, *"See all these things? Show me the dog." "Put your finger on the dog." "Where is the dog?"*
In order ask for: (a) dog, (b) ball, (c) engine (train, choo-choo), (d) bed, (e) doll, (f) scissors (shears). It is not permissible to ask for the objects by any special names other than those specified in the instructions.

SCORE: 5 plus. The child must point to the objects.

YEAR II-6

1. * IDENTIFYING OBJECTS BY USE

MATERIAL: Card with cup, shoe, penny, knife, automobile, and iron attached.

PROCEDURE: Show the card with the six small objects attached and say: *"Show me what . . . ."* or *"Which one . . . ."* or *"Show me the one that . . . . . ."*

(a) *". . . . . . we drink out of."*
(b) *". . . . . . goes on our feet."*
(c) *". . . . . . we can buy candy with."*
(d) *". . . . . . we can cut with."*
(e) *". . . . . . we ride in."*
(f) *". . . . . . we use to iron clothes."*

SCORE: 3 plus. The child must designate the object by pointing. If he points incorrectly, the response is scored minus even though he may have given the correct name.

2. IDENTIFYING PARTS OF THE BODY (Same as II, 3)

MATERIAL: Large paper doll.

PROCEDURE: Show the paper doll and say, *"Show me the dolly's hair."* Same for *mouth, feet, ear, nose, hands,* and *eyes.*

(a) Hair, (b) mouth, (c) feet, (d) ear, (e) nose, (f) hands, (g) eyes.

SCORE: 6 plus. The child must clearly indicate the parts on the paper doll.

3. *NAMING OBJECTS

MATERIAL: Chair, automobile, box, key, fork, flag.

PROCEDURE: Present the objects one at a time. Have the child name each. Say, *"What is this? What do you call it?"* Present in the order: (a) Chair, (b) automobile, (c) box, (d) key, (e) fork, (f) flag.

SCORE: 5 plus. See scoring standards, page 129.

4. *PICTURE VOCABULARY (Same as II, 5; III, 2; IV, 1)

MATERIAL: Eighteen 2″ × 4″ cards with pictures of common objects.

PROCEDURE: Show the cards one at a time. Say, *"What's this? What do you call it?"*

SCORE: 8 plus. See scoring standards, page 126.

5. *REPEATING 2 DIGITS

PROCEDURE: Say, *"Listen; say 2."* *"Now, say 4-7,"* etc.
(a) 4–7, (b) 6–3, (c) 5–8.
Pronounce the digits distinctly and with perfectly uniform emphasis at the rate of one per second.

SCORE: 1 plus. The series must be repeated in correct order without error.

6. OBEYING SIMPLE COMMANDS

MATERIAL: Block, button, dog, box, scissors.

PROCEDURE: With the objects on the table in a row as follows, block, button, dog, box, scissors, say:

(a) *"Give me the dog."*
(b) *"Put the button in the box."*
(c) *"Put the scissors (shears) beside the block."*

Replace the objects in the same order after each trial. It is sometimes necessary to repeat each command several times if the child has made no move toward carrying out the request.

SCORE: 2 plus.

ALTERNATE

A. THREE-HOLE FORM BOARD: ROTATED (II, 1 must precede)

MATERIAL: Form board used in II, 1.

PROCEDURE: With the board in position 1 (the base of the triangle toward the child), remove the blocks from the board while the child watches. Place each block before its proper recess on the side toward the child. Then rotate the board, while the child watches, to position 2 (with the apex of the triangle toward the child), and say, *"Put them all back where they belong."* No time limit. Give three trials, repeating the same procedure for each trial.

SCORE: 2 plus. All three blocks must be placed correctly. A trial is scored plus if all three blocks are placed correctly.

YEAR III

1. STRINGING BEADS

MATERIAL: Box of 48 kindergarten beads all of the same color, 16 round, 16 square, 16 cylindrical, and a pair of 18-inch shoestrings.

PROCEDURE: String one bead of each shape saying, *"Now let's play this game. Watch."* Then giving S another string, say, *"Let's see how many we can put on."* Continue stringing beads while the child works on his chain, urging as often as necessary to keep the child trying. If S seems to be selecting a particular shape, tell him that any bead will do. Time limit, 2 minutes.

SCORE: 4 beads. Count each bead that has been pulled onto the string beyond the metal tip, even though in manipulation it may have slipped off again.

2. * PICTURE VOCABULARY (Same as II, 5; II–6, 4; IV, 1)

MATERIAL: Eighteen 2" × 4" cards with pictures of common objects.

PROCEDURE: Show the cards one at a time. Say, *"What's this? What do you call it?"*

SCORE: 10 plus. See scoring standards, page 126.

3. * BLOCK BUILDING: BRIDGE

MATERIAL: Twelve 1-inch cubes.

PROCEDURE: Place the blocks in confusion before the child and then proceed to build a bridge of three blocks beyond the child's reach, saying, *"See if you can make one like this."* *"Make yours* (pointing) *right here."* E's bridge is left standing. Illustrate several times if necessary.

SCORE: The structure may be unsteady, but is counted satisfactory if it stands. The base blocks must not be touching. They must be bridged by a third which rests on both. The response is still scored plus if the child continues to build by adding towers to his bridge.

The bridge must be built in response to E's request and not spontaneously at some other time during the test.

4. * PICTURE MEMORIES

MATERIAL: Four cards with animal pictures.

PROCEDURE: Show card (a) and ask, *"What is this?"* *"Yes, it's a cow* (or *moo-cow*)." If the child does not name it correctly, tell him the name. As this card is being removed, say, before showing card (A), **"Now we are going to find it!"** Then show card (A) and ask, **"Where is it?"** If necessary, say, **"Show me,"** or **"Put your finger on it."**

Show card (b) and, pointing to each object, ask, **"What is this?"** If the child does not name it correctly, tell him. As this card is being removed, say, **"Now we are going to find them!"** Then show card (B) and ask, **"Where are they?"** Be careful to avoid naming the objects when you are asking the child to locate them from memory.

SCORE: 1 plus. S must clearly indicate the correct objects. Additional enumeration makes the response minus.

5. *COPYING A CIRCLE

MATERIAL: Circle printed in record booklet.

PROCEDURE: Arrange the record booklet so that the circle is at S's left. Give the child a pencil and, pointing to the circle in the booklet, say, **"Make one just like this. Make it right here."** Give three trials, repeating the directions for each trial. Do not allow S to trace the model.

SCORE: 1 plus. See scoring standards, page 130.

6. DRAWING A VERTICAL LINE

PROCEDURE: Give the child a pencil and, drawing a vertical line, say to him, **"You make one like this. Make it here."** Illustrate once only. Give one trial.

SCORE: See scoring standards, page 132.

ALTERNATE

A. REPEATING 3 DIGITS

PROCEDURE: Say, **"Listen; say 4–2."** **"Now, say 6–4–1,"** etc.
(a) 6–4–1, (b) 3–5–2, (c) 8–3–7.
Pronounce the digits distinctly and with perfectly uniform emphasis at the rate of one per second.

SCORE: 1 plus. The series must be repeated in correct order without error after a single reading.

1. * COMPARISON OF BALLS

MATERIAL: Card with large and small sphere.

PROCEDURE: Show the card and ask, *"Which ball is bigger? Put your finger on the big one."* Give 3 trials alternating the relative positions of the large and small balls. In case one of the first three trials is failed, give 3 additional trials, continuing to alternate the positions of the balls.

SCORE: 3 plus of three trials, or 5 plus of six trials.

2. PATIENCE: PICTURES

MATERIAL: Two cards with pictures cut in two vertically.

PROCEDURE: Place the two halves of the card before the child so that the cut edges are toward the outside, as indicated in the figure.

(a) Say, *"Put these two pieces together and make a ball."*

(b) Place the two halves of the other card before him and say, *"Put these two pieces together and make a pig."*

SCORE: 1 plus. See scoring standards, page 132.

3. * DISCRIMINATION OF ANIMAL PICTURES

MATERIAL: Two cards with pictures of animals.

PROCEDURE: Superimpose Card A over Card B, arranged so that the rabbit in the lower left corner is framed by the rectangular slit in Card A. Say, *"See all of these animals? Find me another one just like this up here,"* pointing to the rabbit in the frame.

Correct an error on the rabbit by saying, *"No, find me one just like this,"* again pointing to the rabbit. If S still fails, show him the rabbit. S is *not* given credit for finding the rabbit after correction. Proceed from left to right in order. R to L for the middle row, and L to R for the top row. Say, *"Find me another one just like this one,"* for each animal. Since the items of this test have not been arranged in the order of their difficulty, it is not safe to assume that failure on the first few items indicates inability to pass the test.

SCORE: 4 plus.

4. * RESPONSE TO PICTURES: LEVEL I (Same as VI, A)

MATERIAL: Three pictures, Grandmother's Story, Birthday Party, Wash Day.

PROCEDURE: Present the pictures in the following order: Grandmother's Story, Birthday Party, Wash Day. Say, *"Look at this picture and tell me all about it."* If there is no response, repeat the request, *"Tell me all about it."* If the child names one or two things in a picture and then stops, urge him on by saying, *"Tell me more about it."* Only one question of this type, however, is permissible in a trial. Do not remove the picture until it is clear that no further response is forthcoming.

SCORE: Level I, 2 plus. See scoring standards, page 133.

5. SORTING BUTTONS

MATERIAL: Twenty half-inch buttons, 10 black and 10 white. Small box.

PROCEDURE: Empty the button box onto the table in front of the child and place the box cover beside the box ready for sorting the buttons. Take a button of each color from the mixed pile in front of the boxes, saying, as you illustrate: *"See, the black buttons go in this box, and the white buttons go in that box. Now you put all the black buttons in that box and all the white buttons in this box."* Time limit, 2 minutes.

SCORE: No error. Errors made in the process of sorting, if corrected spontaneously, are disregarded in scoring.

6. * COMPREHENSION I

PROCEDURE: Ask:

(a) *"What must you do when you are thirsty?"*
(b) *"Why do we have stoves?"*
If there is no response, repeat the question.

SCORE: 1 plus. See scoring standards, page 135.

A. COMPARISON OF STICKS

MATERIAL: Match sticks, cut to 2-inch and 2½-inch lengths.

PROCEDURE: Place the two sticks on the table before the child in the positions indicated below and about an inch apart. Say, *"Which stick is longer? Put your finger on the long one."* Give three trials, alternating the relative positions of the long and the short sticks. In case one of the first three trials is failed, give three additional trials, continuing to alternate the positions of the sticks.

(a) _____   (b)_____   (c)_____
_____   _____   _____

SCORE: 3 plus of three trials, or 5 plus of six trials.

YEAR IV

1. *PICTURE VOCABULARY   (Same as II, 5; II–6, 4; III, 2)

MATERIAL: Eighteen 2″ × 4″ cards with pictures of common objects.

PROCEDURE: Show the cards one at a time. Say, *"What's this?   What do you call it?"*

SCORE: 14 plus. See scoring standards, page 126.

2. *NAMING OBJECTS FROM MEMORY

MATERIAL: Automobile, dog, shoe, cat, spoon, engine, doll, scissors, thimble, box.

PROCEDURE: Place the automobile, dog, and shoe in a row before the child in the order indicated from his left to his right. Call his attention to each object, asking him to name it. Accept whatever name he gives. If he hesitates, name it for him. Then say, *"Now shut your eyes tight so that you can't see them."* Screen the test objects from his sight and cover the *dog* with the small box cover. Remove the screen and say, *"Open your eyes. Look! Which one did I hide?"* If the child points without naming the hidden object, say, *"Yes, what is it?"* Repeat the procedure for (b) and (c), hiding in turn the engine and then the doll.

E must be careful to prevent the child from lifting the box cover before he has named the hidden object, thus defeating the purpose of the test. It is not necessary to be overly insistent that the child close his eyes while the object is being hidden since the screen hides the procedure.

(a) Automobile, *dog,* shoe.
(b) Cat, spoon, *engine.*
(c) *Doll,* scissors, thimble.

SCORE: 2 plus. The child must designate the object either by its correct name or by the name he used when it was first shown to him.

3. * OPPOSITE ANALOGIES I (Same as IV–6, 2)

PROCEDURE: Say:

(a) *"Brother is a boy; sister is a . . . . . ."*
(b) *"In daytime it is light; at night it is . . . . . ."*
(c) *"Father is a man; mother is a . . . . . ."*
(d) *"The snail is slow; the rabbit is . . . . . ."*
(e) *"The sun shines during the day; the moon at . . . . . ."*

SCORE: 2 plus. See scoring standards, page 136.

4. * PICTORIAL IDENTIFICATION (Same as IV–6, A)

MATERIAL: Card with pictures of objects.

PROCEDURE: Show the card and say: *"Show me what . . . . . ."* or *"Which one . . . . . ."* or *"Show me the one that . . . . . ."*

(a) ". . . . . . *we cook on."*
(b) ". . . . . . *we carry when it is raining."*
(c) ". . . . . . *gives us milk."*
(d) ". . . . . . *has the longest ears."*
(e) ". . . . . . *shines in the sky at night."*
(f) ". . . . . . *catches mice."*
If S names the object without pointing to it, ask him to point.

SCORE: 3 plus. Naming the object is not sufficient. The child must point to it on the card.

5. DISCRIMINATION OF FORMS

MATERIAL: Card with 10 forms and an "✕"; 10 duplicate forms to be placed, one at a time, on "✕".

PROCEDURE: Show the card with the ten forms and say, *"See all of these things?"* Place the circle of the duplicate set at "✕" and say, *"Find me another one just like this,"* at the same time passing your finger around the circumference of the circle. If there is no response, say, *"Do you see all of these things?"* indicating the other forms. *"And do you see this one?"* pointing to the circle at "✕" again. *"Now find me another one just like this."* Correct an error on the circle by saying, *"No, find one just like this,"* again passing the finger around the outline of the figure. If S still fails to find the circle, show him. S is not given credit for finding the circle after correction. Give no further help. Present the square next, then the triangle, and then the other forms in any random order that differs from the order of their arrangement on the large card.

SCORE: 8 plus.

6. COMPREHENSION II

PROCEDURE: Ask:

(a) *"Why do we have houses?"*
(b) *"Why do we have books?"*

SCORE: 2 plus. See scoring standards, page 137.

ALTERNATE

A. MEMORY FOR SENTENCES I

PROCEDURE: Say, *"I want you to say something for me. Say, 'big boy'* (or *'big girl'*). *Now say, 'I am a big boy'* (or *'girl'*). *Now say . . . . . ."* Introduce the second sentence by repeating, *"Now say . . . . . ."*

(a) *"We are going to buy some candy for mother."*
(b) *"Jack likes to feed the little puppies in the barn."*

If S hesitates, urge him to try by asking him to *"Say it."* It is, of course, never permissible to repeat the sentence.

SCORE: 1 plus. No error. Errors include omissions, substitutions, additions, changes in words or in the order of words, but *not* contractions, e.g., "we're" for "we are."

1. AESTHETIC COMPARISON

MATERIAL: Three cards with pairs of pictures for comparison.

PROCEDURE: Show each card in turn and ask, *"Which one is prettier?"*

SCORE: 3 plus.

2. *OPPOSITE ANALOGIES I (Same as IV, 3)

PROCEDURE: Say:

(a) *"Brother is a boy; sister is a . . . . . ."*
(b) *"In daytime it is light; at night it is . . . . . ."*
(c) *"Father is a man; mother is a . . . . . ."*
(d) *"The snail is slow; the rabbit is . . . . . ."*
(e) *"The sun shines during the day; the moon at . . . . . ."*

SCORE: 3 plus. See scoring standards, page 138.

3. *PICTORIAL SIMILARITIES AND DIFFERENCES I

MATERIAL: Six cards with pictures.

PROCEDURE: Present card (a) and say, *"See these crosses that are just alike? Here's one* (pointing) *that is not like the others. Put your finger on the one that is not the same as the others."* Make sure that S points out the one that is different. No further illustration. E may repeat for any of the following cards, *"Put your finger on the one that is not the same as the others."* Card (a) is used for illustration only.

SCORE: 3 plus. Card (a) is not included in the score.

4. MATERIALS

PROCEDURE: Say, *"What is a house made of?"* Same for *window* and *book.*

(a) House, (b) window, (c) book.

SCORE: 2 plus. See scoring standards, page 138.

5. *THREE COMMISSIONS

PROCEDURE: Arrange the setting before beginning the test; that is, see that a chair is available, the door open (or shut), and a box in place, all in plain sight. Have the child accompany you to the center of the room, saying, *"Now I want you to do something for me."* Make sure that you have the child's attention as you continue the instructions, saying, *"Here's a pencil. I want you to put it on the chair; then I want you to shut (open) the door; and then bring me the box which you see over there."* Point in turn to each object designated and make sure that the child does not start until the instructions have been completed and repeated by saying, *"Do you under-stand? Be sure to get it right. First you put the pencil on the chair, then you shut (open) the door, and then bring me the box."* Give no further help. If S asks what to do next say merely, *"Go ahead."* If the child stops or hesitates it is not permissible to prompt by asking what comes next.

SCORE: All three commissions must be executed and in the proper order. See scoring standards, page 139.

6. *COMPREHENSION III

PROCEDURE: Ask:

(a) *"What do we do with our eyes?"*
(b) *"What do we do with our ears?"*

SCORE: 1 plus. See scoring standards, page 139.

ALTERNATE

A. PICTORIAL IDENTIFICATION (Same as IV, 4)

MATERIAL: Card with pictures of objects.

PROCEDURE: Show the card and say: *"Show me what . . . ."* or *"Which one . . . . . ."* or *"Show me the one that . . . . . ."*

(a) "*. . . . . . we cook on.*"
(b) "*. . . . . . we carry when it is raining.*"
(c) "*. . . . . . gives us milk.*"
(d) "*. . . . . . has the longest ears.*"

(e) "...... *shines in the sky at night.*"
(f) "...... *catches mice.*"

If S names the object without pointing to it, ask him to point.

SCORE: 4 plus. Naming of object is not sufficient. S must designate it on the card.

YEAR V

1. * PICTURE COMPLETION: MAN

MATERIAL: Incomplete drawing of a man.

PROCEDURE: Point to the incomplete drawing in the record booklet and say, "*What is this?*" Whether the child recognizes it or not, say, "*It is a man, isn't it?* (or *Yes, it's a man*). *See, he has only one leg. You finish him. Make all the rest of him.*" If S stops after making the missing leg only, believing he has completed the task, say, "*Make all the rest of him.*" If, however, S begins with an arm or some part other than the leg and then stops, accept the response as complete without further urging. If S's addition is unrecognizable, ask, "*What is this?*"

SCORE: 2 points plus. See scoring standards, page 140.

2. PAPER FOLDING: TRIANGLE

MATERIAL: Six-inch squares of paper.

PROCEDURE: Say, "*Watch what I do.*" Make sure that the child is watching while you fold one of the 6" × 6" sheets once along the diagonal making a triangle; then fold this triangle once through the middle to make a triangle half as large.

Give the child another square of paper and say, "*Now you do it. Make one just like this.*" Leave the folded paper exposed, but pressed flat against the table.

SCORE: See scoring standards, page 142.

3. * DEFINITIONS

PROCEDURE: Say, "*What is a ball?*" If necessary, urge by saying, "*You know what a ball is. Tell me what a ball is."* Use the same formula for *hat* and *stove.*

(a) Ball,   (b) hat,   (c) stove.

SCORE: 2 plus. See scoring standards, page 142.

4. * COPYING A SQUARE

MATERIAL: Square printed in the record booklet.

PROCEDURE: Give the child a pencil and say, pointing to the square in the booklet, *"Make one just like this. Make it right here."* Give three trials, repeating the directions for each trial. Do not allow S to use the side of one square as part of another, or to trace the model.

SCORE: 1 plus. See scoring standards, page 143.

5. PICTORIAL SIMILARITIES AND DIFFERENCES ⅱ

MATERIAL: Twelve cards with pictures.

PROCEDURE: Present card (a) and say, *"See these two trees? They are just alike, aren't they? Just the same."* Then show card (b), *"But these two aren't alike* (pointing), *one is round and one is square."* Cards (a) and (b) are used for illustration only. No further illustration. Show card A and say, *"Now look at these two. Are they alike? Are they the same?"* For each successive pair, exposing one card at a time, say, *"And these. Are they alike? Are they the same?"*

SCORE: 9 plus.

6. * PATIENCE: RECTANGLES

MATERIAL: Two rectangular cards, each 2″ × 3″, one divided diagonally into two triangles.

PROCEDURE: Place the uncut card on the table with one of its longer sides toward the child. Beside it lay the two halves of the divided rectangle with their hypotenuses turned from each other, as shown in the figure. Then say, *"One of my cards has been cut in two; you put these two pieces* (touching the two triangles) *together to make a whole one just like this"* (pointing to the uncut card). If the first attempt is a failure, record minus and replace the pieces, saying, *"No, I want you to put these two pieces together to make a whole one just like this."* After a successful trial, return the pieces to their original position and say, *"Do it again."* If a piece is turned over, turn it back and do not count that trial. A trial is counted when the child leaves the pieces in some position. Give 3 trials. No time limit.

SCORE: 2 plus.

ALTERNATE

A. KNOT

MATERIAL: Pair of 18-inch shoestrings. Pencil.

PROCEDURE: Say, *"Watch what I do. I'm tying a knot around this pencil."* Tie a single knot (not a bow), then present the other shoelace and say to the child, *"You take this other piece of string and tie the same kind of knot around my finger. Make one just like this one"* (pointing to the examiner's knot).

SCORE: Any sort of knot which does not come undone is acceptable.

YEAR VI

1. * VOCABULARY

MATERIAL: Vocabulary card.

PROCEDURE: Say, *"I want to find out how many words you know. Listen, and when I say a word, you tell me what it means. What is an orange?"* Vary the form of the question to avoid a stilted manner of presentation, e.g., *"What does . . . . . . mean?"*, *"Tell me what a . . . . . . is"*, or give just the word without further question. If S hesitates, urge him to try by saying, *"Just tell me in your own words; say it any way you please. All I want to know is whether you know what a . . . . . . is."* Or *"You* know *what a . . . . . . is! Tell me, what is a . . . . . . ?"* If the child can read, give him the vocabulary card and let him look at each word as you read it.

If the child's meaning is not clear, that is, if his response can't be scored either plus or minus without further explanation, say, *"Tell me what you mean,"* or *"Tell me more about it."*

The words have been re-arranged in the order of their present difficulty for subjects tested in 1950–54. We have found that there is very little likelihood of success beyond the point where six consecutive words have been failed.

SCORE: 6 plus. See scoring standards, page 232.

2. * DIFFERENCES

PROCEDURE: Say: *"What is the difference between . . . . . ."*
(a) *"A bird and a dog?"*
(b) *"A slipper and a boot?"*
(c) *"Wood and glass?"*

If S does not seem to understand, say, *"You've seen a bird and you've seen dogs. Now, tell me the difference between a bird and a dog."*

SCORE: 2 plus. See scoring standards, page 145.

3. MUTILATED PICTURES

MATERIAL: Card with mutilated pictures.

PROCEDURE: Show S the card with the mutilated pictures and, pointing to each in turn, ask, *"What is gone in this picture?"* or *"What part is gone?"* If the child hesitates, further urging is sometimes necessary to elicit a response. Vary the question by asking, *"What isn't there?"* Avoid pointing to the missing part in designating the object.
(a) Wagon, (b) shoe, (c) teapot, (d) rabbit, (e) glove.

SCORE: 4 plus. See scoring standards, page 146.

4. * NUMBER CONCEPTS

MATERIAL: Twelve 1-inch cubes.

PROCEDURE: Place the blocks in a pile on the table before S. In order that the examiner may be sure just how many blocks the child means to indicate, we use a sheet of white paper for him to put his blocks on. Say, *"Give me . . . . . . blocks. Put them here,"* pointing to the sheet of paper. After each choice replace the blocks in the pile. Ask, in turn, for *three* blocks, *ten, six, nine* and *seven.* Sometimes the child thinks that in order to designate the correct number of blocks he has to pick them all up in his hand at once. In such a case say, **"You don't have to take them all in your hand at once."** It is important for the examiner to avoid suggesting the correct response; for example, do not wait expectantly when S stops after having placed too few blocks on the paper, nor should you hasten to remove the blocks, after he has given you the correct number, without making sure that he has really finished.

(a) 3, (b) 10, (c) 6, (d) 9, (e) 7.

SCORE: 4 plus.

5. *OPPOSITE ANALOGIES II

PROCEDURE: Say:

(a) *"A table is made of wood; a window of . . . . . ."*
(b) *"A bird flies; a fish . . . . . ."*
(c) *"The point of a cane is blunt; the point of a knife is . . . . . ."*
(d) *"An inch is short; a mile is . . . . . ."*

SCORE: 3 plus. See scoring standards, page 148.

6. MAZE TRACING

MATERIAL: Maze paths with three positions marked (see record booklet).

PROCEDURE: Show S the first maze and say, pointing to the little figure on the path, **"This little boy lives here, and here** (pointing) *is the schoolhouse. The little boy wants to go to school the shortest way without getting off the sidewalk. Here is the sidewalk.* (Point with the eraser end of the pencil to the path where the boy stands.) *Show me the shortest way. Mark it with your pencil, but don't go off the sidewalk. Start here and take the little boy to school the shortest way."*

Then show the second maze and say, **"This other little boy lives here** (position 2). *Show me the shortest way for him to go to school. Don't go off the sidewalk."*

Likewise, for the third maze say, **"And this boy lives here** (position 3). *Show me the shortest way for him to go to school. Don't go off the sidewalk."*

Make sure that the booklet is turned in each case so that the schoolhouse is in the correct (upright) position with relation to the child. Be careful to avoid suggesting a choice of pathway when pointing to the sidewalk.

In case the child starts tracing without marking the path with the pencil, say, *"Mark it so I can see it."*

SCORE: 2 plus. See scoring standards, page 149.

ALTERNATE

A. RESPONSE TO PICTURES LEVEL II (Same as III–6, 4)

MATERIAL: Three pictures, Grandmother's Story, Birthday Party, and Wash Day.

PROCEDURE: Present the pictures in the following order: Grandmother's Story, Birthday Party, Wash Day. Say, *"Look at this picture and tell me all about it."*

SCORE: Level II, 2 plus. See scoring standards, page 149.

YEAR VII

1. PICTURE ABSURDITIES I

MATERIAL: Five pictures: (a) Man with umbrella, (b) man with saw, (c) dog and rabbit, (d) man and woman sitting in the rain, (e) cat and mice.

PROCEDURE: Show the pictures in the order indicated and ask for each in turn, *"What's funny (foolish) about that picture?"* If the child's response is ambiguous without further explanation, ask, *"Why is that funny (foolish)?"*

SCORE: 4 plus. See scoring standards, page 151.

2. *SIMILARITIES: TWO THINGS

PROCEDURE: Say: *"In what way are . . . . . . and . . . . . . alike?"*

(a) *Wood and coal.*
(b) *Apple and peach.*
(c) *Ship and automobile.*
(d) *Iron and silver.*

It is often necessary to insist a little if S is silent or says he doesn't know. It is permissible to repeat the original question or to add, *"How are they the same?"* or *"In what way are they alike?"* When a difference is given for (a) say, *"No, I want you to tell me how they are* alike. *In what way are wood and coal the same?"* If the child persists in giving differences, make no further comment after the other pairs.

SCORE: 2 plus. See scoring standards, page 154.

3. * COPYING A DIAMOND

MATERIAL: Diamond printed in the record booklet.

PROCEDURE: Point to the model in the booklet and, giving S a pencil, say, *"Make one just like this. Make it right here."* Give 3 trials. For the second and third trials say, *"Now, make another one just like this. Make it here."*

SCORE: 1 plus. See scoring standards, page 155.

4. * COMPREHENSION IV (Same as VIII, 5)

PROCEDURE: Ask:

(a) *"What should you do if you found on the streets of a city a three-year-old baby that was lost from its parents?"*
(b) *"What's the thing for you to do when you have broken something that belongs to someone else?"*
(c) *"What's the thing for you to do when you are on your way to school and see that you are in danger of being late?"*
(d) *"What makes a sailboat move?"*
(e) *"What's the thing for you to do if another boy* (or girl, depending on the sex of the subject; or another person, for adults) *hits you without meaning to do it?"*
(f) *"What should you say when you are in a strange city and someone asks you how to find a certain address?"*

SCORE: 3 plus. See scoring standards, page 157.

5. OPPOSITE ANALOGIES III

PROCEDURE: Say:

(a) *"The rabbit's ears are long; the rat's ears are . . . . . ."*
(b) *"Snow is white; coal is . . . . . ."*

(c) *"The dog has hair; the bird has* . . . . . ."
(d) *"Wolves are wild; dogs are* . . . . . ."

SCORE: 2 plus. See scoring standards, page 159.

6. *REPEATING 5 DIGITS

PROCEDURE: Say, *"I am going to say some numbers and when I am through I want you to say them just the way I do. Listen carefully, and get them just right."* Before each series repeat, *"Listen carefully, and get them just right."* Pronounce the digits distinctly and with perfectly uniform emphasis at the rate of one per second.
   (a) 3–1–8–5–9,   (b) 4–8–3–7–2, (c) 9–6–1–8–3.

SCORE: 1 plus. The series must be repeated in correct order without error after a single reading.

ALTERNATE

A. REPEATING 3 DIGITS REVERSED

PROCEDURE: Say, *"I am going to say some numbers, and I want you to say them backwards. For example, if I should say 5–1–4, you would say 4–1–5. Ready now; listen carefully, and be sure to say the numbers backwards."* Before each series repeat, *"Ready now; listen carefully, and be sure to say the numbers backwards."* Pronounce the digits distinctly and with perfectly uniform emphasis at the rate of one per second.

   (a) 2–9–5,   (b) 8–1–6,   (c) 4–7–3.

SCORE: 1 plus. The series must be repeated backwards in correct order without error after a single reading.

YEAR VIII

1. *VOCABULARY

MATERIAL: Vocabulary card.

PROCEDURE: Say, *"I want to find out how many words you know. Listen, and when I say a word, you tell me what it means. What is an orange?"*

Vary the form of the question to avoid a stilted manner of presentation, e.g., *"What does . . . . . . mean?"*, *"Tell me what a . . . . . . is"*, or give just the word without further question. If S hesitates, urge him to try by saying: *"Just tell me in your own words; say it any way you please. All I want to know is whether you know what a . . . . . . is."* Or *"You know what a . . . . . . is! Tell me, what is a . . . . . . ?"* If the child can read, give him a printed copy of the word list and let him look at each word as you read it.

If the child's meaning is not clear, that is, if his response can't be scored either plus or minus without further explanation, say, *"Tell me what you mean,"* or *"Tell me more about it."* Continue until six consecutive words have been failed.

SCORE: 8 plus. See scoring standards, page 232.

2. MEMORY FOR STORIES: THE WET FALL

MATERIAL: Card with printed selection on it.

PROCEDURE: Say, *"Here is a story about 'The Wet Fall.' Listen carefully while I read it because I shall ask you questions about it."* Give the child a copy of the selection and let him follow it as you read it aloud.

"The Wet Fall"

"Once there was a little girl named Betty. She lived on a farm with her brother Dick. One day their father gave them a Shetland pony. They had lots of fun with it. One day, when Dick was riding on it, the pony became frightened and ran away. Poor Dick fell into a ditch. How Betty laughed when she saw him! He was covered with mud from head to foot."

Remove the child's copy of the selection and proceed to ask him the following questions:

(a) *"What is the name of this story?"*
(b) *"What was Betty's brother's name?"*
(c) *"Where did they live?"*
(d) *"Who gave the pony to them?"*
(e) *"What did the pony do?"*
(f) *"What happened?"*

SCORE: 5 of 6. See scoring standards, page 160.

3. *VERBAL ABSURDITIES I

PROCEDURE: Read each statement and, after each one, ask, *"What is foolish about that?"* The response is frequently ambiguous without further explanation. If it is not clear whether the subject sees the absurdity E must ask, *"Why is that foolish?"*

(a) "A man had flu (influenza) twice. The first time it killed him, but the second time he got well quickly."

(b) "Walter now has to write with his left hand because two years ago he lost both his arms in an accident."

(c) "A man said, 'I know a road from my house to the city which is downhill all the way to the city and downhill all the way back home.'"

(d) "An old gentleman complained that he could no longer walk around the park as he used to; he said he could now go only halfway around and back again."

SCORE: 3 plus. See scoring standards, page 162.

4. *SIMILARITIES AND DIFFERENCES

PROCEDURE: Say, *"I'm going to name two things and I want you to tell me how they are* alike *and how they are* different. *In what way are* . . . . . . *and* . . . . . . *alike, and how are they different?"* If in (a) or (b) S omits either of the comparisons, ask, *"And how are they the same* (or *different)?"* Make no comment concerning omissions in (c) and (d).

(a) *Baseball and orange.*   (c) *Ocean and river.*
(b) *Airplane and kite.*   (d) *Penny and quarter.*

If his response indicates that S has failed to recall the item correctly, for example, *baseball* as *football, orange* as *lemon,* or *river* as *lake,* repeat the original question.

SCORE: 3 plus. See scoring standards, page 164.

5. *COMPREHENSION IV (Same as VII, 4)

PROCEDURE: Ask:
(a) *"What should you do if you found on the streets of a city a three-year-old baby that was lost from its parents?"*
(b) *"What's the thing for you to do when you have broken something that belongs to someone else?"*

(c) *"What's the thing for you to do when you are on your way to school and see that you are in danger of being late?"*

(d) *"What makes a sailboat move?"*

(e) *"What's the thing for you to do if another boy"* (or girl, depending on the sex of the subject; or another person, for adults) *"hits you without meaning to do it?"*

(f) *"What should you say when you are in a strange city and someone asks you how to find a certain address?"*

SCORE: 4 plus. See scoring standards, page 157.

6. NAMING THE DAYS OF THE WEEK

PROCEDURE: Say, *"Name the days of the week for me."* If S fails to comprehend the task and begins to name the various holidays or the like, say, *"No, that is not what I mean. I want you to name the days of the week."* It is not permissible to start S off by naming one day. If S names them all in correct order, give three checks by asking, *"What day comes before . . . . . . ?"*

(a) Tuesday, (b) Thursday, (c) Friday.

SCORE: All must be named in the correct order. 2 of 3 checks correct.

ALTERNATE

A. PROBLEM SITUATIONS I

PROCEDURE: Say:

(a) "About two o'clock one afternoon a number of boys and girls dressed in their best clothes rang the bell at Alice's house. Alice opened the door. *What was happening?"*

(b) "Helen heard a big 'Bang' and came running outdoors. There were nails all over the road, and an automobile had just stopped beside the road. *What was the 'Bang'?"*

(c) "A young man and lady were sitting in a restaurant. They had nearly finished eating a big dinner. The waiter brought the bill. The young man looked at it, and then seemed worried and embarrassed. *Why?"*

SCORE: 2 plus. See scoring standards, page 167.

1. PAPER CUTTING (Same as XIII, A)

MATERIAL: Six-inch squares of paper and scissors.

PROCEDURE: Taking one of the sheets, say,

(a) *"Watch carefully what I do. See, I fold the paper this way* (folding it over once through the middle, making a rectangle). *Now I will cut out a piece right here"* (indicating). At the center of the creased edge cut out a half-inch *square*. (If the paper were unfolded the cut would be rectangular.) Leave the folded paper exposed, but pressed flat against the table. The fragment cut from the paper should be kept out of sight. Indicating the 3" × 3" square in the booklet, say, *"Make a drawing here to show how this paper would look if it were un-folded (opened). Draw lines to show where the paper would be creased and show how and where it would be cut."* If S omits either the creases or the cuts, repeat, *"Draw lines to show where the paper would be creased and show how and where it would be cut,"* emphasizing the pertinent words.

(b) For the second sheet say, *"Now watch what I do. See, I fold the paper this way* (folding the sheet over in the middle). *Then I fold it this way* (folding it again in the middle, but at right angles to the first fold). *And now I will cut out a piece right here."* Cut off the corner formed by the intersection of the folds. The cut should be made about three quarters of an inch from the corner. Then say, as before, *"Make a drawing here to show how this paper would look if it were unfolded (opened). Draw lines to show where the paper would be creased and show how and where it would be cut."*

SCORE: 1 plus. See scoring standards, page 168.

2. VERBAL ABSURDITIES II (Same as XII, 2)

PROCEDURE: Read each statement and, after each one, ask, *"What is foolish about that?"* The response is frequently ambiguous without further explanation. If it is not clear that the subject sees the absurdity E must say, *"Why is that foolish?"*

(a) "Bill Jones's feet are so big that he has to pull his trousers on over his head."

(b) "A man went one day to the post office and asked if there was a letter waiting for him. 'What is your name?' asked the postmaster. 'Why,' said the man, 'you will find my name on the envelope.'"

(c) "The fireman hurried to the burning house, got his fire hose ready, and after smoking a cigar, put out the fire."

(d) "In an old graveyard in Spain they have discovered a small skull which they believe to be that of Christopher Columbus when he was about ten years old."

(e) "One day we saw several icebergs that had been entirely melted by the warmth of the Gulf Stream."

SCORE: 3 plus. See scoring standards, page 171.

3. *MEMORY FOR DESIGNS I (Same as XI, 1)

MATERIAL: Card with two designs.

PROCEDURE: With the card in your hand, but before showing the designs say, *"This card has two drawings on it. I am going to show them to you for ten seconds, then I will take the card away and let you draw from memory what you have seen. Be sure to look at both drawings carefully."* Then show the card for 10 seconds, holding it at right angles to the child's line of vision and with the designs in the position given in the plate. At the end of approximately 4 seconds say quietly, *"Look at both."* Have S reproduce the designs immediately, and note which is the top of his drawing.

SCORE: 1 plus or 2 with half credit each. See scoring standards, page 174.

4. *RHYMES: NEW FORM

PROCEDURE: Say, *"You know what a rhyme is, of course. A rhyme is a word that sounds like another word. Two words rhyme if they end in the same sound, like 'hat' and 'sat.' Now I want you to:*
(a) *"Tell me the name of a color that rhymes with* head."
(b) *"Tell me a number that rhymes with* tree."
(c) *"Tell me the name of an animal that rhymes with* fair."
(d) *"Tell me the name of a flower that rhymes with* nose."

SCORE: 3 plus. See scoring standards, page 179.

5. *MAKING CHANGE

PROCEDURE: Ask, *"If I were to buy four cents' worth of candy and should give the storekeeper ten cents, how much money would I get back?"* Same for 12–15; 4–25 cents.

SCORE: 2 plus.

6. *REPEATING 4 DIGITS REVERSED

PROCEDURE: Say, *"I am going to say some numbers, and I want you to say them backwards. For example, if I should say 5–1–4, you would say 4–1–5. Ready now; listen carefully, and be sure to say the numbers backwards."* Before each series repeat, *"Ready now; listen carefully, and be sure to say the numbers backwards."* Rate, one per second.
   (a) 8–5–2–6,   (b) 4–9–3–7,   (c) 3–6–2–9.

SCORE: 1 plus. The series must be repeated backwards in correct order without error after a single reading.

ALTERNATE

A. RHYMES: OLD FORM

PROCEDURE: Say:
   (a) *"You know what a rhyme is, of course. A rhyme is a word that sounds like another word. Two words rhyme if they end in the same sound. For example, 'hat,' 'bat,' 'rat,' 'sat,' all rhyme with cat. Now see how many words you can name that rhyme with* date. *Ready; go ahead."*
   (b) *"Now see how many words you can name that rhyme with* head.*"*
   (c) *"Now see how many words you can name that rhyme with* cap.*"*
   Time limit, 30 seconds each.

SCORE: 2 plus with 3 rhymes each. See scoring standards, page 180.

YEAR X

1. *VOCABULARY

MATERIAL: Vocabulary card.

PROCEDURE: Say, *"I want to find out how many words you know. Listen, and when I say a word, you tell me what it means. What is an orange?"*

Vary the form of the question to avoid a stilted manner of presentation, e.g., *"What does . . . . . . mean?"*, *"Tell me what a . . . . . . is"*, or give just the word without further question. If S hesitates, urge him to try by saying, *"Just tell me in your own words; say it any way you please. All I want to know is whether you know what a . . . . . . is."* Or, *"You know what a . . . . . . is! Tell me, what is a . . . . . . ?"* Give S a printed copy of the word list and let him look at each word as you read it.

If the child's meaning is not clear, that is, if his response can't be scored either plus or minus without further explanation, say, *"Tell me what you mean,"* or *"Tell me more about it."* Continue until six consecutive words have been failed.

SCORE: 11 plus. See scoring standards, page 232.

2. BLOCK COUNTING

MATERIAL: Card with picture of piles of cubes arranged in 2 rows.

PROCEDURE: Show the card and, pointing to the first illustration, ask, *"How many blocks are there here?"* Then point to the second pile of blocks and ask, *"And here there are how many?"* Then the third and ask, *"And here?"* These first three are for illustration only and are not counted toward the score. Correct any errors which the subject makes on the samples and show him how the count should be made to include the unseen blocks. Then point to the rows below and say, *"Now count them and tell me how many there are in each square, beginning here* (at the subject's left) *and working along each row."* Point to the first square and ask, *"How many here?"* For the second square ask, *"And here?"* Record the count for each square in order from S's left to his right. Do not allow S to point to each block with a pencil while counting.

SCORE: 8 plus

Key:

6	9	6	6	5	12	5
4	10	11	8	9	11	10

3. *ABSTRACT WORDS I (Same as XII, 5)

PROCEDURE: Say, *"What do we mean by . . . . . . ?"* or *"What is . . . . . . ?"*

(a) Pity, (b) curiosity, (c) grief, (d) surprise.

Responses defining abstract words are often ambiguous. In asking for further clarification of a response say, *"Yes, but what do we mean by*

. . . . . . *?"* or *"Yes, but what is* . . . . . . *?"*

SCORE: 2 plus. See scoring standards, page 181.

4. FINDING REASONS I

PROCEDURE: Say:

(a) *"Give two reasons why children should not be too noisy in school."*

(b) *"Give two reasons why most people would rather have an automobile than a bicycle."*

If S gives only one reason and stops, do not try to elicit the second by further questioning, but, before giving the next item, hesitate long enough to give S an opportunity to remember for himself that he is expected to give two reasons. If in either case S asks how many reasons he has given, read his response to him so that he may decide for himself.

SCORE: 2 plus. See scoring standards, page 183.

5. * WORD NAMING

PROCEDURE: Say, *"Now I want to see how many different words you can name in one minute. Just any words will do, like 'clouds,' 'dog,' 'chair,' 'happy.' When I say, 'Ready,' you begin and say the words as fast as you can and I will count them. Ready; go ahead."* Do no urging unless the child hesitates for 10 seconds, in which case say, *"Go ahead as fast as you can. Any words will do."* If S gives sentences or counts, stop him, saying, *"Counting* (or *sentences*) *not allowed. You must name separate words. Go ahead as fast as you can."*

SCORE: 28 words in one minute. See scoring standards, page 185.

6. * REPEATING 6 DIGITS

PROCEDURE: Say, *"I am going to say some numbers and when I am through I want you to say them just the way I do. Listen carefully, and get them just right."* Before each series repeat, *"Listen carefully, and get them just right."* Pronounce the digits distinctly and with perfectly uniform emphasis at the rate of one per second.

(a) 4–7–3–8–5–9, (b) 5–2–9–7–4–6, (c) 7–2–8–3–9–4.

SCORE: 1 plus. The series must be repeated in correct order without error after a single reading.

ALTERNATE

A. VERBAL ABSURDITIES III

PROCEDURE: Read each statement and after each one ask, "*What is foolish about that?*" The response is frequently ambiguous without further explanation. If it is not clear that the subject sees the absurdity E must say, "*Why is that foolish?*"

(a) "In the year 1951 many more women than men got married in the United States."

(b) "A man wished to dig a hole in which to bury some rubbish, but could not decide what to do with the dirt from the hole. A friend suggested that he dig a hole large enough to hold the dirt, too."

(c) "They began the meeting late, but they set the hands of the clock back so that the meeting might surely close before sunset."

SCORE: 2 plus. See scoring standards, page 185.

YEAR XI

1. *MEMORY FOR DESIGNS I (Same as IX, 3)

MATERIAL: Card with two designs.

PROCEDURE: With the card in your hand, but before showing the designs, say, "*This card has two drawings on it. I am going to show them to you for ten seconds, then I will take the card away and let you draw from memory what you have seen. Be sure to look at both drawings carefully.*" Then show the card for 10 seconds, holding it at right angles to the child's line of vision and with the designs in the position given in the plate. At the end of approximately 4 seconds say, quietly, "*Look at both.*" Have S reproduce the designs immediately, and note which is the top of his drawing.

SCORE: 1½ plus. See scoring standards, page 174.

2. *VERBAL ABSURDITIES IV

PROCEDURE: Read each statement and, after each one, ask, "*What is foolish about that?*" The response is frequently ambiguous. If it is not clear that the subject sees the absurdity say, "*Why is that foolish?*"

(a) "The judge said to the prisoner, 'You are to be hanged, and I hope it will be a warning to you.' "

(b) "A well-known railroad had its last accident five years ago and since that time it has killed only one person in a collision."

(c) "When there is a collision the last car of the train is usually damaged most. So they have decided that it will be best if the last car is always taken off before the train starts."

SCORE: 2 plus. See scoring standards, page 188.

3. * ABSTRACT WORDS II (Same as XIII, 2)

PROCEDURE: Say, "*What is . . . . . . ?*" or "*What do we mean by . . . . . . ?*"

(a) Connection, (b) compare, (c) conquer, (d) obedience, (e) revenge.

Responses defining abstract words are often ambiguous. In asking for a further clarification, say, "*Yes, but what do we mean by . . . . . . ?*" or "*Yes, but what is . . . . . . ?*"

SCORE: 3 plus. See scoring standards, page 189.

4. MEMORY FOR SENTENCES II

PROCEDURE: Say, before giving each sentence, "*Now listen, and be sure to say exactly what I say.*"

(a) "*At the summer camp the children get up early in the morning to go swimming.*"

(b) "*Yesterday we went for a ride in our car along the road that crosses the bridge.*"

SCORE: 1 plus. No error. Errors include omissions, substitutions, additions, changes in words or in the order of words.

5. PROBLEM SITUATION II

PROCEDURE: Say, "*Listen, and see if you can understand what I read.*"
"Donald went walking in the woods. He saw a pretty little animal that

he tried to take home for a pet. It got away from him, but when he got home, his family immediately burned all his clothes. **Why?**"

SCORE: See scoring standards, page 192.

6. * SIMILARITIES: THREE THINGS

PROCEDURE: Say: "*In what way are* . . . . . . , ... , *and* . . . . . . *alike?*"
  (a) *Snake, cow, sparrow.*
  (b) *Rose, potato, tree.*
  (c) *Wool, cotton, leather.*
  (d) *Knife-blade, penny, piece of wire.*
  (e) *Book, teacher, newspaper.*
A little urging is sometimes necessary to secure a response. If S hesitates or says he doesn't know, urge him to try by repeating the question or asking, "*How are they alike?*"

SCORE: 3 plus. See scoring standards, page 192.

ALTERNATE

A. FINDING REASONS II

PROCEDURE: Say:
  (a) "*Give two reasons why children should obey their parents.*"
  (b) "*Give two reasons why there should be plenty of railroads in the United States.*"

SCORE: 2 plus with 2 reasons each. See scoring standards, page 195.

YEAR XII

1. * VOCABULARY

MATERIAL: Vocabulary card.

PROCEDURE: Say, "*I want to find out how many words you know. Listen, and when I say a word, you tell me what it means. What is an orange?*"

Vary the form of the question to avoid a stilted manner of presentation, e.g., *"What does* . . . . . . *mean?"*, *"Tell me what a* . . . . . . *is"*, or give just the word without any further question. If S hesitates, urge him to try by saying, *"Just tell me in your own words; say it any way you please. All I want to know is whether you know what a* . . . . . . *is."* Or *"You* know *what a* . . . . . . *is! Tell me, what is a* . . . . . . *?"* Give S a printed copy of the word list and let him look at each word as you read it.

If the subject's meaning is not clear, that is, if his response can't be scored plus or minus without further explanation, say, *"Tell me what you mean,"* or *"Tell me more about it."* Continue until six consecutive words have been failed.

SCORE: 15 plus. See scoring standards, page 232.

2. * VERBAL ABSURDITIES II (Same as IX, 2)

PROCEDURE: Read each statement and, after each one, ask, *"What is foolish about that?"* The response is frequently ambiguous. If it is not clear that the subject sees the absurdity say, *"Why is that foolish?"*

(a) "Bill Jones's feet are so big that he has to pull his trousers on over his head."

(b) "A man went one day to the post office and asked if there was a letter waiting for him. 'What is your name?' asked the postmaster. 'Why,' said the man, 'you will find my name on the envelope.' "

(c) "The fireman hurried to the burning house, got his fire hose ready, and after smoking a cigar, put out the fire."

(d) "In an old graveyard in Spain they have discovered a small skull which they believe to be that of Christopher Columbus when he was about ten years old."

(e) "One day we saw several icebergs that had been entirely melted by the warmth of the Gulf Stream."

SCORE: 4 plus. See scoring standards, page 171.

3. PICTURE ABSURDITIES II

MATERIAL: Picture, The Shadow.

PROCEDURE: Showing the picture, ask, *"What's foolish about that picture?"* If the response is ambiguous, say, *"Why is that foolish?"*

SCORE: See scoring standards, page 196.

4. REPEATING 5 DIGITS REVERSED

PROCEDURE: Say, "*I am going to say some numbers, and I want you to say them backwards. For example, if I should say 5–1–4, you would say 4–1–5. Ready now; listen carefully, and be sure to say the numbers backwards.*" Before each series repeat, "*Ready now; listen carefully, and be sure to say the numbers backwards.*" Rate, one per second.

(a) 8–1–3–7–9, (b) 6–9–5–8–2, (c) 9–2–5–1–8.

SCORE: 1 plus. The series must be repeated backwards in correct order without error after a single reading.

5. *ABSTRACT WORDS I (Same as X, 3)

PROCEDURE: Say, "*What do we mean by* . . . . . .? or "*What is* . . . . . .?*"
(a) Pity, (b) curiosity, (c) grief, (d) surprise
Responses defining abstract words are often ambiguous. In asking for further clarification of a response, say, "*Yes, but what do we mean by* . . . . . .?*" or "*What is* . . . . . .?*"

SCORE: 3 plus. See scoring standards, page 181.

6. *MINKUS COMPLETION I

MATERIAL: Selection printed in record booklet.

PROCEDURE: Have S fill in the missing word for each blank in the selection printed in the record booklet. Say, "*Write the missing word in each blank. Put just one word in each.*"

(a) We like to pop corn . . . . . . to roast chestnuts over the fire.
(b) One cannot always be a hero, ... one can always be a man.
(c) The streams are dry . . . . . . there has been little rain.
(d) Lincoln aroused no jealousy . . . . . . he was not selfish.

If S cannot read, it is permissible to read the words for him, indicating each. If necessary, write in the missing word that S dictates.
Time limit, 5 minutes.

SCORE: 3 sentences plus. See scoring standards, page 197.

A. MEMORY FOR DESIGNS II

MATERIAL: Card with design.

PROCEDURE: Before showing the card say, *"This card has a drawing on it. I am going to show it to you for ten seconds, then I will take the card away and let you draw from memory what you have seen. Be sure to look at the drawing carefully."* Show the card for 10 seconds. Have S reproduce the design immediately, and note which is the top of his drawing.

SCORE: See scoring standards, page 198.

YEAR XIII

1. *PLAN OF SEARCH

MATERIAL: Diamond-shaped figure (in record booklet) with a small gap in the angle nearest the subject.

PROCEDURE: Give S a pencil and, showing him the figure, say, *"Let's suppose that your purse with a lot of money in it has been lost in this big field. Take this pencil and start here* (pointing) *at the gate, and show me where you would go to hunt for the purse so as to be sure not to miss it."* If S fails to understand that he is to mark the path, add, *"Mark it with the pencil to show me where you would go to hunt for the purse."*

If S stops before there is evidence whether or not any plan governs his procedure, say, *"But suppose you hadn't found it yet, show me everywhere you would go to look for it."* No further questioning or urging.

SCORE: See scoring standards, page 200.

2. *ABSTRACT WORDS II (Same as XI, 3)

PROCEDURE: *Say, "What is a . . . . . . ?"* or *"What do we mean by . . . . . . ?"*

(a) Connection, (b) compare, (c) conquer, (d) obedience, (e) revenge.

Responses defining abstract words are often ambiguous. In asking for further clarification of a response, say, *"Yes, but what do we mean by . . . . . .?"* or *"Yes, but what is . . . . . .?"*

SCORE: 4 plus. See scoring standards, page 189.

3. MEMORY FOR SENTENCES III

PROCEDURE: Say before giving each sentence, *"Listen, and be sure to say exactly what I say."*

(a) *"The airplane made a careful landing in the space which had been prepared for it."*

(b) *"Tom Brown's dog ran quickly down the road with a huge bone in his mouth."*

SCORE: 1 plus. No error. Errors include omissions, substitutions, additions, changes in words or in order of words.

4. * PROBLEMS OF FACT

PROCEDURE: Say, *"Listen . . . ."*

(a) "A man who was walking in the woods near a city stopped suddenly, very much frightened, and then ran to the nearest policeman, saying that he had just seen hanging from the limb of a tree a . . . . . . *a what?"* (If the reply is *"man,"* say, *"Tell me what you mean; explain it."*)

(b) "My neighbor has been having queer visitors. First a doctor came to his house, then a lawyer, then a minister (preacher, priest, or rabbi). *What do you think happened there?"* If the response appears to be at all plausible, check by asking, *"Why did the lawyer come?"*

(c) "An Indian who had come to town for the first time in his life saw a boy riding along the street. As the boy rode by the Indian said, 'The white boy is lazy; he walks sitting down.' *What was the boy riding on that caused the Indian to say, 'He walks sitting down'?"*

SCORE: 2 plus. See scoring standards, page 200.

5. * DISSECTED SENTENCES

MATERIAL: Cards on which disarranged words are printed in capitals.

PROCEDURE: Show the sentences one at a time in the order indicated.

Before giving S the first sentence, say, with the card in your hand but held so that S can't see the words until you have completed your instructions: *"Here is a sentence that has the words all mixed up so that they don't make any sense. If the words were changed around in the right order they would make a good sentence. Look carefully, and tell me how the sentence ought to read."* Pronounce for S any word he does not know, but give no further help. For (b) and (c) say, *"Now tell me how this one ought to read."* Time, 1 minute each.

(a) FOR THE STARTED AN WE COUNTRY EARLY AT HOUR.
(b) TO ASKED PAPER MY TEACHER CORRECT I MY.
(c) A DEFENDS DOG GOOD HIS BRAVELY MASTER.

SCORE: 2 plus, or equivalent in half credits. See scoring standards, page 203.

6. COPYING A BEAD CHAIN FROM MEMORY

MATERIAL: Box of 48 kindergarten beads all of the same color, 16 round, 16 square, and 16 cylindrical.

PROCEDURE: Make a 9-bead chain, holding the string so that S can see, and say, *"Watch carefully what I am making because I am going to take this one away and see if you can make one just like it."* Use, in order, 2 round, 1 square, 1 round, 1 cylindrical, 1 round, 1 square, and 2 round beads, making a chain like the sample: ○○□○▭○□○○ .
When complete, let S look at it for 5 seconds. Remove the chain and tell him to make one just like it. Time limit, 2 minutes.

SCORE: No error.

ALTERNATE

A. PAPER CUTTING (Same as IX, 1)

MATERIAL: Six-inch squares of paper.

PROCEDURE: Taking one of the sheets, say,
(a) *"Watch carefully what I do. See, I fold the paper this way* (folding it over once through the middle, making a rectangle). *Now I will cut*

out a piece right here" (indicating). At the center of the creased edge cut out a half-inch *square*. (If the paper were unfolded, the cut would be rectangular.) Leave the folded paper exposed, but pressed flat against the table. The fragments cut from the paper should be kept out of sight. Indicating the 3″ × 3″ square in the record booklet, say: *"Make a drawing here to show how this paper would look if it were unfolded (opened). Draw lines to show where the paper would be creased and show how and where it would be cut."* If S omits either the creases or cuts, repeat, *"Draw lines to show* where *the paper would be creased and show* how *and* where *it would be cut,"* emphasizing the pertinent words.

(b) Fold the second sheet once in the middle, and then fold it again in the middle but at right angles to the first fold. Then cut off the corner formed by the intersection of the folds. The cut should be made about three quarters of an inch from the corner. Repeat the instructions as before.

SCORE: 2 plus. See scoring standards, page 168.

YEAR XIV

1. *VOCABULARY

MATERIAL: Vocabulary card.

PROCEDURE: Say, *"I want to find out how many words you know. Listen, and when I say a word, you tell me what it means. What is an orange?"* Vary the form of the question to avoid a stilted manner of presentation, e.g., *"What does . . . . . . mean?"*, *"Tell me what a . . . . . . is"*, or give just the word without further question. If S hesitates, urge him to try by saying, *"Just tell me in your own words; say it any way you please. All I want to know is whether you know what a . . . . . . is."* Or *"You* know *what a . . . . . . is! Tell me, what is a . . . . . ?"* Give S the vocabulary card containing the word list and let him look at each word as you read it.

If the subject's meaning is not clear, that is, if his response can't be scored plus or minus without further explanation, say, *"Tell me what you mean,"* or *"Tell me more about it."* Continue until six consecutive words have been failed.

SCORE: 17 plus. See scoring standards, page 232.

2. * INDUCTION

MATERIAL: Six sheets of tissue paper 8½″ × 11″.

PROCEDURE: Take the first sheet, and saying, *"Watch what I do,"* fold it through the middle and then, in the center of the folded edge, cut out a small notch. Then say, *"How many holes will there be when the paper is unfolded?"* Unfold the sheet and spread it out so S can count the holes, thus calling his attention to the correct number.

Take a second sheet of paper and fold it as before, saying, *"When I folded it this way and cut out a piece, you remember it made one hole in the paper. This time we will give the paper another fold and see how many holes there will be."* Then proceed to fold the paper again, this time at right angles to the first fold, cut out a notch from the folded edge, and ask, *"How many holes will there be this time when the paper is unfolded?"* Let S see the result as before and place this sheet on the other, proceeding to the third sheet.

Continue in the same manner with sheets 3, 4, 5, and 6, adding one fold each time at right angles to the preceding one. In folding each sheet recapitulate the results, saying thus, with the sixth sheet, *"When we folded it this way there was* one *hole; when we folded it again there were* two; *when we folded it again there were* four; *when we folded it again there were* eight; *when we folded it again there were* sixteen; *now tell me how many holes there will be if we fold it once more?"* Be careful to avoid saying, "When we folded it once, twice, three times . . . . . ." It is not necessary to cut or unfold the last sheet, but this time express approval regardless of the correctness of the response, and if S gives the correct response for the sixth sheet, say, *"Give me a rule so that I can know each time how many holes there are going to be."*

If the rule is given spontaneously before the sixth folding it is not necessary to continue. It is not permissible to ask for the rule until all six parts have been given. Nothing must be said which could remotely suggest the operation of the rule.

SCORE: Plus if the rule is grasped by the time the sixth sheet is reached; that is, S may pass after five incorrect responses, provided the sixth is correct and the governing rule can then be given. See scoring standards, page 204.

3. * REASONING I

MATERIAL: Card on which the problem is stated.

PROCEDURE: Give S a copy of the problem and let him have it to look at as you read it aloud and while he is solving it.

"My house was burglarized last Saturday. I was at home all of the morning but out during the afternoon until 5 o'clock. My father left the house at 3 o'clock and my brother was there until 4. At what time did the burglary occur?"

If the response is either *"after 4"* or *"before 5,"* ask S to explain what he means.

SCORE: See scoring standards, page 205.

4. * INGENUITY I (Same as AA, 2; SA II, 4)

PROCEDURE: The problem is given orally and may be repeated if necessary. (a) *"A mother sent her boy to the river to bring back exactly 2 pints of water. She gave him a 5-pint can and a 3-pint can. Show me how the boy can measure out exactly 2 pints of water using nothing but these two cans and not guessing at the amount. You should begin by filling the 5-pint can first. Remember, you have a 5-pint can and a 3-pint can and you must bring back exactly 2 pints of water."*

(b) *"This time he has to bring back exactly 13 pints of water. He has a 9-pint can and a 5-pint can. Show me how he can measure out exactly 13 pints of water using nothing but these two cans and not guessing at the amount. You should begin by filling the 9-pint can first. Remember, you have a 9-pint can and a 5-pint can and you must bring back exactly 13 pints."*

(c) *"And this time he has to bring back exactly 1 pint of water. He has a 3-pint can and an 8-pint can. Show me how he can measure out exactly 1 pint of water using nothing but these two cans and not guessing at the amount. You should begin by filling the 3-pint can first. Remember, you have a 3-pint can and an 8-pint can and you must bring back exactly 1 pint of water."*

The subject is not allowed to use pencil and paper. If he resorts to a method that involves guessing, tell him that he must *measure* out the water without guessing. Explain, also, if necessary, that it is a fair, not a catch, problem. It is important to encourage him to keep on trying during the full 3-minute period allowed for each problem, but if he has failed on the first problem it is not necessary to go on to (b) and (c).

Begin timing as soon as the problem has been presented.

SCORE: 1 plus. See scoring standards, page 206.

5. ORIENTATION: DIRECTION I

PROCEDURE: Read the following directions distinctly, emphasizing the critical words:

(a) *"Which direction would you have to face so that your* left *hand would be toward the east?"* (S)

(If S points or says, *"That way,"* say, *"What is the* name *of the direction you would have to face?"*)

(b) *"Suppose you are going west, then turn to your right; in what direction are you going now?"* (N)

(c) *"Suppose you are going north, then turn to your left, then turn right; in what direction are you going now?"* (N)

(d) *"Suppose you are going south, then turn left, then turn right, then turn left again; in what direction are you going now?"* (E)

(e) *"Suppose you are going north, then turn left, then left again, then right, and then right again; in what direction are you going now?"* (N)

It is permissible to repeat the directions if S becomes confused or cannot remember the problem.

SCORE: 3 plus.

6. RECONCILIATION OF OPPOSITES (Same as SA I, A)

PROCEDURE: Say, *"In what way are* . . . . . . *and* . . . . . . *alike?"*

(a) Winter and summer.
(b) Happy and sad.
(c) Loud and soft.
(d) Much and little.
(e) Beginning and end.

Even though S is failing the items, all five must be given. If, as sometimes happens, S fails to grasp the idea until several items have been given, a correction of the preceding items is accepted if offered spontaneously. If S says they are opposite, repeat the question with emphasis on *alike.*

SCORE: 2 plus. See scoring standards, page 206.

ALTERNATE

A. INGENUITY II

PROCEDURE: The problem is given orally and may be repeated if necessary.

(a) *"A mother sent her boy to the river to bring back exactly 3 pints of water. She gave him a 7-pint can and a 4-pint can. Show me how the boy can measure out exactly 3 pints of water using nothing but these two cans and not guessing at the amount. You should begin by filling the 7-pint can first. Remember, you have a 7-pint can and a 4-pint can and you must bring back exactly 3 pints of water."*

The subject is not allowed to use pencil and paper. If he resorts to a method that involves guessing, tell him that he must *measure* out the water without guessing. Explain, also, if necessary, that it is a fair, not a catch, problem. It is important to encourage him to keep on trying during the full 3-minute period allowed. Begin timing as soon as the problem has been presented.

SCORE: 1 plus. See scoring standards, page 208.

A V E R A G E   A D U L T

1. * VOCABULARY

MATERIAL: Vocabulary card.

PROCEDURE: Say, *"I want to find out how many words you know. Listen, and when I say a word, you tell me what it means. What is an orange?"* Vary the form of the question to avoid a stilted manner of presentation, e.g., *"What does . . . . . . mean?"* *"Tell me what a . . . . . . is,"* or give just the word without any further question. If S hesitates, urge him to try by saying, *"Just tell me in your own words; say it any way you please. All I want to know is whether you know what a . . . . . . is."* Or *"You know what a . . . . . is! Tell me, what is a . . . . . . ?"* Give S the vocabulary card containing the word list and let him look at each word as you read it.

If the subject's meaning is not clear, that is, if his response can't be scored plus or minus without further explanation, say, *"Tell me what you mean,"* or *"Tell me more about it."* Continue until six consecutive words have been failed.

SCORE: 20 plus. See scoring standards, page 232.

2. * INGENUITY I (Same as XIV, 4; SA II, 4)

PROCEDURE: The problem is given orally and may be repeated if necessary. (a) *"A mother sent her boy to the river to bring back exactly 2 pints of water. She gave him a 5-pint can and a 3-pint can. Show me how the boy can measure out exactly 2 pints of water using nothing but these two cans and not guessing at the amount. You should begin by filling the 5-pint can first. Remember, you have a 5-pint can and a 3-pint can and you must bring back exactly 2 pints of water."*
(b) *"This time he has to bring back exactly 13 pints of water. He has*

a 9-pint can and a 5-pint can. Show me how he can measure out exactly 13 pints of water using nothing but these two cans and not guessing at the amount. You should begin by filling the 9-pint can first. Remember, you have a 9-pint can and a 5-pint can and you must bring back exactly 13 pints."

(c) *"And this time he has to bring back exactly 1 pint of water. He has a 3-pint can and an 8-pint can. Show me how he can measure out exactly 1 pint of water using nothing but these two cans and not guessing at the amount. You should begin by filling the 3-pint can first. Remember, you have a 3-pint can and an 8-pint can and you must bring back exactly 1 pint of water."*

The subject is not allowed to use pencil and paper. If he resorts to a method that involves guessing, tell him that he must *measure* out the water without guessing. Explain also, if necessary, that it is a fair, not a catch, problem. It is important to encourage him to keep on trying during the full three-minute period allowed for each problem, but if he has failed on the first problem it is not necessary to go on to (b) and (c). Begin timing as soon as the problem has been presented.

SCORE: 2 plus. See scoring standards, page 206.

3. * DIFFERENCES BETWEEN ABSTRACT WORDS

PROCEDURE: Say, *"What is the difference between:*
(a) *"Laziness and idleness?"*
(b) *"Poverty and misery?"*
(c) *"Character and reputation?"*

SCORE: 2 plus. See scoring standards, page 208.

4. ARITHMETICAL REASONING

MATERIAL: Three cards on which are printed arithmetical problems.

PROCEDURE: Present each card and say, *"Read this out loud and give me the answer."* Begin timing as soon as S has completed his reading of the problem. With the printed problem still before him, have S find the answer without the use of pencil or paper. It is not permissible, if the subject gives an incorrect answer, to ask him to solve the problem again. The following exception, however, is made to this rule: If the answer given to the third problem indicates that *yard* has been read as *feet*, S is asked to re-read the problem carefully (aloud) and to tell how he solved it. No extension of the time limit is allowed for this correction, however. No further help may be given.

(a) *If a man's salary is $20 a week and he spends $14 a week, how long will it take him to save $300?* (50 weeks)

(b) *If 2 pencils cost 5 cents, how many pencils can you buy for 50 cents?* (20)

(c) *At 15 cents a yard, how much will 7 feet of cloth cost?* (35 cents)

Time limit, 1 minute each.

SCORE: 2 plus.

5. PROVERBS I

PROCEDURE: Say,"*Here is a proverb, and you are supposed to tell what it means. For example, this proverb, 'Large oaks from little acorns grow,' means that great things may have small beginnings. What does this one mean?*"

(a) *"We only know the worth of water when the well is dry."*

(b) *"No wind can do him good who steers for no port."*

(c) *"Don't judge a book by its cover."*

SCORE: 2 plus. See scoring standards, page 211.

6. ORIENTATION: DIRECTION II

PROCEDURE: Read the following directions distinctly, emphasizing the critical words:

(a) *"Which direction would you have to face so your* right *hand would be toward the* north?" (W)

(If S points or says, *"That way,"* say, *"What is the* name *of the direction you would have to face?"*)

(b) *"Suppose you are going* east, *then turn to your* right; *in what direction are you going now?"* (S)

(c) *"Suppose you are going* south, *then turn to your* left, *then turn to your* right; *in what direction are you going now?"* (S)

(d) *"Suppose you are going* north, *then turn* right, *then turn* right *again, then turn* left; *in what direction are you going now?"* (E)

(e) *"Suppose you are going* west, *then turn* right, *then turn* right *again, then turn* right *again, and then* left; *in what direction are you going now?"* (E)

It is permissible to repeat the directions if S becomes confused or cannot remember the problem.

SCORE: 4 plus.

7. *ESSENTIAL DIFFERENCES (Same as SA II, 5)

PROCEDURE: Say, *"What is the principal difference between . . . . . . and . . . . . .?"* Repeat for each item.
   (a) Work and play.
   (b) Ability and achievement.
   (c) Optimist and pessimist.

SCORE: 2 plus. See scoring standards, page 213.

8. ABSTRACT WORDS III

PROCEDURE: Say, *"What is . . . . . .?"* or *"What do we mean by . . . . . .?"*
   (a) Generosity, (b) independent, (c) envy, (d) authority, (e) justice.

Responses defining abstract words are often ambiguous. In asking for further clarification of a response say, *"Yes, but what do we mean by . . . . . .?"* or *"Yes, but what is . . . . . .?"*

SCORE: 4 plus. See scoring standards, page 215.

ALTERNATE

A. BINET PAPER CUTTING

MATERIAL: Six-inch squares of paper.

PROCEDURE: Taking one of the sheets, say, *"Watch carefully what I do. See, I fold the paper this way* (folding it over once in the middle), *then I fold it this way* (folding it again in the middle, but at right angles to the first fold). *Now I will cut out a piece right here"* (indicating). Cut out a small triangular piece from the middle of the side which presents but one edge. Leave the folded paper exposed, but pressed flat against the table. The fragments cut from the paper should be kept out of sight. Indicating the 3″ × 3″ square in the booklet say, *"Make a drawing here to show how this paper would look if it were unfolded* (opened). *Draw lines to show where the paper would be creased and show how and where it would be cut."* If S omits either the creases or the cuts, repeat, *"Draw lines to show where the paper would be creased and show how and where it would be cut."*

SCORE: The test is passed if the creases in the paper are properly represented, if the holes are drawn in the correct number, and if they are located correctly, that is, both on the same crease and each about half way between the center of the paper and the outside. The shape of the holes is disregarded.

SUPERIOR ADULT I

1. *VOCABULARY

MATERIAL: Vocabulary card.

PROCEDURE: Say, *"I want to find out how many words you know. Listen and when I say a word, you will tell me what it means. What is an orange?"* Vary the form of the question to avoid a stilted manner of presentation, e.g., *"What does . . . . . . mean?"*, *"Tell me what a . . . . . . is"*, or give just the word without any further question. If S hesitates, urge him to try by saying, *"Just tell me in your own words; say it any way you please. All I want to know is whether you know what a . . . . . . is."* Or *"You know what a . . . . . . is! Tell me, what is a . . . . . . ?"* Give S the vocabulary card containing the word list and let him look at each word as you read it.

If the subject's meaning is not clear, that is, if his response can't be scored plus or minus without further explanation, say, *"Tell me what you mean,"* or *"Tell me more about it."* Continue until six consecutive words have been failed.

SCORE: 23 plus. See scoring standards, page 232.

2. ENCLOSED BOX PROBLEM

MATERIAL: Any small cardboard box.

PROCEDURE: Show S a box and say:

(a) *"Listen carefully. Let's suppose that this box has 2 smaller boxes inside it, and each one of the smaller boxes contains a little tiny box. How many boxes are there altogether, counting the big one?"* (5)

(b) *"Now let's suppose that this box has 2 smaller boxes inside it and that each of the smaller boxes contains 2 tiny boxes. How many altogether?"* (7)

(c) *"Now suppose that this box has 3 smaller boxes inside it and that* each of the smaller boxes contains 3 tiny boxes. How many boxes are there altogether?" (13)

(d) "Now suppose that this box has 4 smaller boxes inside it and that each of the smaller boxes contains 4 tiny boxes. How many are there altogether?" (21)

SCORE: 4 plus.

3. *MINKUS COMPLETION II

MATERIAL: Selection printed in the record booklet.

PROCEDURE: Have S fill in the missing word for each blank in the selection printed in the record booklet. Say, **"Write the missing word in each blank. Put just one word in each."**

(a) He is . . . . . . well grounded in geography . . . . . . his brother, ... he is not so quick in arithmetic.

(b) . . . . . . he give me his word, I will not trust him.

(c) You must not, ... , imagine that my silence had been due to ignorance of what is going on.

(d) . . . . . . either of us could speak, we were at the bottom of the stairs.

Time limit, 5 minutes.

SCORE: 2 sentences plus. See scoring standards, page 218.

4. *REPEATING 6 DIGITS REVERSED

PROCEDURE: Say, *"I am going to say some numbers, and I want you to say them backwards. For example, if I should say 5-1-4, you would say 4-1-5. Ready now; listen carefully, and be sure to say the numbers backwards."* Before each series repeat, *"Ready now; listen carefully, and be sure to say the numbers backwards."* Rate, one per second.

(a) 4–7–1–9–5–2,   (b) 5–8–3–6–9–4,   (c) 7–5–2–6–1–8.

SCORE: 1 plus. The series must be repeated backwards in correct order without error after a single reading.

5. *SENTENCE BUILDING

PROCEDURE: Say, *"Now make up a sentence that has in it the three words . . . . . ."*

(a) Ceremonial, dignity, impression.
(b) Baffle, cunning, pursuit.
(c) Failure, business, incompetent.

SCORE: 2 plus. See scoring standards, page 219.

6. ESSENTIAL SIMILARITIES

PROCEDURE: Say, *"What is the principal way in which* . . . . . . *and* . . . . . . *are alike?"*
(a) Farming and manufacturing.
(b) Melting and burning.
(c) An egg and a seed.

SCORE: 3 plus. See scoring standards, page 221.

ALTERNATE

A. RECONCILIATION OF OPPOSITES (Same as XIV, 6)

PROCEDURE: Say, *"In what way are* . . . . . . *and* . . . . . . *alike?"*

(a) Winter and summer.   (d) Much and little.
(b) Happy and sad.   (e) Beginning and end.
(c) Loud and soft.

Even though S is failing the items, all five must be given. If, as sometimes happens, S fails to grasp the idea until several items have been given, a correction of the preceding items is accepted if offered spontaneously. If S says they are opposite, repeat the question with emphasis on *alike.*

SCORE: 4 plus. See scoring standards, page 206.

SUPERIOR ADULT II

1. *VOCABULARY

MATERIAL: Vocabulary card.

PROCEDURE: Say, *"I want to find out how many words you know. Listen, and when I say a word, you tell me what it means. What is an orange?"*

Vary the form of the question to avoid a stilted manner of presentation, e.g., *"What does . . . . . mean?"*, *"Tell me what a . . . . . is"*, or give just the word without any further question. If S hesitates, urge him to try by saying, *"Tell me in your own words; say it any way you please. All I want to know is whether you know what a . . . . . is."* Or *"You know what a . . . . . is! Tell me, what is a . . . . . ?"* Give S the vocabulary card containing the word list and let him look at each word as you read it.

If the subject's meaning is not clear, that is, if his response can't be scored either plus or minus without further explanation, say, *"Tell me what you mean,"* or *"Tell me more about it."* Continue until six consecutive words have been failed.

SCORE: 26 plus. See scoring standards, page 232.

2. FINDING REASONS III

PROCEDURE: Say:

(a) *"Give three reasons why some people use typewriters which cost so much when they could get pen and ink for a few cents."*

(b) *"Give three reasons why a man who commits a serious crime should be punished."*

If S stops after giving one or two reasons, do not try to elicit more reasons by further questioning, but, before proceeding to the next item, hesitate long enough to give S an opportunity to continue. If for either (a) or (b) S asks how many reasons he has given, read his responses to him so that he may decide for himself.

It occasionally happens that the subject says he does not believe a man who commits a serious crime should be punished. In such a case, ask him to give the commonly accepted reasons.

SCORE: 2 plus. See scoring standards, page 222.

3. *PROVERBS II

PROCEDURE: Say, *"Here is a proverb, and you are supposed to tell what it means. For example, this proverb, 'Large oaks from little acorns grow,' means that great things may have small beginnings. What does this one mean?"* If another set has preceded, say, *"Here is another proverb. What does this one mean?"*

(a) *"The mouse that has but one hole is easily taken."*

(b) *"You must not throw pearls before swine."*

SCORE: 1 plus. See scoring standards, page 224.

4. *INGENUITY I (Same as XIV, 4; AA, 2)

PROCEDURE: The problem is given orally and may be repeated if necessary. (a) *"A mother sent her boy to the river to bring back exactly 2 pints of water. She gave him a 5-pint can and a 3-pint can. Show me how the boy can measure out exactly 2 pints of water using nothing but these two cans and not guessing at the amount. You should begin by filling the 5-pint can first. Remember, you have a 5-pint can and a 3-pint can and you must bring back exactly 2 pints."*

(b) *"This time he has to bring back exactly 13 pints of water. He has a 9-pint can and a 5-pint can. Show me how he can measure out exactly 13 pints of water using nothing but these two cans and not guessing at the amount. You should begin by filling the 9-pint can first. Remember, you have a 9-pint can and a 5-pint can and you must bring back exactly 13 pints of water."*

(c) *"And this time he has to bring back exactly 1 pint of water. He has a 3-pint can and an 8-pint can. Show me how he can measure out exactly 1 pint of water using nothing but these two cans and not guessing at the amount. You should begin by filling the 3-pint can first. Remember, you have a 3-pint can and an 8-pint can and you must bring back exactly 1 pint of water."*

The subject is not allowed to use pencil and paper. If he resorts to a method that involves guessing, tell him that he must *measure* out the water without guessing. Explain, also, if necessary, that it is a fair, not a catch, problem. It is important to encourage him to keep on trying during the full 3-minute period allowed for each problem, but if he has failed on the first problem it is not necessary to go on to (b) and (c).

SCORE: 3 plus. See scoring standards, page 206.

5. * ESSENTIAL DIFFERENCES (Same as AA, 7)

PROCEDURE: Say, *"What is the principal difference between* . . . . . . *and* . . . . . . *?"* Repeat for each item.
(a) Work and play.
(b) Ability and achievement.
(c) Optimist and pessimist.

SCORE: 3 plus. See scoring standards, page 213.

6. REPEATING THOUGHT OF PASSAGE I: VALUE OF LIFE

PROCEDURE: Say, *"I am going to read a short paragraph. When I am through you are to repeat as much of it as you can. You don't need to remember the exact words, but listen carefully so that you can tell me everything it says."* Then read the following selection:

"Many opinions have been given on the value of life. Some call it good, others call it bad. It would be nearer correct to say that it is mediocre, for on the one hand our happiness is never as great as we should like, and on the other hand our misfortunes are never as great as our enemies would wish for us. It is this mediocrity of life which prevents it from being radically unjust."

SCORE: See scoring standards, page 226.

ALTERNATE

A. CODES

MATERIAL: Message and code printed in capitals in the record booklet.

PROCEDURE: Show S the code given in the record booklet and say, *"Here is a message that has been written two ways. This is what we want to say, 'Come to London'* (pointing) *and here it is in code* (pointing and reading the letters). *Each letter here in the code stands for a letter up here in the message."* Read it aloud as you point to each letter in the code and the corresponding letter in the message. Then say *"You figure out how it goes, what the system is, and then write H U R R Y in code."*

If the first code is solved correctly, it is unnecessary to give (b). If necessary, explain to S that a code is a way of sending secret messages. It is permissible for S to write out the alphabet as an aid if he wishes, but E must in no way suggest his doing so or assist him with the alphabet. Time limit, 3 minutes each.

(a) C O M E   T O   L O N D O N
    D N N D   U N   M N O C P M

(b) C O M E   T O   L O N D O N
    A P K F   R P   J P L E M O

If S gives an incorrect answer to (a), ask, *"What is the rule for this code?"* This question is used as a caution, and if a spontaneous correction is offered, it is accepted if it is within the time limit. The rule must be asked for on (a) even though the full time has been used, in order to guard against careless error in (b). (b) should be given if (a) has been failed or received half-credit.

SCORE: 1 plus or 2 with half-credit each (not more than one error each). See scoring standards, page 227.

SUPERIOR ADULT III

1. *VOCABULARY

MATERIAL: Vocabulary card.

PROCEDURE: Say, *"I want to find out how many words you know. Listen, and when I say a word, you tell me what it means. What is an orange?"* Vary the form of the question to avoid a stilted manner of presentation, e.g., *"What does . . . . . . mean?"*, *"Tell me what a . . . . . . is"*, or give just the word without any further question. If S hesitates, urge him to try by saying, *"Just tell me in your own words; say it any way you please. All I want to know is whether you know what a . . . . . . is."* Or *"You know what a . . . . . is! Tell me, what is a . . . . . .?"* Give S the vocabulary card containing the word list and let him look at each word as you read it.

If the subject's meaning is not clear, that is, if his response can't be scored either plus or minus without further explanation, say, *"Tell me what you mean,"* or *"Tell me more about it."* Continue until six consecutive words have been failed.

SCORE: 30 plus. See scoring standards, page 232.

2. PROVERBS III

PROCEDURE: Say, *Here is a proverb, and you are supposed to tell what it means. For example, this proverb, 'Large oaks from little acorns grow,' means that great things may have small beginnings. What does this one mean?"* If another set has preceded, say, *"Here is another proverb. What does this one mean?"*
  (a) *"Let sleeping dogs lie."*
  (b) *"A bad workman quarrels with his tools."*
  (c) *"It's an ill wind that blows nobody good."*

SCORE: 2 plus. See scoring standards, page 227.

3. *OPPOSITE ANALOGIES IV

PROCEDURE: Say:
  (a) *"A rabbit is timid; a lion is . . . . . ."*

(b) *"The pine tree is evergreen; the poplar is . . . . . ."*
(c) *"A debt is a liability; an income is . . . . . ."*

SCORE: 2 plus. See scoring standards, page 229.

4. ORIENTATION: DIRECTION III

MATERIAL: Card on which the problem is stated.

PROCEDURE: Give S a copy of the problem and let him have it to look at as you read it aloud and while he is solving it. Do not allow S to use pencil and paper.

(a) *"I drove south three miles, turned to my left and drove east two miles, then turned to my left again and drove three miles, and then to my left again and drove one mile. In what direction was I going then?"* (W)

(b) *"How far was I from my starting point when I stopped?"* (1)

SCORE: 2 plus. See scoring standards, page 230.

5. *REASONING II

MATERIAL: Card on which problem is stated.

PROCEDURE: Let S look at the card while you read the problem aloud and while he is solving it.

"I planted a tree that was 8 inches tall. At the end of the first year it was 12 inches tall; at the end of the second year it was 18 inches tall; and at the end of the third year it was 27 inches tall. How tall was it at the end of the fourth year?" (40½ inches.)

Do not allow S to use pencil and paper. If the answer is 40 inches, ask S to explain how he got it. Time limit, 5 minutes.

SCORE: See scoring standards, page 230.

6. *REPEATING THOUGHT OF PASSAGE II: TESTS

PROCEDURE: Say, *"I am going to read a short paragraph. When I am through you are to repeat as much of it as you can. You don't need to remember the exact words, but listen carefully so that you can tell me everything it says."* If SA II has preceded, say only, *"Here is another short selection. Repeat as much of this one as you can."*

"Tests such as we are now making are of value both for the advancement of science and for the information of the person who is tested. It is important for science to learn how people differ and on what factors these differences depend. If we can separate the influence of heredity from the influence of environment we may be able to apply our knowledge so as to guide human development. We may thus in some cases correct defects and develop abilities which we might otherwise neglect."

SCORE: See scoring standards, page 231.

ALTERNATE

A. OPPOSITE ANALOGIES V

PROCEDURE: Say:
(a) *"Ability is native; education is . . . . . ."*
(b) *"Music is harmonious; noise is . . . . . ."*
(c) *"A person who talks a great deal is loquacious; one who has little to say is . . . . . ."*

SCORE: 2 plus. See scoring standards, page 232.

3. SCORING STANDARDS FOR FORM L–M

3. SCORING STANDARDS FOR FORM L–M

SCORING PROCEDURE

In devising the standards for scoring, the first consideration has been to secure objectivity without sacrificing the qualitative values of the individual test method. To this end we have made the instructions as explicit as possible. The principles involved in the scoring of each test have been explained and illustrations given of responses that have been scored plus or minus.

Responses chosen for illustration have been selected from the standardization data supplemented by additional material from the 1950–54 tests. Responses have been given for the most part in the exact words of the subjects. We have included only a few typical examples of successes and failures concerning which there is usually little question once the principle has been grasped. The majority of the examples illustrate responses which are just above or just below the passing line. We have included, also, certain responses which are so ambiguous that they cannot be scored according to our standards without further questioning. It has been obviously impossible, of course, to include all of the doubtful and all of the ambiguous responses, but the examples given should serve to facilitate the scoring of obtained responses with which they are to be compared.

1. Three-Hole Form Board

Score: 1 plus. All three blocks must be correctly placed in one of the two trials.

2. Delayed Response

Score: 2 plus. The child's first choice in each trial must be the correct one. If two boxes are turned over simultaneously in any trial that trial is scored minus.

3. Identifying Parts of the Body (same as II-6, 2)

Score: 4 plus.

4. Block Building: Tower

Score: 4 or more blocks making a tower in imitation of E's tower.

5. Picture Vocabulary (same as II-6, 4; III, 2; IV, 1)

The purpose of this test is to determine whether the sight of a familiar object in a picture provokes recognition and calls up the appropriate name. Responses in terms of use or description are scored minus. Naming a part for the whole is scored minus (i.e., hand for arm), or the whole for the part i.e., leg for foot). *"Thing"* is minus. Plural may be used for singular.

1. *Airplane*

PLUS: Plane. Flying 'chine. Airship. Jet.

MINUS: Ship. Aircar.

2. *Telephone*

PLUS: Phone.

MINUS: Call up. Hello. Talk.

3. *Hat*

PLUS: Straw hat. Summer hat.

MINUS: Cap. Wear.

4. *Ball*

PLUS: Baseball. Tennis ball.

MINUS: Playball thing. Apple. Round circle. Balloon. Football.

5. *Tree*

PLUS: Shade tree.

MINUS: Flowers. Christmas tree.

6. *Key*

PLUS: Key lock.

MINUS: A lock. A door lock.

7. *Horse*

PLUS: Horsie. Pony.

MINUS: Donkey. Mule. Cow.

8. *Knife*

PLUS: Butcher knife. Paring knife.

MINUS: A cutter. Cut thing.

9. *Coat*

PLUS: Jacket.

MINUS: Suit. Shirt. Sweater. Overcoat. Smock. Vest blouse. Clothes. Cape.

10. *Ship*

PLUS: Boat. Steamer. Steamboat. Ferry. Yacht.

MINUS: Boat house. Tent on top of boat.

11. *Umbrella*

PLUS: 'Brella. Parasol. Sunshade.

MINUS: Rain thing. Cane.

12. *Foot*

PLUS: Footie. Feets. Piece of foot. Foot and toes.

MINUS: Shoe. Toes. Leg. Piggies.

13. *Flag*

PLUS: American flag. Flag pole. Banner. Star spangled banner.

MINUS: Pole. Stick. Post. Rag. Kite.

14. *Cane*

PLUS: Stick. Walking stick. Candy cane. A hopping stick.

MINUS: Part of an umbrella. Sword. Thing you walk with. Handle.

15. *Arm*

PLUS: Arm and hand and shoulder. Hand and a arm.

MINUS: Hands. A fist. Muscle. He's going to fight somebody. Elbow. Shoulder.

16. *Pocket knife*

PLUS: Jack knife. Knives.

MINUS: Butcher knife. To eat.

17. *Pitcher*

PLUS: Cream jug. Creamer. Ewer.

MINUS: A mug. Cup. Pot. Cream bottle. Milk. Dish. Dipper. Cream bowl.

18. *Leaf*

PLUS: A tree leaf. Maple leaf.

MINUS: A flower. Tree. Bush. Plant.

Score: 3 plus

6. Word Combinations.

Two or more words must be combined appropriately to meet the requirements of this test. Such word combinations as "See kitty," "Dat bow wow," and "Bye bye car," are, according to the accompanying gestures and inflections, perfectly understandable as declarations, commands, interjections, or other designations of social or affective import. It is this early two-word-sentence stage that meets the requirements for success at this level. The single-word-sentence characteristic of an earlier developmental level, is, of course, not satisfactory, and words repeated parrot-like after mother or examiner do not fulfill the requirements of the test.

PLUS: Mama bye bye. All gone. See man.

MINUS: Bye bye. Night-night. Bow-wow. Good-bye.

Score: 2 or more words combined appropriately.

Alternate. Identifying Objects by Name
Score: 5 plus.

YEAR II–6

1. Identifying Objects by Use
Score: 3 plus. The objects must be designated by pointing.

2. Identifying Parts of the Body (same as II, 3)
Score: 6 plus.

3. Naming Objects

The object must be named. Responses in terms of use or description are minus. *"Thing"* is minus, but plural for singular, and familiar childish names are considered satisfactory. The only item of the six that presents any particular difficulties is automobile. Satisfactory responses include such familiar designations as *"car," "'chine," "motor-car," "bus,"* and *"ambulance."* It is not, however, a *"choo-choo,"* a *"dump-car,"* or *"truck."*

Score: 5 plus.

4. Picture Vocabulary (same as II, 5; III, 2; IV, 1)

Score: 8 plus. See scoring standards, page 126.

5. Repeating 2 Digits

Score: 1 plus. Correct order without error.

6. Obeying Simple Commands.

Score: 2 plus.

Alternate. Three-Hole Form Board: Rotated

Score: 2 plus. All three blocks must be placed in correct holes.

YEAR III

1. Stringing Beads

Score: 4 beads. Each bead pulled onto the string beyond the metal tip counts towards the score.

2. Picture Vocabulary (same as II, 5; II–6, 4; IV, 1)

Score: 10 plus. See scoring standards, page 126.

3. Block Building: Bridge

Score: Base blocks must not be touching. They must be bridged by a third block which rests on both. The addition of extra blocks does not invalidate an otherwise plus response.

4. Picture Memories

Score: 1 plus. Additional enumeration makes the response minus.

5. Copying a Circle

At this level the design and its execution are very simple. All that is required is that the subject shall achieve a rotary movement in reproducing

PLUS

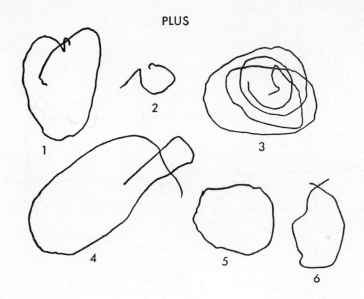

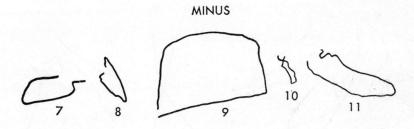

MINUS

the circle. The circle need not be completely closed and, though it must be approximately round, a somewhat elliptical form is scored plus.

Score: 1 plus.

6. Drawing a Vertical Line

Score: 1 plus. See illustrations, page 132, for standards.

Alternate. Repeating 3 Digits.

Score: 1 plus. Correct order without error.

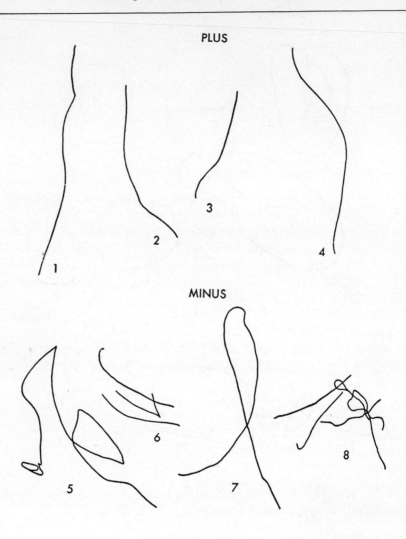

PLUS

MINUS

YEAR III–6

1. Comparison of Balls

Score: 3 plus of three trials or 5 plus of six trials.

2. Patience: Pictures

The arrangement of the cards must indicate that the child is trying to make the picture. There may be slight irregularities of alignment and the cut cards may not quite touch, but they must not be out of alignment by as much as half the diameter of the pig or ball and the two halves should meet within approximately an inch. However, if the two halves are slightly out of alignment they must meet, and if they do not quite meet they must not be out of alignment.

Score: 1 plus.

3. Discrimination of animal pictures.

Score: 4 plus.

4. Response to Pictures: Level I (Level II — VI, A)

Responses to pictures are scored at two difficulty levels, one of which is satisfactory at III-6, the other at the VI-year level.

At level I any one of the following three types of response is satisfactory:

(a) Enumeration. At least three objects must be named *spontaneously*, that is without intervening questions or urging.

(b) Description, which need not refer to more than a single element of the picture.

(c) Interpretation, which may be inadequate or incorrect though not purely fanciful or bizarre.

[For success at level II (Year VI, A) the subject must bring the elements of the picture together either by describing or interpreting. See scoring samples, page 149.]

(a) *Grandmother's Story.*

PLUS

Lady, man, baby, chair.   Boy fall down.
That's mother and boy and that's girl and that's girl.
Don't know it — boy, girl, girl, stove there.
Lady sitting down.   All the boys are sitting down.
She's catching the kids.   Her mama right here.
Here the son and here the son, don't have a tick-tock.
Mother and Helen and daddy and brother and there's her little cousin.
Something cooking on the stove.   Water running on the floor.

Q

Little girl.   I can't.

MINUS

What did the lady do?   Girls, girls, girls, girls.
Girls, lady.   Little girl, big girl, thing.
This here girl. Turn around girl.
Old Mother Hubbard went to the cupboard.

(b) *Birthday Party.*

PLUS

Look — girl — clean. All the girls clean.

He's got the candy.　　　　　　　A cake, a boy, boy, a girl.

Going in the door.　　　　　　　Boy and girl taking a walk.

Those are candles — that's a window — that's a little boy.

That's a boy — going in the door — she can't go in.

Q

Kid, kid (pointing).

MINUS

Boy, girl, things.　　　　　　　All the children.

Babies.　　　　　　　　　　　Pictures — boy — boy — mama.

Here's the back door go out — here's the daddy.

That's a lady and that's a lady and that's a lady.

No ladies here — what is that little girl doing?

(c) *Wash Day*

PLUS

Here dog. Here basket. Lady.　　　The man's shirt is on the dog.

The lady pushed a dog over.　　　The doggie has some pants.

The dog got loose from the lady and she couldn't find him.

I see a mother and a wolf fighting.　What's her running for?

A dog fell down — a girl and a dog.　Here's a line with clothes on.

That is just somebody playing and a dog.

Q

Dog, mother.　　Here's Dorothy.

MINUS

A doggie, a girl, a boy.　　　　A fox — old man and another lady.

Dog — there's a lady, dog, fork.　Basket, wash.

Mother and this a doggie — and this a cat.

That's clothes — that looks like a old rabbit.

That's an ole dog — what's he doing — what's that?

Score: 2 plus. Level I or better.

5. Sorting Buttons

Score: No error.

6. Comprehension I

(a) *What must you do when you are thirsty?*

PLUS

Drink.   Have juice.
Water.   Mama give me drink when I go up.
Go to sink.

Q

Tell my mommy.   Ask.

MINUS

Eat.   Thank you.
Nothing.   I'm hungry.
Go to bed.   Eat dinner.

(b) *Why do we have stoves?*

PLUS

That cook dinner.   To play with.
Cook on.   Warm the house.
Cause to warm.   Burn something, some wood.
Build a fire in.   Heat things.
For make our food.   Stoves for eat.

Q

Turn them on.

MINUS

Stove right here.   Mommy has those.
We have stoves this way (gestures).

Score: 1 plus.

Alternate. Comparison of sticks.

Score: 3 plus of three trials, or 5 plus of six trials.

YEAR IV

1. Picture Vocabulary (same as II, 5; II—6, 4; III, 2)

Score: 14 plus. See scoring standards, page 126.

2. Naming Objects from Memory

Score: 2 plus.

3. Opposite Analogies I (same as IV–6, 2)

In every case the exact word must be used as indicated in the samples.

(a) *Brother is a boy; sister is a* . . . .

PLUS: Girl. Girlie. Little girl.

MINUS: Lady.

(b) *In daytime it is light; at night it is* . . . .

PLUS: Dark.

MINUS: Black. Dark time.

(c) *Father is a man; mother is a* . . . .

PLUS: Woman. Lady. Girl.

MINUS: Wife. Mama.

(d) *The snail is slow; the rabbit is* . . . .

PLUS
Swift.   Speedy.
Quick.   Fast.
Rapid.   Faster.

MINUS
Running faster.

(e) *The sun shines during the day; the moon at* . . . .

PLUS
Night.   Nights.
The night.   Night time.
In the night.   During the night.
The moon shines at night.

MINUS
Midnight.   Lights up at night.
I think the moon is white in the night.

Score: 2 plus.

4. Pictorial Identification (same as IV–6, A)

Naming the object is not sufficient. The child must point to it on the card.

Score: 3 plus.

5. Discrimination of Forms

Score: 8 plus.

6. Comprehension II

(a) *Why do we have houses?*

PLUS

To go in.	To stay in.
To go home.	To play in.
To cook in.	For people.
To make us warm.	'Cause it won't rain on us.
To go in and sleep.	To play with them.
Because we want to sit down.	

Q

Because you need it.

MINUS

This is a house.   I go in make a house.

In houses we have stoves and we have carpets, too, and we have tinker toys and we have lots of things, too.

(b) *Why do we have books?*

PLUS

We read.	Stories in them.
We write in 'em.	See the pictures.
To color in.	For singing.
'Cause to teach something.	To do home works.
To go to school with.	To play with them.

Q

We like them.

MINUS

To look around.

Santa Claus is going to bring lots of books.

Score: 2 plus.

Alternate. Memory for Sentences I

Score: 1 plus. No error.

1. Aesthetic Comparison

Score: 3 plus.

2. Opposite Analogies I (same as IV, 3)

Score: 3 plus. See scoring samples, page 136.

3. Pictorial Similarities and Differences I

Score: 3 plus. Card (a) is not included in the score.

4. Materials

Lack of success in this task often involves failure to comprehend the question, as is indicated by such responses as "open" for window, and "walls" for house.

(a) *House*

PLUS

Wood. Boards. Bricks. Adobe. Cement. Stucco. Shingles. Tile. Stone. Lumber. Blocks. Rocks.

Q

Trees.

MINUS

Walls. Sticks. Nails. To go in. Tree houses.

(b) *Window*

PLUS

Glass. Wood and glass. Glass and steel.

MINUS

Open. Putty. Wood. Screen.

(c) *Book*

PLUS

Paper. Cloth. Leather. Cardboard. Sheepskin. Plastic.
Pieces of paper. Pages are made out of paper and the outsides are made out of something hard.

Q

Cotton.

MINUS

Pictures. Pages. Cards. Pastings. Made out of pictures and covers.

Score: 2 plus.

5. Three Commissions

This test samples the kind of activities demanded in everyday life situations. Success in it depends chiefly on the ability to keep the three commands in mind long enough to carry them out without confusion or error. The test is scored plus if all three commissions are executed in the proper order without further prompting, even though, in the course of carrying out the instructions, the child dawdles on the way.

Permissible variations of performance are the following:

(a) The child may pick up the box and take it with him while he places the pencil on the chair and then opens the door, lastly giving the box to the examiner as directed.

(b) He may put the pencil on the chair and then pick it up again, returning it to the examiner with the box, or he may pick it up again on his way back from the door and so return both articles to the examiner.

It will be noted that in both of the above cases the three commands are carried out in the order laid down. It is particularly important that no look or gesture of commendation or censure on the part of the examiner shall give the child any suggestion.

Score: All three commissions must be carried out in order.

6. Comprehension III

(a) *What do we do with our eyes?*

PLUS

See.	Read.
See the little baby.	Wink 'em.
You can see — better.	Keep them shut.
Keep them open.	Watch TV.

MINUS

Sleep.	There — put glasses on.

(b) *What do we do with our ears?*

PLUS

Hear.	To listen.
Hear through.	To hear the radio.

Put receivers on them if you're telephoning anything.

Wash them with soap. This — (moves them with hand).
Put glasses on them. Put hair over 'em.
They're to make us pretty. On our head.
Keep quiet.

Score: 1 plus.

Alternate. Pictorial identification (same as IV, 4)

Naming the object is not sufficient. The child must point to it on the card.

Score: 4 plus.

YEAR V

1. Picture Completion: Man

This test is one of the many forms of the completion method that have proved to be so satisfactory in measuring intelligence. There is no evidence that the satisfactory completion of the picture is in any way related to drawing ability, even though success depends in part upon the development of motor coordination. Since the ability to observe details rather than artistic ability is involved here, the artistic qualities of the drawing are not taken into account in scoring the test. *The significant thing is the presence or absence of arms, legs, eyes, nose, and mouth.*

The child's interest in drawing a man dates from his earliest attempts to represent things symbolically. In the typical drawings at this level we can trace the characteristic stages of perceptual development of children. The child who drew Figure 3, carefully arranging the five fingers along the arm, illustrates beautifully the phenomenon of "juxtaposition" which Piaget describes as characteristic of one stage of perceptual development. Such distortions do not invalidate the response, and credit is given for arm and hand. However, where the guiding idea of the activity is lost, as in Figure 10, no credit is given. It is obvious here that the child started to draw a leg and then got so interested in the scribbling activity that the end was lost sight of.

Credit is given for this test according to the details which are added. The total possible score is three points. Points are allotted as follows:

One point for leg, even if only crudely indicated. The child is given credit even if more than one leg is added to the original figure.

One point for both arms or for one arm and hand.

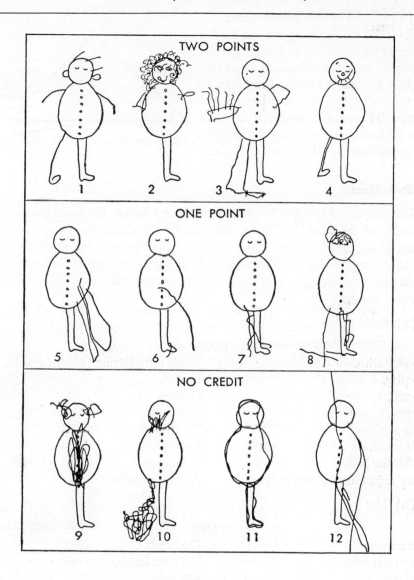

TWO POINTS

1   2   3   4

ONE POINT

5   6   7   8

NO CREDIT

9   10   11   12

One point for attempt to fill in additional features within the outline of the head, i.e., for either nose or mouth. No additional credit for ears or hair or for completing eyes or adding the eyelashes.

The above figures illustrate some of the various possibilities, together with the scoring credits.

Score: 2 points.

2. Paper Folding: Triangle

The scoring of this test is rather liberal. It is not necessary for the folded edges to meet exactly to form a perfect triangle, and the diagonals may be slightly off center causing the edges to be somewhat irregular as shown in the figure. There must, however, be only two folds and the resulting figure must be approximately triangular in shape.

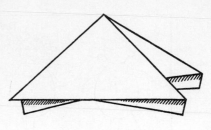

3. Definitions

The purpose of this test is not to determine whether the child knows the meaning of the word, but to see whether he can define it by expressing a usage, giving a description of the object, giving the material of which it is made, or categorizing it. The words which have been chosen include only names of common objects which belong to the everyday experience of five-year-old children.

(a) *Ball*

PLUS

To play with.	Made out of string (rags) (wood).
To play.	Round.
To roll.	Cotton.
Throw.	Kick.
Like a balloon.	To knock.
Ball game.	For baby.
Catch the ball.	It bumps.
They're just like moons, balls are.	A baseball to bat.

(b) *Hat*

PLUS

Put on you.	On head.
To go someplace.	For your heads.
Material.	For lady.
Straw.	Come on here (points to head).
Wool.	One of those kind of round things.
Goods.	A thing that sticks up.
Wear it.	Out of blue ribbon.
Have on boys.	To go in the rain.
Sunday's cap.	That means you go away.

It's round and it's got an open in the bottom.

(c) *Stove*

PLUS

Put wood in.	We put kettle on.
For boil eggs on.	For dinner.
To burn.	Heater.
Metal.	Put wood in.
Iron.	It smokes.
Cook.	To light it.
With gas burners on it.	For put the paper in.

What you get warm on.

Some of 'em gas and some of 'em ain't.

A stove — it's built like that and it has a smoke stack like that (illustrated with gestures).

Score: 2 plus.

4. Copying a Square

This test requires an appreciation of spatial relationships and the ability to make use of visual perception to guide a rather complex set of motor coordinations. The latter is probably the main difficulty in copying the square. The figure appears to be perceived as a whole and not simply as a group of meaningless lines. The ability to make the eye-hand coordinations involved is gauged by execution of the angles, the preservation of the proportions of the square, and the straightness of the lines. As will be seen from the sample responses, the preservation of the angles has been regarded as the most important factor. However, the figure must not be more than half again as long as it is wide, and the lines must not be broken, although they may be bowed slightly. The right angles may be formed by lines that intersect slightly, but must not be decidedly rounded and must not be made by drawing a corner, making ears, as in Figure 8.

The sample squares have been arranged in pairs to contrast the marginal plus with the marginal failure which shows the same fault of construction exaggerated. Although some of the minus examples illustrate more than one typical error, any of the following faults alone would make the response unacceptable.

Example 2: rounded corners.

Example 4: "ear"; roughness of drawing.

Example 6: curved lines; elongated proportions; acute angle.

Example 8: "ears".

Example 10: curved corner; top and left side curved; lines fail to meet at the corner.

Example 12: slanting side obliterates right angles; lines too rough.

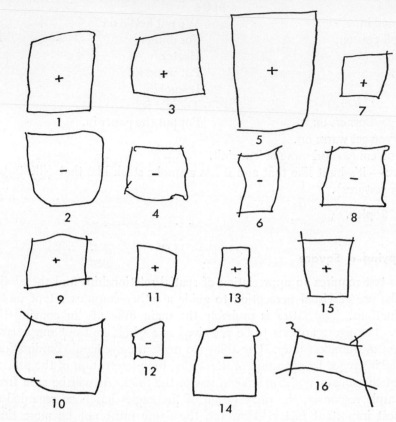

Example 14: "ear"; top line too uneven.

Example 16: elongation of proportions; obliteration of right angles; addition of extra lines.

Score: 1 plus.

5. Pictorial Similarities and Differences II

Score: 9 plus.

6. Patience: Rectangles

Score: 2 plus of three trials.

Alternate. Knot

Score: Any sort of knot which does not come undone is acceptable.

1. Vocabulary

Score: 6 plus. See scoring standards, page 232.

2. Differences

In scoring the differences test, any real difference, whether fundamental or superficial, is counted plus. Reference may be made to just one of the words of a pair provided the distinction is evident from what is said about it.

(a) *What is the difference between a bird and a dog?*

Responses commonly are in terms of locomotion, size, shape, physical attributes, or type of vocalization. Specific differences in color are not satisfactory.

PLUS

A bird flies and a dog runs.　　　　A bird flies.
A bird can't bite.　　　　A bird got wings and a dog got ears.
The dog can run and the bird can't.　　They're different shaped.
A bird has got two feet and a dog hasn't.
Bird says, "Tweet."　　　　Dogs have fur.
A bird flies and a dog runs after the bird when he's down on the ground.
　(Differences clearly implied.)

Q

It's a different kind of animal.　　　'Cause they don't look alike.

MINUS

A bird can go faster than a dog.　　A bird is white and a dog is brown.
If a dog went after a bird the bird would fly up.
A dog chases a bird.
(The last two responses are minus because it is a relationship between the
　two, and not a difference that is emphasized.)

(b) *What is the difference between a slipper and a boot?*

Satisfactory responses usually refer to relative comfort or convenience, protection, differences in shape, material, or use.

PLUS

Slipper is comfortable.　　　　Slipper leaks and boot don't.
A boot is much better than a slipper because it's warmer.

You can get a slipper on much faster than a boot.
A slipper has a little tassel on it, or a little round thing and a shoe hasn't.
Slipper is wool and boot's leather.   A boot's made out of rubber.
Put on the slipper when we get up mornings.
You can't wear a slipper out doors.   The men go out fishing with boots.
The boot is longer.

MINUS

A boot is a shoe and a slipper isn't.   A slipper got laces and a boot hasn't.
'Cause the boot is black and the slipper is red.
The slipper keeps your shoes so the mud won't get on them and the boot
   covers your leg up.

(c) *What is the difference between wood and glass?*

The most frequent difference is in terms of use. Appearances and physical properties are also common bases for differentiation.

PLUS

You can see through glass.   Glass breaks easier.
You drink out of a glass and you make chairs out of wood.
The glass is breakier — it will break — and the wood will crack.
Wood is to saw and make stuff and glass is to put things in.
Wood is stronger than glass.   Wood will burn.
Glass is harder than wood.   Glass can cut you and wood can't.
Glass is to make into a window and wood isn't.
Glass is more shinier.

Q

Glass can hurt you and wood can't.   Glass is lighter than wood.

MINUS

Glass cuts wood.
The wood is darker.   Wood is brown and glass is white.
The glass gets in someone's foot when they walk on it and they are bare-
   footed.

Score: 2 plus.

3. Mutilated Pictures

The missing part must be named or described verbally. Pointing is not enough.

(a) *Wagon*

No front seat and no wheel on the wagon.

Wheel.   Wagon has only three wheels.

The other wheel.   One of the front wheels.

The wheel is broke.   One tire.

Q

This (points correctly).

MINUS

The wheels.   There ought to be a little horse there.

Leg.   Boy.

(b) *Shoes*

PLUS

Lace.   Tie.

Shoe lace.   No shoe strings.

One of the strings.   One shoe tied and one not tied.

Q

No straps.

MINUS

The tongue.   Foot.

Shoe.   Stocking.

(c) *Teapot*

PLUS

The holder.   Holding thing.

The handle.   The thing you hold on.

The thing that you lift it up.   Arm of the tea kettle.

The handle's broke.

Q

Something is off (points correctly).

MINUS

The top (even if the handle is indicated by pointing).

Hangs on (points correctly).

Tea.

(d) *Rabbit*

PLUS

Ear.   Cat's ear.

Other ear.   No ear.

Rabbit with one ear.

Q

Some of the rabbit fell off (points correctly).

MINUS

Ears.   Leg.

(e) *Glove*

PLUS

No finger.   One of those you put your finger in.
One finger broke.   Only has four fingers.
Hasn't got enough fingers.

Q

Part of the glove is gone.

MINUS

Fingers.   Hand.
Some fingers.   Hasn't any snaps.
Part of this finger.   Glove (points correctly).
It's cut.

Score: 4 plus.

4. Number Concepts

Score: 4 plus.

5. Opposite Analogies II

In every case the exact word must be used as indicated in the samples.

(a) *A table is made of wood; a window of* . . . . . .

PLUS

Glass.   Glass and wood.

(b) *A bird flies; a fish* . . . . . .

PLUS

Swims.   Swim.

MINUS

Floats.   Likes to swim.
Floats in the water.   Goes in the water and swims.
Just swims around in the water.

(c) *The point of a cane is blunt; the point of a knife is* . . . . . .

PLUS

Sharp.	Pointed.
Keen.	Very sharp.
Sharper.	

MINUS

Peaked.

(d) *An inch is short; a mile is* . . . . . .

PLUS

Long.   Longer.

MINUS

Too long.   Long ways.

Score: 3 plus.

6. Maze Tracing

In scoring this test motor coordination is not heavily weighted. At this level of development the child may not yet have acquired sufficiently complete control of the complex motor coordinations involved to enable him to trace the path without slipping out from between the two lines which mark the boundaries. He must, of course, choose the shortest path to the goal, but his tracing may waver along the boundary of the path. The rule is that the test is scored plus if the right path is chosen and if the marking is more inside than outside the boundaries of the path. Some children try to trace one of the two lines which form the outlines of the path. Such responses are scored plus.

Score: 2 plus.

Alternate. Response to Pictures: Level II (Level I, III–6, 4)

For success at level II the subject must bring the elements of the picture together either by describing or interpreting. Mere enumeration is not satisfactory at this level. If both description and enumeration are present a fairly low level for each is acceptable.

(a) *Grandmother's Story*

PLUS

The children are in front of the mother and the beans are burning and the hot water is boiling and they're just sitting there playing and don't do nothing about it.
It's boiling over and they don't know it.
Nobody sees that the soup is falling and it's going all over the stove.

Some children playing. Woman sitting in a chair. One of the kettles is boiling over. Tea kettle boiling.

Here's a pot and it's running over. Here's a lady and her three children. Here's a stove.

Two girls and one boy and one mama and the fire is steaming and the stuff is leaking out of the can.

A girl, a lady in a chair and stuff is boiling and things are going all out there.

MINUS

Minimal responses for level I would be scored minus here. Such as —

Lady sitting down.   Water running on the floor.
She's catching the kids.

(b) *Birthday Party*

PLUS

The girl is ringing the door bell and the boy and girl are bringing packages, there's a Christmas cake in the window.

They're going to her teacher. Today's her birthday. They're going to give her a present.

Here's one trying to go in the door on Christmas.

Three children were going visiting one day and they couldn't open the hard door so they rang the door bell and they couldn't get in.

That's a door — she's touching at the knob. This is their home. They have a present for somebody.

They went to buy a box of candy and then they came home.

A boy is bringing this girl a present.

She's ringing the doorbell and there's a cake in the window.

There's a birthday cake in there. Oh, a birthday cake and a present.

That little girl's going up to the door to see if mama's in — she's ringing the doorbell.

MINUS

Minimal responses for level I would be scored minus here. For example,

That's a boy and that's a girl and that's a girl — going to the door.
She can't go in.

(c) *Wash Day*

PLUS

Woman catching a dog and he had clothes, a shirt.
The dog is running and the girl is catchin' the dog.
She's running after these.   Dog ran away with the shirt.
She's chasing the dog.   He's taking the clothes.

He got the clothes down and he pulled the clothes out of the basket.

Some clothes fell and a dog went to get the clothes.

A girl and a house and hanging out the clothes and a basket and some grass and some wood and trees.

There's a house and there's some clothes hanging on clothes line and there's a window and a basket and woman and a dog has got one of her clothes and a dog and a woman.

MINUS

Minimal responses for level I would be scored minus here. For example, There's an old woman and there's a dog running away.

Score: 2 plus.

Y E A R VII

1. Picture Absurdities I

(a) *Man with umbrella*

PLUS

The umbrella is backwards, down, and it's raining on his head.

That guy he's walking in rain with the umbrella on his back.

He's letting him get wet.   'Cause the umbrella's on his back.

It's because he wants his hat to get wet and he wants his back not to get wet.

He's going through rain and he don't know it.

He's got his umbrella crooked, on his back.

Q

About that man carrying his umbrella that way.

MINUS

He's staying out in the rain.

The umbrella is down there and his hat is on and he's walking.

This man's walking along the street and it's raining.

Umbrella leaks and he thinks it's just as well to leave it off'n his head as leave it on.

(b) *Inverted saw*

PLUS

He's sawing the wrong way.   He ain't sawing right.

He is sawing with the thing backwards.

He is sawing on the back of his saw.

He has his saw wrong, the ruffles are on top.

He is going to sleep and sawing a piece of wood upside down.

He is sawing a piece of wood.	That's a crazy way to saw.
It's funny the way he's sawing.	Cutting wood.

MINUS

He's sawing wood off.

Man's sawing and there's a ball right on there.

Because the log's not over — he's standing on it.

(c) *Dog chasing rabbit*

PLUS

The dog's chasing the rabbit the wrong way.

Because the rabbit is running and the dog doesn't know which way the rabbit is running.

The dog thinks the bunny is running over that way, the bunny is running over this way.

He thinks the rabbit's there (points to footprints ahead of dog).

The dog thinks he's chasing the rabbit.

The dog's running straight and the rabbit's running across.

The dog's running and he's not chasing anybody.

The little pooch he's running over here and the rabbit is running up here.

Q

The dog is running after the rabbit.	Dog running there.
Doesn't see the rabbit.	

MINUS

Dog is going that way and bunny is going that way and bunny is going fast so dog can't get him.

The dog is running after those footprints.

The dog's not running after the rabbit — he's running after something else.

The dog's chasing after the rabbit's tracks.

A rabbit and a dog, the dog didn't see the little rabbit.

(d) *Sitting in the rain.*

PLUS

The lady and man are sitting in the rain.

They think they're not getting wet, but they do get wet.

It's raining and they're sitting out on the porch.

They're on the porch, they haven't got an umbrella and are gettin' their clothes all wet.

The house is getting all wet too.

They are sitting outdoors without any raincoat or umbrella when it's raining.

They're sitting out doors.   Oh, it's raining.

MINUS

The man is smoking a pipe in the rain.
The door is open and the man is smoking while it's raining.
It's raining inside the house.

(e) *Cat and mice*

Any of the following aspects of the absurdity is scored plus:
1. The cat not going after the mice.
2. The mice not afraid of the cat.
3. An abnormal family group.

PLUS

'Cause they're all running around and one is on the cat. He should get up
   and eat them all.
Because the mice are so tame.
He's coming up to the cat — the cat might bite him.
This is on top of his back. Cats love to eat mouses. Gee, those mouses don't
   seem to be very scared, do they?
The mouses are dumb. They don't know the cat will eat them and they're
   walking all around the cat instead of running away.
Because the mouse came up to the cat. He wouldn't.
A kitty has some little mouses instead of a mama mouse having little
   mouses.
'Cause cats eat mice.

Q

The mouse runs on the cat.   A mouse is on the cat's back.
'Cause the cat is with the mice.   All the mouses are around the cat.
These two eating cheese and drinking milk.
A mouse, a cat, a mouse, a mouse.

MINUS

Mouses, why are they doing that? Is cat going to eat them up?
The mouse is up on top of the cat and the mouse is talking to the cat and
   the cat is laying down and two little mouses are eating (description of
   the picture).
A mice is going on the pussy cat and there's a mice talking to him.
Here's two mouses drinking his milk up.
(These two responses seem also to contain nothing beyond description.)
A mouse couldn't walk on his two hind legs.
Mice don't drink milk.

Score: 4 plus.

2. Similarities: Two things

In scoring the similarities test, any real likeness, whether fundamental or superficial, is counted satisfactory.

(a) *Wood and coal*

PLUS

Both burn.

They burn and both are wood.

Both keep you warm.

Burn coal with wood.

You could put both of them in the fire and coal don't burn so easy as wood does.

Both come from the ground.

Both hard.

The coal is made out of trees and the wood is made out of trees.

You can burn coal and you can burn wood and you can chop wood.

Both got the letter 'o.'

Coal is pressed wood about 100 years old.

Fuel.

Q

Coal is made out of wood — same kind of thing.

MINUS

Both are black.

Both the same color.

Coal's dirty and wood is dirty.

You can't break them.

Coal burns better.

Coal is round and wood is long and round.

(b) *Apple and peach*

PLUS

Both of them are red. Sometimes an apple is green.

Almost the same color.

Apple is juicy and so is peach.

Both the same size.

Both the same shape.

Peach is red and apple sometimes gets red. Both nearly always have some red on them.

Both got 'a.'

Both round.

Both have a stem (or seeds, skin, etc.).

They're good.

Q

They look alike.

Like pie.

MINUS

Both have a fuzzy skin.

Both taste the same.

Both hard (or soft).

Both have a lot of seeds.

Just the same inside.

(c) *Ship and automobile*

PLUS

Good to ride in.   Ship has iron in it and so does a car.
Both go.   Both of 'em runs with gas.
They both got windows.   They both carry freight.
Ship has a horn and an automobile has a horn.
Both have engines in them.
Both have a steering wheel.

Q

They ride.   Both have wheels.

MINUS

Machine rides on the street and boat rides on water.
Ship goes on water and automobile sometimes goes in water.
Both got tops on.   Both made alike.

(d) *Iron and silver*

PLUS

Both metals (or minerals).   Both solid (or strong, heavy, etc.).
Both used to make things.   Make dishes out of them.
Because they are hard.
Iron don't break and silver don't break.
They're both valuable (or worth something).
Both you make knives and things out of.
Can't bend the silver with your hand or you can't bend iron.
Both can be bent.   Both shiny.

Q

You can use them both.   Same color.

MINUS

Good to cut with.   Both thin (thick).
Sometimes they are the same shape.   Iron is white and silver is white.

Score: 2 plus.

3. Copying a Diamond.

The scoring takes account of the formation of the angles, of the equi-
lateral character of the sides, and of the positions of sides and angles in
relation to each other. Thus, a satisfactory drawing must have four well-
defined angles, it must be more diamond-shaped than square or kite-shaped,
and the pairs of angles must be approximately opposite.

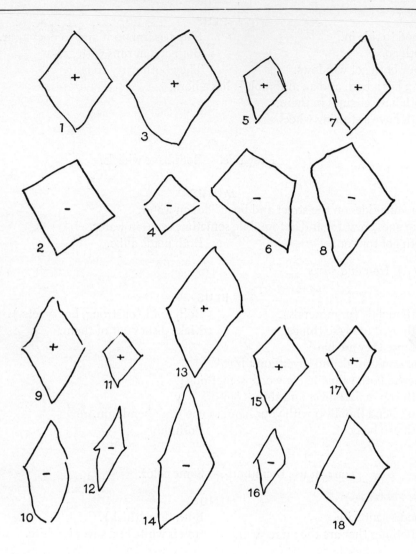

Sample drawings are shown above.

The diamonds have been arranged in pairs to contrast the marginal plus with marginal failure which shows the same fault of construction exaggerated. Although some of the minus examples illustrate more than one typical error, any of the following faults occurring alone would make the response unacceptable.

Example 2: too square shaped.

Example 4: sides fail to meet; two sides elongated.

Example 6: shape too irregular; angles not opposite each other; sides unequal; kite-shaped.

Example 8: corner rounded; angles not opposite each other; sides unequal; kite-shaped.

Example 10: angles obliterated; sides do not meet; lines curved.

Examples 12 and 14: "ear"; angles of unequal size.

Example 16: corner rounded.

Example 18: angles not opposite each other.

Score: 1 plus.

4. Comprehension IV (same as VIII, 5)

(a) *What should you do if you found on the streets of a city a three-year-old baby that was lost from its parents?*

PLUS

Take it to a lost and found place.
Take her home and ask her where she lives.
Ask it its name.   Advertise in the paper.
Find the parents.   Take it to the police station.
Bring him home until he is found.   Try to take her home.

Q

Take it home.   Go tell somebody.
Take him in.   Give it back to the lady.

MINUS

Don't do nothing with it.   Say, "You mustn't cry."
Find it.   Play with it.

(b) *What's the thing for you to do when you've broken something that belongs to someone else?*

Restitution or apology, or both, must be suggested. Mere confession is not satisfactory.

PLUS

I'd be scared that I had to buy another for 'em.
If I have one I give it to him.   Fix it.
Say, "Excuse me."   Tell them I'm sorry.
Give them something.   Pay for it.

Q

Give it back.   Respect their property.
Bring it to them again.

MINUS

Be ashamed.   Tell 'em I did it.
Tell my mother.   My mother will spank me.
Feel sorry.

(c) *What's the thing for you to do when you are on your way to school and notice that you are in danger of being late?*

Only those responses which suggest hurrying are acceptable. Local conditions and customs and the child's particular circumstances should be taken into account in evaluating responses.

PLUS

Hurry.

Go right ahead to school. (Here it seems clear that the child's idea is to proceed with dispatch and no loitering.)

I don't want to hurry and get run over. I'd rather walk than run. (In this case it is evident that the child understands the expected response.)

Take the street bus.

Q

Run home.   Walk.

Bring a note.

MINUS

Go on to school and tell my teacher why I'm late.

Not stop.	Get a late card.
Take a motor cycle.	Ask them what time it is.
Just keep on going.	Go early.

(d) *What makes a sailboat move?*

PLUS

Wind.   Wind and sails.

Wind and water.

Q

The sails.   The big things on top.

Sails and the waves.

MINUS

Water.   Sails make the boat go.

The motor.

(e) *What is the thing to do if another boy (girl, person) hits you without meaning to do it?*

The only satisfactory responses are those which suggest excusing or overlooking the act.

PLUS

Go and tell my mother they didn't mean to do it.

Tell them it didn't hurt.	If they say "excuse you" it's all right.
Don't say they done it on purpose.	Tell 'em they never meant to do it.
Go right on playing.	

I wouldn't hit them back. I would say, "Please don't do it again."
If they apologize, take the apology.   Ask them to be more careful.

MINUS

Not to tell, you'd get in trouble if you did.
He'd say excuse me.   Would not play with him.
I would hit them back.   They say they're sorry.
Leave it or go tell the teacher.   They should do something about it.
Tell my mama.

    (f) *What should you say when you are in a strange city and someone asks you how to find a certain address?*

PLUS

I'd say if I didn't know the address, "I'll ask my folks where it is."
You wouldn't know because you don't live there.
I'm a visitor.   I just came here.
Say you live somewhere else.   Tell him to ask someone else.

Q

I don't know. (Not clear whether this is what he would say or means that
  he doesn't know the answer.)

MINUS

Wouldn't know what to say.   Give him a phone book.
Say, "No."   Look at the numbers of the houses.

Score: 3 plus.

5. Opposite Analogies III

  (a) *The rabbit's ears are long; the rat's ears are* . . . . . .

PLUS
Short.

MINUS
Small.

  (b) *Snow is white; coal is* . . . . . .

PLUS
Black.

MINUS
Dark.

  (c) *The dog has hair; the bird has* . . . . . .

PLUS
Feathers.

MINUS
Wings.

(d) *Wolves are wild; dogs are* . . . . . .

PLUS
Tame.   Very tame.
Tamed.   Tamed — or civilized.
Domestic.

MINUS
Tameful.   Gentle.
Pets.   Calm.
Playful.   Friendly.
Timid.   Quiet.
Mild.

Score: 2 plus.

6. Repeating 5 Digits.

Score: 1 plus. Correct order without error.

Alternate. Repeating 3 digits reversed.

Score: 1 plus. Correct order without error.

YEAR VIII

1. Vocabulary

Score: 8 plus. See scoring standards, page 232.

2. Memory for Stories: The Wet Fall

Once there was a little girl named Betty. She lived on a farm with her brother Dick. One day their father gave them a Shetland pony. They had lots of fun with it. One day, when Dick was riding on it, the pony became frightened and ran away. Poor Dick fell into a ditch. How Betty laughed when she saw him! He was covered with mud from head to foot.

(a) *What is the name of this story?*

PLUS
A Wet Fall.   One Wet Fall.
A Wet — something about Fall.

The Wet Falls.   A Fall.

(b) *What was Betty's brother's name?*

PLUS

Dick.   Dickie.

MINUS

Ned.   Bill.

(c) *Where did they live?*

PLUS

On a farm.   On their father's ranch.

MINUS

With their mother and father.   In the country.

(d) *Who gave the pony to them?*

PLUS

Their father.   Dick's father.

MINUS

Their father and mother.

(e) *What did the pony do?*

It happens sometimes that in responding to (e) the child spontaneously gives the rest of the story, thus volunteering the answer for (f). In such cases, of course, he receives credit for both (e) and (f), and it is unnecessary for the examiner to ask for (f).

PLUS

Became frightened and ran away.   Dumped Dick in a ditch.
Gave Dick a ride.   Throwed him.
Ran away with Dick.   Ran away from them.
Got frightened from Dick.

MINUS

He got mad and let Dick fall into a ditch.
Carried them on his back.   Fell in a ditch.
Kicked.   Fall in the mud.
They got on it and the pony went.

(f) *What happened?*

(Dick fell into a ditch. He was covered with mud from head to foot. Betty laughed when she saw him.) The expected answer for (f) varies according to what has been given for (e).

When a child recalls the boy's name incorrectly, e.g., Ned for Dick, his response is, of course, minus for (b); but if the incorrect name is employed in an otherwise acceptable answer for a succeeding question, the child is given credit for that question. On the other hand, if he gives an incorrect name for (b) but uses "Dick" in later responses (b) is still scored minus.

PLUS

The pony got scared (when the response to (e) was "Gave Dick a ride").
Then Betty laughed and laughed (response to (e) "He got frightened and ran away").
Dick fell into the water and was full of mud.
John got all dirty and fell in the mud and was covered all up and the Shetland pony laughed.
Mud got all over him.   He fell into the mud.
The pony ran away — he'd got frightened.

MINUS

He fell into the well.   They laughed.
Then Dick laughed.   They both fell into a ditch.

Score: 5 plus of the six questions.

3. Verbal Absurdities I

The purpose of this test is to discover whether the subject can point out the intellectually irreconcilable elements of the situation presented. The only difficulty is in judging whether the response shows that the subject has seen the incongruity. The child who has seen the point instantly often indicates that fact by repeating the critical phrase, and the dull, uncomprehending child may just try to say over what you have said. For example, you ask concerning the man with influenza, "*What is foolish about that?*" and the child replies, "*He got well quickly.*" He may be pointing out just the crucial element or he may be repeating parrot-fashion the last words you've said. Additional questioning will bring out the distinction.

(a) *A man had flu (influenza) twice. The first time it killed him, but the second time he got well quickly.*

PLUS

He can't have it twice if it killed him once.
If the first time it killed him, he couldn't get it again.
Just got it backwards.
It should be the first time he got well and the second time he died.
He couldn't have got well if it killed him the first time.
'Cause he got dead and got well quickly.

The second time he couldn't get well.
He can only die once.
Because the first time it killed him and the second it didn't.
He got well quickly.

MINUS
When he had it the first time he couldn't have it again.
Because the first time he died and the next time he didn't die.
He got well the next day.

(b) *Walter now has to write with his left hand because two years ago he lost both his arms in an accident.*

PLUS
He can't write if both arms are broken.   He hasn't got no arms.
Writing and he's lost both hands!   How'd he get another one?
He couldn't write.
If he hurt one arm and he wrote with the left one then how could both of
   them be hurt.
If he lost his arms he'd lose his hands, too.
Both arms were gone.

Q
He couldn't write none with his left hand.

MINUS
He could use the other arm, too.

(c) *A man said, "I know a road from my house to the city which is downhill all the way to the city and down hill all the way back home."*

PLUS
It can't be downhill both directions.
Have to go uphill one way or have to change. You couldn't go down the hill
   all the time.
Have to be uphill one way.
Going down to the city and going down coming back.
If it was downhill going to the city it would have to be uphill going home.
He'd be taking another road if he was going home and it was downhill.
The hill can't change up and down for him — can't be downhill coming
   back.

Q
Downhill all the way back home.
He goes downhill when he goes to the city and downhill when he comes
   home.

If it's downhill to the village he'll have to climb.

I guess it's a very crooked road.

'Cause it isn't downhill all the way to the city, it's uphill too.

(d) *An old gentleman complained that he could no longer walk around the park as he used to; he said he could now go only halfway around and back again.*

PLUS

Says he can't walk around and he can walk one halfway around and back, he should be able to walk all the way around then.

He said he couldn't walk around it all and said he could walk around it one half way and back again.

If he could walk one half way round and back again he could walk all the way round.

If he can't walk around it how could he go one half way and back.

If he's getting too old to walk around the park he couldn't walk around one half way and back.

Q

He said he couldn't walk around it all and he said he could.

He could go all the way around.

MINUS

Because he said he couldn't walk around the park any longer and then he said he could walk around.

'Cause if you go one half way round and back again you would walk around it twice.

Score: 3 plus.

4. Similarities and Differences

(a) *Baseball and orange*

PLUS

Both are round and baseball is a game and orange is a fruit.

Both healthy for you, one's fruit and one's wood.

An orange you can throw and a ball you can throw, a ball can sink and you can eat an orange.

You can't hit an orange and a ball you can. They both are round.

Ball's different colors than a orange is and they're round.

A ball is hard and an orange ain't and you can play baseball with a ball and with an orange too if it don't bust open.

Baseball is as round as an orange.   Baseball is made of rubber.
Because a ball is harder than an orange.

MINUS

Baseball is lighter than an orange and both of them are round.

When a ball is yellow and an orange is yellow they are alike and an orange
   is softer.

The baseball and orange have tough skin and the baseball is different inside
   and so is the orange.

'Cause they are both round and the baseball is a little bit pointed.

You can use them both. Orange you can use for fruit and baseball to play ball
   with.

(b) *Airplane and kite*

PLUS

They're made out of paper and they could fly same as airplanes and airship
   is made out of iron.

Airplane goes up in air and so does a kite and an airplane hasn't got sticks
   and a kite has.

They both fly and an airplane goes straight and a kite doesn't (gesturing).

Airplane and kite can fly — kite of paper, airship of wood.

Difference because the kite has a different shape. Both have wood on.

They both fly in air and kite is thin and airship is not thin.

They fly in the air but the kite won't fly unless you hold a string to it.

Q

Airplane can fly all the time that it wants to and a kite can't.

One's flying up high and one's down low.

MINUS

A kite and an airplane flies up in the air and a kite won't go up in the air
   if it got a hole in it and an airplane will go up in the air if it got a hole in
   it.

'Cause, they can both fly in the air and they're different because they're
   different colors.

Both fly and one is paper and the other is rag.

(c) *Ocean and river*

PLUS

The ocean is water and the river is water, and different because ocean don't
   run along like the river does.

They're both water and ocean starts with 'o' and river starts with 'r'.

Ocean has water and river has water. Ocean is bigger and longer and river is quite big but not as big and not half as long. (If "longer" had been the only difference given the response would have been unsatisfactory.)

Both of them have water in 'em and a ocean is grayish and a river is red and an ocean has bigger ships and bigger waves than a river has. (We have ignored the incorrect element in view of the satisfactory elements of the response.)

They're both water and one's smaller than the other.

The ocean floats like the river does, but river isn't as wide, deep, and big as the ocean is.

They both got water in them and the rivers are usually between the states and the oceans between the countries.

They're both water. In the one water runs both ways and in the river it just runs one way.

An ocean is round and a river isn't round, is it? An ocean's got water and river's got water.

River is same as ocean only a river is smaller body of water and it runs through valleys to the ocean.

MINUS

Ocean is lots of water and a river some water.

Both have water in them but they're different places, the ocean is in one place and the river in another.

The ocean is long and deep and a river is long but it isn't deep.

They both have water and an ocean is longer than a river.

They're both big and an ocean is bigger than a river.

(d) *Penny and quarter*

PLUS

They are money and one is silver looking and the other looks like brass.

Both metal, but a quarter amounts to more than a penny.

Both round. A quarter is silver.

Both have cents and you can get more with a quarter.

A penny is made out of hard stuff like a quarter and a quarter is made out of silver and a penny is made out of that tin stuff like on the gutters on your roof.

They're both round but they haven't got the same pictures on them.

Penny is red and quarter is gold — a quarter is silver and they're both round. They're both small.

Penny, as soon as you spend it you don't have any more left, and quarter, when you spend it you have some left and they're both the same thing and only one thing is different, when you spend a penny you don't have nothing left and they're both round.

Penny is little and round and quarter is big and round.

Both of them are round and one's black and one's white and they are
  bigger.
The penny is littler and the quarter is bigger and you can buy lots of things
  with a penny and more things with a quarter.

Score: 3 plus.

5. Comprehension IV (same as VII, 4)

Score: 4 plus. See scoring standards, page 157.

6. Naming the Days of the Week

The test is passed if the days of the week are all named, and in correct
order, and if the subject succeeds in at least two of the check questions. It
is not necessary for him to begin with the first day of the week.

Score: All named in correct order. 2 of the check questions correct.

Alternate. Problem Situations I

(a) *About two o'clock one afternoon a number of boys and girls, dressed
in their best clothes, rang the bell at Alice's house. Alice opened the door.
What was happening?*

PLUS

A party.	It was Alice's birthday.
A dance.	They were surprising her.
Give 'em a Valentine or a birthday party or a basket of Easter eggs.	
Christmas day.	Going to be a play.
They wanted her to come to a party.	

MINUS

The following responses have been scored minus because they are too
vague and do not indicate that account is being taken of the various elements in the situation.

They came to see her.	Some company were coming.
They went to visit that little girl.	They wanted to play with her.
They were coming to her house.	They wanted her to go somewhere.

(b) *Helen heard a big "bang" and came running outdoors. There were
nails all over the road, and an automobile had just stopped beside the road.
What was the "bang"?*

PLUS

Puncture.   Tire busted.
Blow out.   The tire.
Flat tire.   Automobile got nails in the wheels.

Q

Car ran over the nails.

MINUS

Box of nails fell out.   Machine got smashed.
The nails.   Wreck.
Backfire.

(c) *A young man and lady were sitting in a restaurant. They had nearly finished eating a big dinner. The waiter brought the bill. The young man looked at it and then seemed worried and embarrassed. Why?*

PLUS

Not enough money.   He had to pay a lot of money.
Because he didn't have the money.   It cost too high.
Didn't have no money to pay for it.

Q

Because he ate a big dinner.   Because the bill was wrong.
It was eight dollars.

MINUS

Because he didn't want to pay.
It might not even have had any writing on it.
He swallowed something bad and the waiter brought too much money and
    the stuff wasn't good.

Score: 2 plus.

YEAR IX

1. Paper Cutting (same as XIII, A)

Scoring is liberal. (a) There must be only one crease and it must be nearer to the center than it is to either edge of the paper. The cut must be longer than it is wide and must be intersected by the crease, but its location on the crease may be off center and it may be incorrectly placed with reference to its lengthwise dimension. The illustrations on pages 169 and 170 indicate the standard of accuracy required for passing and kind of response that has been scored minus.

(a)

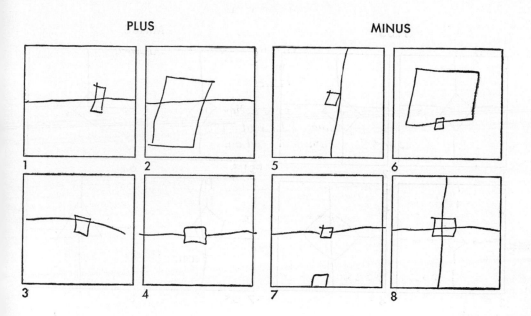

PLUS   MINUS

(a)

Figure 3. Plus because cut is longer than it is wide.

Figure 4. Plus even though cut is incorrectly placed with reference to lengthwise dimension.

Figure 5. Minus because cut is not intersected by crease and because cut is square.

Figure 6. Addition of irrelevant details makes response minus.

Figure 7. Irrelevant detail and square cut.

Figure 8. Shows two creases.

(b)

PLUS   MINUS

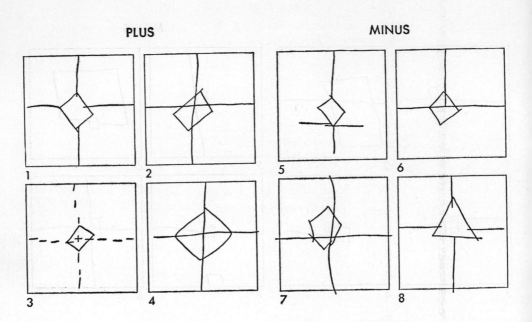

(b) The cut must be in the center of the square and must be approximately diamond-shaped, with each corner located approximately on the crease. Slight inaccuracies resulting from careless execution are disregarded.

(b)

Figure 5. Cut incorrectly located with reference to horizontal line; horizontal line incorrectly drawn.
Figure 6. One line incomplete.
Figures 7 & 8. Cut incorrectly represented.

Score: 1 plus.

2. Verbal Absurdities II (same as XII, 2)

(a) *Bill Jones's feet are so big that he has to pull his trousers on over his head.*

This absurdity is rather difficult to explain. The point is, of course, that people and trousers just aren't made in such a way that it would be possible to pull a pair of trousers over one's head. We have scored a response plus if it indicated that the child was fumbling for this explanation and really saw the point even though he hadn't expressed it exactly.

PLUS

He couldn't do that, his head would be too big.
Because you usually can't put 'em on over your head.
That his trousers would stick up on his shoulders.
He couldn't.   Trousers don't go over his head.
The trousers couldn't fit his head.   'Cause his body's bigger than his feet.
He'd have to put his feet through the legs of his trousers anyway.
No hole for his head to go through.
How can he!

Q

Because he pulls his trousers over his head.
He puts 'em over his head because his feet are too big.
Pulls his trousers on over his head.
It's foolish because he had to put them over his head.

MINUS

You're not supposed to wear trousers over your head.
His feet would get cold.
Have to pull his pants over his head — you're not supposed to.
He wouldn't be able to see if he put them over his head.
He can't get them over his head because the legs are too long.
His trousers are 'sposed to go over your feet.

(b) *A man went one day to the post office and asked if there was a letter waiting for him. "What is your name?" asked the postmaster. "Why," said the man, "you will find my name on the envelope."*

PLUS
The man wouldn't know which one it was.

He doesn't know on the envelope if that's his name.

The postmaster wouldn't know what his name was.

He calls up when he's at the post office and expects him to know if there is a letter for him when he don't tell his name.

If the postmaster found the letter he wouldn't know who he was.

You can't find his name on the envelope (child laughs), he has to tell the man.

There's bound to be more than one envelope.

That wouldn't help because there's a name on every envelope.

If he didn't know his name how could he!

Q
He oughta told his name.　　　　　　It could be anybody.

Because he might take the wrong envelope.

Foolish to say, "You will find my name on the envelope."

How would the postmaster know if the letter was for him?

He shouldn't be that way — he should tell his name.

Telling his name.

MINUS
The postman brings it to him, to his address.

I guess because he didn't really have any letter.

He should get it from his mail box.

Some one might have written the wrong name — he might have taken the letter.

He should tell him because maybe he won't find it.

They didn't have the envelope to find his name in it.

Didn't know his name — and he lived right in the town.

If he don't have any envelope there he had to tell him his name.

Because the man didn't want to look at the envelope.

Might not have been an envelope there for him.

(c) *The fireman hurried to the burning house, got his fire hose ready, and after smoking a cigar, put out the fire.*

PLUS
He should have put out the fire and then smoked.

He wouldn't do it. He'd get the hose and put it out.

Because he didn't put it out quick enough.

After he smoked a cigar the house would be all burned down.

He ought to put it out soon as he got there.

If you sit down and smoke a cigar and don't turn the water on, that don't put out a fire.

He wouldn't smoke a cigar.

Q

He couldn't because the fire would be all over then.

Put the fire out after smoking a cigar.

It was foolish to smoke a cigar.　　　　　He was a pretty poor fireman.

MINUS

Smoking would make the fire bigger.

It's against the rules to smoke while you're working.

It's foolish to say the cigar put out the fire.

He shouldn't smoke a cigar at the fire because it is liable to start another fire.

The other men would put out the fire ahead of him and he wouldn't have to.

He smoked a cigar and made all the more smoke instead of putting water on it.

He smoked his cigar while the rest of them put out the fire.

He was smoking and he was putting out the fire.

(d) *In an old graveyard in Spain they have discovered a small skull which is believed to have been that of Christopher Columbus when he was about ten years old.*

PLUS

Christopher Columbus didn't die when he was ten years old.

Christopher Columbus didn't discover nothing when he was ten years old. When he's older he discovered things.

He didn't come over here then; he was twenty-five years old when he came over.

When you was ten years old and buried you couldn't come alive again.

He didn't sail over when he was ten.

Couldn't have had two heads.

Because, how could he have sailed on his voyage?

It couldn't be his face when he was twelve years old because the face would be bigger — he growed up to be a big man.

They thought he was in that grave and he was still alive — wasn't ten years old and buried.

Q

Because they said he was ten years old.

He had a bigger skull!

It reads wrong.　　　　　　　　　If he was that old they couldn't.

MINUS

Christopher Columbus wasn't living then — so they couldn't have thought that he was.

He didn't live in Spain, he lived in Italy.

He wasn't killed like that, Christopher Columbus wasn't; he was killed in prison.

How did they know it was Christopher Columbus' skull?

He wasn't buried in Spain.

He came to America and his skull couldn't be there.

He was bigger. They wouldn't know how old he was.

(e) *One day we saw several icebergs that had been entirely melted by the warmth of the Gulf Stream.*

PLUS

They came to some and said they saw some and they were already melted.

If they had been melted they wouldn't be there.

Wasn't any icebergs (laughed).

There'd have been water instead of icebergs.

Said he seen them after they was melted.

'Cause you say you saw some icebergs and they was melted.

Q

About icebergs that were entirely melted.

It was melted.   It was water.

MINUS

They wouldn't be in the Gulf Stream.

If icebergs were in the Gulf Stream they would get all knocked to pieces.

Icebergs can't melt because it's all wet.

The Gulf Stream couldn't be warm; it would have to be cold.

They couldn't melt that fast.

You can't see them when it is warm weather.

Icebergs are too big — they wouldn't be all melted by the Gulf Stream.

Score: 3 plus

3. Memory for Designs I (same as XI, 1)

For *full credit* on design (a) all of the elements of the design must be reproduced and the relationship between these elements maintained. Slight irregularities due to lack of motor skill or hasty execution are disregarded.

For *half-credit* all of the elements must be present, but inaccuracies due to omission or addition of details or to irregularities in size and shape of the figures are overlooked. The samples on pages 175–176 indicate the standard for plus, half-credit, and minus.

(a)
FULL CREDIT

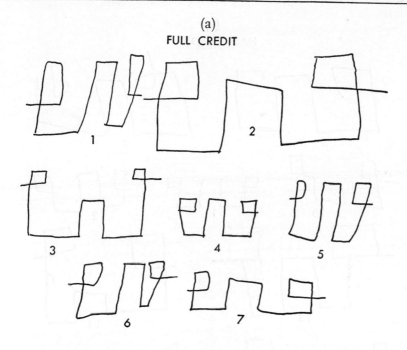

(a)
HALF-CREDIT

Figure 8. Lower part of right and left details missing.

Figure 9. Uprights cross at the wrong place.

Figure 10. Irregularity of right detail.

Figure 11. Uprights turned out instead of in.

Figure 12. One of the uprights turned out.

Figure 13. Incorrect right and left details.

Figure 14. Irregularity in proportions; center detail too much below uprights.

Figure 15. Uprights turned out; irregularity of drawing center detail.

Figures 16 & 18. Too little attention to details of execution.

Figure 17. Lines fail to cross right and left uprights.

NO CREDIT

Figure 19. Center detail incorrect.

Figure 22. Poor proportions (center detail too much below uprights); figure drawn upside down.

Figure 25. Omission of center.

Figure 26. Omission of right and left uprights.

(a)
HALF CREDIT

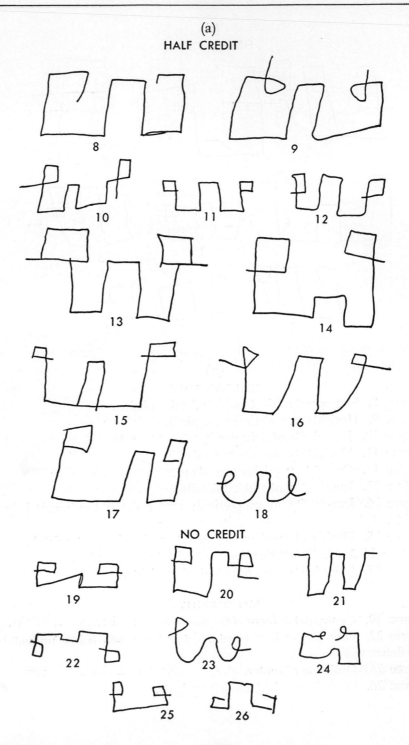

NO CREDIT

(b)

FULL CREDIT

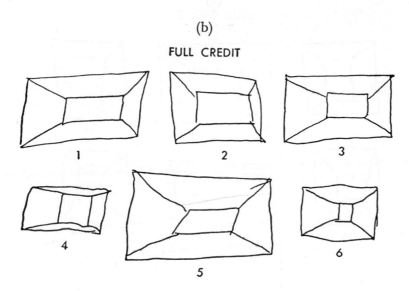

For *full credit* on design (b) the essential plan of the design must have been grasped and reproduced. Ordinary irregularities due to lack of motor skill or too hasty execution are disregarded. Four conditions must be met:

(1) The outer figure must be rectangular.

(2) The inner rectangle must be off center to the right.

(3) The inner figure may appear square but must not be noticeably higher than wide.

(4) The lines from the corners of the inner rectangle must meet the corners of the outer rectangle fairly accurately.

For *half-credit* no essential part must be omitted or any part added, but there is greater latitude in scoring than above.

An inverted design or one whose inner rectangle is in the center or off center to the left receives half-credit.

The inner rectangle may be taller than wide in relation to the outer figure.

The outer rectangle may be square or may be rectangular in the opposite direction from the original figure. Less accuracy is required of the radiating lines, but they must show a tendency to meet the corners, otherwise the score is minus.

On pages 177–178 are samples of full credit, half-credit, and minus responses.

(b)
HALF CREDIT

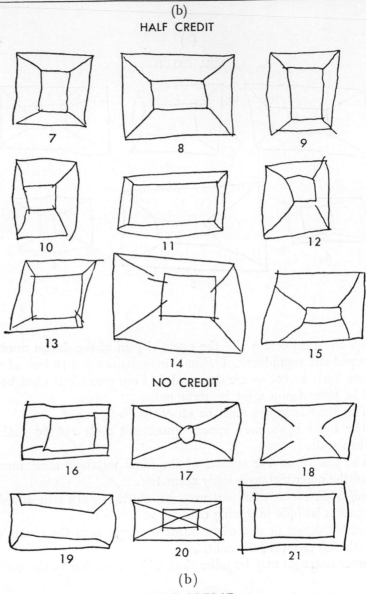

(b)

HALF-CREDIT

Figure 7. Outer figure not rectangular; inner rectangle longer than it is wide, and not off center.

Figure 8. Inner rectangle not off center.

Figure 10. Designs poorly executed; outer figure not rectangular; inner rectangle off center in the wrong direction.

Figure 11. Inner figure disproportionately large.
Figure 12. Irregularities of drawing; outer figure not rectangular.
Figures 14 and 15. Irregularity of execution.

NO CREDIT
Figure 16. Center figure too large; lines fail to meet corners.
Figure 17. Center figure round and not off center.
Figure 21. Center figure too large and lines omitted.

Score: 1 plus or 2 with half-credit each.

4. Rhymes: New Form

(a) *Tell me the name of a **color** that rhymes with head.*

PLUS
Red.   Dark red.   Lead.

(b) *Tell me a **number** that rhymes with tree.*

PLUS
Three.   Twenty-three.

(c) *Tell me the name of an **animal** that rhymes with fair.*

PLUS
Hare.   Bear.   Mare.

(d) *Tell me the name of a **flower** that rhymes with nose.*

PLUS
Rose.   Primrose.

Score: 3 plus.

5. Making Change
Score: 2 plus.

6. Repeating 4 Digits Reversed
Score: 1 plus. Correct order without error.

Alternate. Rhymes: Old Form

There must be three words in addition to the stimulus word. These must be real words, not nonsense syllables or made-up words. The child is given credit for the rhyming words even though there may occur, interspersed among the proper rhymes, nonsense syllables or words that do not rhyme. Of course, if the child is just reeling off nonsense syllables among which occur by chance some real words, the item should be scored minus.

All common words are credited. Occasionally obscure or rarely used words are given which are mere nonsense syllables as far as the subject is concerned but which can be found in the dictionary or occasionally are used as proper names. Unless there is reason to believe that the child is using such words meaningfully we do not give credit for them. Words of more than one syllable are given credit when the last syllable rhymes with the stimulus word. Words with the same pronunciation but different meaning, when differentiated by the child, are each given credit. Sometimes the child gives another meaning for the stimulus word, for example, "date that you don't eat"; this does not count as a rhyme for it. A word repeated is counted only the first time it is given.

(a) *Rhymes with date*

PLUS

Rate.

Debate.

Originate.

Mate and playmate (counted as two).

Bait and rebate (counted as two).

Accumulate.

Pate.

Concentrate.

MINUS

Drate.   Zate.   Flate.   Sedate.

(b) *Rhymes with head*

PLUS

Said.

Jed.

Ted.

Two reds — read a book, and red a color (credit for two).

Two sheds — shed a building, and a tree sheds its leaves (credit for two).

Ked (singular of keds).

Zed (a cracker).

Ced — short for Cedric.

Pled.

MINUS

Married.   Shredded.   Med.   Ped.   Cred.

(c) *Rhymes with cap*

PLUS

Crap.   Flap.   Slap.   Hap.

MINUS

Swap.   Drap.   Blap.   Ap.   Fap.   Bap.

Score: 2 plus with three rhymes each.

YEAR X

1. Vocabulary

Score: 11 plus. See scoring standards, page 232.

2. Block Counting

Score: 8 plus.

3. Abstract Words I (same as XII, 5)

(a) *Pity.* (A feeling of compassion for the sufferings of others.)

PLUS

To feel compassion or sympathy.   You feel for people.
Feel sorry for.   Feel bad for somebody.
Person gets hurt — you pity them — feel bad.
Means you help a person out and don't like to have 'em suffer.
If somebody was awful poor or anything you'd pity 'em — might give 'em
    something to help 'em out.
You take mercy on some one, you'll take them in if they're hungry and give
    them something to eat.
You see something that's wrong and have your feelings aroused.

Q

If a person is sick you pity them.   Sorry.
Have mercy on anyone.
If somebody went away to some other country you'd pity them.
If you are liable to get a lickin' and the kids say, "I pity you."
Something that is going to happen to you later.

MINUS

Sad.   Sorrow.
You'd pity somebody that was going away because you don't like to see
    them go.

181

Means you are going to get a whippin'.
If you pity some cripple it means not to start laughing at them.
Like if you killed somebody they might take pity on you — let you go.
When you take pity on anybody you hope they'll do better if they've done
    something wrong.
It means something is going to happen to you and you'd better watch out.

(b) *Curiosity.* (Disposition to inquire into anything, especially something new or strange, often implying meddlesomeness; desire to know.
That which is curious, or fitted to excite or reward attention.)

PLUS

Wondering what it is.   Means that you are nosey.
Want to know something.   Want to know everything.
You're always curious and want to look into something. If there is some-
    thing, you want to see it.
It means you're very interested or anxious.
You're trying to find out about other people's business.
Like you think something is queer.
That they are different from other people.

Q

Asking too many questions.   You get into things.
Like you're out in the woods and you're watching for birds.

MINUS

Not to know.   You hardly believe it.
Anxious.   Stare at people.
You're afraid to ask questions, but you ask anyway.
If you go to see somebody for the fun of it.
Like someone is curious and never will believe you.
Somebody is always butting into someone else's business.

(c) *Grief.* (Suffering, distress, a cause of suffering, remorse, disaster.)

PLUS

Suffer.   We have sadness.
You're in misery.   You're not happy.
You feel hurt over something.   Sort of mournful.
Like mourning.   You're sorry.
Sorrow.
A feeling you have when you lose something or someone.

Q

When you say, "Good grief, I've lost my purse."
Death.   If a lady is sobbing.
Trouble.   To be sorry for.
If somebody dies you're in grief.

Means it's hard to get you out of trouble.
It's grief when you haven't got your lesson. Means you get a bad mark.
Means pity.   When you bear anything.

(d) *Surprise.* (To be struck with wonder, astonishment, or confusion by something unexpected, sudden, or remarkable.)

PLUS
The showing of something unexpected — your emotion to that.
A sudden feeling over some one thing.
To take anyone unawares.   Something comes off suddenly.
Astonishment.   Startled.
The feeling toward something that thrills you or amazes you.
Something that comes that you didn't know about.
If you didn't expect somebody you'd be surprised to see them.
Like something somebody has hidden for you — like at Christmas — they
    want to surprise you by giving you something.
You are surprised — well — you are taken off your guard or something like
    that.

Q
Somebody wants to give you a surprise.
A party.

MINUS
You get alarmed by something or good news — or hear of an accident or
    something.
Something new that you never saw before, or heard.
A present.   Something to fool them.
Means you don't know what to think about.

Score: 2 plus.

4. Finding Reasons I

Finding reasons involves seeing the relationship between cause and effect in situations with which the child is familiar. The relationship pointed out needn't be an essential one, indeed at this level any plausible connection may be considered satisfactory. It often happens that the child continues to elaborate instead of being guided by the instruction to give two reasons. He thinks in terms of the particular situations which the task recalls and loses his goal in the details which present themselves, as, for instance, the child who starts out to give two reasons why children shouldn't be too noisy in school and then gets lost in his own description — "They can't do their lessons because they'd be too noisy and would run around and bump their arms and scribble all over the paper."

Our scoring standards are very lenient. We have credited the child with two reasons even when the reasons overlap somewhat, or when they belong in the same category, provided different aspects are presented that can be distinguished in any way.

(a) *Give two reasons why children should not be too noisy in school.*

PLUS

'Cause they'll get a lickin'. They'll have to sit in dunce chair.

Because the teacher don't want 'em to be, and then they'll have to go up to the office if they won't do what the teacher says.

So they won't disturb them working, and won't disturb them reading.

'Cause they ought not to be noisy when they have class reading. 'Cause they ought not to be noisy when the teacher's talking.

Because the other pupils couldn't hear and if they couldn't hear what the teacher was saying then they couldn't do the problems and things.

They wouldn't know what their lessons was about. Wouldn't be paying attention to the teacher and wouldn't know what she was saying.

They don't learn and they're not supposed to.

MINUS

Because they're supposed to sit down and be still and do their studying when the teacher tells them to.

Because it will disturb the other classes upstairs. They might be reading, doing arithmetic, geography.

Some other children are working and they are quiet and you make them be noisy.

Because helps 'em out so they could study and they learn a lot when they grow up.

If they were noisy in school everybody would hear them over the school and it would disturb other ones from their lessons.

(b) *Give two reasons why most people would rather have an automobile than a bicycle.*

PLUS

Because an automobile can go faster than a bicycle. Because you fall down on a bicycle.

Automobile can travel more, go more miles. Bicycle can't go as fast.

People don't want bicycle because they don't last long and machines you can ride for a long time and go all over the country.

An automobile can go faster and a bicycle can get in more trouble.

Because an auto can go faster. And a bicycle is too slow. You have to pump a lot.

Because you can travel from land to land in an automobile and you can just ride around the city on a bicycle. An automobile is more convenient than a bicycle.

Can go better in an automobile and can go faster.

Automobile is easier to ride and doesn't tire you out.

MINUS

They can go faster in an auto. Don't take as much time to get there.

An auto is bigger than a bicycle. Holds more people.

An automobile can ride in the gutters and a bicycle can't, a bicycle lot of people can't stay on, but an automobile they could.

Bicycle don't run like a auto in the street because they might get runned over on street and they can't run on sidewalk because they'll run into people.

Score: 2 plus with two reasons each.

5. Word Naming

Although scoring takes account only of the number of words given, very characteristic qualitative differences are observable between different age levels and from individual to individual in this free association test. Some subjects, more often the younger ones, give mainly isolated words. Objects immediately present contribute largely to the responses of some children and abstract words are of rarer occurrence. Most responses include a mixture of isolated words, objects immediately seen, and various word groups.

The test is passed if 28 words, exclusive of repetitions, are named in one minute. Only real words are counted. As noted in the procedure, the subject is not allowed to count or to give sentences. However, he is given credit for as many as three numbers in counting and for that portion of a sentence up to the point where the examiner discovers and stops him. Sequences such as months and days of the week are allowed, and proper names are credited.

Score: 28 words in one minute exclusive of repetitions.

6. Repeating 6 Digits

Score: 1 plus. Correct order without error.

Alternate. Verbal Absurdities III

(a) *In the year 1951 many more women than men got married in the United States.*

They couldn't get married if they didn't have men.

That women have to get married to men — they can't get married to women.

It couldn't. There'd be two women married at the same time together.

In some places that could be possible because of polygamy, but in any other place where there aren't Mormons we need as many men as women to get married.

There has to be as many men as women to get married.

Q

There wouldn't be enough men married to the women.

'Cause there's not as many men as women.

They couldn't do it.

MINUS

'Cause just one at a time gets married don't they?

More people couldn't be married because lots of people were married already.

Because the women gets married more than the men.

Men don't get married, only women get married because the men are the husbands and they don't do the marrying, the wife does it.

How could there be enough men?

(b) *A man wished to dig a hole in which to bury some rubbish, but could not decide what to do with the dirt from the hole. A friend suggested that he dig the hole large enough to hold the dirt, too.*

PLUS

He couldn't dig a hole big enough to put the dirt in, too.

Well, he'd have more dirt and he'd just keep on digging holes.

It would be foolish; a larger hole would get more dirt.

He'd still have some dirt from the other hole.

There'd be just as much dirt coming out.

Because if he dug a hole and put all the dirt back in the hole there wouldn't be any room for the other rubbish.

If he dug a hole deep it would just hold the dirt that he dug out of it.

The bigger the hole the more dirt he'd have to put in.

He couldn't dig a hole large enough to hold the dirt, too, unless there were a lot of rocks in the ground he threw away.

Well, if you dig a hole, if you leave the dirt in there it wouldn't be a hole at all.

Q

Because he couldn't do that.　　　　He would have to dig it out again.

He couldn't dig a hole that would hold the dirt because if he dug the hole he would have to throw the dirt aside.

He should put the dirt on top.

Couldn't get every scrap of the dirt back in the hole.

Don't have to dig a hole large enough to put the dirt in. Just pack the dirt in and step on it, it'll go down after a rain or two.

If he just dug a little hole the dirt would have went back in. It don't matter how big he dug it.

If he just dug one hole he could put the rubbish in that and leave the dirt where it was.

He can't bury the rubbish without putting the dirt over the top of it.

(c) *They began the meeting late, but they set the hands of the clock back so that the meeting might surely close before sunset.*

PLUS

It don't matter if they put it back. It would be sunset at the same time anyway.

They couldn't do that because it'd just be as late anyway.

The time would go on anyway. The clock would just be wrong, that's all.

They set the hands back and thought it would be later — or earlier when it's the same time.

Because the clock would be slow.   It would still be late.

Q

It would be dark when they got through.

It wouldn't make any difference.   They set the hands of the clock back.

MINUS

It was foolish to set the hands of the clock back because then they couldn't tell what time it was.

The sun can set any time.

Then the sun would go down before the clock would strike the time it was.

It would be sunset and past by the time they got through with their meeting.

If they started it early, they wouldn't have to set it back.

It wouldn't do any good because they might have watches.

If they wanted the meeting to close before sunset they could watch when the sun was going down, they could stop the meeting.

It'll shorten the meeting instead of lengthening it.

Score: 2 plus.

YEAR XI

1. Memory for Designs I (same as IX, 3)

Score: 1½ plus. See scoring standards, page 174.

2. Verbal Absurdities IV

(a) *The judge said to the prisoner, "You are to be hanged, and I hope it will be a warning to you."*

PLUS

After he was hung it wouldn't be any warning to him because he'd be dead.
If he is hung he can't never live again and so how would he know it?
If he got hanged he wouldn't be alive — he'd be dead.
Well, can't be a warning to him that he's going to be hanged because he's going to be hanged already.
That isn't a warning — judge should have said, "Next time you do a crime like that you *will* be hanged."
He won't need a warning after he's hanged.

Q

He is going to give him a warning and he is going to hang him.
He said he hoped it would be a warning to him.
He is dead and it is a warning.

MINUS

He should say hung not hanged.
It is his fault. Why should he give him a warning?
If he's going to be hanged what's he going to warn it to him? He's just about going to die. What's warn?
Well if he's going to be hung why should they warn him about it. They've already got him.
He warned the prisoner that he can't escape and the prisoner would have to die anyway.
The judge gave him warning he was going to be hanged.
If he warned him he couldn't get out of it anyway, if he did warn him.
If he was going to be hanged, he wouldn't know when the warning would come.

(b) *A well-known railroad had its last accident five years ago and since that time it has killed only one person in a collision.*

PLUS

If they had one five years ago and one since it would have been two accidents in five years.
He couldn't kill nobody if there was no train wreck.
It's had two accidents.
It wouldn't kill anybody if it hadn't had any wrecks.
It had another wreck.

Q

Killed only one person in a collision.
It said it had a collision and it said it had its last accident five years ago.

They had to have an accident if they killed a person.
What's the difference between accident and collision?

MINUS

If it had an accident five years ago it couldn't of just killed one person
since that time.
If it had a accident five years ago it couldn't have killed anybody in a collision.
And if it had its last wreck it couldn't have any more — if it's wrecked real
bad it can't be fixed.
It's had its last accident, it is funny they're still riding on it.

(c) *When there is a collision the last car of the train is usually damaged
most. So they have decided that it will be best if the last car is always taken
off before the train starts.*

PLUS

There will be another last car.
Should not be taken off because the last one would be crashed most. Have
to take all off.
'Cause the other one will get hurt the worst.

Q

Taking the last car off before the train starts!
It's usually the first one that gets wrecked the most and the next to the last
will be the last.

MINUS

It won't go if the last train is off.   They should take the front car away.
They wouldn't know whether they were going to have an accident or not.
They made a mistake. It is the front car that gets damaged the most.

Score: 2 plus.

3. Abstract Words II (same as XIII, 2)

(a) *Connection.* (That which joins things together. A relationship.)

PLUS

Joins two or more things together.   Connect two things together.
Sometimes to get in touch with someone, or also putting two parties to-
gether over the 'phone.
The relation between things.
You're kin to 'em.   Like you add another part to a train.
If somebody had a broken rope they'd tie the rope together, connect it.

Like you connect two wires.   When you connect anything.

My father has connections to get him show tickets.

Means you connect another car.

MINUS

We go with one another.   Something is broken and you fix it.

You connect the lights — you shut off the lights.

(b) *Compare*. (To examine for the discovery of resemblances or differences. To represent as similar.)

PLUS

To compare two things you try to find out which is the best thing.

When you take one thing and put it alongside of another and see in what ways they're alike and in what ways they aren't alike.

When you compare two things you check them as to their value — what they're worth.

To compare two things to see if they are both the same.

You have two automobiles or two dresses and you try to decide which one you want — to compare them together.

To show difference.

You liken her to her mother.

Q

You compare two things.

You compare her to her mother.

Like you compare one number to another.

MINUS

Take two things that's just alike and put them together.

If you have two words you can compare them together, but if they're not the same you can't compare them together.

Put together.

To compare two answers together to correct 'em.

Like two words meaning the same.

(c) *Conquer*. (To gain or acquire by force or by mental or moral power. To be victorious; to prevail.)

PLUS

To win over our enemies.   You capture them.

If you're fighting you conquer the other nation if it loses.

You've got that under your power; you're going to get something and it belongs to you now.

When they conquer a city they take it away from the people that own it, that are ruling it.

Like your studies, you'd have to get it, have to understand it.

To get something.
To take something away from someone.
Win.   Like if you would hurt them.
Conquer something, like in school, if you had something you had to do
   like mathematics, you'd have to conquer your mathematics.
Like you conquer Mexico.

MINUS

Means you'll shoot someone.   You fight.
To make anything better.   To surrender.
You stop anything.   You conk her on the head.
You hurt someone, go up and push them down just for meanness.
You conquer Mexico, you discover parts of it like Cortez.

  (d) *Obedience.* (Submission or compliance).

PLUS

To mind.   Keeping the law.
A person does what they're told.
If somebody tells you to do it, like your teacher, you do it right away, and
   don't hesitate.
You do what other people want you to.
To have manners and do what you're told.

Q

Being good.   To be quiet.
To have manners.   Be nice.
To obey them.

MINUS

Not talk out all the time in your classroom and street car 'n' everything.
Be kind to your parents.
To obey and not be bad or anything.

  (e) *Revenge.* (To inflict harm in return for wrong or injury. To avenge.)

PLUS

Harming someone to make up for something bad done to somebody you
   like.
The desire to return a grudge.   Get even.
Getting back at a person who's done you harm.
If somebody gets you into trouble, you want to make them get the blame
   for something or get into trouble for making you get into trouble.
If they've been harmed they get revenge and that satisfies 'em then.
You hate someone for something he's done and you want to get back at
   him some way.

He done something to you. You want to do something to him.
Try to get something over on somebody.
Like you revenge anything.

MINUS

When you get ahead of somebody they want to get revenge right away.
You want to win something for yourself.
To come back at a person, doublecross them.
If you're mad at someone and you wanted revenge on them you'd do something dirty to them, that's revenge.
You hate a person.
Keep somebody from doing what they want to do.
Someone is going to hit you, you do something back.

Score: 3 plus.

4. Memory for Sentences II

Score: 1 plus. No error. Errors include omissions, substitutions, additions, changes in words or in order of words.

5. Problem Situation II

PLUS

It was a skunk.   It was a bad smelling animal.
That kitty was a pole!   Because it stunk.

MINUS

That animal had a disease or something.
That animal was poison.   Because his clothes were so dirty.
Because the animal probably had fleas or something.
The animal chewed his clothes all up.

6. Similarities: Three things

Any real similarity is acceptable whether fundamental or superficial. This test sometimes provokes doubtful responses such as the indefinite statements, "*all are useful*," or "*all made of the same material*," and in order to score these a supplementary explanation must be called for.

(a) *Snake — Cow — Sparrow*

PLUS

All are animals.   They can eat.
All move.   All have babies.
They can all make a noise.   None of them can talk.
They all stay out in the pasture.
They have tails (eyes, tongue, skin, etc.).

They are not human.   They can all do something.
They like grass.

MINUS

They are all on the ground.   All can walk.
They make noise.   All have legs.
They eat the same food.   They all lay down.
They can all hurt you.   They're all mammals.
All animals — no, sparrow isn't an animal.
A snake crawls, a cow walks, and a sparrow flies (or some other difference).
All eat grass.

(b) *Rose — Potato — Tree*

PLUS

They grow in the ground.   All have roots.
Both got leaves.   All are plants.
All of them bloom.   All green at the same season.
They all produce food — rose for the bees, and potato and tree for human
    being or livestock.
All part of nature.   All part of a garden.

Q

All useful.   All vegetable.
They are on the ground.

MINUS

They're all wild plants.   All give us sap.
They can rust.   They are vegetables.
Rose grows like a tree and a potato grows in the ground.
All grow from nearly the same things.

(c) *Wool — Cotton — Leather*

PLUS

All used for clothing.   To wear.
You can make coats out of them.   They're all cloth-like.
They can all make gloves.   They're all goods.
Wool will keep you warm, cotton keeps you warm, leather will keep your
    feet warm.
Because they are all worn, wool and cotton makes wool and cotton dresses,
    and leather, they make shoes out of.
They're all grown in the United States.

Q

You can make things out of them.   They are all useful.

MINUS

You make shoes out of leather and you make clothes out of cotton and you
  make clothes out of wool.
They're made out of the same kind of stuff that comes out of the ground.
All soft.   Come from animals.
Because they make clothing out of them and shoes.
They are all necessities of life.

(d) *Knife-blade — Penny — Piece of wire*

PLUS

They are all minerals.
They're all made out of something hard.
They're made out of some kind of stuff that comes from the ground.
They're made out of different metals.
They're all copper, no I guess a knife isn't copper — all metals.

Q

They are all made of the same thing.
You can do something with all of them.
All the same substance.   You can use them all.

MINUS

All made of copper.   They are articles.
They won't break.   You can use 'em for different things.
Steel.   They're all shiny.
They are both strong.

(e) *Book — Teacher — Newspaper*

PLUS

You learn from all.   They all use words.
All teach.   They all serve the public.
You can read a book and read a newspaper and learn something and a
  teacher talks to you and you learn something.
All help you get an education.

Q

All useful.

MINUS

They belong to school — newspaper has reading on it and you use it some-
  times in school.
The teacher teaches you something from a book and newspaper, too,
  teaches you something.
To learn to read.   All give you news.   All read.
Teacher tells you something and newspaper does, too.

Score: 3 plus.

Alternate. Finding Reasons II

This test is scored very leniently. Any reason that is at all plausible is credited. Even if the reasons proposed by the child overlap or belong in the same category, provided different aspects are presented that can be distinguished, they are counted as two. Failure usually consists of inability to give two reasons and is manifested in a rambling account of some particular situation that the task recalls.

(a) *Give two reasons why children should obey their parents.*

Some of the commonest reasons mentioned are: To avoid punishment, for their own good, to avoid getting into trouble, because they should, because it is the right thing to do, and because parents know best.

PLUS

Because their parents know best and because they might get a whipping.

Because they'll do something wrong and they'll get in trouble.

If their mother tells them not to go out on the street and they disobey they might get run over. They can get in trouble if they disobey their mother, like if they go to some house and they wreck things.

They would get things done quicker and they would leave more time to go places.

Because if they don't then the parents won't get 'em anything. They have to obey their parents or they won't like 'em.

To be kind to the parents and because their parents want them to do it.

It'll help you learn to be good and they wouldn't have to put you in jail when you grow up.

Because they might get a whipping and they might be sent to bed.

So they wouldn't get so many whippings. They should obey their parents anyway.

MINUS

Because their parents wouldn't like it if they went off somewhere without their parents knowing where they're going and they wouldn't want them to.

Their parents know more than the children because parents was once children and they should obey them because they know better.

Because if you didn't you might get a whipping and if you do you might not.

Children should obey their parents 'cause if they don't they might not pass — they might not get good grades.

Because the mothers and daddies want to have a nice child and they would have to be ashamed.

Because the parents is bigger than the children and they should obey them.

(b) *Give two reasons why there should be plenty of railroads in the United States.*

PLUS

So they can go to a lot of towns without using their car. Should have 'em because maybe the people haven't got cars to go in.

To carry passengers and to take fruit and cattle and things like that to different towns and cities.

So men won't have to buy automobiles in order to go down town and it's quicker than to take a taxi or bus.

To bring people from states to states and if there was a robbery and needed cops out there you could go by train — easier, quicker.

So they can carry people that have no cars and to make the United States popular.

People can get places quicker and easier.

When there's plenty of railroads there's a easy way of transportation. They'll make the country more prosperous.

To carry people. More comfortable than driving.

MINUS

So people can travel and so they can go different places.

Because there's lots of people going out of town and comin' in.

So people won't have to walk to the place — maybe they haven't got a car and they can go by train and won't have to walk.

So the trains can run on them — there'd be too much trains to run on one track.

The trains has to haul cars and go every place and you need the railroad.

So the trains and the street cars can go on 'em.

Score: 2 plus with two reasons each.

Y E A R   XII

1. Vocabulary

Score: 15 plus. See scoring standards, page 232.

2. Verbal Absurdities II (same as IX, 2)

Score: 4 plus.

3. Picture Absurdities II

PLUS

If the sun is shining his shadow would be on the other side of him.

His shadow wouldn't be like that — if the sun was shining that way.

His shadow's on the wrong side.
The shadow is going the wrong way.
His shadow's shining against the sun.
When the sun is there his shadow would be in front.
It's the shadow — it would be away from the sun.
The man should be between the sun and his shadow.
The shadow wouldn't point towards the sun.

Q

His shadow is in front of him.   His shadow shouldn't be there.
That line isn't straight — the horizon and the shadow should be more to the
   back.
When the sun is just rising his shadow wouldn't be like that.

MINUS

The sun is rising in the west.
The man's walking through the woods and the sun is shining and his
   shadow is in front of him and your shadow always goes in back of you
   most of the time.
Because your shadow is always in back of you on a hot day.
The shadow, because it's facing a different way than he is.
He's walking this way and his shadow goes that way.
The sun hasn't risen and the man sees his shadow.

4. Repeating 5 Digits reversed.

Score: 1 plus. Correct order without error.

5. Abstract Words I (same as X, 3)

Score: 3 plus.

6. Minkus Completion I

(a) *We like to pop corn* . . . . . . *to roast chestnuts over the fire.*

PLUS
and,   or.

(b) *One cannot always be a hero,* . . . . . . *one can always be a man.*

PLUS
nevertheless,
although,   though,
while,   however,
yet,   but.

(c) *The streams are dry* . . . . . . *there has been little rain.*

PLUS

if, so,
therefore, because,
where, when,
after, since,
as, for.

(d) *Lincoln aroused no jealousy* . . . . . . *he was not selfish.*

PLUS

because, as,
since, but.
for,

Score: 3 plus within the time limit of 5 minutes.

Alternate: Memory for Designs II

This test was used in the United States Army during World War I.[1] The design is made up of three diamond-shaped figures. The plan of the design is the important thing to consider in scoring rather than neatness of execution. The diamonds may be somewhat irregular if the essential characteristics of the plan are carried out; that is, there must be an outer diamond, an inner diamond crosswise within, whose acute angles meet the obtuse angles of the outer diamond, and a still smaller diamond within the second diamond which maintains the same relationship to the second diamond as the second diamond does to the first.

Figure 11. Corners do not meet.
Figure 12. Second diamond more rectangular than diamond-shaped; corners of the third diamond do not meet those of the second.
Figure 15. Second diamond is not crosswise.
Figures 16 and 17. Second diamond has rounded lines instead of obtuse angles.

[1] "Psychological Examining in the United States Army." Robert M. Yerkes, ed. *Nat'l. Acad. of Sc. Mem.*, pp. 185–87; 199; Washington, Gov't Printing Office, 1921.

PLUS

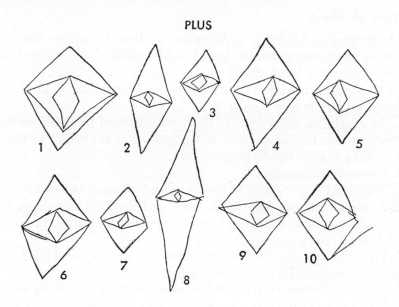

MINUS

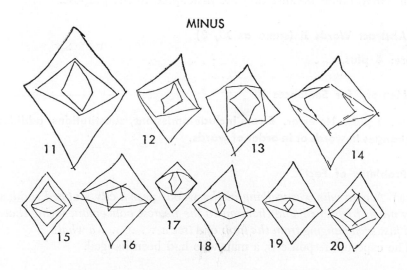

1. Plan of Search

The purpose of this test is to determine whether the subject can execute a plan of search that meets the logical requirements of the problem. Satisfactory evidence is based chiefly on the type of plan evolved. The paths must be almost parallel and there must be no intersections or breaks. The satisfactory types include mainly:

1. An adaptation of the spiral to the requirements of the diamond-shaped field with a line beginning either at the gate or at the center of the field and made up of fairly regular lines.

2. Concentric diamonds.

3. Transverse lines, parallel or almost so, and joined at the ends.

4. A line around the field which turns back on itself, then goes round again making an inner diamond before turning back on itself to go round the field again, and so on covering the field.

5. Field divided into quarters and filled in with lines making spiral or concentric triangular figures in each quarter.

Superimposed plans are not satisfactory unless both are clearly adequate (conform to one of the above types) and are presumably given as alternative choices.

The samples on page 201 indicate the main types of satisfactory plans and give a few illustrations of the almost unlimited kinds of plans that have been scored minus because they are ill-adapted to the purpose.

2. Abstract Words II (same as XI, 3)

Score: 4 plus.

3. Memory for Sentences III

Score: 1 plus. No error. Errors include omissions, substitutions, additions, changes in words or in order of words.

4. Problems of Fact

(a) *A man who was walking in the woods near a city stopped suddenly, very much frightened, and then ran to the nearest policeman, saying that he had just seen hanging from the limb of a tree a . . . . . . a what?*

The expected response is, a man who had been hanged.

PLUS

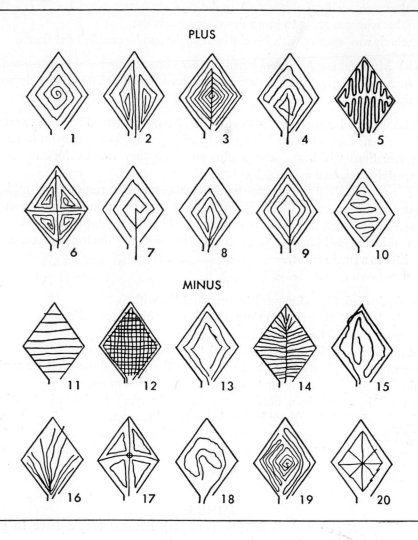

MINUS

PLUS

A dead man.

A man who had been hung.

A man who had been lynched.

A man who had hung himself.

A skeleton.

Somebody dying — hanging there.

A body of a person.

Q

A man.   A person.   A robber.   A man hanging from a limb.

Monkey.   Leaf.   A snake.

A robber who was going to jump down on somebody.

Somebody was hanging with his clothes caught and he couldn't get down.

(b) *My neighbor has been having queer visitors. First a doctor came to his house, then a lawyer, then a minister (preacher or priest). What do you think happened there?*

The expected answer is "a death," or "someone has died." However, this problem brings forth a wide variety of ingenious but rather far-fetched interpretations which are scored plus provided they can be *logically* and adequately explained by the subject.

It is almost always necessary to check the subject's response by asking what the lawyer came for and occasionally why the minister and doctor came. These must be correctly explained. The interpretation, in order to be considered satisfactory, must relate the visits of doctor, lawyer, and minister to a single event.

PLUS

Somebody died. (Q) (Lawyer) to see about the will.

Somebody died. (Q) (Lawyer) to see about the insurance policy.

Someone died and the lawyer came to settle the estate.

Got run over and killed. (Q) (Lawyer) to try to settle the case.

A murder. (Q) (Lawyer) came to look over the case and see what he could do about it. The minister to preach the funeral sermon.

He must have got in a crash — got hurt (Lawyer) to investigate what happened, (Minister) maybe he died and said prayers.

Might have been some crime committed. If a man was shot the doctor came to fix up his wounds, the lawyer came to see who did it and the minister to preach a sermon if he died.

MINUS

Somebody got sick and died. (Q) (Lawyer) Because they'd have to get their doctor bills straightened.

Somebody was dying. (Q) Doctor for his money, lawyer for his money, minister came to pray for him.

Somebody died and the lawyer told him what to do.

A boy died or a girl or somebody. (Q) (Lawyer) To see about fixing up things.

They were sick. (Q) (Lawyer) to see what the damage was done, minister to pray.

Someone was sick and then there was some trouble and then someone got married.

Doctor came with a baby and they have to have a license from the lawyer and the minister came to marry them.

Maybe this lady was getting a divorce.

(c) *An Indian who had come to town for the first time in his life saw a boy riding along the street. As the boy rode by, the Indian said, "The white boy is lazy; he walks sitting down." What was the boy riding on that caused the Indian to say "he walks sitting down"?*

PLUS
Bike. Bicycle. Kiddy car.

MINUS
Horse. A car. Scooter.

Score: 2 plus.

5. Dissected Sentences

A sentence is not counted correct if any word is omitted, altered, or inserted, or if the order given fails to make perfect sense. Certain responses are not absolutely incorrect, but are objectionable as regards sentence structure, or else fail to give the exact meaning intended. These are half-credit.

(a) FOR THE STARTED AN WE COUNTRY EARLY AT HOUR

PLUS
We started for the country at an early hour.
At an early hour we started for the country.
We started at an early hour for the country.

HALF-CREDIT
For the country at an early hour we started.
For the country we started at an early hour.

MINUS
We started early at an hour for the country.
We started early for the country.
And we started for the country at an early hour.

(b) TO ASKED PAPER MY TEACHER CORRECT I MY

PLUS
I asked my teacher to correct my paper.

HALF-CREDIT
My teacher I asked to correct my paper.
To correct my paper I asked my teacher.

My teacher asked to correct my paper.
I asked my teacher to correct the paper.
I asked the teacher to correct my paper.

(c) A DEFENDS DOG GOOD HIS BRAVELY MASTER

PLUS

A good dog defends his master bravely.
A good dog bravely defends his master.
A dog defends his good master bravely.
A dog bravely defends his good master.

HALF-CREDIT

A good master bravely defends his dog.
His good dog bravely defends a master.
Bravely a master defends his good dog.
His good dog defends a master bravely.

MINUS

A dog defends his master bravely.
A bravely dog defends his master.
A good dog defends his bravely master.
A good brave dog defends his master.

Score: 2 plus.

6. Copying a Bead Chain from Memory

Score: No error.

Alternate. Paper Cutting. (same as IX, 1)

Score: 2 plus.

Y E A R   X I V

1. Vocabulary

Score: 17 plus. See scoring standards, page 232.

2. Induction

This test presents a series of events which affords a basis for making a generalization stating the governing principle involved. The subject must observe that each unfolded sheet contains twice as many holes as the previous one, and must infer that folding the paper again will double the number. He must then state that doubling the number of holes contained in the preceding sheet, or multiplying that number by two, will predict the number in the succeeding sheet. It is ordinarily only after one or more mistakes have been made and have been disclosed by the examiner's unfolding the sheet for inspection that the correct principle is grasped.

The test is scored plus only if the rule is grasped and correctly stated. The criteria by which the examiner determines whether the rule has been grasped are:

1. Statement of the principle spontaneously before the sixth folding has been reached.

2. Giving the correct number of holes for the sixth folding regardless of the correctness or incorrectness of the responses for the preceding sheets, and then stating the correct principle.

Recapitulation of the correct number of holes for each folding does *not* constitute a statement of the principle. The following samples are illustrations of the standards which govern the scoring of responses to this test:

PLUS

Double it each time.

Two times the number that it is, if it was 4 when you folded it, it'd make 8.

Add the amount — like you have 8 and fold it again, add 8 more equals 16.

Every fold you make in the paper there'll be double the amount of holes.

MINUS

If you fold it once there is 1 hole, twice there's 2 holes, 3 times there's 4 holes, 4 times there's 8 holes, 5 times and there are 16 holes and then 6 times and there are 32.

By doubling it after it gets to 8.   Add more on every one.

At first you know it's 1 hole, or second it's 2 holes and on third it's 4 holes and then it gains 4 and then goes to 8 and gains 8 more and goes to 16 and gains 16 more and then goes to 32.

Multiply the last number by how many more times you fold it.

The number of times you fold it.

Score: Plus if the rule is grasped by the time the sixth sheet is reached; that is, S may pass after five incorrect responses, provided the sixth is correct and the governing rule can then be stated.

3. Reasoning I

PLUS

(Any specific time between four and five o'clock is plus.)

Between four and five.   Four-fifteen.   Four-thirty.

About half-past four.   About ten minutes to five.

After four.   Before five.

MINUS

Four o'clock.   About five.
About four.   About dinner time.
Five o'clock.   During the afternoon.

4. Ingenuity I (same as AA, 2; SA II, 4)

Score: 1 plus. To receive credit on the test the subject must demonstrate the successive steps followed in his solution of the problem.

5. Orientation: Direction I

Score: 3 plus.

6. Reconciliation of Opposites (same as SA I, A)

(a) *Winter and summer*

PLUS

They're seasons.   Both a climate.
They're both parts of the year.   Both weather.
They both get three months in 'em.   Have atmospheric changes.
Same amount of months (or days).   Both are temperatures.
They're both time.

MINUS

Both of them are months.   Summer and winter both have winds.
Winter is the cold part of the year and summer is the warm part.
There are vacations in both of them — in both seasons.

(b) *Happy and sad*

PLUS

Both state of mind (or action of mind, state of being, conditions of mind).
Both tell the mind of a person.   Both have to do with feelings.
Both natures (or characters).   Both mental.
Both conditions, tell whether you're happy or sad.
Both emotions (or moods, spirit, humor, disposition).
Both adjectives describing how a person feels.

A way you act.   Different appearance of people.
Both ways you can be.   Both expressions of the face.
Same capacity — sad is height of bereavement and happy is the result of joy.
Both in your life.

(c) *Loud and soft*

Vibrations.   Both affect the ear.
Both detected by the senses.   Both sounds (noise, voice).
Both amount of sound (noise, voice).
Both extremes of sound (noise, voice).
Both tones (pitch).
Both a manner of making a noise or speaking.

You can hear both of them.   Talk.
You can make a soft sound and you can make a loud sound.
Both make a noise.
Can be made by the same instrument.
Both contain the same number of letters. (Should repeat question.)

(d) *Much and little*

Both measurements of weight (or size).
Measurements.   Both are quantitative adjectives.
Used for measuring.   Both tell how much.
Both a certain amount of anything.

It's some.   Both commodities.
They're something.
You can have much of something and little of something.
One's a large quantity and one's a small quantity.

(e) *Beginning and end*

This item is the hardest of the series. It is difficult to grasp the point and difficult to express the answer. The examiner must be on his guard against fine-sounding phrases which miss the point.

They are both terminals.   Both a certain point.
Both places.   Tell when.
Both determinants.   They are both times.
They mark position of progress.

Both where some action of some sort terminates.

They're both parts in doing a thing — that isn't very clear though; time at the end of which you do something.

MINUS

Because attached on to the same thing.

Beginning and end of a thing.	Start with both of them.
You can begin at both ends.	Both ends of stories.

Because they're both parts. (Very common.)

Both a part of something — one part beginning and other part the end. (Example of inadequate explanation.)

Because they are both terms of stopping.

If there's a beginning there must be an end, so they're connected.

They both determine how the thing turns out.

Both definite proceedings.

Score: 2 plus.

Alternate. Ingenuity II

Score: 1 plus. The subject must demonstrate the successive steps followed in his solution of the problem.

A V E R A G E   A D U L T

1. Vocabulary

Score: 20 plus. See scoring standards, page 232.

2. Ingenuity I (same as XIV, 4; SA II, 4)

Score: 2 plus. See scoring standards, page 206.

3. Differences between Abstract Words

Success on this test depends upon the ability to point out the essential distinction between the pairs of stimulus words, a requirement which imposes a difficult task upon the powers of linguistic expression. For this reason, it is necessary in scoring to disregard clumsiness of expression and consider, rather, the essential correctness or incorrectness of the thought.

(a) *Laziness and idleness*

The essential contrast is that laziness refers to unwillingness to work; idleness to inactivity. This contrast must be expressed, however clumsily.

When you're lazy you won't work and when you're idle you can't work because you haven't anything to do.

Laziness you just don't want to do anything, while idleness you stop and rest or something like that.

If you're lazy you'll do something but you don't like to do it and, if you're idle you don't do anything.

When you're lazy you don't want to do anything — just want to sit down and read or something like that, and when you're idle you're willing to do something.

If a person's out of work he's idle, but that doesn't make him necessarily lazy.

Q

Laziness is temperamental, but idleness is temporary!

If you're idle you are fooling around. Laziness is your nature.

MINUS

If you're lazy you are just lying around, but if you're idle you don't want to do anything.

Laziness you're too lazy to do something, idleness you're not quite lazy — just don't want to do it.

Laziness is wanting to sleep all the time and idleness is don't want to work.

Laziness you don't want to do nothing and idleness you have something to do but you don't do it — you just sit there.

They're both the same. (Frequent type of failure.)

Laziness you don't do anything at all and idleness you're just idle for the time being.

(b) *Poverty and misery*

PLUS

Poverty means to be in want; misery comes from any kind of suffering or anguish.

Misery is how you feel, like if you are cold, and poverty is when you are poor.

Poverty is to be poor, misery is to be sick or ill.

Can be poor but you don't have to be miserable.

Poverty means poor and misery means lack of food or water or to be sick.

You don't always have to be in poverty to be in misery, but poverty is usually misery.

Q

You can be rich and sad and poor and happy.

If you're in pain you are miserable and poverty means hardship.

Environmental versus physical.

MINUS

Misery you don't feel good and otherwise you feel good.

In poverty you're happy, in misery you're not happy.

One's in pain and the other is just the thought.

Misery — you're miserable, you don't feel good and I don't know poverty.
  (Frequent.)

Poverty some people owe a lot and that's their poverty, and misery you're
  in misery.

(c) *Character and reputation*

The essential distinction is, of course, that character is what you are and
reputation is what is thought about you.

PLUS

Character is made up of all the qualities you possess and reputation is something you have acquired by acting out these qualities.

Character is what you really are and your reputation is what you're noted
  for.

Character tells what kind of a person you are and reputation is what you
  make, what people think of you.

Character is how you do things and reputation is what people think of you.

Reputation means your name and what you do, if you're good or bad, and
  character means yourself.

Your reputation is how you stand in your town or city and your character
  is your habits.

Character is what you are now and reputation is what you seem to be.

Q

Character is your personality. Reputation is gossip.

You may have a bad reputation and character is the person.

MINUS

When you have good character you're smart and know everything and have
  reputation, everybody knows you're doing good.

Character you do anything and reputation a lot of people know you.

Your character is yourself and reputation is the way you act.

Reputation is what you do, whether it's right or wrong, and character is
  your ideals and if you live up to them.

Score: 2 plus.

4. Arithmetical Reasoning.

Score: 2 plus.

PART TWO   **AA, 4**   **210**

5. Proverbs I

The task is a difficult one, even for adults, since a pertinent generalization is required, based on the rather cryptic, homely situations into which folkways of thinking have become crystallized. Thus the proverb must be analyzed, abstracted, and applied to life situations. Particularized or literal interpretation is not satisfactory. The interpretation of a given proverb in terms of another pertinent proverbial saying is satisfactory because in order to arrive at such a response the subject must not only have generalized from the particular situation presented by the given proverb but have gone a step farther and reapplied the generalization. Awkwardness of verbal expression is disregarded if the generalization is correct. Failures are of three types: (a) inability to respond; (b) literal interpretation, i.e., explaining the statement without generalization; and (c) incorrect or inappropriate generalizations.

(a) *We only know the worth of water when the well is dry.* (We don't appreciate the value of things until we are deprived of them.)

PLUS

We don't know how to appreciate a thing when it is with us.

We wait until it's too late to know the use of things.

Means the same as locking the door after the horse is stolen — means you don't know how much you want a thing 'til the chance has gone by to get it.

We don't know when we're well off until we're poor.

Might have a whole lot of money and spend it and you wouldn't care, and then when it's gone you know what it's worth.

You pay more attention to things after they're gone than when they're around you.

If you have plenty of a thing you don't care so much — just as soon as it's taken away you miss it.

Means when you have a lot of something you don't think about it until you haven't anything.

MINUS

You don't know what it means to do without water or anything 'til your well goes dry and you don't have it.

Whenever you haven't anything you realize what it is.

Do not waste when you have lots.

Should take care of things when we have them because we'll miss them when we haven't.

It's too late to begin things when they're already done.

Maybe you might have a whole lot of money and waste it and later have

only a little — remember they had a whole lot and wish they hadn't been so wasteful.
We don't appreciate it when we have it. (Too vague.)

(b) *No wind can do him good who steers for no port.* (Unless one has an objective in life, assistance is of no avail.)

PLUS

No one can help a person unless they have an aim themselves and work for it.
All the advantages you have — if you don't concentrate them on something — won't amount to much.
Nothing can do you much good unless you are going some place.
Education can't do a person any good unless he goes out for some certain thing.
If a person doesn't know what he wants to do — no one can help him — until he decides.
Nothing will do him any good in life if he hasn't any ambition.
Nothing can do a person any good if he don't try to do something.

MINUS

If you don't go for a certain place, that you won't get there.
Can't do what he don't try.
Nobody helps anybody who hasn't got any ideal.
He's got to have some goal — or he'll just blow all round.
No person can get anywhere and nobody will help him unless he shows what he wants to do and don't keep changing his ideas.
Nothing can do any good if you don't try.
No help can do him any good if he don't want to have opportunities.
Nothing will come to you if you don't get it yourself.
You have to help yourself if you want somebody else to.

(c) *Don't judge a book by its cover.* (External appearances may be deceiving.)

PLUS

Don't judge people by their clumsiness outside.
That we shouldn't judge things by their reputation or names.
Don't judge anybody by the way they dress.
Means good things sometimes don't look it.
Bad things sometimes have good outsides or don't show their bad parts.
Look into a thing before you decide what it means.
At first sight you might think things are good, but you have to learn later on.
Look into things thoroughly.

Not to make any statements about what you see on the outside of a person or thing.

Can't tell how a person is by the way he acts.

You have to find out what's inside.

Sometimes the books don't have a good name — don't judge them by the cover — the name.

Score: 2 plus.

6. Orientation: Direction II

Score: 4 plus.

7. Essential Differences (same as SA II, 5)

(a) *Work and play*

In pointing out the difference between work and play, several characteristic contrasts appear to be about equally valid according to one's philosophy. One of the most frequent contrasts brought out is that of *necessity* vs. *freedom*; the *duty* aspect of work is contrasted with the *leisure* or *recreation* aspect of play; *usefulness* vs. *uselessness* constitutes a third contrast; and lastly a contrast in attitudes is emphasized, the *pleasant feeling tone* vs. the *irksomeness* or *disliked character* of the activity.

PLUS

You work to earn money and you play for the fun.

One is for amusement and the other for a living.

Play is a pleasure and work is something you should do, your duty.

Work is energy used for doing something useful and play is just wasting energy.

One's recreation — and one's labor. I mean play is an enjoyment and work is something you have to do. Sometimes you enjoy it and sometimes you don't.

When you're working you're generally doing something that has to be done — when you're playing you're just doing what you feel like.

One is something that most people like to do and the other is a duty.

The attitude towards whatever you're doing — if you're playing baseball and don't like to play baseball then it's work — if you're working at mathematics and you like to do it — then it's not work to you anymore.

Work you take seriously and play you don't.

MINUS

Work is hard and play is easy.

You can go to work and make money, but when you play, you just play games, hide-and-go-seek and things like that.

Work you're doing something and play you're just playing around and not working.

You'd rather play than to work.

Work, you get tired more quickly.

One is helping you and the other one isn't.

(b) *Ability and achievement*

PLUS

Ability is a thing you have, and achievement is a thing you work for.

Because if you have ability you can get somewhere and if you have achieved something you've done it already.

Have to work to have achievement — don't have to work to have ability.

You're able to do it — but it is the difference — if you *do* it or not.

One, you have the ability to do something and the other — what you have done.

Achievement is a product of ability because if you have the ability most always you can achieve the thing you want.

Ability means you can or can't do it and achievement means you will or won't do it.

Q

If you have ability you might someday have a big achievement.

He has the ability to do it, but he just can't achieve it.

MINUS

Ability means you can try to do something and achievement is when you have accomplished it.

Ability you want to do it and achievement means you done it.

Ability is to do something and achievement is when it's already done.

(c) *Optimist and pessimist*

PLUS

Optimist is always looking at the right side of things and the pessimist always sees the wrong side.

Optimist believes he can do it and pessimist thinks he can't.

Pessimist knows something bad is going to happen and the other knows it won't happen.

Pessimist is always against everything and optimist is just the opposite, thinks things are all right as they are.

A pessimist looks at the evil of the future and optimist is the opposite.

An optimist likes life and a pessimist dreads it.

An optimist looks towards better times and towards the future, and the pessimist feels that the world is all against him and owes him something.

They take the exact opposite views.

You'd like to have an optimist around, but not a pessimist.

One is a good guy and the other a square.

MINUS

One is for it and the other is always against — one man would say something and they'd all agree to it and there'd be just one man in the bunch who'd say something different and wouldn't give in to them.

A pessimist isn't an optimist — a pessimist just tries to be somebody that doesn't agree — an optimist doesn't.

A pessimist is constantly bothering you while an optimist may sometimes help you.

(The most common incorrect meaning given for pessimist is pest.)

Optimist is always looking ahead and pessimist he don't look at or believe in much of anything.

Optimistic person thinks greater thoughts than pessimists. Pessimist has a narrow mind.

Score: 2 plus.

8. Abstract Words III

(a) *Generosity.* (Liberality, magnanimity.)

PLUS

Generosity is unselfishness.

It means you're giving people a lot of things.

Generous — not stingy.

Well, if somebody asks you for anything you're generous you give it to them or do what you can for them.

When you're generous to anybody you're kind-hearted — do all you can for them.

It's being generous when you want to help.

Q

To be generous.

The art of being generous.

Kind.

Means when your generous to anybody.

MINUS

Be nice.

Means be nice to people when they talk to you.

When you're in a crowd don't push — just go on easy with everything.

Being generous. You're gentle with anybody.

(b) *Independent.* (Free from external control. Self-directing. Self-reliant.)

Independent is frequently confused with dependable. The slang use of independent as haughty, proud, or demanding is scored minus.

PLUS

Self-ruling.   Free from anything.

Nobody owns you.   When you're free to do things.

Somebody don't have anybody to tell 'em what to do.

Free — if you're independent, it isn't under the rule of any other country.

You have no one bossing you around.

Can give up his job whenever he wants to — has enough money saved to live on — he's free.

Means that you earn your own living.

Q

You don't belong to anybody.   Means liberty.

Free.

MINUS

You're kind of — put your head up in the air — like that.

Always want their own way.   They want it right then.

Always particular what you get — if you get the right thing or not.

You demand your rights.   Somebody thinks they are the boss.

Somebody that won't do anything.   Fourth of July.

It's a place where you can do what you want to and nobody has to tell you what to do.

(c) *Envy.* (Envy must carry the implication of grudging and must be distinguished from admiration.)

PLUS

It's the way you feel when you see somebody with something nicer than you have.

When somebody is envied — somebody else has got something and you are mad you haven't got it.

Somebody has things you haven't and you get sore about it.

Like somebody is a good talker and you're jealous you can't be one — you envy them.

Somebody got a car and you haven't — you're not their friend — you don't like 'em and you wish you had a car.

You dislike a person — like I'd dislike a girl because she had a new dress and I didn't.

Jealous. You hate somebody 'cause he's got more than you have.

You wish you had the thing that somebody else had.

It's like you're jealous. Your girl friend has a new coat and you wish you
   had it.

Q

Jealous.   Means to envy somebody.
You don't like somebody.

MINUS

When you envy somebody you hate them.
Means that they don't like a person — they don't like his manner or style.
When you tell somebody that you like their hat or coat or something.
You envy her — wish you had a coat like hers.

   (d) *Authority.* (Jurisdiction. Power due to opinion or esteem.)

PLUS

The right to rule.   The legal right to do something.
Have the privilege of commanding someone to do something.
Like a policeman is backed by the government — he has authority, he has
   the right to do whatever he is doing.
Authority means somebody that has high office.
Some high person in authority has some large responsibility.
You're good on some subject and you know practically everything about it.

Q

The right to do something.   Some high person in authority.
When somebody tells you to do something.
The teacher has authority.

MINUS

Means somebody has done something and they are going to take him to
   court.
Authority is a man who keeps people out of trouble.
Always coming in and taking something that doesn't belong to them.
A company of people that decide on some laws of the state.
Give you a whipping.
Your mother tells you to do something. They can do a lot that they want
   to.

   (e) *Justice.* (Fairness. Rendering to everyone his due.)

PLUS

Doing the right thing by everybody.   You get treated right.
To give the people their rights.   Punishment given correctly and fairly.
Having everyone be treated alike.   It's giving a person an even break.
To be just — do the right thing by a person.
They look on both sides and then they think the best thing to do.

Giving people what they have coming to them.
To do what's right. Like the judge gives justice to the man.

Q

To do what's right.   To be just.
The right thing.
If you have done something you would want to have justice.

MINUS

Means justice of the peace.   Don't do anything wrong.
It means we are doing the right thing — like helping other people.
Means to do the right thing. Like if you tell me to do something.
Doing right means — I think I'll give you a sentence, "I think I am doing
    justice to try to learn."
You want to have somebody be lenient with you if you've done something.
Be just. Be nice to people.

Score: 4 plus.

Alternate. Binet Paper Cutting.

**Score: The test is passed if the creases are drawn, if the correct number
of holes is indicated, and if the holes are correctly located.**

SUPERIOR ADULT I

1. Vocabulary

Score: 23 plus. See scoring standards, page 232.

2. Enclosed Box Problem

Score: 4 plus.

3. Minkus Completion II

(a) *He is* . . . . . . *well grounded in geography* . . . . . . *his brother,*
. . . . . . *he is not so quick in arithmetic.*

PLUS

as — as — but (however, nevertheless, although, and)
also — like — and (although, but)
very — like — yet (although, while, but, and)
considered — by — but (however, nevertheless, although, and)

quite — like — but (however, nevertheless, although, and)
very — unlike — but (however, nevertheless, although, and)
isn't — like — and (although, but)
"He is *very* well grounded in geography," *said* his brother, *"but* he is not so
quick in arithmetic."

(b) . . . . . . *he give me his word, I will not trust him.*

PLUS
although   though   if   should   unless

(c) *You must not, ... , imagine that my silence has been due*
to ignorance of what is going on.

PLUS

however	nevertheless	moreover	then
therefore	understand	though	really
indeed	Mary	surely	sir

(d) . . . . . . *either of us could speak, we were at the bottom of the*
stairs.

PLUS
before

Score: 2 sentences plus.

4. Repeating 6 Digits Reversed

Score: 1 plus. Correct order without error.

5. Sentence Building

All three words must be included in one sentence. The words must be
correctly used and the sentence must not be ungrammatical. The only
change permitted in the form of the key words is in number; plural may be
used for singular. Nouns must not be changed to verbs. Failure to comprehend the meaning of a word results either in inability to respond or
guessing, revealed in the bizarre character of the sentence.

(a) *Ceremonial — Dignity — Impression*

PLUS

The ceremonial dances and dignity of the Indians made an impression on
the people watching.
The ceremonial had much dignity and left a big impression.
He made an impression of dignity in his ceremonial actions.

A king gave a ceremonial banquet with much dignity and made a large
impression on all of his subjects.

The man had ceremonial dignity and made a good impression.

MINUS

He made an impression on their dignity at a ceremonial place.

The ceremonial rites gave an impression of dignity upon the people.

The lecture on dignity was very ceremonial and made a deep impression.

A man that has dignity sometimes likes to give a ceremonial impression.

The ceremonial was alive with dignity and the people were very much impressed with the part done by the ladies.

(b) *Baffle — Cunning — Pursuit*

PLUS

The cunning criminal will baffle the police unless they start in pursuit
quickly.

The rabbit was able to baffle by his cunning the pursuit of him by hunters.

The Germans baffled the pursuit plane with cunning dexterity.

A cunning pursuit baffled the fugitive.

The criminal baffled the detectives because he was very cunning and the
detectives were always in pursuit after him.

The cunning man baffled the pursuit.

MINUS

He led a baffling, cunning pursuit.

He was a cunning man and the police had to baffle the mystery to pursue
him.

The police are pursuing the cunning baffler.

He was a cunning man, and the man baffled him in the pursuit.

The pursuit was very baffling and cunning.

The cunning man had to baffle the pursuit that was following him.

(c) *Failure — Business — Incompetent*

PLUS

He was a business failure and an incompetent.

The incompetent man was a failure in his business.

He made a business of failure because he was incompetent.

The incompetent president caused a failure of his business.

His failure in business was due to his incompetent manner.

Because of his failure in business he was incompetent.

MINUS

My business was very incompetent and therefore it was a failure.

He made an incompetent failure in business.

Incompetent business is generally a failure.

Score: 2 plus.

6. Essential Similarities

(a) *Farming and manufacturing*

It is permissible to place the emphasis either on the activity of *producing*, or on *providing* that which supplies human needs.

PLUS

Both are creative.   Both make products.
Both put out something that people use.
Both produce goods from raw materials.
They both produce food and clothing for people.
They're both making something. In farming you're making new plants and manufacturing you're making new clothes or shoes or things. They're both the processes of making.
Both make things for human consumption.
They both supply the cities with goods.

MINUS

Both of them helps to make our country bigger.
You get things out of both of them.   Both sell things.
Both employ a lot of people.   They are both working places.
Both bring in money.

(b) *Melting and burning*

For this essential similarity the subject may give consideration either to the effect in changing the form of substances, or to the necessity for accompanying heat.

PLUS

The form of substances is altered by either process.
Melting is changing that substance into a different form and fire is changing that substance into a different form.
Both changes, one chemical and the other physical.
They both change the thing that burns or melts.
Both destroy the shapes of things.   Both require heat.

MINUS

When you melt something and burn something you bring it down to a smaller substance.
Both solid at the beginning and not when you get through.
Melting usually never comes back into the same shape and burning never does.
They both have to do with cooking and heating.
Giving off water in both processes.
They both produce a great heat.   Both are hot.

(c) *Egg and seed*

PLUS

Both undeveloped plants or animals.   Both become something.
Life is hatched from egg and life grows from seed, too.
They're both for making new animals.   Both form plants or animals.
Raise more stuff with either one of 'em.
They both bring forth fruit.   Both grow.

MINUS

Eggs you can hatch chickens and seeds you can grow plants out of them.
They are both products of something else.
Seed is produced by the parent plant and egg is produced by the parent hen.
A plant comes out of a seed and a chicken comes out of an egg.
Both hatch out of something.   Both produce a food.

Score: 3 plus.

Alternate. Reconciliation of Opposites (same as XIV, 6)

Score: 4 plus. See page 206.

SUPERIOR ADULT II

1. Vocabulary

Score: 26 plus. See scoring standards, page 232.

2. Finding Reasons III

At this level, we expect a response of a better quality than was required in the Finding Reasons test at year X. The reasons, while not limited to the most essential, must be valid, definite, and clearly differentiated. Failure is due chiefly to inability to give three reasons, and the examiner must be on the watch for the same reason repeated in different words.

(a) *Give three reasons why some people use typewriters which cost so much when they could get pen and ink for a few cents.*

Acceptable reasons include chiefly those which mention: (a) ease and convenience in use; (b) neatness and appearance; (c) speed; (d) legibility; (e) custom; (f) carbon copy; and (g) economy.

PLUS

They're faster, easier, more legible.
A typewriter's so much quicker. Shows up neater. It's printed.

The typewriter is more convenient, and it can be read by other people easily, and it is cheaper to run a typewriter than it is to write with pen and ink.

They can do the work quicker, and better, and you can read it better.

You can read typewritten things better. If you've got a typewriter it's easier to get a position from some people by typing a letter to them. When you write stories to a magazine some magazines only want typewritten stories.

MINUS

A typewriter is better and it's faster, and you can do it quicker with a typewriter.

Because they can do their work faster and get more money by doing it faster and save time.

Typewriter can go faster than pen and ink. You can read it sometimes better than pen and ink. You don't have to help it.

(b) *Give three reasons why a man who commits a serious crime should be punished.*

The following categories include most of the acceptable reasons:

(a) To teach him a lesson.
(b) To set an example for others.
(c) To prevent his doing it again.
(d) To prevent his doing something worse.
(e) To protect society.
(f) To make him suffer for his wrong-doing.
(g) To uphold the law.

PLUS

So that he wouldn't do it again. To show people what they'd get if they did it themselves. To show the person who did it that that was the wrong thing to do.

'Cause if they let him go he may do it over again. Next time he might do something worse. If they don't, other people will start doing it.

So he won't do it again. So he'd repay for the crime he's done. To see how wrong the thing he's done is.

So he won't do it again. To teach a lesson for others. Doing bad is a sin.

So he won't hurt anybody else. He committed the crime and made the person suffer so he has to suffer. If you commit a crime it's against the law so you have to be punished for it.

If he isn't punished he might think he can get by with it again. It would show young boys — teach them a lesson. The laws have to be enforced.

To keep him from committing other crimes. When a man commits a crime and is not punished by law someone usually tries to punish him in some way. It wouldn't be fair to let him go.

Avenge society. To make an example of him for others. Make him pay for his folly.

If he isn't punished he'll repeat the crime. He is dangerous to the community. He is liable to influence someone else into committing crimes.

MINUS

Because if they don't punish him he might kill somebody else. And then he might steal something and then he might go and burn up something. (Stated in terms of the concrete situation.)

Because he shouldn't kill no one. And he's breakin' the law and no one lets anyone get away with committing a serious crime.

The other fellow's got as much rights as he has. He's disobeying the law. Spoiling family reputation.

A man ought to be punished so he won't think he can do anything and get away with it. He ought to be punished because it will probably give compensation to the person against whom he did the crime. And I think he ought to be punished because if he's punished it would teach him a good lesson so he won't do it again.

Because if he isn't he'll do it again and somebody else will do it again and the city won't like the people that got him free.

If he did the act willfully he should be punished, if it was against someone else's property. Because if he was let go it would serve as a bad example for the courts.

Score: 2 plus with three reasons each.

3. Proverbs II

(a) *The mouse that has but one hole is easily taken.* (Disaster is less likely where there are several alternatives.)

PLUS

It's like "Don't put all your eggs in one basket." If you depend too much on one thing, it may go back on you.

You should not always depend on one thing because that might easily fail. Like if you're investing your money, should not invest it all in one thing but divide it up.

A man who has just one thing to turn to, is easily broke.

If you only have one way to defend yourself you're more easily overtaken than if you had two or three ways.

Means you should make your knowledge more extensive.

Do more than one thing because that one thing may fail.

A person who has but one method is easily fooled.

A person who has a single-track mind is easily confused.

If you have only one means of escape you're easily caught. (The proverb practically repeated.)

A person that has one place of business and one piece of property is easily taken up by a big concern or by people that are more well-to-do.

Like if you just do one thing — you'll soon be overcome with it.

Well, a person that has only one object in life is soon stopped.

A person who has but one thought may be easily persuaded.

There ought to always be two ways out of anything.

If we only have one way of learning things and know one side of anything we don't succeed so easily.

You should have several views of life.

(b) *You must not throw pearls before swine.* (Don't offer people things they can't appreciate.)

PLUS

Only people with fine sensibilities can appreciate the finer things.

It's no use to try to teach those that do not know what you're talking about and aren't interested in what you're talking about.

You shouldn't try and give beauty to ignorant things — people that don't understand — you can't show them beauty — they can't understand — so it's no use.

Swine have no appreciation of the value of pearls and if a person is uneducated he has no appreciation of fine things in life, they won't do him any good.

Should not waste good things for people that don't appreciate them, it doesn't do 'em any good.

It doesn't do any good to give some people a chance in life because they don't know what to do with it, don't know its value.

Don't waste your time on people who don't appreciate it.

Give the people something that they can appreciate and understand.

MINUS

They wouldn't know what to do with it — you should not be giving money to people who beg for it because they don't know how to spend it — they waste it.

Not to throw away something that you could accomplish and let someone else come along and take it up and do it and get the benefit of it.

Don't make foolish offers to people who don't know what they're getting.

No use to give things away unless they are going to be made use of.

Score: 1 plus.

4. Ingenuity I (same as XIV, 4; AA, 2)

Score: 3 plus.

5. Essential Differences (same as AA, 7)

Score: 3 plus.

6. Repeating Thought of Passage I: Value of Life

This passage can be divided into the following component ideas:
(a) Many opinions have been given on the value of life.
(b) Some call it good,
(c) others call it bad.
(d) It would be nearer correct to say that it is mediocre,
(e) for on the one hand our happiness is never as great as we should like,
(f) and on the other hand our misfortunes are never as great as our enemies would wish for us.
(g) It is this mediocrity of life which prevents it from being radically unjust.

Satisfactory responses include those in which there is accurate reproduction of at least four of these seven divisions, except that in case (a), (b), and (c) are given, there must be two in addition. In any other combination four are sufficient for a satisfactory response, providing gratuitous invention does not contradict the theme and thus invalidate the response. Accurate recall is taken to be an index of comprehension of the passage. The ideas may, of course, be expressed in the subject's own language. Neither elegance of expression nor verbatim repetition is expected.

PLUS

Many opinions have been given on life. Some say it is good, some bad, but it is mediocrity. We can not have as much as our enemies wish and we can't have as much happiness as we wish. (a b c d e f)

There have been many opinions of life made. Some are good and some are bad. Our misfortunes are not as great as our enemies would like and our miseries are not as little as we would like, but these are the med — I don't know how to say it — medriocolus of life — something like that. (a b c e f)

Some — many opinions have been given about life. Some say it is good and some say it is bad but it is termed mediocre, because the goodness is not as good as we would want it to be and the badness is not as bad as our enemies would want it to be so life is unfair. (So many elements have been reproduced correctly that misunderstanding of the final idea does not invalidate this response.) (a b c d e f)

Many definitions have been given life. Some say it is good and some say it is not. But it is never as good as we could make it and is never as bad as it could be. These are both wrong. It is really medium. (a b c d e f)

Many people's opinions are that life is good or bad, but it is better to think it is medium because our misfortunes are not as great as our enemies might wish them. (b c d f)

It is better to say that life is medium than to say it is good or bad because we never have the discomforts that our enemies would wish us to have or never have the pleasant things that we and our friends would want to have. (b c d e, f slightly inaccurate.)

MINUS

There's — many things — in the value of life — some call it good and some call it bad, but it really is mediocre because our happiness is never what we like and mediocre takes in all the things. (b c d, e reproduced incorrectly.)

Great opinions have been given to life, some say it's good and some say it's bad — our misfortunes are never as great as our enemies would like for it to be. (a b c d)

There are many opinions given about our life, but even though there are many disappointments and many times our happiness is greater than might be and misfortunes are not so many but our enemies wish they were more. This keeps us medium, we can live through it if we have some happiness with our unhappiness. (Note invention.) (a f d)

Many things have been said about our life, but our happiness is never as great as we would wish it and our misfortunes are never as great as our enemies would wish it to be. (a e f)

Score: Accurate reproduction of component ideas.

Alternate. Codes

To receive full credit for a code there must be no error. The rule is not scored. Half-credit is allowed in either (a) or (b) where the response contains one error. One letter incorrectly coded constitutes an error. The correct response for (a) is ITSQZ; for (b) FVPSW.

Score: 1 plus or two with half-credit each.

S U P E R I O R   A D U L T   III

1. Vocabulary

Score: 30 plus. See scoring standards, page 232.

2. Proverbs III

(a) *Let sleeping dogs lie.* (Don't seek trouble if you can avoid it.)

PLUS

If you see something that is getting along all right left alone — leave it alone or it might cause trouble.

Don't stir up trouble.   Do not revive past happenings.
Leave well enough alone.
Let anyone who isn't bothering you alone.
Don't bother trouble till trouble troubles you.
Don't bring up something that is best kept quiet.
After a thing is gone and done with not to be continually bringing it up
    and harping on it.

MINUS

Let a person who does not care to accomplish anything alone.
Don't get into any task that would cause you great danger or injury.
You shouldn't bother with anything that's not to be bothered with.
Let something that might be dangerous alone.
Don't disturb anybody if you have nothing to say.
It's better to leave things alone that you don't know anything about.
If something is still and you disturb it, something might happen.
Let things alone that don't concern you.
Don't try to change it or make it different — leave it the way it was first.

(b) *A bad workman quarrels with his tools.* (The incompetent always
finds excuses for his failure.)

PLUS

That when we make mistakes we're likely to put the blame on anything
    that's handy — take it out on someone else and not put the blame where
    it really belongs.
A man that is not doing the thing right himself finds fault with everybody
    else.
A person who does bad blames it on somebody else.
Because if a worker isn't a good worker he has to take his spite out on some-
    body or something.
A person who is incompetent blames his helpers or his tools when it is really
    himself that is to blame.

MINUS

If he doesn't like his work he will blame everything onto the implements
    he is using.
A person who is unhappy usually quarrels with what he has to do.
Because he has no one else to quarrel with, he quarrels with his tools.
A person who is unskilled at something can't get along with his associates.
He lays his failure on his tools instead of on himself.
An inefficient person will find something to fight about.

(c) *It's an ill wind that blows nobody good.* (Someone usually benefits
even by a calamity which brings general misfortune.)

PLUS

Everything that happens in life must do someone good so that it doesn't
  do to moan too much if it doesn't benefit you especially.
Nearly everything does somebody some good.
Something has to be pretty bad not to do someone some good.
Somebody always gets something out of whatever happens.
Whatever comes along ought to be an opportunity for somebody.

MINUS

Something that's meant to do you harm never does you any good.
A person that goes around talking or whispering things about certain people
  doesn't bring anybody in this world any good.
An ill-minded person does nobody any good.
Something bad never does anybody any good.
Things that aren't likely to be beneficial to anyone are better left undone.
Every little something is of some importance.

Score: 2 plus.

3. Opposite Analogies IV

(a) A *rabbit is timid; a lion is* . . . . . .

PLUS
Courageous.   Bold.
Unafraid.   Brave.
Fearless.

MINUS
Not afraid.   Vicious.
Wild.   Fierce.
Ferocious   Dangerous.
Savage.

(b) *The pine tree is evergreen; the poplar is* . . . . . .

PLUS
Deciduous.

MINUS
Dies in winter.   Tree that sheds its leaves.
Leaf-falling tree. Changeable.

(c) A *debt is a liability; an income is* . . . . . .

PLUS
An asset.   Resource.

MINUS

Help.   Salary.
Profit.   Money coming in.
Credit.

Score: 2 plus.

4. Orientation: Direction III

(a) The correct answer is West.
(b) The only correct answer is 1 mile.

The most frequent failure, aside from inability to answer, is 9, at which, of course, the subject arrives by calculating the distance he has traversed rather than the actual distance that he is now from the starting point.

Score: 2 plus.

5. Reasoning II

The expected answer is 40½ inches. Since, however, one can, by considering the growth increment in terms of arithmetic ratio rather than geometric, arrive at 40 (inches) as the answer, credit is given for this response also, but *only* when the subject can satisfactorily explain how he arrived at it, for this answer is frequently only a guess. The two methods are as follows:

Geometric:

1st year $8 + \frac{1}{2} = 12$	i.e., the tree increases each year
2nd year $12 + \frac{1}{2} = 18$	at the rate of ½ its total height
3rd year $18 + \frac{1}{2} = 27$	at the beginning of the year.
4th year $27 + \frac{1}{2} = 40\frac{1}{2}$	

Arithmetic:

1st year $8 + \ \ 4 = 12$	
2nd year $12 + \ \ 6 = 18$	(2 inches greater increment than 1st year)
3rd year $18 + \ \ 9 = 27$	(3 inches greater increment than 2d year)
4th year $27 + 13 = 40$	(4 inches greater increment than 3d year)

Guessing at the answer is very common, particularly in the case of students, and the guesses are often very close, such as "40" and "41." However, the response "40½," not being a round number, is not likely to be guessed and does not need to be explained; nor should the examiner ask for an explanation of any other answer except "40," since to do so would be equivalent to giving the subject a second chance.

6. Repeating Thought of Passage II: Tests

This passage may be divided into the following component ideas:

(a) Tests such as we are now making are of value both for the advancement of science and

(b) for the information of the person who is tested.

(c) It is important for science to learn how people differ and

(d) on what factors these differences depend.

(e) If we can separate the influence of heredity from the influence of environment,

(f) we may be able to apply our knowledge so as to guide human development.

(g) We may thus in some cases correct defects and

(h) develop abilities which we might otherwise neglect.

Satisfactory responses include those in which there is accurate reproduction of at least four of these eight divisions. The idea contained in the section must be stated or clearly implied, although it may, of course, be expressed in the subject's own way.

PLUS

Tests are important both to science and to the person who takes them. They find out how people differ and they want to try out how people are in regard to heredity and environment, and in this way they can correct defects. (a b c e g)

Tests of this kind aid science as well as find out about the person who is receiving this test. Science says that certain abilities can be developed and certain defects will be overcome. If they can take heredity instead of so much of what comes on the home things will be better. (a b e g)

Tests that we are taking now are good for advancing knowledge and learning about the person who is being tested. It advances science to learn how people differ and it might help the person to find out defects and to have abilities in more things. (a b c g h)

Tests such as we are now making are for the benefit of the people who are taking them and for science. We can separate the heredity from environment and see how much people differ. (a b c e)

These tests that we are having are for the help of the person given the test and we are giving them for science 'cause it might help the development of people and science tells how people differ and on what facts these differences depend upon. (a b c d f)

Tests such as we are now making are a great advantage to us and to scientists so they may see how people differ and thus correct the defects. (a b c g)

MINUS

Tests which we are taking are of great value to both science and the person, to see how much he knows and so persons can tell how people differ and the amount the person knows who is being tested. (a b c)

Tests which we are now making are very important. They are useful to science to find out the difference in people. Sometimes used to correct faults which might otherwise be neglected. (a c g)

Examinations such as are being made are important to science and to the knowledge of the one who is being tested. You may in some cases fix defects and correct mistakes which are being made. (a b g)

Score: Accurate reproduction of component ideas.

Alternate. Opposite Analogies V

(a) *Ability is native; education is* . . . . . .

PLUS
acquired.   achieved

MINUS

learned.	culture.
achievement.	something to be learned.
foreign.	

(b) *Music is harmonious; noise is* . . . . . .

PLUS
dissonant.   discordant.

MINUS

discord.	inharmonious.
deafening.	pandemonious.

(c) *A person who talks a great deal is loquacious; one who has little to say is* . . . . . .

PLUS

taciturn.	silent.
laconic.	quiet.

MINUS

conservative.	not talkative.
lackadaisical.	

Score: 2 plus.

VOCABULARY

(VI, 1; VIII, 1; X, 1; XII, 1; XIV, 1; AA, 1; SA I, 1; SA II, 1; SA III, 1)

It is important for the examiner to realize that the purpose of this vocabulary test is to determine whether the subject knows the meaning of the word, not whether he can give a completely logical definition. Awkwardness of expression is disregarded. It is often necessary to determine by additional questions, as indicated in the testing procedure, whether the meaning is apprehended.

Standard for Passing

Year	Score
VI	6
VIII	8
X	11
XII	15
XIV	17
AA	20
SA I	23
SA II	26
SA III	30

Vocabulary

1. *Orange*

PLUS

A fruit.   An orange is sweet.
Like a tangerine.   It's round.
Tree.   It's yellow.
A drink.   An orange is orange color.
It's orange juice.   A jello.
What you drink (eat, squeeze, cut, suck).

Q
Orange.

MINUS
Lemon.   Red.

2. *Envelope*

PLUS

For a letter.   An envelope is straight and has a cover.
What you send.   It's sticky on the top so you can paste it down.
To put things in.

Q
To read.   Paper.
To write.   A letter.
To open.

MINUS
A sheet of paper.

3. *Straw*

PLUS

You suck it.	It's a fiber of some sort.
For orange juice.	It's used for baskets and hats.
To blow through.	Straw is what you make a straw house out of.
Kind of round stick.	What chickens lay on.
Dried grass.	Make chairs like this.
Hay.	Brooms have it.
It's a plant.	You tickle people with it.

Q

Paper.	Easy to burn.
Plastic.	Covers it up.
To eat.	You can put it on strawberries and things.
Use it for cows.	Like — bale straw.
Play in.	It bends.

MINUS

It's the same as a leaf that grows on a tree.	Piece of wood.
Straw is something that's in piles.	Long.

4. *Puddle*

PLUS

A puddle of water.	What you step in.
Water.	You can sail boats in.
Rain makes it.	You can play in puddles.
Mud.	For little frogs.
Little pond.	That's what the baby does.
A puddle is when it's raining.	

Q

In the street.   Lots of water.

MINUS

A puddle is where some fishes swim.	You go in bathing.
A plaything.	To play games.
Just a puddle of water that people swim in.	A brook of water.

5. *Tap*

PLUS

You make a little noise.	Dance.
Tap your foot.	Tap a shoe.
You tap a bell.	Like a heel plate on your shoes.
Somebody is at the door.	Faucet.
Rain on the roof.	Tap trees.

Tap on the door (or floor, table, blocks, etc.).
Tap is to hold some water in somewhere.

(S just illustrates tapping with hand or foot.)

Q

Shoes.   That makes music.
Something that you take out of a hole.

MINUS

Hammers things down. Nails.

6. *Gown*

PLUS

A nightgown.   Night-night pajamas or something.
To sleep in.   Put on.
When you go to bed.   Sort of a cloak.
Wear to a party.

Q

King's wedding gown.

7. *Roar*

E should take special pains to pronounce this word distinctly. If it is understood as "raw" or "oar" the word should be repeated.

PLUS

Noise.   Bomb roars (jet, boat).
A wolf or somebody goes roarrrrr. Big noise like a tiger makes.
A lion roars (car, wild animal, ocean, seashell).
Like an airplane is roaring down the runway.
When you're fierce.

Q

Angry. You laugh.

8. *Eyelash*

It is often necessary to ask the child to point if it is not clear that he has differentiated eyelash from eyelid or eyebrow.

PLUS

Hair that protects your eyes.   Keeps dirt out of your eye.
When you blink your eyes the eyelash keeps it from going too far back.

Q

Part of your eyelid.   It covers your eyes.
Hair over the eyes.   Keeps your eyes warm.
Comes over your eye when you go to sleep.

MINUS

The top part of the skin that comes down over the eye.
Hair right over your eye it's either these (lashes) or these (brows) I always
forget.
Helps you see better.
Eyelid.   Eyebrow.

9. *Mars*

To the specialized use of Mars applied correctly to some such object as a
candy bar or an airplane, the examiner should say, "Yes, but what *else* does
Mars mean?"

PLUS

Mars is something like Venus and travels around.
Some kind of a comet like the world.
A space ship will go up in the air and hit Mars.
Star.   A world.
Land out in space.   Scratch something that's painted.
Up by the moon.   It's a god of war.

Q

Man.   Mars is a different kind of people.
The name of a place.   A group of stars.

MINUS

Means clouds — up near the clouds.   Someone in the sky.
Things up in the sky — them round balls.

10. *Juggler*

PLUS

A man that juggles balls up and down.   A man that performs tricks.
A man that juggles a stick — he puts his hand out like that and he has a
stick balancing on it.
Somebody knows how to juggle things and he juggles a lot of them at a time.

Q

A man who throws balls.   A person who juggles.
A magician.   A man who mixes up things.
When you juggle something on your fingers.   A circus man.

MINUS

A juggler goes around and tells jokes and plays an instrument.
A man who sells jugs.

11. *Scorch*

It's to burn.   When something gets awful hot.
Burn your clothes with an iron.   Singe.
Means you make something brown.   The sun burns you.
A person could be scorched by touched the stove — part of a burn.

Q

Scorch a dress.   It's a hot day.
Burn your pants up.   Hot.
Stain.

MINUS

Takes whitening out of clothes.   You got too much starch.
You burn yourself with hot water (scald).   Just burnt to pieces.

12. *Lecture*

PLUS

A speech.   Explain it to somebody.
Lecture is a man who talks.   Tell people not to do it.
Like somebody tells you something.
Some place where you go and they tell you something.
What they have in church — somebody preaches.
Get a lecture if you do something you shouldn't do.

Q

On TV.   If you did something.
Something you go to.   You give a lecture.
Meeting.

MINUS

When you vote, elect a president.   Sit straight.
Turn on the radio.   When a man's mad.
Church.

13. *Skill*

PLUS

If you do something real well.   You're talented.
Ease and gracefulness at doing a thing.
Ability.   Trained.
Means sly or smart at some tricks.   How you do a thing.
Practiced.   He can work good.
Skill means to have a great deal of knowledge.
Very clever, smart.
Done by energy and work — isn't luck — opposite of luck.

Like you're skilled in playing basketball.
People that do things with great skill.
Brains. Like you're a skilled workman.
Succeed. A saw.

MINUS

Do many things. To be brave.
Show how you can paint or whatever you know.
When you're not afraid to go up on tall buildings.
A man has great skill — he has the energy to do it.
You don't mind working.

14. *Brunette*

PLUS

Somebody with black hair (or brown).
Brunette means dark. Lady that isn't a blonde.
Black hair. Dark complected.
Somebody that's dark in features.

Q

A brunette is a woman. Color.
You have brunette hair. Something you put on hair.
Sometimes if your hair's a certain color they'd call you a brunette.

MINUS

Kind of light colored hair. Light brown.
Reddish. Reddish brown. Auburn colored.
Something you wear on your hair.
You go to a brunette, and they curl your hair.

15. *Muzzle*

PLUS

Anybody's nose. Part of a face.
Mouth. Top of the gun barrel.
You put it on a dog to keep him from biting.
Thing you put on a calf to keep it from sucking a cow.
It's the round hole at the end of a gun.

Q

Muzzle is for a dog. What you put on your horse.
Harness. A mask.
Prevent a thing from doing something.
Muzzle of a gun.

MINUS

Something you put on a dog so it can't get away.
A little round thing that dogs wear — you put it around his neck.
It's something you wear over your face. (catcher's mask)
The barrel of a gun.   The long part of a gun.
If there's a big roaring sound they'd put something over it so make it not so
   noisy. (muffle)
It's on your arm. (muscle)   Muzzle is on hose. (nozzle)

16. *Haste*

PLUS

Hurry.   Not to lose time.
Run.   Right away.
If I had to haste to go I'd have to go right then.
Better be shaking along.

Q

Want to do something.   Make haste.
Haste to get something.   Haste makes waste.
If you run away from somebody or make haste for somebody.

MINUS

Haste is to get ready.   It means get out.
Haste is like you're going some place.   You don't like somebody. (hate)
When you run away. You don't like it.
It means go — like you say, haste for some water.

17. *Peculiarity*

PLUS

Something that's rare.   Queer.
Strange.   Odd.
Sort of exception.   Something unusual.
Something somebody does and it's different from other things.
Somebody that's kind of funny looking.
The different ways certain people act.
Some people are peculiar. They don't talk much and they're awful still.
Somebody with pink eyes — you'd call them peculiar.
Don't happen every time. Once in a while.
Fellow that's peculiar — he don't act like the other fellow is acting, you
   know.

Q

Some people are peculiar.   Something funny.
When something peculiar happens you have to see it.
Something new — you've never seen it before.

MINUS

You don't know what thing it is and you are kind of peculiar about it.
They're finicky. (particular)   Like people talk too fast or stutter.
Like a man — he chews his cigar and you call that a peculiarity.
Some people won't drink out of a dirty cup — that's peculiar.
High-toned.

18. *Priceless*

PLUS

Invaluable.   When the price is out of reach.
Something very old and antique — costs very much.
Something that takes a whole lot of money to buy.
More than money can buy.

Q

Something that hasn't a price.   No price.
Something that you can't buy.   Costs a lot.
Means that something's gone up real high.

MINUS

Beyond, below price, almost nothing.   Not worth anything.
No price on it, not marked.   Doesn't cost anything.
Somebody gives you a bill and it's high.
Some lettuce real low and then jumped up high, the price.
If you wanted to buy something in the window and it wasn't for sale, it
     would be priceless.

19. *Regard*

E, in scoring this word, must be sure that S is not confusing regard with
guard, a very common error and one sometimes difficult to recognize from
the wording. A definition of *regardless* is not satisfactory.

PLUS

Can mean two things, to observe something, and then can mean compli-
     ments.
You look at something.   You study a person or anything.
To watch — take notice.   Consider.
To listen to a person when he's talking.
To think of a person.   To care for something.
Your feeling.   Respect for a person.
Like I'd take a certain person and say I don't think she's a nice person to
     play with and that's how I regard her.
To pertain to.   To wish luck.
Related to.   To remember somebody.

When you write a letter you send regards to them.
Like learning to regard other people's property.
Trust somebody.   Regarding anything for anyone.
Have an opinion about a thing.

MINUS

Take care.   You like what a person does.
Not to heed something.   A person who watches things. (guards)
When you send your congratulations.
Do anything anyhow regardless of what your mother says.
Well, if you give your regards to a person you ask about them — wonder
   how they are.

20. *Tolerate*

The responses to this word are considerably affected by the prevalent use
of it by school teachers in the form of "I can't tolerate" — such and such.
As a result we have *tolerate* defined as "Won't stand for something," or
"Can't stand it." In some cases this is merely a reiteration of the teacher's
expression without knowledge of the connotation of the word to be defined,
and is scored minus unless it can be satisfactorily explained.

PLUS

You don't like something and you bear it because you have to.
To stand.   To just barely stand something.
Endure.   Let anything — let them do it.
You put up with something too long.
Keep someone — when you don't really want them — whether you want
   them or not.
To take something against your will.
To — if you don't like a person you can still play up to it — not act as if
   you hate it.
To be patient and to understand.
To be kind — to tolerate another's belief is to see their side of the question.
Take things off of people even if they do aggravate you.
If someone thinks different than you do, do not oppress them or condemn
   them because they hold different ideas.
To get along with.

Q

Allow.   You can't stand something.
Have toleration for.   To tolerate a person.
Broadminded.

Like you tolerate somebody. Make friends with them and go around with
  them.

Nice or kind.

Agree with someone — think it is alright.

To tolerate a person. You wouldn't have to like them or have anything to
  do with them.

Something that you can't do — like sometimes you say you can't tolerate
  something you can't do it.

21. *Disproportionate*

PLUS

Not of the right formation.	Not in proportion.
Out of size — out of shape.	Opposite from proportionate.
Out of proportion — ungainly.	To give too much of or too less of.

Out of proportion — out of its natural size.

Something that is not in shape — hasn't got the right proportions.

Take a rich person and a poor person and that would be disproportionate.

You have an apple and cut in half and one half in quarters — disproportionate.

I think if somebody had a big head and little shoulders and arms — something like that.

To have something on one side different from on the other.

They're not equal.

Like you're dividing a cake and you don't give the right amount.

Q

Not the right proportion.	Have too much.
Not built right.	Not have any proportion.

You haven't got quite enough of something.

MINUS

Portioning out things.	It isn't in the right place.
Something doesn't fit.	Not in portion.

Isn't where it should be — supposed to be somewhere else and it isn't.

You haven't got quite enough of something that you are making.

Too much in proportion.

A boy had something and it wasn't the same as the other boys.

22. *Lotus*

PLUS

Lotus is a plant — a supposed plant that whoever ate it was to forget where
  he came from or where he was going.

The name of a blossom.	Chinese flower.
A lily.	Some kind of a tree.

That is a person that eats flowers.
A weed — lotus weed. (loco weed)   A bug.
An animal.   A sort of food.

23. *Shrewd*

PLUS

Discerning.   Wily.
Very quick thinking.   Sharp.
Wise.   Intelligent.
Calculating.   Sly.
Cunning.   Ingenious.
Means kind of foxy — they can do things awful easy, or something.
A shrewd business man wouldn't put his money into something he wasn't
    sure of.
If a person is shrewd it's a person that no one can cheat them out of some-
    thing.
Generally a very careful person, sometimes miserly.
You can see through something quickly — not always a desirable character.
Best you can get out of a deal.
Somebody that's tricky, or something like that.
Hard to get around — hard to deal with — and make anything out of.

Q

Might mean careful sometimes.   Jewish.
A man is a shrewd businessman.   Close.
Not to be cheated.

MINUS

A mean person.
Nasty — something like a nasty person.
Sort of queer fellow that gets by easy.
Miserly. (minus without additional characteristics of clever or careful)
They're bad.   Thrifty.

24. *Mosaic*

Mosaic may be defined as a form of art, in which pictures or designs are
    made with stone, pieces of glass, tile, wood, paper, or straw; as a variety of
    tile; or as relating to Moses.

PLUS

Work in small squares of glass or stone — color.
Little stone they set into flowers and brooches.
Picture made out of little blocks.   Inlaid work.
Some kind of stuff used in Italy — put parts together and make pretty
    things.

It's wood inlaid — little different shapes and make designs with it.
Mosaic law — the law God gave to Moses.
Something that was in the time of Moses.

Little stones.	Lot of little colors.
Decoration.	Painting.
Picture.	Some sort of glass.
A form of art.	A design.
Inlaid pieces of wood.	A religion.

MINUS

Stone — little stones they have over in Italy.
Someone does a little mosaic work, little figures with little mosaic.
Kind of painting — I don't know what kind.
In early Greek art the way they made tapestries and did drawings on buildings.

It's an odd kind of designing.   Pertaining to the Middle Ages.
A character of the Bible.

25. *Stave*

There is considerable confusion of the words "stave" with similar sounding words. A definition in terms of stake, stay, or picket is minus.

The noun stave is satisfactorily defined as one of the parts making up the sides of a barrel, as a stick (used as a support or weapon), staff, cane, slat, a round (rung), a musical term, or a metrical portion in poetry.

PLUS

A part of a barrel — like a curved board.
One of those boards in a barrel — is a barrel stave.
Part of a barrel.   It is a slat.
A walking stick.   A thing in music — five lines.
Sort of a stick that they would fight each other with — about five feet long mostly made of oak wood.
Stave in the bottom of a chair — a small rod.
In a book — old fashioned book — same as calling it a chapter — call it Stave I, II, ...
To fight away, stave off or ward off.
If you stave in a barrel means you hit the barrel and broke it.

A piece of wood.	A stick like.
To break.	Support.

Ring that goes round a barrel.   Like a post.
Iron that binds a barrel.   Sort of a stick in a fence.
Something that you stick in the ground and tie a horse or cow to.
Corset stave— kind of iron thing that supports you.
Bread is the main stave of life — thing that keeps you living.

26. *Bewail* (To wail over; weep for; lament; mourn; complain about.)

PLUS

To complain.   When you cry for somebody.
To grieve.   Feel sorry about something.
Regret.   Wail over something.
To be in despair.   A cry of distress.
If you lost something you want very much and it's very valuable you'd feel
    very badly about it.
People bewail something — bewail things that have gone wrong — haven't
    gone the way they should and bewail the fact.

Q

You cry.   Somebody is hollering.
Sad.

MINUS

Bewail because somebody is hurting 'em or something.   To wail.
Gave a loud wail because you're frightened or something.   Anxious.
A shrill noise or something.

27. *Ochre* (An earthy clay containing iron ore, usually yellow or reddish
brown in color; used as a pigment in paints. The color of ochre; especially
dark yellow.)

PLUS

It's kind of yellow, but it isn't quite yellow — medium brown and yellow
    color.
Kind of a tannish-reddish color.   You use it in oil paints.
Something you use for paint.   It's sort of an orange color.

Q

A color.   A shade of color.
Has something to do with color.

MINUS

A gray color. (deep red; deep blue; purple)   A drug.
Sort of a mixture of colors.   Vegetable coloring.

28. *Repose* (To rest; to depend; calm, tranquillity, composure.)

This word is often confused with "pose." Responses that could apply equally well to "pose" and "repose" should be questioned.

PLUS

Peacefulness — of mind or body.   To rest.
To sleep or something like that.   Take it easy.
When you are tired you lay down — say you repose.
Like you can say that the can reposes on the table.
To stand or be at ease.   Retiring — to retire.
Someone is sitting still or — not doing anything.   Someone with poise.

Q

Stay in one place.   Stay still.
Stand where you are.   Certain position that you take.

MINUS

If you was in a movie you'd take a certain position, you'd repose.
Repose on something — you sit on it, I guess some position.
To lay or sit or stand in a certain way.   You pose over again.
To put something on a desk.   You take it back.

29. *Ambergris* (A grayish waxy substance, secreted by sperm whales — used in making perfumes.)

Use, origin, or description of the substance is acceptable for ambergris.

PLUS

Some kind of jelly they take off of whales — use it to make perfume.
A product of whaling — or seal fishing valued very highly by chemists.
Something they make perfume out of.   Stuff spit up from a sick whale.
Material from a whale — it's very valuable.
Substance that comes out of a whale. I think it's kind of fat.
Substance obtained from the head of a whale.
Sort of a rather, very bad smell — it's quite valuable.

Q

A substance found in the ocean.   It's some kind of substance.

MINUS

Something that has to do with plants — no, it's a fluid.
It's what they make amber out of.   A mineral.

30. *Limpet* (Any of several varieties of shellfish.)

PLUS

Some kind of mollusk — found in the rocks — conical shape.
Shellfish.   Sea food.

Kind of fish.   An animal.

MINUS

A man who limps.   Somebody who has no energy.
Wilted — limp.   Clear, deep water.

31. *Frustrate* (To cause to have no effect. Foil, baffle, defeat.)

PLUS

To prevent or foil an attempt.   Not to let, or keep from.
Spoil — frustrate somebody's plans, means you spoil their plans.
To stop when a person is doing something bad and stop them in the act of
    doing it.

Q

To interfere with.   To be discouraged.
To fool somebody.   To aggravate.

MINUS

If somebody thinks you are doing one thing and you do another.
To have something on your mind that you don't think you can do.
To make somebody uneasy or uncomfortable.
Means you don't know quite what to do — you're kind of startled.
Like if somebody is bothering you.   To get confused. (excited)

32. *Flaunt* (To make a gaudy, ostentatious, or defiant display. To show
off proudly or impudently.)

Care should be taken to make sure that "flaunt" has not been confused
with "taunt."

PLUS

To display saucily.   To show off.
To be especially proud of something and to show it to everybody.
Proud — flaunted her skirts — whisked them in a certain way.
It shows its petals, a flower flaunts its petals, shows them.
To wave — wave something in front of everybody else.
To wave a flag — bull fighters in Spain flaunt a red flag in front of the bull.
To flirt — to make a show of yourself.

Q

To wave something.   To not think much of — to laugh at.
If you go against something — flaunt it.

MINUS

Make fun of.   When you sneer at somebody.
A dare.   To unfold.

A rich person might flaunt a poor person — kind of ignore him.
If someone was going off on a boat and you waved a handkerchief at them.
If somebody puts up a rule and you don't want to abide by it, you flaunt it.

33. *Incrustation* (A hard outer layer or coating.)

PLUS

Crust formed by evaporation of water from hard particles.
Inclosed by some substance.　　　　　The forming of a crust.
When anything is beginning to form on the top of anything.
Something that's incrusted on a shield or on a ship, like barnacles.
Things gets incrusted, covered with rust or something.
It's a covering over the outside of something.
Something with crust on it — incrusted.
The hard cover on the top of snow.
They might say his hands were incrusted with dirt.

Q

The crust of something.　　With a crust.
A covering.　　　　　　　Something that's dried up.
Incrusted.

MINUS

To have a thing incrusted is something stuck in it.
In a crust, maybe.　　　　　　Something without a crust.
The crust of something is the foundation of something.
Indented in the crust — creased or something like that.
Bread in the form of a crust.　　Penetration of something.

34. *Retroactive* (Having application to or effect on things prior to its enactment or effectuation.)

PLUS

It affects events previous to a present enactment.
A retroactive law — one that governs things that happened before it was
　　passed.
If they passed a law that if somebody stole a loaf of bread he should be put
　　in prison, and he'd stolen the loaf of bread before they made the law,
　　and it was a retroactive law, they'd put him in prison.
Something that takes effect in the past.

Q

Acting back upon.　　　　　　Backward — going backward kind of.
Action that's gone on before.　　It acts back upon you.

MINUS

If a thing is retroactive it reacts.
Something that's happened before and you're doing it again.

A retroactive method in writing — method goes back and picks up things that have gone by.

In chemistry — something that reacts back. Like you do something and it acts back.

Something that reverts back to the original.

35. *Philanthropy* (Love of mankind. Desire to help mankind. Something that helps mankind.)

PLUS

Broad outlook toward others, helpful outlook.

Charity.   Giving away money to some cause.

Good feeling — trying to do good.   Doing things for other people.

A practice where people are kind to other people — sometimes they endow colleges.

Brotherly — treat everybody nice — study of love, I suppose.

A fostering of arts or better things.

One who gives to the public good.

Philanthropy is the act of giving out things to the poor folks.

Q

Generousness.   Giving things away.

Being benevolent.   It's being kind.

MINUS

It's a place where they take in old clothes for the needy people.

A creed or something you go by.

A study.   Deep thinking.

Good natured.   Something you study in college.

Pertaining to the study of man and his problems.

36. *Piscatorial* (of fishes, fishermen, or fishing.)

PLUS

Pertaining to fishes.

Sort of fishy — study of fish or something.

37. *Milksop* (Unmanly man or boy; mollycoddle, sissy.)

PLUS

A mollycoddle.   A spineless creature.

Might be a man that doesn't amount to much — hasn't got any courage.

Someone that has no back bone and is easily pushed around.

Somebody that is a sissy or something.

A man that is very weak — like a womanish man.

A slang term that is given to a rich person or a person that is used to having other people do things for him.

A person that is sort of sleepy looking — seeming afraid of doing something — of hurting themselves.

Babyish — a slang expression.

Something that's like bread and that's sopped up — soaked in milk — call the dumb guys that.

Q

It's an expression of disgust.   Means insipid.

A term used to call somebody.

MINUS

People call people who haven't done exactly what they wanted a milksop.

Bread soaked in milk.   You take up milk with it.

A drunkard.   An inexperienced person.

38. Harpy

The only acceptable definitions of harpy are as a mythical character; a creature half bird and half woman; the creatures who took food away from Ulysses or his men; birds or women who prey on humans; a rapacious or plundering person; an extortioner; a type of eagle. Any definition of harpy as a scold or shrew is minus.

PLUS

Mythical being in one of the seas around Greece.

A myth — birds — women with wings.

A harpy is a mythical woman.

Name of one kind of eagle — harpy eagle.

An imaginary beast — part person and part animal.

Kind of bird the Greeks believed in — head of a man and body of a bird.

A person who preys upon other people or upon weaker people.

A bird that preys upon human flesh.

Q

A certain kind of people in the ancient myths.   A bird.

A person of a race of people over in North Africa that what's his name met on his journey.

MINUS

Women that sang songs and anybody that heard them never wanted to leave.

Beautiful girls in the Idylls of the Kings and stories like that.

A witch.   A loud-voiced woman.

A scold.   Kind of always complaining.

39. Depredation (A plundering or laying waste; robbery.)

PLUS

A raid that has done some damage or something like that.

Injury to property — malicious intent to do harm — perhaps not malicious, but harm done.

Outlawry, robbery, killing.   Something like marauding.
An attack made on something with a view to decreasing its value.
Ruin something or nearly ruin.
To destroy.   Some mischievous act.
Could be stealing and destroying things — not for personal gain so much
    as revenge.

Q
Thievery — theft.   To tear someone down.
A lowering of.

MINUS
Demoralizing.   Sort of a depression.
Being deprived of something.   To cause somebody's downfall.
To depreciate something, don't like it, let it go to waste.
To say derogatory things about someone.

40. *Perfunctory* (Done without care or interest or merely as a form,
routinely.)

A satisfactory definition must take cognizance of lack of interest in the
thing done perfunctorily. This word is often confused with punctual.

PLUS
Necessarily done with a sense of duty — no feeling.
In an offhand manner with no particular significance.
Something you do — you don't care about it, but it's a social necessity and
    you have to do it.
You do something that you've done so long it just becomes a second
    nature — casually.
Just doing something — sort of a duty — sort of a habit.
Usually a short curt greeting or something that is done in a mediocre sort of
    way.
Something that has to be done because it has to be done.
Usual duties — perfunctory duties.   Careless.

Q
To be very deliberate in everything you do.
Casually, non-committally.

MINUS
Regular.   Performing your duties.
Everything you do, do it in a certain way and always do it that way.
Means not well — a thing isn't well done if it is done in a perfunctory
    manner.
Means a short manner.

41. *Achromatic* (Colorless. In music without accidentals.)

PLUS

Without color.   Uncolored.
Refracting light without breaking it up into its constituent colors.
A musical scale that is not chromatic — the diatonic or whole tone scale.
A form of musical scale.

Q

A scale that is played on the piano.   Musical.
It has something to do with color.
It's on the piano key-board — not every key.

MINUS

Nothing to do with chromatic, is it? — means to go up by small degrees,
   doesn't it?
Have one octave and play every note that is the scale. (chromatic)
Part of a telescope — the lens.   A series of colors.
Means you're not sensitive to colors.

42. *Casuistry* (The solving of special cases of right and wrong in conduct
by applying general principles of ethics, and deciding how far circumstances
alter cases. Often used disparagingly of subtle but evasive reasoning.)

PLUS

A branch of philosophy.   Sophistry.
A branch of philosophy generally dealing with theology.
Dealing with questions of right and wrong in conduct.

Q

Reasoning that — well, it's reasoning.
Giving reasons that aren't true.

MINUS

It deals with causes.   It's not natural.
Don't know unless it comes from casual.
Somebody who argues on fine points.

43. *Homunculus* (A little man; dwarf. A model of a human being used
for demonstrating anatomy.)

PLUS

Some sort or variety of dwarf.   Small man.

Q

Used of a man in a derogatory sense.   To do with man.

MINUS

Pertaining to the species of man.   Homologous.
Something done by a man.   Means similar.

44. *Sudorific* (Causing or increasing sweat. A medicine that causes sweat.)

PLUS

Pertaining to perspiration.   Having to do with sweat.
Sweaty.

Q

There's a sudorific medicine.

MINUS

It has something to do with odor.   Means an inactive state.
Sleepy-like. (soporific)

45. *Parterre* (Part of a theatre beneath the balcony and behind the parquet. Garden area in which the flower beds and paths form a pattern.)

PLUS

Part of the lower floor of a theatre.   A terraced garden.
Part of a theatre under the balcony.   Flower beds with paths between.

Q

Sort of an outdoor terrace.

MINUS

Under the ground.   The theatre — its boxes.
Pertaining to the earth or part of the earth.   You portion things out.

PART THREE ▶

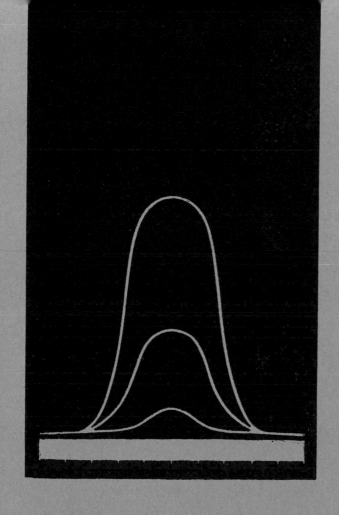

Pinneau Revised IQ Tables

PINNEAU REVISED IQ TABLES

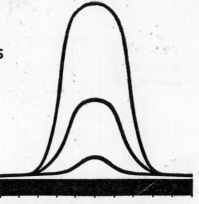

The revised IQ tables enable one to determine a subject's standard score or deviation IQ from the mental age score he obtains on the 1937 Revision of the Stanford-Binet (Form L or Form M), or from a mental age score obtained on the 1960 scale Form L-M.

To find a subject's IQ in the revised tables one first finds the table appropriate to his mental age score as indicated in table headings. In these tables one goes down the chronological age column until he finds the subject's chronological age and then horizontally across to the column appropriate to his mental age in years and months (as indicated at the top of the columns) or in months (as indicated at the bottom of the columns).

YEARS MONTHS	2-0	2-1	2-2	2-3	2-4	2-5	2-6	2-7	2-8	2-9	2-10	2-11	
2-00	98	102	106	110	114	118	122	127	131	135	139	143	24
2-01	94	98	102	105	109	113	117	121	125	129	132	136	25
2-02	90	94	98	101	105	108	112	116	119	123	127	130	26
2-03	87	91	94	98	101	104	108	111	115	118	122	125	27
2-04	84	88	91	94	97	101	104	107	110	114	117	120	28
2-05	82	85	88	91	94	97	100	103	106	110	112	116	29
2-06	80	83	86	89	91	94	97	100	103	106	109	112	30
2-07	77	80	83	86	89	91	94	97	100	103	106	108	31
2-08	75	78	81	83	86	89	91	94	97	100	102	105	32
2-09	73	76	78	81	84	86	89	92	94	97	99	102	33
2-10	71	74	76	79	81	84	86	89	92	94	97	99	34
2-11	69	71	74	76	79	81	84	87	89	92	94	97	35
3-00	67	70	72	74	77	79	82	84	87	89	92	94	36
3-01	66	68	70	73	75	77	80	82	85	87	89	92	37
3-02	64	66	69	71	73	76	78	80	83	85	88	90	38
3-03	62	65	67	69	72	74	76	79	81	83	86	88	39
3-04	61	63	66	68	70	73	75	77	79	82	84	86	40
3-05	60	62	64	66	69	71	73	75	78	80	82	84	41
3-06	58	61	63	65	67	69	72	74	76	78	80	83	42
3-07	57	59	61	63	66	68	70	72	74	76	79	81	43
3-08	55	57	60	62	64	66	68	70	72	75	77	79	44
3-09	54	56	58	60	62	64	67	69	71	73	75	77	45
3-10	52	54	57	59	61	63	65	67	69	71	73	75	46
3-11	51	53	55	57	59	61	63	65	67	70	72	74	47
4-00	50	52	54	56	58	60	62	64	66	68	70	72	48
4-01	48	50	52	54	56	58	60	62	64	66	68	70	49
4-02	47	49	51	53	55	57	59	61	63	65	67	69	50
4-03	46	47	49	51	53	55	57	59	61	63	65	67	51
4-04	44	46	48	50	52	54	56	58	60	62	64	66	52
4-05	43	45	47	49	51	53	55	57	58	60	62	64	53
4-06	42	44	46	47	49	51	53	55	57	59	61	63	54
4-07	40	42	44	46	48	50	52	54	56	58	59	61	55
4-08	39	41	43	45	47	49	50	52	54	56	58	60	56
4-09	38	40	42	44	45	47	49	51	53	55	57	58	57
4-10	37	39	40	42	44	46	48	50	52	53	55	57	58
4-11	35	37	39	41	43	45	46	48	50	52	54	56	59
TOTAL MONTHS	24	25	26	27	28	29	30	31	32	33	34	35	

CHRONOLOGICAL AGE

MA 2-0 / CA 2-0

258

CHRONOLOGICAL AGE (YEARS-MONTHS)	2-0	2-1	2-2	2-3	2-4	2-5	2-6	2-7	2-8	2-9	2-10	2-11	TOTAL MONTHS
5-00	34	36	38	40	42	43	45	47	49	51	52	54	60
5-01	33	35	37	39	41	42	44	46	48	49	51	53	61
5-02	32	34	36	38	39	41	43	45	46	48	50	52	62
5-03	31	33	35	37	38	40	42	44	45	47	49	51	63
5-04	30	32	34	36	37	39	41	43	44	46	48	50	64
5-05		31	33	35	36	38	40	41	43	45	47	48	65
5-06		30	32	34	35	37	39	40	42	44	46	47	66
5-07		30	31	33	35	36	38	40	41	43	45	46	67
5-08			31	33	34	36	38	39	41	42	44	46	68
5-09			30	32	34	35	37	39	40	42	43	45	69
5-10			30	32	33	35	36	38	40	41	43	44	70
5-11				31	33	34	36	37	39	41	42	44	71
6-00				31	32	34	35	37	38	40	41	43	72
6-01				30	32	33	35	36	38	39	41	42	73
6-02				30	31	33	34	36	37	39	40	42	74
6-03				30	31	32	34	35	37	38	40	41	75
6-04					31	32	33	35	36	38	39	41	76
6-05					30	32	33	34	36	37	39	40	77
6-06					30	31	33	34	35	37	38	40	78
6-07						31	32	34	35	36	38	39	79
6-08						30	32	33	35	36	37	39	80
6-09						30	32	33	34	36	37	38	81
6-10						30	31	32	34	35	36	38	82
6-11						30	31	32	33	35	36	37	83
7-00								32	33	34	36	37	84
7-01								31	33	34	35	36	85
7-02								31	32	34	35	36	86
7-03								31	32	33	35	36	87
7-04								31	32	33	34	35	88
7-05								30	32	33	34	35	89
7-06								30	31	33	34	35	90
7-07								30	31	32	33	35	91
7-08								30	31	32	33	34	92
7-09								30	31	32	33	34	93
7-10									31	32	33	34	94
7-11									30	31	32	34	95
TOTAL MONTHS	24	25	26	27	28	29	30	31	32	33	34	35	

259

MA 2-0 / CA 5-0

CHRONOLOGICAL AGE YEARS MONTHS	2 0	2 1	2 2	2 3	2 4	2 5	2 6	2 7	2 8	2 9	2 10	2 11	TOTAL
8–00									30	31	32	33	96
8–01									30	31	32	33	97
8–02									30	31	32	33	98
8–03									30	31	32	33	99
8–04										30	31	32	100
8–05										30	31	32	101
8–06										30	31	32	102
8–07										30	31	32	103
8–08										30	31	32	104
8–09										30	31	32	105
8–10											30	31	106
8–11											30	31	107
9–00											30	31	108
9–01											30	31	109
9–02											30	31	110
9–03											30	31	111
9–04											30	31	112
9–05											30	31	113
9–06											30	31	114
9–07											30	30	115
9–08											30	30	116
9–09											30	30	117
9–10												30	118
9–11												30	119
10–00												30	120
10–01												30	121
10–02												30	122
10–03													123
10–04													124
10–05													125
10–06													126
10–07													127
10–08													128
10–09													129
10–10													130
10–11													131
TOTAL MONTHS	24	25	26	27	28	29	30	31	32	33	34	35	

MA 2–0 / CA 8–0

YEARS / MONTHS	3 0	3 1	3 2	3 3	3 4	3 5	3 6	3 7	3 8	3 9	3 10	3 11	TOTAL MONTHS
2–00	147	151	155	160	164	168	172						24
2–01	140	144	148	152	156	160	164	167	171				25
2–02	134	138	141	145	148	152	156	160	163	167	170		26
2–03	128	132	135	139	142	146	149	152	156	159	163	166	27
2–04	123	126	130	133	136	140	143	146	149	152	156	159	28
2–05	119	122	125	128	131	134	137	140	143	146	149	152	29
2–06	115	117	120	123	126	129	132	135	138	141	143	146	30
2–07	111	114	117	120	122	125	128	131	134	136	139	142	31
2–08	108	111	113	116	119	121	124	127	130	132	135	138	32
2–09	105	107	110	113	115	118	121	123	126	129	131	134	33
2–10	102	104	107	110	112	115	117	120	122	125	128	130	34
2–11	99	102	104	107	109	112	114	117	119	122	124	127	35
3–00	96	99	101	104	106	109	111	114	116	118	121	123	36
3–01	94	97	99	101	104	106	109	111	113	116	118	121	37
3–02	92	95	97	99	102	104	106	109	111	113	116	118	38
3–03	90	93	95	97	99	102	104	106	109	111	113	116	39
3–04	88	91	93	95	98	100	102	104	107	109	111	113	40
3–05	87	89	91	93	96	98	100	102	104	107	109	111	41
3–06	85	87	89	91	94	96	98	100	102	105	107	109	42
3–07	83	85	87	89	92	94	96	98	100	102	105	107	43
3–08	81	83	85	87	90	92	94	96	98	100	102	105	44
3–09	79	81	83	86	88	90	92	94	96	98	100	102	45
3–10	77	80	82	84	86	88	90	92	94	96	98	100	46
3–11	76	78	80	82	84	86	88	90	92	94	96	98	47
4–00	74	76	78	80	82	84	86	88	90	92	94	96	48
4–01	72	74	76	78	80	82	84	86	88	90	93	95	49
4–02	71	73	75	77	79	81	83	85	87	89	91	93	50
4–03	69	71	73	75	77	79	81	83	85	87	89	91	51
4–04	68	70	72	74	75	77	79	81	83	85	87	89	52
4–05	66	68	70	72	74	76	78	80	82	84	86	88	53
4–06	65	67	69	70	72	74	76	78	80	82	84	86	54
4–07	63	65	67	69	71	73	75	77	78	80	82	84	55
4–08	62	64	65	67	69	71	73	75	77	79	81	82	56
4–09	60	62	64	66	68	70	71	73	75	77	79	81	57
4–10	59	61	63	64	66	68	70	72	74	76	77	79	58
4–11	57	59	61	63	65	67	68	70	72	74	76	78	59
TOTAL MONTHS	36	37	38	39	40	41	42	43	44	45	46	47	

MA 3–0 / CA 2–0

YEARS / MONTHS	3 0	3 1	3 2	3 3	3 4	3 5	3 6	3 7	3 8	3 9	3 10	3 11	
5–00	56	58	60	62	63	65	67	69	71	72	74	76	60
5–01	55	57	58	60	62	64	66	67	69	71	73	75	61
5–02	54	55	57	59	61	62	64	66	68	70	71	73	62
5–03	52	54	56	58	59	61	63	65	66	68	70	72	63
5–04	51	53	55	56	58	60	62	63	65	67	69	70	64
5–05	50	52	53	55	57	59	60	62	64	66	67	69	65
5–06	49	51	52	54	56	57	59	61	63	64	66	68	66
5–07	48	50	51	53	55	57	58	60	62	63	65	67	67
5–08	47	49	51	52	54	56	57	59	61	62	64	66	68
5–09	47	48	50	52	53	55	56	58	60	61	63	64	69
5–10	46	47	49	51	52	54	55	57	59	60	62	63	70
5–11	45	47	48	50	52	53	55	56	58	59	61	63	71
6–00	45	46	48	49	51	52	54	55	57	58	60	62	72
6–01	44	45	47	48	50	51	53	55	56	58	59	61	73
6–02	43	45	46	48	49	51	52	54	55	57	58	60	74
6–03	43	44	46	47	49	50	52	53	54	56	57	59	75
6–04	42	44	45	46	48	49	51	52	54	55	57	58	76
6–05	42	43	44	46	47	49	50	51	53	54	56	57	77
6–06	41	42	44	45	47	48	49	51	52	54	55	56	78
6–07	40	42	43	45	46	47	49	50	51	53	54	56	79
6–08	40	41	43	44	45	47	48	49	51	52	53	55	80
6–09	40	41	42	44	45	46	48	49	50	52	53	54	81
6–10	39	40	42	43	44	46	47	48	50	51	52	53	82
6–11	39	40	41	42	44	45	46	48	49	50	52	53	83
7–00	38	39	41	42	43	45	46	47	48	50	51	52	84
7–01	38	39	40	42	43	44	45	47	48	49	50	52	85
7–02	37	39	40	41	42	44	45	46	47	48	50	51	86
7–03	37	38	39	41	42	43	44	45	47	48	49	50	87
7–04	37	38	39	40	41	43	44	45	46	47	49	50	88
7–05	36	38	39	40	41	42	43	45	46	47	48	49	89
7–06	36	37	38	39	41	42	43	44	45	46	48	49	90
7–07	36	37	38	39	40	41	43	44	45	46	47	48	91
7–08	35	37	38	39	40	41	42	43	44	46	47	48	92
7–09	35	36	37	38	40	41	42	43	44	45	46	47	93
7–10	35	36	37	38	39	40	41	43	44	45	46	47	94
7–11	35	36	37	38	39	40	41	42	43	44	45	46	95
	36	37	38	39	40	41	42	43	44	45	46	47	TOTAL MONTHS

CHRONOLOGICAL AGE

MA 3–0 / CA 5–0

YEARS MONTHS	3 0	3 1	3 2	3 3	3 4	3 5	3 6	3 7	3 8	3 9	3 10	3 11	
8–00	34	35	37	38	39	40	41	42	43	44	45	46	96
8–01	34	35	36	37	38	39	40	42	43	44	45	46	97
8–02	34	35	36	37	38	39	40	41	42	43	44	45	98
8–03	34	35	36	37	38	39	40	41	42	43	44	45	99
8–04	33	34	35	36	37	38	39	40	42	43	44	45	100
8–05	33	34	35	36	37	38	39	40	41	42	43	44	101
8–06	33	34	35	36	37	38	39	40	41	42	43	44	102
8–07	33	34	35	36	37	38	39	40	41	42	42	43	103
8–08	33	34	34	35	36	37	38	39	40	41	42	43	104
8–09	32	33	34	35	36	37	38	39	40	41	42	43	105
8–10	32	33	34	35	36	37	38	39	40	41	41	42	106
8–11	32	33	34	35	36	37	38	39	39	40	41	42	107
9–00	32	33	34	35	36	36	37	38	39	40	41	42	108
9–01	32	33	34	35	35	36	37	38	39	40	41	42	109
9–02	32	33	33	34	35	36	37	38	39	40	41	41	110
9–03	32	32	33	34	35	36	37	38	39	39	40	41	111
9–04	32	32	33	34	35	36	37	38	38	39	40	41	112
9–05	32	32	33	34	35	36	37	38	38	39	40	41	113
9–06	31	32	33	34	35	36	37	37	38	39	40	41	114
9–07	31	32	33	34	35	35	36	37	38	39	40	40	115
9–08	31	32	33	34	35	35	36	37	38	39	40	40	116
9–09	31	32	33	34	34	35	36	37	38	39	39	40	117
9–10	31	32	33	34	34	35	36	37	38	38	39	40	118
9–11	31	32	33	33	34	35	36	37	37	38	39	40	119
10–00	31	32	33	33	34	35	36	37	37	38	39	40	120
10–01	31	32	33	33	34	35	36	37	37	38	39	40	121
10–02	31	32	33	34	34	35	36	37	37	38	39	40	122
10–03	31	32	33	34	34	35	36	37	37	38	39	40	123
10–04	31	32	33	34	34	35	36	37	37	38	39	40	124
10–05	31	32	33	34	34	35	36	37	37	38	39	40	125
10–06	31	32	33	34	34	35	36	37	37	38	39	40	126
10–07	32	32	33	34	35	35	36	37	37	38	39	40	127
10–08	32	32	33	34	35	35	36	37	37	38	39	40	128
10–09	32	33	33	34	35	35	36	37	37	38	39	40	129
10–10	32	33	33	34	35	36	36	37	38	38	39	40	130
10–11	32	33	33	34	35	36	36	37	38	38	39	40	131
	36	37	38	39	40	41	42	43	44	45	46	47	TOTAL MONTHS

MA 3–0 / CA 8–0

YEARS → MONTHS ↓	3 0	3 1	3 2	3 3	3 4	3 5	3 6	3 7	3 8	3 9	3 10	3 11	
11–00	32	33	34	34	35	36	36	37	38	38	39	40	132
11–01	32	33	33	34	35	36	36	37	38	38	39	40	133
11–02	32	33	34	34	35	36	36	37	38	38	39	40	134
11–03	32	33	34	34	35	36	36	37	38	38	39	40	135
11–04	32	33	33	34	35	35	36	37	37	38	39	39	136
11–05	32	33	33	34	35	35	36	37	37	38	39	39	137
11–06	32	33	33	34	35	35	36	37	37	38	39	39	138
11–07	32	33	34	34	35	35	36	37	37	38	39	39	139
11–08	32	33	34	34	35	35	36	37	37	38	39	39	140
11–09	32	33	34	34	35	35	36	37	37	38	39	39	141
11–10	32	33	34	34	35	35	36	37	37	38	39	39	142
11–11	32	33	34	34	35	35	36	37	37	38	39	39	143
12–00	32	33	34	34	35	35	36	37	37	38	38	39	144
12–01	32	33	33	34	35	35	36	36	37	38	38	39	145
12–02	32	33	33	34	34	35	36	36	37	37	38	39	146
12–03	32	33	33	34	34	35	36	36	37	37	38	39	147
12–04	32	32	33	34	34	35	35	36	37	37	38	38	148
12–05	32	32	33	33	34	35	35	36	36	37	38	38	149
12–06	32	32	33	33	34	35	35	36	36	37	37	38	150
12–07	32	32	33	33	34	34	35	36	36	37	37	38	151
12–08	31	32	32	33	34	34	35	35	36	37	37	38	152
12–09	31	32	32	33	33	34	35	35	36	36	37	38	153
12–10	31	32	32	33	33	34	35	35	36	36	37	37	154
12–11	31	32	32	33	33	34	34	35	36	36	37	37	155
13–00	31	31	32	33	33	34	34	35	35	36	37	37	156
13–01	31	31	32	32	33	33	34	35	35	36	36	37	157
13–02	31	31	32	32	33	33	34	35	35	36	36	37	158
13–03	30	31	31	32	32	33	34	34	35	35	36	36	159
13–04	30	31	31	32	32	33	33	34	34	35	36	36	160
13–05	30	30	31	32	32	33	33	34	34	35	36	36	161
13–06		30	31	31	32	32	33	34	34	35	35	36	162
13–07		30	31	31	32	32	33	33	34	34	35	36	163
13–08			30	31	32	32	33	33	34	34	35	35	164
13–09			30	31	31	32	32	33	34	34	35	35	165
13–10			30	30	31	32	32	33	33	34	34	35	166
13–11				30	31	31	32	33	33	34	34	35	167
	36	37	38	39	40	41	42	43	44	45	46	47	TOTAL MONTHS

CHRONOLOGICAL AGE

CHRONOLOGICAL AGE

YEARS MONTHS	3 0	3 1	3 2	3 3	3 4	3 5	3 6	3 7	3 8	3 9	3 10	3 11	
14-00				30	31	31	32	32	33	33	34	35	168
14-01				30	30	31	32	32	33	33	34	34	169
14-02					30	31	31	32	33	33	34	34	170
14-03					30	31	31	32	32	33	33	34	171
14-04						30	31	32	32	33	33	34	172
14-05						30	31	31	32	32	33	34	173
14-06						30	31	31	32	32	33	33	174
14-07							30	31	31	32	33	33	175
14-08							30	31	31	32	32	33	176
14-09							30	31	31	32	32	33	177
14-10								30	31	31	32	33	178
14-11								30	31	31	32	32	179
15-00								30	30	31	32	32	180
15-01									30	31	31	32	181
15-02									30	31	31		182
15-03										30	31		183
15-04											30		184
15-05													185
15-06													186
15-07													187
15-08													188
15-09													189
15-10													190
15-11													191
16-00													192
	36	37	38	39	40	41	42	43	44	45	46	47	TOTAL MONTHS

265

MA 3-0 / CA 14-0

YEARS → MONTHS ↓	4-0	4-1	4-2	4-3	4-4	4-5	4-6	4-7	4-8	4-9	4-10	4-11	TOTAL MONTHS
2–00													24
2–01													25
2–02													26
2–03	170												27
2–04	162	166	169	172									28
2–05	155	158	162	165	168	171							29
2–06	149	152	155	158	161	164	167	170					30
2–07	145	148	150	153	156	159	162	164	167	170			31
2–08	141	143	146	149	151	154	157	160	162	165	168	170	32
2–09	137	139	142	144	147	150	152	155	158	160	163	166	33
2–10	133	135	138	141	143	146	148	151	153	156	159	161	34
2–11	129	132	134	137	139	142	144	147	149	152	154	157	35
3–00	126	128	131	133	136	138	140	143	145	148	150	153	36
3–01	123	125	128	130	133	135	137	140	142	145	147	149	37
3–02	120	123	125	128	130	132	135	137	139	142	144	146	38
3–03	118	120	123	125	127	130	132	134	136	139	141	143	39
3–04	116	118	120	123	125	127	129	132	134	136	138	141	40
3–05	113	116	118	120	122	125	127	129	131	134	136	138	41
3–06	111	113	116	118	120	122	124	127	129	131	133	135	42
3–07	109	111	113	115	118	120	122	124	126	128	131	133	43
3–08	107	109	111	113	115	117	120	122	124	126	128	130	44
3–09	105	107	109	111	113	115	117	119	121	124	126	128	45
3–10	102	105	107	109	111	113	115	117	119	121	123	125	46
3–11	100	103	105	107	109	111	113	115	117	119	121	123	47
4–00	98	101	103	105	107	109	111	113	115	117	119	121	48
4–01	97	99	101	103	105	107	109	111	113	115	117	119	49
4–02	95	97	99	101	103	105	107	109	111	113	115	117	50
4–03	93	95	97	99	101	103	105	107	109	111	113	115	51
4–04	91	93	95	97	99	101	103	105	107	109	111	113	52
4–05	89	91	93	95	97	99	101	103	105	107	109	111	53
4–06	88	90	92	93	95	97	99	101	103	105	107	109	54
4–07	86	88	90	92	94	96	97	99	101	103	105	107	55
4–08	84	86	88	90	92	94	96	97	99	101	103	105	56
4–09	83	85	86	88	90	92	94	96	98	99	101	103	57
4–10	81	83	85	87	88	90	92	94	96	98	100	101	58
4–11	79	81	83	85	87	89	90	92	94	96	98	100	59
TOTAL MONTHS	48	49	50	51	52	53	54	55	56	57	58	59	

CHRONOLOGICAL AGE

MA 4–0 / CA 2–0

CHRONOLOGICAL AGE

YEARS MONTHS	4 0	4 1	4 2	4 3	4 4	4 5	4 6	4 7	4 8	4 9	4 10	4 11	TOTAL MONTHS
5–00	78	80	81	83	85	87	89	91	92	94	96	98	60
5–01	76	78	80	82	84	85	87	89	91	93	94	96	61
5–02	75	77	78	80	82	84	86	87	89	91	93	94	62
5–03	73	75	77	79	81	82	84	86	88	89	91	93	63
5–04	72	74	76	77	79	81	83	84	86	88	90	91	64
5–05	71	72	74	76	78	79	81	83	84	86	88	90	65
5–06	69	71	73	75	76	78	80	81	83	85	86	88	66
5–07	68	70	72	73	75	77	78	80	82	83	85	87	67
5–08	67	69	70	72	74	75	77	79	80	82	84	85	68
5–09	66	68	69	71	73	74	76	77	79	81	82	84	69
5–10	65	67	68	70	71	73	75	76	78	79	81	83	70
5–11	64	66	67	69	70	72	74	75	77	78	80	81	71
6–00	63	65	66	68	69	71	72	74	76	77	79	80	72
6–01	62	64	65	67	68	70	71	73	74	76	77	79	73
6–02	61	63	64	66	67	69	70	72	73	75	76	78	74
6–03	60	62	63	65	66	68	69	71	72	74	75	77	75
6–04	59	61	62	64	65	67	68	70	71	72	74	75	76
6–05	59	60	61	63	64	66	67	69	70	71	73	74	77
6–06	58	59	61	62	63	65	66	68	69	70	72	73	78
6–07	57	58	60	61	62	64	65	67	68	69	71	72	79
6–08	56	58	59	60	62	63	64	66	67	68	70	71	80
6–09	56	57	58	60	61	62	64	65	66	68	69	70	81
6–10	55	56	57	59	60	61	63	64	65	67	68	69	82
6–11	54	55	57	58	59	61	62	63	64	66	67	68	83
7–00	53	55	56	57	59	60	61	62	64	65	66	67	84
7–01	53	54	55	57	58	59	60	62	63	64	65	67	85
7–02	52	53	55	56	57	58	60	61	62	63	64	66	86
7–03	52	53	54	55	56	58	59	60	61	62	64	65	87
7–04	51	52	53	55	56	57	58	59	61	62	63	64	88
7–05	50	52	53	54	55	56	58	59	60	61	62	63	89
7–06	50	51	52	53	55	56	57	58	59	60	62	63	90
7–07	49	51	52	53	54	55	56	57	59	60	61	62	91
7–08	49	50	51	52	53	55	56	57	58	59	60	61	92
7–09	48	50	51	52	53	54	55	56	57	58	60	61	93
7–10	48	49	50	51	52	53	55	56	57	58	59	60	94
7–11	48	49	50	51	52	53	54	55	56	57	58	59	95
	48	49	50	51	52	53	54	55	56	57	58	59	TOTAL MONTHS

MA 4–0 / CA 5–0

CHRONOLOGICAL AGE — YEARS / MONTHS	4-0	4-1	4-2	4-3	4-4	4-5	4-6	4-7	4-8	4-9	4-10	4-11	TOTAL MONTHS
8-00	47	48	49	50	51	52	53	55	56	57	58	59	96
8-01	47	48	49	50	51	52	53	54	55	56	57	58	97
8-02	46	47	48	49	50	51	52	54	55	56	57	58	98
8-03	46	47	48	49	50	51	52	53	54	55	56	57	99
8-04	46	47	48	49	50	51	52	53	54	55	56	57	100
8-05	45	46	47	48	49	50	51	52	53	54	55	56	101
8-06	45	46	47	48	49	50	51	52	53	54	55	56	102
8-07	44	45	46	47	48	49	50	51	52	53	54	55	103
8-08	44	45	46	47	48	49	50	51	52	53	54	55	104
8-09	44	45	46	47	48	48	49	50	51	52	53	54	105
8-10	43	44	45	46	47	48	49	50	51	52	53	54	106
8-11	43	44	45	46	47	47	49	50	51	51	52	53	107
9-00	43	44	45	46	46	47	48	49	50	51	52	53	108
9-01	43	44	44	45	46	47	48	49	50	51	52	52	109
9-02	42	43	44	45	46	47	48	49	49	50	51	52	110
9-03	42	43	44	45	46	46	47	48	49	50	51	52	111
9-04	42	43	44	44	45	46	47	48	49	50	51	51	112
9-05	42	43	43	44	45	46	47	48	49	49	50	51	113
9-06	42	42	43	44	45	46	47	48	48	49	50	51	114
9-07	41	42	43	44	45	46	46	47	48	49	50	51	115
9-08	41	42	43	44	44	45	46	47	48	49	49	50	116
9-09	41	42	43	43	44	45	46	47	48	48	49	50	117
9-10	41	42	42	43	44	45	46	46	47	48	49	50	118
9-11	41	41	42	43	44	45	45	46	47	48	49	49	119
10-00	41	41	42	43	44	44	45	46	47	48	48	49	120
10-01	40	41	42	43	44	44	45	46	47	47	48	49	121
10-02	40	41	42	43	44	44	45	46	47	47	48	49	122
10-03	40	41	42	43	43	44	45	46	46	47	48	49	123
10-04	40	41	42	43	43	44	45	46	46	47	48	49	124
10-05	40	41	42	43	43	44	45	46	46	47	48	48	125
10-06	40	41	42	43	43	44	45	45	46	47	48	48	126
10-07	40	41	42	43	43	44	45	45	46	47	48	48	127
10-08	40	41	42	42	43	44	45	45	46	47	47	48	128
10-09	40	41	42	42	43	44	45	45	46	47	47	48	129
10-10	40	41	42	43	43	44	45	45	46	47	47	48	130
10-11	40	41	42	42	43	44	45	45	46	47	47	48	131
TOTAL MONTHS	48	49	50	51	52	53	54	55	56	57	58	59	

MA 4-0 / CA 8-0

YEARS MONTHS	4 0	4 1	4 2	4 3	4 4	4 5	4 6	4 7	4 8	4 9	4 10	4 11	
11–00	40	41	42	42	43	44	45	45	46	47	47	48	132
11–01	40	41	42	42	43	44	44	45	46	46	47	48	133
11–02	40	41	42	42	43	44	44	45	46	46	47	48	134
11–03	40	41	42	42	43	44	44	45	46	46	47	48	135
11–04	40	41	41	42	43	43	44	45	45	46	47	47	136
11–05	40	41	41	42	43	43	44	45	45	46	47	47	137
11–06	40	41	41	42	43	43	44	45	45	46	46	47	138
11–07	40	41	41	42	43	43	44	44	45	46	46	47	139
11–08	40	41	41	42	42	43	44	44	45	46	46	47	140
11–09	40	40	41	42	42	43	44	44	45	45	46	47	141
11–10	40	40	41	42	42	43	44	44	45	45	46	47	142
11–11	40	40	41	42	42	43	43	44	45	45	46	47	143
12–00	40	40	41	42	42	43	43	44	45	45	46	46	144
12–01	39	40	41	41	42	43	43	44	44	45	46	46	145
12–02	39	40	41	41	42	42	43	44	44	45	45	46	146
12–03	39	40	40	41	42	42	43	43	44	45	45	46	147
12–04	39	40	40	41	41	42	43	43	44	44	45	46	148
12–05	39	39	40	41	41	42	42	43	44	44	45	45	149
12–06	39	39	40	40	41	42	42	43	43	44	45	45	150
12–07	39	39	40	40	41	41	42	43	43	44	44	45	151
12–08	38	39	39	40	41	41	42	42	43	44	44	45	152
12–09	38	39	39	40	40	41	42	42	43	43	44	44	153
12–10	38	39	39	40	40	41	41	42	43	43	44	44	154
12–11	38	38	39	40	40	41	41	42	42	43	44	44	155
13–00	38	38	39	39	40	41	41	42	42	43	43	44	156
13–01	37	38	39	39	40	40	41	41	42	43	43	44	157
13–02	37	38	38	39	40	40	41	41	42	42	43	44	158
13–03	37	38	38	39	39	40	40	41	41	42	43	43	159
13–04	37	37	38	38	39	40	40	41	41	42	42	43	160
13–05	37	37	38	38	39	39	40	41	41	42	42	43	161
13–06	36	37	37	38	39	39	40	40	41	41	42	42	162
13–07	36	37	37	38	38	39	39	40	41	41	42	42	163
13–08	36	37	37	38	38	39	39	40	40	41	42	42	164
13–09	36	36	37	37	38	39	39	40	40	41	41	42	165
13–10	35	36	37	37	38	38	39	39	40	40	41	42	166
13–11	35	36	36	37	38	38	39	39	40	40	41	41	167
	48	49	50	51	52	53	54	55	56	57	58	59	TOTAL MONTHS

MA 4–0 / CA 11–0

YEARS	4	4	4	4	4	4	4	4	4	4	4	4	
MONTHS	0	1	2	3	4	5	6	7	8	9	10	11	
14–00	35	36	36	37	37	38	38	39	39	40	41	41	168
14–01	35	35	36	36	37	38	38	39	39	40	40	41	169
14–02	35	35	36	36	37	37	38	39	39	40	40	41	170
14–03	34	35	36	36	37	37	38	38	39	39	40	40	171
14–04	34	35	35	36	36	37	37	38	39	39	40	40	172
14–05	34	35	35	36	36	37	37	38	38	39	40	40	173
14–06	34	34	35	35	36	37	37	38	38	39	39	40	174
14–07	34	34	35	35	36	36	37	37	38	38	39	40	175
14–08	33	34	35	35	36	36	37	37	38	38	39	39	176
14–09	33	34	34	35	35	36	36	37	38	38	39	39	177
14–10	33	34	34	35	35	36	36	37	37	38	38	39	178
14–11	33	33	34	35	35	36	36	37	37	38	38	39	179
15–00	33	33	34	34	35	35	36	36	37	37	38	39	180
15–01	32	33	33	34	34	35	35	36	36	37	37	38	181
15–02	32	32	33	33	34	35	35	36	36	37	37	38	182
15–03	31	32	32	33	33	34	35	35	36	36	37	37	183
15–04	31	31	32	32	33	33	34	34	35	36	36	37	184
15–05	31	31	32	32	33	33	34	34	35	35	36	36	185
15–06		31	31	32	32	33	33	34	34	35	35	36	186
15–07			30	31	32	32	33	33	34	34	35	35	187
15–08				31	31	32	32	33	33	34	34	35	188
15–09					31	31	32	32	33	33	34	34	189
15–10						31	31	32	32	33	33	34	190
14–11							30	31	32	32	33	33	34	191
16–00 } 16–02 }							30	31	31	32	32	33	{ 192 { 194
16–03 } 16–07 }								30	30	31	31	32	{ 195 { 199
16–08 } 17–00 }										30	30	31	{ 200 { 204
17–01 } 17–05 }												30	{ 205 { 209
17–06 } 17–10 }													{ 210 { 214
17–11 } 18–00 }													{ 215 { 216
	48	49	50	51	52	53	54	55	56	57	58	59	**TOTAL MONTHS**

CHRONOLOGICAL AGE

MENTAL AGE

YEARS → MONTHS ↓ (CHRONOLOGICAL AGE)	5 / 0	5 / 1	5 / 2	5 / 3	5 / 4	5 / 5	5 / 6	5 / 7	5 / 8	5 / 9	5 / 10	5 / 11	TOTAL MONTHS
2–00													24
2–01													25
2–02													26
2–03													27
2–04													28
2–05													29
2–06													30
2–07													31
2–08													32
2–09	168	171											33
2–10	164	166	169	171									34
2–11	159	162	164	167	169								35
3–00	155	158	160	162	165	167	170						36
3–01	152	154	157	159	161	164	166	169	171				37
3–02	149	151	153	156	158	160	163	165	167	170			38
3–03	146	148	150	153	155	157	160	162	164	167	169	171	39
3–04	143	145	147	150	152	154	157	159	161	163	166	168	40
3–05	140	142	145	147	149	151	154	156	158	160	163	165	41
3–06	138	140	142	144	146	149	151	153	155	157	160	162	42
3–07	135	137	139	141	144	146	148	150	152	154	157	159	43
3–08	132	135	137	139	141	143	145	147	150	152	154	156	44
3–09	130	132	134	136	138	141	143	145	147	149	151	153	45
3–10	128	130	132	134	136	138	140	142	144	146	148	150	46
3–11	125	127	129	131	133	136	138	140	142	144	146	148	47
4–00	123	125	127	129	131	133	135	137	139	141	143	145	48
4–01	121	123	125	127	129	131	133	135	137	139	141	143	49
4–02	119	121	123	125	127	129	131	133	135	137	139	141	50
4–03	117	119	121	123	125	126	128	130	132	134	136	138	51
4–04	115	117	118	120	122	124	126	128	130	132	134	136	52
4–05	113	115	117	118	120	122	124	126	128	130	132	134	53
4–06	111	113	115	116	118	120	122	124	126	128	130	132	54
4–07	109	111	113	114	116	118	120	122	124	126	128	130	55
4–08	107	109	111	112	114	116	118	120	122	124	126	128	56
4–09	105	107	109	111	112	114	116	118	120	122	124	125	57
4–10	103	105	107	109	111	112	114	116	118	120	122	123	58
4–11	101	103	105	107	109	110	112	114	116	118	120	121	59
TOTAL MONTHS	60	61	62	63	64	65	66	67	68	69	70	71	

CHRONOLOGICAL AGE

271

MA 5–0 / CA 2–0

YEARS }	5	5	5	5	5	5	5	5	5	5	5	5	
MONTHS }	0	1	2	3	4	5	6	7	8	9	10	11	
5–00	100	101	103	105	107	109	110	112	114	116	118	120	60
5–01	98	100	102	103	105	107	109	110	112	114	116	118	61
5–02	96	98	100	101	103	105	107	109	110	112	114	116	62
5–03	95	96	98	100	102	103	105	107	109	110	112	114	63
5–04	93	95	96	98	100	102	103	105	107	109	110	112	64
5–05	91	93	95	96	98	100	102	103	105	107	109	110	65
5–06	90	92	93	95	97	98	100	102	103	105	107	109	66
5–07	88	90	92	93	95	97	98	100	102	103	105	107	67
5–08	87	89	90	92	94	95	97	99	100	102	103	105	68
5–09	86	87	89	90	92	94	95	97	99	100	102	103	69
5–10	84	86	87	89	91	92	94	95	97	99	100	102	70
5–11	83	85	86	88	89	91	92	94	96	97	99	100	71
6–00	82	83	85	86	88	89	91	93	94	96	97	99	72
6–01	80	82	83	85	86	88	90	91	93	94	96	97	73
6–02	79	81	82	84	85	87	88	90	91	93	94	96	74
6–03	78	79	81	82	84	85	87	88	90	91	93	94	75
6–04	77	78	80	81	83	84	85	87	88	90	91	93	76
6–05	76	77	78	80	81	83	84	86	87	88	90	91	77
6–06	75	76	77	79	80	82	83	84	86	87	89	90	78
6–07	73	75	76	78	79	80	82	83	84	86	87	89	79
6–08	72	74	75	76	78	79	81	82	83	85	86	87	80
6–09	72	73	74	76	77	78	80	81	82	84	85	86	81
6–10	71	72	73	74	76	77	78	80	81	82	84	85	82
6–11	70	71	72	73	75	76	77	79	80	81	83	84	83
7–00	69	70	71	72	74	75	76	78	79	80	81	83	84
7–01	68	69	70	72	73	74	75	77	78	79	80	82	85
7–02	67	68	69	71	72	73	74	76	77	78	79	80	86
7–03	66	67	69	70	71	72	73	75	76	77	78	79	87
7–04	65	67	68	69	70	71	73	74	75	76	77	78	88
7–05	65	66	67	68	69	70	72	73	74	75	76	78	89
7–06	64	65	66	67	68	70	71	72	73	74	75	77	90
7–07	63	64	65	67	68	69	70	71	72	73	75	76	91
7–08	62	64	65	66	67	68	69	70	71	73	74	75	92
7–09	62	63	64	65	66	67	68	70	71	72	73	74	93
7–10	61	62	63	64	65	67	68	69	70	71	72	73	94
7–11	60	62	63	64	65	66	67	68	69	70	71	72	95
	60	61	62	63	64	65	66	67	68	69	70	71	TOTAL MONTHS }

CHRONOLOGICAL AGE

MA 5–0 / CA 5–0

MENTAL AGE

YEARS → MONTHS ↓ (CHRONOLOGICAL AGE)	5-0	5-1	5-2	5-3	5-4	5-5	5-6	5-7	5-8	5-9	5-10	5-11	TOTAL MONTHS
8-00	60	61	62	63	64	65	66	67	68	69	70	71	96
8-01	59	60	61	62	63	65	66	67	68	69	70	71	97
8-02	59	60	61	62	63	64	65	66	67	68	69	70	98
8-03	58	59	60	61	62	63	64	65	66	67	68	69	99
8-04	58	59	60	61	62	63	64	65	66	67	68	69	100
8-05	57	58	59	60	61	62	63	64	65	66	67	68	101
8-06	57	58	59	60	60	61	62	63	64	65	66	67	102
8-07	56	57	58	59	60	61	62	63	64	65	66	67	103
8-08	56	56	57	58	59	60	61	62	63	64	65	66	104
8-09	55	56	57	58	59	60	61	62	63	64	65	65	105
8-10	55	56	56	57	58	59	60	61	62	63	64	65	106
8-11	54	55	56	57	58	59	60	61	62	63	63	64	107
9-00	54	55	56	56	57	58	59	60	61	62	63	64	108
9-01	53	54	55	56	57	58	59	60	61	61	62	63	109
9-02	53	54	55	56	57	57	58	59	60	61	62	63	110
9-03	53	53	54	55	56	57	58	59	60	61	61	62	111
9-04	52	53	54	55	56	57	57	58	59	60	61	62	112
9-05	52	53	54	55	55	56	57	58	59	60	61	61	113
9-06	52	53	53	54	55	56	57	58	58	59	60	61	114
9-07	51	52	53	54	55	56	56	57	58	59	60	61	115
9-08	51	52	53	54	54	55	56	57	58	58	59	60	116
9-09	51	52	52	53	54	55	56	57	57	58	59	60	117
9-10	50	51	52	53	54	54	55	56	57	58	59	59	118
9-11	50	51	52	53	53	54	55	56	57	57	58	59	119
10-00	50	51	52	52	53	54	55	55	56	57	58	59	120
10-01	50	51	51	52	53	54	54	55	56	57	58	58	121
10-02	50	50	51	52	53	53	54	55	56	57	57	58	122
10-03	50	50	51	52	53	53	54	55	56	56	57	58	123
10-04	49	50	51	52	52	53	54	55	55	56	57	58	124
10-05	49	50	51	51	52	53	54	54	55	56	57	57	125
10-06	49	50	51	51	52	53	54	54	55	56	56	57	126
10-07	49	50	51	51	52	53	53	54	55	56	56	57	127
10-08	49	50	50	51	52	53	53	54	55	55	56	57	128
10-09	49	50	50	51	52	52	53	54	55	55	56	57	129
10-10	49	50	50	51	52	52	53	54	54	55	56	57	130
10-11	49	49	50	51	51	52	53	54	54	55	56	56	131
TOTAL MONTHS	60	61	62	63	64	65	66	67	68	69	70	71	

MA 5-0 / CA 8-0

YEARS MONTHS	5 0	5 1	5 2	5 3	5 4	5 5	5 6	5 7	5 8	5 9	5 10	5 11	TOTAL MONTHS
11–00	49	49	50	51	51	52	53	53	54	55	56	56	132
11–01	48	49	50	50	51	52	53	53	54	55	55	56	133
11–02	48	49	50	50	51	52	52	53	54	54	55	56	134
11–03	48	49	50	50	51	52	52	53	54	54	55	56	135
11–04	48	49	49	50	51	51	52	53	53	54	55	55	136
11–05	48	48	49	50	50	51	52	52	53	54	54	55	137
11–06	48	48	49	50	50	51	52	52	53	54	54	55	138
11–07	48	48	49	50	50	51	52	52	53	53	54	55	139
11–08	48	48	49	49	50	51	51	52	53	53	54	55	140
11–09	47	48	49	49	50	51	51	52	52	53	54	54	141
11–10	47	48	49	49	50	50	51	52	52	53	54	54	142
11–11	47	48	48	49	50	50	51	52	52	53	53	54	143
12–00	47	48	48	49	50	50	51	51	52	53	53	54	144
12–01	47	47	48	49	49	50	50	51	52	52	53	54	145
12–02	47	47	48	48	49	50	50	51	51	52	53	53	146
12–03	46	47	48	48	49	49	50	51	51	52	52	53	147
12–04	46	47	47	48	49	49	50	50	51	52	52	53	148
12–05	46	46	47	48	48	49	49	50	51	51	52	52	149
12–06	46	46	47	48	48	49	49	50	50	51	52	52	150
12–07	46	46	47	47	48	49	49	50	50	51	51	52	151
12–08	45	46	46	47	48	48	49	49	50	51	51	52	152
12–09	45	46	46	47	47	48	49	49	50	50	51	51	153
12–10	45	46	46	47	47	48	48	49	50	50	51	51	154
12–11	45	45	46	46	47	48	48	49	49	50	50	51	155
13–00	45	45	46	46	47	47	48	48	49	50	50	51	156
13–01	44	45	45	46	46	47	48	48	49	49	50	50	157
13–02	44	45	45	46	46	47	48	48	49	49	50	50	158
13–03	44	44	45	45	46	47	47	48	48	49	49	50	159
13–04	43	44	45	45	46	46	47	47	48	49	49	50	160
13–05	43	44	45	45	46	46	47	47	48	48	49	50	161
13–06	43	44	44	45	45	46	46	47	48	48	49	49	162
13–07	43	43	44	44	45	46	46	47	47	48	48	49	163
13–08	43	43	44	44	45	45	46	47	47	48	48	49	164
13–09	42	43	44	44	45	45	46	46	47	47	48	49	165
13–10	42	43	43	44	44	45	45	46	47	47	48	48	166
13–11	42	42	43	44	44	45	45	46	46	47	47	48	167
TOTAL MONTHS	60	61	62	63	64	65	66	67	68	69	70	71	

CHRONOLOGICAL AGE

CHRONOLOGICAL AGE YEARS–MONTHS	5–0	5–1	5–2	5–3	5–4	5–5	5–6	5–7	5–8	5–9	5–10	5–11	TOTAL MONTHS
14–00	42	42	43	43	44	44	45	46	46	47	47	48	168
14–01	41	42	43	43	44	44	45	45	46	46	47	47	169
14–02	41	42	42	43	43	44	45	45	46	46	47	47	170
14–03	41	42	42	43	43	44	44	45	45	46	46	47	171
14–04	41	41	42	42	43	43	44	45	45	46	46	47	172
14–05	41	41	42	42	43	43	44	44	45	46	46	47	173
14–06	40	41	41	42	43	43	44	44	44	45	46	46	174
14–07	40	41	41	42	42	43	43	44	44	45	45	46	175
14–08	40	41	41	42	42	43	43	44	44	45	45	46	176
14–09	40	40	41	41	42	42	43	43	44	45	45	46	177
14–10	39	40	41	41	42	42	43	43	44	44	45	45	178
14–11	39	40	40	41	41	42	43	43	44	44	45	45	179
15–00	39	40	40	41	41	42	42	43	43	44	44	45	180
15–01	39	39	40	40	41	41	42	42	43	43	44	44	181
15–02	38	39	39	40	40	41	41	42	43	43	44	44	182
15–03	38	38	39	39	40	40	41	41	42	42	43	44	183
15–04	37	38	38	39	39	40	40	41	41	42	42	43	184
15–05	37	37	38	39	39	40	40	41	41	42	42	43	185
15–06	36	37	37	38	38	39	40	40	41	41	42	42	186
15–07	36	36	37	37	38	38	39	39	40	41	41	42	187
15–08	36	36	37	37	38	38	39	39	40	40	41	41	188
15–09	35	35	36	37	37	38	38	39	39	40	40	41	189
15–10	34	35	35	36	36	37	38	38	39	39	40	40	190
15–11	34	35	35	36	36	37	37	38	38	39	39	40	191
16–00 / 16–02	33	34	34	35	35	36	37	37	38	38	39	39	192 / 194
16–03 / 16–07	32	33	33	34	34	35	36	36	37	37	38	38	195 / 199
16–08 / 17–00	31	32	32	33	33	34	35	35	36	36	37	37	200 / 204
17–01 / 17–05	30	31	31	32	32	33	34	34	35	35	36	36	205 / 209
17–06 / 17–10		30	30	31	31	32	33	33	34	34	35	35	210 / 214
17–11 / 18–00				30	31	31	32	32	33	33	34	34	215 / 216
TOTAL MONTHS	60	61	62	63	64	65	66	67	68	69	70	71	

MA 5–0 / CA 14–0

MENTAL AGE

YEARS MONTHS	6 0	6 1	6 2	6 3	6 4	6 5	6 6	6 7	6 8	6 9	6 10	6 11	
2-00													24
2-01													25
2-02													26
2-03													27
2-04													28
2-05													29
2-06													30
2-07													31
2-08													32
2-09													33
2-10													34
2-11													35
3-00													36
3-01													37
3-02													38
3-03													39
3-04	170												40
3-05	167	169											41
3-06	164	166	168	171									42
3-07	161	163	165	167	170								43
3-08	158	160	162	165	167	169	171						44
3-09	155	157	160	162	164	166	168	170					45
3-10	153	155	157	159	161	163	165	167	169				46
3-11	150	152	154	156	158	160	162	164	167	169	171		47
4-00	147	149	152	154	156	158	160	162	164	166	168	170	48
4-01	145	147	149	151	153	155	157	159	161	163	165	167	49
4-02	143	145	147	149	151	153	155	157	159	161	163	165	50
4-03	140	142	144	146	148	150	152	154	156	158	160	162	51
4-04	138	140	142	144	146	148	150	152	154	156	158	159	52
4-05	136	138	140	142	144	146	148	149	151	153	155	157	53
4-06	134	136	138	139	141	143	145	147	149	151	153	155	54
4-07	132	133	135	137	139	141	143	145	147	149	151	152	55
4-08	129	131	133	135	137	139	141	143	144	146	148	150	56
4-09	127	129	131	133	135	137	139	140	142	144	146	148	57
4-10	125	127	129	131	133	135	136	138	140	142	144	146	58
4-11	123	125	127	129	131	132	134	136	138	140	142	143	59
	72	73	74	75	76	77	78	79	80	81	82	83	TOTAL MONTHS

CHRONOLOGICAL AGE

YEARS → MONTHS ↓ / CHRONOLOGICAL AGE	6-0	6-1	6-2	6-3	6-4	6-5	6-6	6-7	6-8	6-9	6-10	6-11	TOTAL MONTHS
5-00	121	123	125	127	129	130	132	134	136	138	140	141	60
5-01	119	121	123	125	127	128	130	132	134	136	137	139	61
5-02	117	119	121	123	125	126	128	130	132	133	135	137	62
5-03	116	117	119	121	123	124	126	128	130	131	133	135	63
5-04	114	116	117	119	121	123	124	126	128	129	131	133	64
5-05	112	114	115	117	119	121	122	124	126	127	129	131	65
5-06	110	112	114	115	117	119	120	122	124	126	127	129	66
5-07	108	110	112	113	115	117	118	120	122	123	125	127	67
5-08	107	108	110	112	113	115	117	118	120	122	123	125	68
5-09	105	107	108	110	112	113	115	116	118	120	121	123	69
5-10	103	105	107	108	110	111	113	115	116	118	119	121	70
5-11	102	103	105	107	108	110	111	113	114	116	118	119	71
6-00	100	102	103	105	106	108	110	111	113	114	116	117	72
6-01	99	100	102	103	105	106	108	109	111	112	114	115	73
6-02	97	99	100	102	103	105	106	108	109	111	112	113	74
6-03	96	97	99	100	102	103	104	106	107	109	110	112	75
6-04	94	96	97	98	100	101	103	104	106	107	109	110	76
6-05	93	94	96	97	98	100	101	103	104	106	107	108	77
6-06	91	93	94	96	97	98	100	101	103	104	105	107	78
6-07	90	91	93	94	95	97	98	100	101	102	104	105	79
6-08	89	90	91	93	94	95	97	98	100	101	102	104	80
6-09	88	89	90	92	93	94	96	97	98	100	101	102	81
6-10	86	88	89	90	92	93	94	95	97	98	99	101	82
6-11	85	86	88	89	90	92	93	94	95	97	98	99	83
7-00	84	85	86	88	89	90	92	93	94	95	97	98	84
7-01	83	84	85	87	88	89	90	92	93	94	95	97	85
7-02	82	83	84	85	87	88	89	90	92	93	94	95	86
7-03	81	82	83	84	86	87	88	89	90	92	93	94	87
7-04	80	81	82	83	84	86	87	88	89	90	92	93	88
7-05	79	80	81	82	83	85	86	87	88	89	90	92	89
7-06	78	79	80	81	82	84	85	86	87	88	89	90	90
7-07	77	78	79	80	81	83	84	85	86	87	88	89	91
7-08	76	77	78	79	80	82	83	84	85	86	87	88	92
7-09	75	76	77	78	79	81	82	83	84	85	86	87	93
7-10	74	75	76	77	79	80	81	82	83	84	85	86	94
7-11	73	74	76	77	78	79	80	81	82	83	84	85	95
TOTAL MONTHS	72	73	74	75	76	77	78	79	80	81	82	83	

MA 6-0 / CA 5-0

CHRONOLOGICAL AGE	YEARS 6 MONTHS 0	6 1	6 2	6 3	6 4	6 5	6 6	6 7	6 8	6 9	6 10	6 11	TOTAL MONTHS
8–00	73	74	75	76	77	78	79	80	81	82	83	84	96
8–01	72	73	74	75	76	77	78	79	80	81	82	83	97
8–02	71	72	73	74	75	76	77	78	79	80	81	82	98
8–03	70	71	72	73	74	75	76	77	78	79	80	82	99
8–04	70	71	72	73	74	75	76	77	78	79	80	81	100
8–05	69	70	71	72	73	74	75	76	77	78	79	80	101
8–06	68	69	70	71	72	73	74	75	76	77	78	79	102
8–07	68	69	70	71	72	72	73	74	75	76	77	78	103
8–08	67	68	69	70	71	72	73	74	75	76	77	77	104
8–09	66	67	68	69	70	71	72	73	74	75	76	77	105
8–10	66	67	68	69	70	70	71	72	73	74	75	76	106
8–11	65	66	67	68	69	70	71	72	73	74	74	75	107
9–00	65	66	66	67	68	69	70	71	72	73	74	75	108
9–01	64	65	66	67	68	69	70	70	71	72	73	74	109
9–02	64	64	65	66	67	68	69	70	71	72	72	73	110
9–03	63	64	65	66	67	68	68	69	70	71	72	73	111
9–04	63	64	64	65	66	67	68	69	70	70	71	72	112
9–05	62	63	64	65	66	67	67	68	69	70	71	72	113
9–06	62	63	64	64	65	66	67	68	69	69	70	71	114
9–07	61	62	63	64	65	66	66	67	68	69	70	71	115
9–08	61	62	63	63	64	65	66	67	68	68	69	70	116
9–09	61	61	62	63	64	65	65	66	67	68	69	70	117
9–10	60	61	62	63	63	64	65	66	67	67	68	69	118
9–11	60	61	61	62	63	64	65	65	66	67	68	69	119
10–00	59	60	61	62	63	63	64	65	66	67	67	68	120
10–01	59	60	61	62	62	63	64	65	65	66	67	68	121
10–02	59	60	60	61	62	63	63	64	65	66	67	67	122
10–03	59	59	60	61	62	62	63	64	65	66	66	67	123
10–04	58	59	60	61	61	62	63	64	64	65	66	67	124
10–05	58	59	60	60	61	62	63	63	64	65	66	66	125
10–06	58	59	59	60	61	62	62	63	64	65	65	66	126
10–07	58	59	59	60	61	61	62	63	64	64	65	66	127
10–08	58	58	59	60	60	61	62	63	63	64	65	65	128
10–09	57	58	59	59	60	61	62	62	63	64	64	65	129
10–10	57	58	59	59	60	61	61	62	63	64	64	65	130
10–11	57	58	58	59	60	60	61	62	63	63	64	65	131
TOTAL MONTHS	72	73	74	75	76	77	78	79	80	81	82	83	

MA 6–0 / CA 8–0

278

CHRONOLOGICAL AGE

YEARS	6	6	6	6	6	6	6	6	6	6	6	6	
MONTHS	0	1	2	3	4	5	6	7	8	9	10	11	
11–00	57	58	58	59	60	60	61	62	62	63	64	64	132
11–01	57	57	58	59	59	60	61	61	62	63	63	64	133
11–02	56	57	58	58	59	60	60	61	62	62	63	64	134
11–03	56	57	58	58	59	60	60	61	62	62	63	64	135
11–04	56	57	57	58	59	59	60	61	61	62	63	63	136
11–05	56	56	57	58	58	59	60	60	61	62	62	63	137
11–06	56	56	57	57	58	59	59	60	61	61	62	63	138
11–07	55	56	57	57	58	59	59	60	61	61	62	62	139
11–08	55	56	56	57	58	58	59	60	60	61	62	62	140
11–09	55	56	56	57	57	58	59	59	60	61	61	62	141
11–10	55	55	56	57	57	58	59	59	60	60	61	62	142
11–11	55	55	56	56	57	58	58	59	60	60	61	61	143
12–00	54	55	56	56	57	58	58	59	59	60	61	61	144
12–01	54	55	55	56	57	57	58	58	59	60	60	61	145
12–02	54	54	55	56	56	57	57	58	59	59	60	61	146
12–03	54	54	55	55	56	57	57	58	58	59	60	60	147
12–04	53	54	55	55	56	56	57	58	58	59	59	60	148
12–05	53	54	54	55	55	56	57	57	58	58	59	60	149
12–06	53	53	54	55	55	56	56	57	58	58	59	59	150
12–07	53	53	54	54	55	56	56	57	57	58	58	59	151
12–08	52	53	53	54	55	55	56	56	57	58	58	59	152
12–09	52	53	53	54	54	55	56	56	57	57	58	58	153
12–10	52	52	53	54	54	55	55	56	56	57	58	58	154
12–11	52	52	53	53	54	54	55	56	56	57	57	58	155
13–00	51	52	52	53	54	54	55	55	56	56	57	58	156
13–01	51	52	52	53	53	54	54	55	56	56	57	57	157
13–02	51	52	52	53	53	54	54	55	56	56	57	57	158
13–03	51	51	52	52	53	53	54	54	55	56	56	57	159
13–04	50	51	51	52	52	53	54	54	55	55	56	56	160
13–05	50	51	51	52	52	53	54	54	55	55	56	56	161
13–06	50	50	51	51	52	53	53	54	54	55	55	56	162
13–07	49	50	51	51	52	52	53	53	54	54	55	56	163
13–08	49	50	50	51	52	52	53	53	54	54	55	56	164
13–09	49	50	50	51	51	52	52	53	54	54	55	55	165
13–10	49	49	50	50	51	51	52	53	53	54	54	55	166
13–11	49	49	50	50	51	51	52	52	53	54	54	55	167
	72	73	74	75	76	77	78	79	80	81	82	83	TOTAL MONTHS

MA 6–0 / CA 11–0

CHRONOLOGICAL AGE YEARS MONTHS	6 0	6 1	6 2	6 3	6 4	6 5	6 6	6 7	6 8	6 9	6 10	6 11	
14–00	48	49	49	50	50	51	52	52	53	53	54	54	168
14–01	48	49	49	50	50	51	51	52	52	53	53	54	169
14–02	48	48	49	50	50	51	51	52	52	53	53	54	170
14–03	48	48	49	49	50	50	51	51	52	52	53	54	171
14–04	47	48	48	49	49	50	51	51	52	52	53	53	172
14–05	47	48	48	49	49	50	50	51	52	52	53	53	173
14–06	47	47	48	48	49	50	50	51	51	52	52	53	174
14–07	47	47	48	48	49	49	50	50	51	51	52	53	175
14–08	46	47	48	48	49	49	50	50	51	51	52	52	176
14–09	46	47	47	48	48	49	49	50	50	51	52	52	177
14–10	46	46	47	47	48	49	49	50	50	51	51	52	178
14–11	46	46	47	47	48	48	49	50	50	51	51	52	179
15–00	45	46	47	47	48	48	49	49	50	50	51	51	180
15–01	45	45	46	46	47	48	48	49	49	50	50	51	181
15–02	45	45	46	46	47	47	48	48	49	49	50	51	182
15–03	44	45	45	46	46	47	47	48	48	49	49	50	183
15–04	44	44	45	45	46	46	47	47	48	48	49	49	184
15–05	43	44	44	45	45	46	46	47	48	48	49	49	185
15–06	43	43	44	44	45	45	46	46	47	47	48	49	186
15–07	42	43	43	44	44	45	45	46	46	47	47	48	187
15–08	42	42	43	43	44	45	45	46	46	47	47	48	188
15–09	41	42	42	43	43	44	44	45	46	46	47	47	189
15–10	41	41	42	42	43	43	44	44	45	45	46	47	190
15–11	41	41	42	42	43	43	44	44	45	45	46	46	191
16–00 } 16–02 }	40	40	41	41	42	43	43	44	44	45	45	46	{ 192 { 194
16–03 } 16–07 }	39	40	40	41	41	42	42	43	43	44	44	45	{ 195 { 199
16–08 } 17–00 }	38	39	39	40	40	41	41	42	42	43	43	44	{ 200 { 204
17–01 } 17–05 }	37	38	38	39	39	40	40	41	41	42	42	43	{ 205 { 209
17–06 } 17–10 }	36	37	37	38	38	39	39	40	40	41	41	42	{ 210 { 214
17–11 } 18–00 }	35	36	36	37	37	38	38	39	39	40	41	41	{ 215 { 216
	72	73	74	75	76	77	78	79	80	81	82	83	TOTAL MONTHS

YEARS MONTHS	7-0	7-1	7-2	7-3	7-4	7-5	7-6	7-7	7-8	7-9	7-10	7-11	TOTAL MONTHS
2–00													24
2–01													25
2–02													26
2–03													27
2–04													28
2–05													29
2–06													30
2–07													31
2–08													32
2–09													33
2–10													34
2–11													35
3–00													36
3–01													37
3–02													38
3–03													39
3–04													40
3–05													41
3–06													42
3–07													43
3–08													44
3–09													45
3–10													46
3–11													47
4–00													48
4–01	169												49
4–02	167	169	171										50
4–03	164	166	168	170									51
4–04	161	163	165	167	169								52
4–05	159	161	163	165	167	169	171						53
4–06	157	159	161	162	164	166	168	170					54
4–07	154	156	158	160	162	164	166	168	170				55
4–08	152	154	156	158	159	161	163	165	167	169	171		56
4–09	150	152	153	155	157	159	161	163	165	166	168	170	57
4–10	147	149	151	153	155	157	159	160	162	164	166	168	58
4–11	145	147	149	151	153	154	156	158	160	162	164	165	59
	84	85	86	87	88	89	90	91	92	93	94	95	TOTAL MONTHS

281

MA 7–0 / CA 2–0

YEARS → MONTHS ↓	7 0	7 1	7 2	7 3	7 4	7 5	7 6	7 7	7 8	7 9	7 10	7 11	TOTAL MONTHS
5–00	143	145	147	149	150	152	154	156	158	159	161	163	60
5–01	141	143	145	146	148	150	152	154	155	157	159	161	61
5–02	139	141	142	144	146	148	149	151	153	155	156	158	62
5–03	137	138	140	142	144	145	147	149	151	152	154	156	63
5–04	135	136	138	140	142	143	145	147	149	150	152	154	64
5–05	133	134	136	138	139	141	143	145	146	148	150	152	65
5–06	131	132	134	136	138	139	141	143	144	146	148	149	66
5–07	129	130	132	134	135	137	139	140	142	144	145	147	67
5–08	127	128	130	131	133	135	136	138	140	141	143	145	68
5–09	124	126	128	129	131	133	134	136	137	139	141	142	69
5–10	123	124	126	127	129	130	132	134	135	137	138	140	70
5–11	121	122	124	125	127	129	130	132	133	135	136	138	71
6–00	119	120	122	123	125	127	128	130	131	133	134	136	72
6–01	117	118	120	121	123	124	126	128	129	131	132	134	73
6–02	115	116	118	119	121	122	124	125	127	128	130	131	74
6–03	113	115	116	118	119	121	122	124	125	126	128	129	75
6–04	112	113	114	116	117	119	120	122	123	125	126	127	76
6–05	110	111	113	114	115	117	118	120	121	123	124	125	77
6–06	108	110	111	112	114	115	117	118	119	121	122	123	78
6–07	106	108	109	111	112	113	115	116	117	119	120	122	79
6–08	105	106	108	109	110	112	113	114	116	117	118	120	80
6–09	104	105	106	107	109	110	111	113	114	115	117	118	81
6–10	102	103	105	106	107	109	110	111	113	114	115	116	82
6–11	101	102	103	104	106	107	108	110	111	112	114	115	83
7–00	99	100	102	103	104	106	107	108	109	111	112	113	84
7–01	98	99	100	102	103	104	105	107	108	109	110	112	85
7–02	97	98	99	100	101	103	104	105	106	108	109	110	86
7–03	95	96	98	99	100	101	103	104	105	106	107	109	87
7–04	94	95	96	98	99	100	101	102	104	105	106	107	88
7–05	93	94	95	96	98	99	100	101	102	103	105	106	89
7–06	92	93	94	95	96	97	99	100	101	102	103	104	90
7–07	90	92	93	94	95	96	97	98	100	101	102	103	91
7–08	89	91	92	93	94	95	96	97	98	100	101	102	92
7–09	88	89	91	92	93	94	95	96	97	98	99	101	93
7–10	87	88	89	91	92	93	94	95	96	97	98	99	94
7–11	86	87	88	89	91	92	93	94	95	96	97	98	95
TOTAL MONTHS	84	85	86	87	88	89	90	91	92	93	94	95	

CHRONOLOGICAL AGE

CHRONOLOGICAL AGE (YEARS-MONTHS)	7-0	7-1	7-2	7-3	7-4	7-5	7-6	7-7	7-8	7-9	7-10	7-11	TOTAL MONTHS
8-00	85	86	87	88	90	91	92	93	94	95	96	97	96
8-01	84	85	86	88	89	90	91	92	93	94	95	96	97
8-02	83	84	86	87	88	89	90	91	92	93	94	95	98
8-03	83	84	85	86	87	88	89	90	91	92	93	94	99
8-04	82	83	84	85	86	87	88	89	90	91	92	93	100
8-05	81	82	83	84	85	86	87	88	89	90	91	92	101
8-06	80	81	82	83	84	85	86	87	88	89	90	91	102
8-07	79	80	81	82	83	84	85	86	87	88	89	90	103
8-08	78	79	80	81	82	83	84	85	86	87	88	89	104
8-09	78	79	80	81	82	82	83	84	85	86	87	88	105
8-10	77	78	79	80	81	82	83	83	84	85	86	87	106
8-11	76	77	78	79	80	81	82	83	84	85	86	86	107
9-00	76	76	77	78	79	80	81	82	83	84	85	86	108
9-01	75	76	77	78	79	79	80	81	82	83	84	85	109
9-02	74	75	76	77	78	79	80	80	81	82	83	84	110
9-03	74	75	75	76	77	78	79	80	81	82	82	83	111
9-04	73	74	75	76	77	77	78	79	80	81	82	83	112
9-05	73	73	74	75	76	77	78	79	79	80	81	82	113
9-06	72	73	74	75	75	76	77	78	79	80	80	81	114
9-07	71	72	73	74	75	76	76	77	78	79	80	81	115
9-08	71	72	73	73	74	75	76	77	77	78	79	80	116
9-09	70	71	72	73	74	74	75	76	77	78	79	79	117
9-10	70	71	71	72	73	74	75	75	76	77	78	79	118
9-11	69	70	71	72	73	73	74	75	76	76	77	78	119
10-00	69	70	70	71	72	73	74	74	75	76	77	78	120
10-01	69	69	70	71	72	72	73	74	75	76	76	77	121
10-02	68	69	70	70	71	72	73	73	74	75	76	77	122
10-03	68	69	69	70	71	72	72	73	74	75	75	76	123
10-04	67	68	69	70	70	71	72	73	73	74	75	76	124
10-05	67	68	69	69	70	71	72	72	73	74	75	75	125
10-06	67	68	68	69	70	70	71	72	73	73	74	75	126
10-07	67	67	68	69	69	70	71	72	72	73	74	75	127
10-08	66	67	68	68	69	70	70	71	72	73	73	74	128
10-09	66	67	67	68	69	69	70	71	72	72	73	74	129
10-10	66	66	67	68	68	69	70	71	71	72	73	73	130
10-11	65	66	67	67	68	69	70	70	71	72	72	73	131
TOTAL MONTHS	84	85	86	87	88	89	90	91	92	93	94	95	

MA 7-0 / CA 8-0

YEARS	7	7	7	7	7	7	7	7	7	7	7	7	
MONTHS	0	1	2	3	4	5	6	7	8	9	10	11	
11–00	65	66	66	67	68	69	69	70	71	71	72	73	132
11–01	65	65	66	67	67	68	69	70	70	71	72	72	133
11–02	64	65	66	67	67	68	69	69	70	71	71	72	134
11–03	64	65	66	66	67	68	68	69	70	70	71	72	135
11–04	64	65	65	66	67	67	68	69	69	70	70	71	136
11–05	64	64	65	66	66	67	67	68	69	69	70	71	137
11–06	63	64	65	65	66	67	67	68	69	69	70	70	138
11–07	63	64	64	65	66	66	67	68	68	69	70	70	139
11–08	63	63	64	65	65	66	67	67	68	69	69	70	140
11–09	63	63	64	64	65	66	66	67	68	68	69	69	141
11–10	62	63	64	64	65	65	66	67	67	68	69	69	142
11–11	62	63	63	64	65	65	66	66	67	68	68	69	143
12–00	62	62	63	64	64	65	65	66	67	67	68	69	144
12–01	61	62	63	63	64	64	65	66	66	67	68	68	145
12–02	61	62	62	63	64	64	65	65	66	67	67	68	146
12–03	61	61	62	63	63	64	64	65	66	66	67	67	147
12–04	61	61	62	62	63	64	64	65	65	66	67	67	148
12–05	60	61	61	62	63	63	64	64	65	66	66	67	149
12–06	60	60	61	62	62	63	63	64	65	65	66	66	150
12–07	60	60	61	61	62	63	63	64	64	65	66	66	151
12–08	59	60	60	61	62	62	63	63	64	65	65	66	152
12–09	59	60	60	61	61	62	62	63	64	64	65	65	153
12–10	59	59	60	60	61	62	62	63	63	64	65	65	154
12–11	58	59	60	60	61	61	62	62	63	64	64	65	155
13–00	58	59	59	60	60	61	62	62	63	63	64	64	156
13–01	58	58	59	60	60	61	61	62	62	63	63	64	157
13–02	58	58	59	59	60	61	61	62	62	63	63	64	158
13–03	57	58	58	59	60	60	61	61	62	62	63	63	159
13–04	57	57	58	59	59	60	60	61	61	62	63	63	160
13–05	57	57	58	59	59	60	60	61	61	62	63	63	161
13–06	56	57	58	58	59	59	60	60	61	61	62	63	162
13–07	56	57	57	58	58	59	59	60	61	61	62	62	163
13–08	56	57	57	58	58	59	59	60	61	61	62	62	164
13–09	56	56	57	57	58	58	59	60	60	61	61	62	165
13–10	55	56	56	57	58	58	59	59	60	60	61	61	166
13–11	55	56	56	57	57	58	59	59	60	60	61	61	167
	84	85	86	87	88	89	90	91	92	93	94	95	TOTAL MONTHS

CHRONOLOGICAL AGE

YEARS → MONTHS →	7 0	7 1	7 2	7 3	7 4	7 5	7 6	7 7	7 8	7 9	7 10	7 11	
14-00	55	55	56	57	57	58	58	59	59	60	60	61	168
14-01	55	55	56	56	57	57	58	58	59	59	60	61	169
14-02	54	55	56	56	57	57	58	58	59	59	60	60	170
14-03	54	55	55	56	56	57	57	58	58	59	60	60	171
14-04	54	54	55	55	56	57	57	58	58	59	59	60	172
14-05	54	54	55	55	56	56	57	57	58	59	59	60	173
14-06	53	54	54	55	56	56	57	57	58	58	59	59	174
14-07	53	54	54	55	55	56	56	57	57	58	58	59	175
14-08	53	53	54	55	55	56	56	57	57	58	58	59	176
14-09	53	53	54	54	55	55	56	56	57	57	58	59	177
14-10	52	53	53	54	54	55	56	56	57	57	58	58	178
14-11	52	53	53	54	54	55	55	56	56	57	58	58	179
15-00	52	52	53	53	54	55	55	56	56	57	57	58	180
15-01	51	52	52	53	53	54	54	55	56	56	57	57	181
15-02	51	52	52	53	53	54	54	55	55	56	56	57	182
15-03	50	51	52	52	53	53	54	54	55	55	56	56	183
15-04	50	50	51	51	52	53	53	54	54	55	55	56	184
15-05	50	50	51	51	52	52	53	53	54	54	55	56	185
15-06	49	50	50	51	51	52	52	53	53	54	54	55	186
15-07	48	49	50	50	51	51	52	52	53	53	54	54	187
15-08	48	49	49	50	50	51	51	52	53	53	54	54	188
15-09	48	48	49	49	50	50	51	51	52	52	53	53	189
15-10	47	48	48	49	49	50	50	51	51	52	52	53	190
15-11	47	47	48	48	49	49	50	51	51	52	52	53	191
16-00 / 16-02	46	47	47	48	48	49	49	50	50	51	51	52	192 / 194
16-03 / 16-07	45	46	46	47	47	48	48	49	49	50	50	51	195 / 199
16-08 / 17-00	44	45	45	46	46	47	47	48	48	49	49	50	200 / 204
17-01 / 17-05	43	44	44	45	45	46	46	47	47	48	48	49	205 / 209
17-06 / 17-10	42	43	43	44	44	45	45	46	46	47	47	48	210 / 214
17-11 / 18-00	42	42	43	43	44	44	45	46	46	47	47	48	215 / 216
	84	85	86	87	88	89	90	91	92	93	94	95	TOTAL MONTHS

CHRONOLOGICAL AGE

285

MA 7-0 / CA 14-0

YEARS / MONTHS	8 0	8 1	8 2	8 3	8 4	8 5	8 6	8 7	8 8	8 9	8 10	8 11	TOTAL MONTHS
4–00													48
4–01													49
4–02													50
4–03													51
4–04													52
4–05													53
4–06													54
4–07													55
4–08													56
4–09													57
4–10	170												58
4–11	167	169	171										59
5–00	165	167	169	170									60
5–01	162	164	166	168	170								61
5–02	160	162	164	165	167	169	171						62
5–03	158	160	161	163	165	167	168	170					63
5–04	156	157	159	161	162	164	166	168	169				64
5–05	153	155	157	158	160	162	164	165	167	169	170		65
5–06	151	153	155	156	158	160	161	163	165	166	168	170	66
5–07	149	150	152	154	155	157	159	160	162	164	165	167	67
5–08	146	148	150	151	153	155	156	158	160	161	163	164	68
5–09	144	146	147	149	150	152	154	155	157	159	160	162	69
5–10	142	143	145	146	148	150	151	153	154	156	158	159	70
5–11	140	141	143	144	146	147	149	151	152	154	155	157	71
6–00	137	139	140	142	144	145	147	148	150	151	153	154	72
6–01	135	137	138	140	141	143	144	146	147	149	150	152	73
6–02	133	134	136	137	139	140	142	143	145	146	148	149	74
6–03	131	132	134	135	137	138	140	141	143	144	146	147	75
6–04	129	130	132	133	135	136	138	139	140	142	143	145	76
6–05	127	128	130	131	133	134	135	137	138	140	141	142	77
6–06	125	126	128	129	130	132	133	135	136	137	139	140	78
6–07	123	124	126	127	129	130	131	133	134	135	137	138	79
6–08	121	123	124	125	127	128	129	131	132	133	135	136	80
6–09	119	121	122	123	125	126	127	129	130	131	133	134	81
6–10	118	119	120	122	123	124	126	127	128	130	131	132	82
6–11	116	117	119	120	121	123	124	125	126	128	129	130	83
	96	97	98	99	100	101	102	103	104	105	106	107	TOTAL MONTHS

CHRONOLOGICAL AGE

MENTAL AGE

CHRONOLOGICAL AGE (YEARS–MONTHS)	8-0	8-1	8-2	8-3	8-4	8-5	8-6	8-7	8-8	8-9	8-10	8-11	TOTAL MONTHS
7–00	114	116	117	118	120	121	122	123	125	126	127	128	84
7–01	113	114	115	117	118	119	120	122	123	124	125	127	85
7–02	111	113	114	115	116	117	119	120	121	122	124	125	86
7–03	110	111	112	113	115	116	117	118	120	121	122	123	87
7–04	108	110	111	112	113	114	115	117	118	119	120	121	88
7–05	107	108	109	110	112	113	114	115	116	118	119	120	89
7–06	106	107	108	109	110	111	112	114	115	116	117	118	90
7–07	104	105	106	108	109	110	111	112	113	114	116	117	91
7–08	103	104	105	106	107	109	110	111	112	113	114	115	92
7–09	102	103	104	105	106	107	108	109	110	112	113	114	93
7–10	100	101	103	104	105	106	107	108	109	110	111	112	94
7–11	99	100	101	102	103	105	106	107	108	109	110	111	95
8–00	98	99	100	101	102	103	104	105	106	108	109	110	96
8–01	97	98	99	100	101	102	103	104	105	106	107	108	97
8–02	96	97	98	99	100	101	102	103	104	105	106	107	98
8–03	95	96	97	98	99	100	101	102	103	104	105	106	99
8–04	94	95	96	97	98	99	100	101	102	103	104	105	100
8–05	93	94	95	96	97	98	99	100	101	102	103	104	101
8–06	92	93	94	95	96	97	98	99	100	101	102	103	102
8–07	91	92	93	94	95	96	97	98	99	100	101	102	103
8–08	90	91	92	93	94	95	96	97	98	99	99	100	104
8–09	89	90	91	92	93	94	95	96	97	98	99	99	105
8–10	88	89	90	91	92	93	94	95	96	97	97	98	106
8–11	87	88	89	90	91	92	93	94	95	96	97	97	107
9–00	86	87	88	89	90	91	92	93	94	95	96	96	108
9–01	86	87	88	88	89	90	91	92	93	94	95	96	109
9–02	85	86	87	88	88	89	90	91	92	93	94	95	110
9–03	84	85	86	87	88	89	89	90	91	92	93	94	111
9–04	83	84	85	86	87	88	89	90	90	91	92	93	112
9–05	83	84	85	85	86	87	88	89	90	91	91	92	113
9–06	82	83	84	85	86	86	87	88	89	90	91	91	114
9–07	81	82	83	84	85	86	86	87	88	89	90	91	115
9–08	81	82	82	83	84	85	86	87	87	88	89	90	116
9–09	80	81	82	83	83	84	85	86	87	87	88	89	117
9–10	79	80	81	82	83	83	84	85	86	87	88	88	118
9–11	79	80	80	81	82	83	84	84	85	86	87	88	119
TOTAL MONTHS	96	97	98	99	100	101	102	103	104	105	106	107	

287

MA 8–0 / CA 7–0

YEARS MONTHS	8 0	8 1	8 2	8 3	8 4	8 5	8 6	8 7	8 8	8 9	8 10	8 11	
10–00	78	79	80	81	81	82	83	84	85	85	86	87	120
10–01	78	79	79	80	81	82	83	83	84	85	86	86	121
10–02	77	78	79	80	80	81	82	83	83	84	85	86	122
10–03	77	78	78	79	80	81	81	82	83	84	85	85	123
10–04	76	77	78	79	79	80	81	82	83	83	84	85	124
10–05	76	77	77	78	79	80	80	81	82	83	83	84	125
10–06	76	76	77	78	79	79	80	81	81	82	83	84	126
10–07	75	76	77	77	78	79	80	80	81	82	82	83	127
10–08	75	75	76	77	78	78	79	80	81	81	82	83	128
10–09	74	75	76	77	77	78	79	79	80	81	82	82	129
10–10	74	75	75	76	77	78	78	79	80	80	81	82	130
10–11	74	74	75	76	76	77	78	79	79	80	81	81	131
11–00	73	74	75	75	76	77	77	78	79	80	80	81	132
11–01	73	74	74	75	76	76	77	78	78	79	80	80	133
11–02	73	73	74	75	75	76	77	77	78	79	79	80	134
11–03	72	73	74	74	75	76	76	77	78	78	79	80	135
11–04	72	72	73	74	74	75	76	76	77	78	78	79	136
11–05	71	72	73	73	74	75	75	76	77	77	78	79	137
11–06	71	72	72	73	74	74	75	76	76	77	78	78	138
11–07	71	71	72	73	73	74	75	75	76	77	77	78	139
11–08	70	71	72	72	73	74	74	75	76	76	77	77	140
11–09	70	71	71	72	73	73	74	74	75	76	76	77	141
11–10	70	70	71	72	72	73	74	74	75	75	76	77	142
11–11	70	70	71	71	72	73	73	74	74	75	76	76	143
12–00	69	70	70	71	72	72	73	73	74	75	75	76	144
12–01	69	69	70	71	71	72	72	73	74	74	75	75	145
12–02	68	69	70	70	71	71	72	73	73	74	74	75	146
12–03	68	69	69	70	71	71	72	72	73	74	74	75	147
12–04	68	68	69	70	70	71	71	72	72	73	74	74	148
12–05	67	68	68	69	70	70	71	71	72	73	73	74	149
12–06	67	68	68	69	69	70	71	71	72	72	73	73	150
12–07	67	67	68	68	69	70	70	71	71	72	73	73	151
12–08	66	67	67	68	69	69	70	70	71	72	72	73	152
12–09	66	67	67	68	68	69	69	70	71	71	72	72	153
12–10	66	66	67	67	68	69	69	70	70	71	71	72	154
12–11	65	66	67	67	68	68	69	69	70	71	71	72	155
	96	97	98	99	100	101	102	103	104	105	106	107	TOTAL MONTHS

CHRONOLOGICAL AGE

MA 8–0 / CA 10–0

288

YEARS MONTHS	8 0	8 1	8 2	8 3	8 4	8 5	8 6	8 7	8 8	8 9	8 10	8 11	
13–00	65	66	66	67	67	68	68	69	70	70	71	71	156
13–01	65	65	66	66	67	67	68	69	69	70	70	71	157
13–02	65	65	66	66	67	67	68	69	69	70	70	71	158
13–03	64	65	65	66	66	67	67	68	69	69	70	70	159
13–04	64	64	65	65	66	66	67	68	68	69	69	70	160
13–05	64	64	65	65	66	66	67	68	68	69	69	70	161
13–06	63	64	64	65	65	66	67	67	68	68	69	69	162
13–07	63	63	64	64	65	66	66	67	67	68	68	69	163
13–08	63	63	64	64	65	66	66	67	67	68	68	69	164
13–09	62	63	63	64	65	65	66	66	67	67	68	68	165
13–10	62	63	63	64	64	65	65	66	66	67	67	68	166
13–11	62	62	63	63	64	65	65	66	66	67	67	68	167
14–00	61	62	63	63	64	64	65	65	66	66	67	68	168
14–01	61	62	62	63	63	64	64	65	65	66	67	67	169
14–02	61	62	62	63	63	64	64	65	65	66	67	67	170
14–03	61	61	62	62	63	63	64	64	65	66	66	67	171
14–04	60	61	61	62	62	63	64	64	65	65	66	66	172
14–05	60	61	61	62	62	63	63	64	65	65	66	66	173
14–06	60	60	61	61	62	63	63	64	64	65	65	66	174
14–07	60	60	61	61	62	62	63	63	64	64	65	65	175
14–08	59	60	60	61	62	62	63	63	64	64	65	65	176
14–09	59	60	60	61	61	62	62	63	63	64	64	65	177
14–10	59	59	60	60	61	61	62	62	63	64	64	65	178
14–11	59	59	60	60	61	61	62	62	63	63	64	65	179
15–00	58	59	59	60	60	61	61	62	63	63	64	64	180
15–01	58	58	59	59	60	60	61	61	62	62	63	64	181
15–02	57	58	59	59	60	60	61	61	62	62	63	63	182
15–03	57	57	58	58	59	60	60	61	61	62	62	63	183
15–04	56	57	57	58	58	59	59	60	60	61	62	62	184
15–05	56	57	57	58	58	59	59	60	60	61	61	62	185
15–06	55	56	57	57	58	58	59	59	60	60	61	61	186
15–07	55	55	56	56	57	57	58	59	59	60	60	61	187
15–08	55	55	56	56	57	57	58	58	59	59	60	60	188
15–09	54	55	55	56	56	57	57	58	58	59	59	60	189
15–10	53	54	54	55	56	56	57	57	58	58	59	59	190
15–11	53	54	54	55	55	56	56	57	57	58	58	59	191
	96	97	98	99	100	101	102	103	104	105	106	107	TOTAL MONTHS

CHRONOLOGICAL AGE

MA 8–0 / CA 13–0

YEARS	8	8	8	8	8	8	8	8	8	8	8	8	
MONTHS	0	1	2	3	4	5	6	7	8	9	10	11	
16–00 } 16–02 }	52	53	53	54	55	55	56	56	57	57	58	58	{ 192 { 194
16–03 } 16–07 }	51	52	52	53	54	54	55	55	56	56	57	57	{ 195 { 199
16–08 } 17–00 }	50	51	51	52	53	53	54	54	55	55	56	56	{ 200 { 204
17–01 } 17–05 }	49	50	50	51	52	52	53	53	54	54	55	55	{ 205 { 209
17–06 } 17–10 }	48	49	49	50	51	51	52	52	53	53	54	54	{ 210 { 214
17–11 } 18–00 }	48	49	49	50	51	51	52	52	53	53	54	54	{ 215 { 216
	96	97	98	99	100	101	102	103	104	105	106	107	TOTAL MONTHS

CHRONOLOGICAL AGE

YEARS MONTHS	9 0	9 1	9 2	9 3	9 4	9 5	9 6	9 7	9 8	9 9	9 10	9 11	TOTAL MONTHS
4–00													48
4–01													49
4–02													50
4–03													51
4–04													52
4–05													53
4–06													54
4–07													55
4–08													56
4–09													57
4–10													58
4–11													59
5–00													60
5–01													61
5–02													62
5–03													63
5–04													64
5–05													65
5–06													66
5–07	169	170											67
5–08	166	168	169										68
5–09	163	165	167	168	170								69
5–10	161	162	164	166	167	169	170						70
5–11	158	160	162	163	165	166	168	169					71
6–00	156	158	159	161	162	164	165	167	168	170			72
6–01	153	155	156	158	159	161	162	164	166	167	169	170	73
6–02	151	152	154	155	157	158	160	161	163	164	166	167	74
6–03	149	150	151	153	154	156	157	159	160	162	163	165	75
6–04	146	148	149	151	152	153	155	156	158	159	161	162	76
6–05	144	145	147	148	150	151	152	154	155	157	158	160	77
6–06	142	143	144	146	147	149	150	151	153	154	156	157	78
6–07	140	141	142	144	145	146	148	149	151	152	153	155	79
6–08	137	139	140	141	143	144	146	147	148	150	151	152	80
6–09	135	137	138	139	141	142	143	145	146	147	149	150	81
6–10	134	135	136	137	139	140	141	143	144	145	147	148	82
6–11	132	133	134	135	137	138	139	141	142	143	144	146	83
TOTAL MONTHS	108	109	110	111	112	113	114	115	116	117	118	119	

CHRONOLOGICAL AGE

291

MA 9–0 / CA 4–0

YEARS MONTHS	9-0	9-1	9-2	9-3	9-4	9-5	9-6	9-7	9-8	9-9	9-10	9-11	
7-00	130	131	132	134	135	136	137	139	140	141	142	144	84
7-01	128	129	130	132	133	134	135	137	138	139	140	142	85
7-02	126	127	129	130	131	132	133	135	136	137	138	140	86
7-03	124	126	127	128	129	130	132	133	134	135	137	138	87
7-04	123	124	125	126	127	129	130	131	132	133	135	136	88
7-05	121	122	123	125	126	127	128	129	130	132	133	134	89
7-06	119	121	122	123	124	125	126	128	129	130	131	132	90
7-07	118	119	120	121	122	124	125	126	127	128	129	130	91
7-08	116	118	119	120	121	122	123	124	125	127	128	129	92
7-09	115	116	117	118	119	120	122	123	124	125	126	127	93
7-10	113	115	116	117	118	119	120	121	122	123	124	125	94
7-11	112	113	114	115	116	117	119	120	121	122	123	124	95
8-00	111	112	113	114	115	116	117	118	119	120	121	122	96
8-01	110	111	112	113	114	115	116	117	118	119	120	121	97
8-02	108	109	110	111	112	113	114	115	117	118	119	120	98
8-03	107	108	109	110	111	112	113	114	115	116	117	118	99
8-04	106	107	108	109	110	111	112	113	114	115	116	117	100
8-05	105	106	107	108	109	110	111	112	113	114	115	116	101
8-06	104	105	106	107	108	109	110	110	111	112	113	114	102
8-07	102	103	104	105	106	107	108	109	110	111	112	113	103
8-08	101	102	103	104	105	106	107	108	109	110	111	112	104
8-09	100	101	102	103	104	105	106	107	108	109	110	111	105
8-10	99	100	101	102	103	104	105	106	107	108	109	110	106
8-11	98	99	100	101	102	103	104	105	106	107	108	109	107
9-00	97	98	99	100	101	102	103	104	105	106	106	107	108
9-01	97	97	98	99	100	101	102	103	104	105	105	106	109
9-02	96	96	97	98	99	100	101	102	103	104	104	105	110
9-03	95	96	96	97	98	99	100	101	102	103	103	104	111
9-04	94	95	96	96	97	98	99	100	101	102	103	103	112
9-05	93	94	95	96	96	97	98	99	100	101	102	102	113
9-06	92	93	94	95	96	97	97	98	99	100	101	102	114
9-07	91	92	93	94	95	96	96	97	98	99	100	101	115
9-08	91	91	92	93	94	95	96	96	97	98	99	100	116
9-09	90	91	92	92	93	94	95	96	96	97	98	99	117
9-10	89	90	91	92	92	93	94	95	96	96	97	98	118
9-11	88	89	90	91	92	92	93	94	95	96	96	97	119
TOTAL MONTHS	108	109	110	111	112	113	114	115	116	117	118	119	

CHRONOLOGICAL AGE

CHRONOLOGICAL AGE (YEARS–MONTHS)	9-0	9-1	9-2	9-3	9-4	9-5	9-6	9-7	9-8	9-9	9-10	9-11	TOTAL MONTHS
10–00	88	89	89	90	91	92	92	93	94	95	96	96	120
10–01	87	88	89	90	90	91	92	93	93	94	95	96	121
10–02	87	87	88	89	90	90	91	92	93	93	94	95	122
10–03	86	87	88	88	89	90	91	91	92	93	94	94	123
10–04	86	86	87	88	89	89	90	91	92	92	93	94	124
10–05	85	86	86	87	88	89	89	90	91	92	92	93	125
10–06	84	85	86	87	87	88	89	90	90	91	92	92	126
10–07	84	85	85	86	87	88	88	89	90	90	91	92	127
10–08	83	84	85	86	86	87	88	88	89	90	91	91	128
10–09	83	84	84	85	86	86	87	88	89	89	90	91	129
10–10	83	83	84	85	85	86	87	87	88	89	90	90	130
10–11	82	83	83	84	85	85	86	87	88	88	89	90	131
11–00	82	82	83	84	84	85	86	86	87	88	88	89	132
11–01	81	82	82	83	84	84	85	86	86	87	88	89	133
11–02	81	81	82	83	83	84	85	85	86	87	87	88	134
11–03	80	81	82	82	83	84	84	85	86	86	87	88	135
11–04	80	80	81	82	82	83	84	84	85	86	86	87	136
11–05	79	80	81	81	82	83	83	84	85	85	86	86	137
11–06	79	80	80	81	81	82	83	83	84	85	85	86	138
11–07	79	79	80	80	81	82	82	83	84	84	85	86	139
11–08	78	79	79	80	81	81	82	83	83	84	84	85	140
11–09	78	78	79	80	80	81	81	82	83	83	84	85	141
11–10	77	78	79	79	80	80	81	82	82	83	84	84	142
11–11	77	78	78	79	79	80	81	81	82	83	83	84	143
12–00	77	77	78	78	79	80	80	81	81	82	83	83	144
12–01	76	77	77	78	79	79	80	80	81	82	82	83	145
12–02	76	76	77	78	78	79	79	80	81	81	82	82	146
12–03	75	76	77	77	78	78	79	80	80	81	81	82	147
12–04	75	75	76	77	77	78	78	79	80	80	81	81	148
12–05	74	75	76	76	77	77	78	79	79	80	80	81	149
12–06	74	75	75	76	76	77	78	78	79	79	80	81	150
12–07	74	74	75	76	76	77	77	78	78	79	80	80	151
12–08	73	74	74	75	76	76	77	77	78	79	79	80	152
12–09	73	73	74	75	75	76	76	77	78	78	79	79	153
12–10	73	73	74	74	75	75	76	77	77	78	78	79	154
12–11	72	73	73	74	75	75	76	76	77	77	78	79	155
TOTAL MONTHS	108	109	110	111	112	113	114	115	116	117	118	119	

MA 9–0 / CA 10–0

YEARS MONTHS	9 0	9 1	9 2	9 3	9 4	9 5	9 6	9 7	9 8	9 9	9 10	9 11	
13–00	72	72	73	74	74	75	75	76	76	77	78	78	156
13–01	71	72	73	73	74	74	75	75	76	77	77	78	157
13–02	71	72	73	73	74	74	75	75	76	76	77	78	158
13–03	71	71	72	73	73	74	74	75	75	76	76	77	159
13–04	70	71	72	72	73	73	74	74	75	75	76	77	160
13–05	70	71	72	72	73	73	74	74	75	75	76	77	161
13–06	70	70	71	72	72	73	73	74	74	75	75	76	162
13–07	69	70	71	71	72	72	73	73	74	74	75	76	163
13–08	69	70	71	71	72	72	73	73	74	74	75	76	164
13–09	69	70	70	71	71	72	72	73	73	74	75	75	165
13–10	69	69	70	70	71	71	72	72	73	74	74	75	166
13–11	68	69	70	70	71	71	72	72	73	73	74	75	167
14–00	68	69	69	70	70	71	71	72	72	73	74	74	168
14–01	68	68	69	69	70	70	71	72	72	73	73	74	169
14–02	68	68	69	69	70	70	71	71	72	73	73	74	170
14–03	67	68	68	69	69	70	70	71	72	72	73	73	171
14–04	67	67	68	68	69	70	70	71	71	72	72	73	172
14–05	67	67	68	68	69	69	70	71	71	72	72	73	173
14–06	66	67	67	68	69	69	70	70	71	71	72	72	174
14–07	66	67	67	68	68	69	69	70	70	71	71	72	175
14–08	66	66	67	68	68	69	69	70	70	71	71	72	176
14–09	66	66	67	67	68	68	69	69	70	70	71	71	177
14–10	65	66	66	67	67	68	68	69	69	70	70	71	178
14–11	65	66	66	67	67	68	68	69	69	70	70	71	179
15–00	65	65	66	66	67	67	68	68	69	69	70	71	180
15–01	64	65	65	66	66	67	67	68	68	69	69	70	181
15–02	64	64	65	65	66	67	67	68	68	69	69	70	182
15–03	63	64	64	65	65	66	66	67	68	68	69	69	183
15–04	63	63	64	64	65	65	66	66	67	67	68	68	184
15–05	62	63	64	64	65	65	66	66	67	67	68	68	185
15–06	62	62	63	63	64	64	65	66	66	67	67	68	186
15–07	61	62	62	63	63	64	64	65	65	66	66	67	187
15–08	61	62	62	63	63	64	64	65	65	66	66	67	188
15–09	60	61	61	62	62	63	64	64	65	65	66	66	189
15–10	60	60	61	61	62	62	63	63	64	64	65	66	190
15–11	60	60	61	61	62	62	63	63	64	64	65	65	191
TOTAL MONTHS	108	109	110	111	112	113	114	115	116	117	118	119	

CHRONOLOGICAL AGE

YEARS MONTHS	9 0	9 1	9 2	9 3	9 4	9 5	9 6	9 7	9 8	9 9	9 10	9 11	
16–00 ⎰ 16–02 ⎱	59	59	60	60	61	62	62	63	63	64	64	65	⎰192 ⎱194
16–03 ⎰ 16–07 ⎱	58	59	59	60	60	61	61	62	62	63	64	64	⎰195 ⎱199
16–08 ⎰ 17–00 ⎱	57	58	58	59	59	60	60	61	61	62	63	63	⎰200 ⎱204
17–01 ⎰ 17–05 ⎱	56	57	57	58	58	59	59	60	60	61	62	62	⎰205 ⎱209
17–06 ⎰ 17–10 ⎱	55	56	56	57	57	58	58	59	59	60	61	61	⎰210 ⎱214
17–11 ⎰ 18–00 ⎱	55	56	56	57	57	58	58	59	59	60	61	61	⎰215 ⎱216
	108	109	110	111	112	113	114	115	116	117	118	119	TOTAL MONTHS

CHRONOLOGICAL AGE

MA 9–0 / CA 16–0

YEARS MONTHS	10 0	10 1	10 2	10 3	10 4	10 5	10 6	10 7	10 8	10 9	10 10	10 11	
5–00													60
5–01													61
5–02													62
5–03													63
5–04													64
5–05													65
5–06													66
5–07													67
5–08													68
5–09													69
5–10													70
5–11													71
6–00													72
6–01													73
6–02	169	170											74
6–03	166	168	169	171									75
6–04	164	165	166	168	169								76
6–05	161	162	164	165	167	168	170						77
6–06	158	160	161	163	164	165	167	168	170				78
6–07	156	157	159	160	162	163	164	166	167	168	170		79
6–08	154	155	156	158	159	160	162	163	164	166	167	169	80
6–09	151	153	154	155	157	158	159	161	162	163	165	166	81
6–10	149	151	152	153	155	156	157	158	160	161	162	164	82
6–11	147	148	150	151	152	154	155	156	157	159	160	161	83
7–00	145	146	148	149	150	151	153	154	155	156	158	159	84
7–01	143	144	145	147	148	149	150	152	153	154	155	157	85
7–02	141	142	143	145	146	147	148	150	151	152	153	154	86
7–03	139	140	141	143	144	145	146	147	149	150	151	152	87
7–04	137	138	139	141	142	143	144	145	147	148	149	150	88
7–05	135	136	138	139	140	141	142	143	145	146	147	148	89
7–06	133	135	136	137	138	139	140	141	143	144	145	146	90
7–07	132	133	134	135	136	137	138	140	141	142	143	144	91
7–08	130	131	132	133	134	136	137	138	139	140	141	142	92
7–09	128	129	130	132	133	134	135	136	137	138	139	140	93
7–10	127	128	129	130	131	132	133	134	135	136	137	139	94
7–11	125	126	127	128	129	130	131	133	134	135	136	137	95
TOTAL MONTHS	120	121	122	123	124	125	126	127	128	129	130	131	

CHRONOLOGICAL AGE

MA 10–0 / CA 5–0

MENTAL AGE

YEARS / MONTHS	10 0	10 1	10 2	10 3	10 4	10 5	10 6	10 7	10 8	10 9	10 10	10 11	
8–00	123	125	126	127	128	129	130	131	132	133	134	135	96
8–01	122	123	124	125	126	127	128	129	130	131	133	134	97
8–02	121	122	123	124	125	126	127	128	129	130	131	132	98
8–03	119	120	121	122	123	124	125	126	127	128	129	130	99
8–04	118	119	120	121	122	123	124	125	126	127	128	129	100
8–05	117	118	119	120	121	122	123	124	125	126	127	128	101
8–06	115	116	117	118	119	120	121	122	123	124	125	126	102
8–07	114	115	116	117	118	119	120	121	122	123	124	125	103
8–08	113	114	115	116	117	118	119	120	120	121	122	123	104
8–09	112	113	114	115	115	116	117	118	119	120	121	122	105
8–10	111	111	112	113	114	115	116	117	118	119	120	121	106
8–11	109	110	111	112	113	114	115	116	117	118	119	120	107
9–00	108	109	110	111	112	113	114	115	116	116	117	118	108
9–01	107	108	109	110	111	112	113	114	114	115	116	117	109
9–02	106	107	108	109	110	111	112	112	113	114	115	116	110
9–03	105	106	107	108	109	110	110	111	112	113	114	115	111
9–04	104	105	106	107	108	109	109	110	111	112	113	114	112
9–05	103	104	105	106	107	108	108	109	110	111	112	113	113
9–06	102	103	104	105	106	107	107	108	109	110	111	112	114
9–07	101	102	103	104	105	106	106	107	108	109	110	111	115
9–08	101	101	102	103	104	105	106	106	107	108	109	110	116
9–09	100	101	101	102	103	104	105	105	106	107	108	109	117
9–10	99	100	100	101	102	103	104	104	105	106	107	108	118
9–11	98	99	100	100	101	102	103	104	104	105	106	107	119
10–00	97	98	99	100	100	101	102	103	104	104	105	106	120
10–01	97	97	98	99	100	100	101	102	103	104	104	105	121
10–02	96	97	97	98	99	100	100	101	102	103	103	104	122
10–03	95	96	97	97	98	99	100	100	101	102	103	104	123
10–04	95	95	96	97	98	98	99	100	101	101	102	103	124
10–05	94	95	95	96	97	98	98	99	100	101	101	102	125
10–06	93	94	95	95	96	97	98	98	99	100	101	101	126
10–07	93	93	94	95	96	96	97	98	98	99	100	101	127
10–08	92	93	93	94	95	96	96	97	98	98	99	100	128
10–09	91	92	93	94	94	95	96	96	97	98	99	99	129
10–10	91	92	92	93	94	94	95	96	97	97	98	99	130
10–11	90	91	92	92	93	94	94	95	96	97	97	98	131
TOTAL MONTHS	120	121	122	123	124	125	126	127	128	129	130	131	

CHRONOLOGICAL AGE

MA 10–0 / CA 8–0

YEARS → MONTHS ↓	10 0	10 1	10 2	10 3	10 4	10 5	10 6	10 7	10 8	10 9	10 10	10 11	TOTAL MONTHS
11–00	90	91	91	92	93	93	94	95	95	96	97	97	132
11–01	89	90	91	91	92	93	93	94	95	95	96	97	133
11–02	89	89	90	91	91	92	93	93	94	95	95	96	134
11–03	88	89	90	90	91	92	92	93	94	94	95	96	135
11–04	88	88	89	90	90	91	92	92	93	94	94	95	136
11–05	87	88	88	89	90	90	91	92	92	93	94	94	137
11–06	87	87	88	89	89	90	91	91	92	93	93	94	138
11–07	86	87	88	88	89	89	90	91	91	92	93	93	139
11–08	86	86	87	88	88	89	90	90	91	91	92	93	140
11–09	85	86	86	87	88	88	89	90	90	91	92	92	141
11–10	85	85	86	87	87	88	89	89	90	90	91	92	142
11–11	84	85	86	86	87	87	88	89	89	90	91	91	143
12–00	84	85	85	86	86	87	88	88	89	89	90	91	144
12–01	83	84	85	85	86	86	87	88	88	89	89	90	145
12–02	83	84	84	85	85	86	87	87	88	88	89	90	146
12–03	83	83	84	84	85	86	86	87	87	88	89	89	147
12–04	82	83	83	84	84	85	86	86	87	87	88	89	148
12–05	82	82	83	83	84	85	85	86	86	87	88	88	149
12–06	81	82	82	83	84	84	85	85	86	86	87	88	150
12–07	81	81	82	83	83	84	84	85	85	86	87	87	151
12–08	80	81	81	82	83	83	84	84	85	86	86	87	152
12–09	80	80	81	82	82	83	83	84	84	85	86	86	153
12–10	79	80	81	81	82	82	83	84	84	85	85	86	154
12–11	79	80	80	81	81	82	83	83	84	84	85	85	155
13–00	79	79	80	80	81	82	82	83	83	84	84	85	156
13–01	78	79	79	80	80	81	82	82	83	83	84	84	157
13–02	78	79	79	80	80	81	82	82	83	83	84	84	158
13–03	78	78	79	79	80	80	81	82	82	83	83	84	159
13–04	77	78	78	79	79	80	81	81	82	82	83	83	160
13–05	77	78	78	79	79	80	81	81	82	82	83	83	161
13–06	77	77	78	78	79	79	80	81	81	82	82	83	162
13–07	76	77	77	78	78	79	79	80	81	81	82	82	163
13–08	76	77	77	78	78	79	79	80	81	81	82	82	164
13–09	76	76	77	77	78	78	79	80	80	81	81	82	165
13–10	75	76	76	77	77	78	79	79	80	80	81	81	166
13–11	75	76	76	77	77	78	78	79	80	80	81	81	167
TOTAL MONTHS	120	121	122	123	124	125	126	127	128	129	130	131	

CHRONOLOGICAL AGE

MA 10–0 / CA 11–0

YEARS MONTHS	10 0	10 1	10 2	10 3	10 4	10 5	10 6	10 7	10 8	10 9	10 10	10 11	
14–00	75	75	76	76	77	77	78	79	79	80	80	81	168
14–01	74	75	75	76	76	77	78	78	79	79	80	80	169
14–02	74	75	75	76	76	77	77	78	79	79	80	80	170
14–03	74	74	75	75	76	76	77	78	78	79	79	80	171
14–04	73	74	74	75	76	76	77	77	78	78	79	79	172
14–05	73	74	74	75	75	76	77	77	78	78	79	79	173
14–06	73	73	74	74	75	76	76	77	77	78	78	79	174
14–07	72	73	74	74	75	75	76	76	77	77	78	78	175
14–08	72	73	73	74	75	75	76	76	77	77	78	78	176
14–09	72	73	73	74	74	75	75	76	76	77	77	78	177
14–10	72	72	73	73	74	74	75	75	76	76	77	77	178
14–11	72	72	73	73	74	74	75	75	76	76	77	77	179
15–00	71	72	72	73	73	74	74	75	75	76	76	77	180
15–01	70	71	72	72	73	73	74	74	75	75	76	76	181
15–02	70	71	71	72	72	73	73	74	75	75	76	76	182
15–03	70	70	71	71	72	72	73	73	74	74	75	75	183
15–04	69	70	70	71	71	72	72	73	73	74	74	75	184
15–05	69	69	70	70	71	71	72	73	73	74	74	75	185
15–06	68	69	69	70	70	71	71	72	72	73	73	74	186
15–07	68	68	69	69	70	70	71	71	72	72	73	73	187
15–08	67	68	68	69	69	70	71	71	72	72	73	73	188
15–09	67	67	68	68	69	69	70	70	71	71	72	73	189
15–10	66	67	67	68	68	69	69	70	70	71	71	72	190
15–11	66	66	67	67	68	69	69	70	70	71	71	72	191
16–00 / 16–02	65	66	66	67	67	68	68	69	69	70	71	71	192 / 194
16–03 / 16–07	65	65	66	66	67	67	68	69	69	70	70	71	195 / 199
16–08 / 17–00	64	64	65	65	66	66	67	68	68	69	69	70	200 / 204
17–01 / 17–05	63	63	64	64	65	65	66	67	67	68	68	69	205 / 209
17–06 / 17–10	62	62	63	63	64	64	65	66	66	67	67	68	210 / 214
17–11 / 18–00	62	62	63	63	64	64	65	66	66	67	67	68	215 / 216
	120	121	122	123	124	125	126	127	128	129	130	131	TOTAL MONTHS

CHRONOLOGICAL AGE

MA 10-0 / CA 14-0

YEARS MONTHS	11 0	11 1	11 2	11 3	11 4	11 5	11 6	11 7	11 8	11 9	11 10	11 11	
5–00													60
5–01													61
5–02													62
5–03													63
5–04													64
5–05													65
5–06													66
5–07													67
5–08													68
5–09													69
5–10													70
5–11													71
6–00													72
6–01													73
6–02													74
6–03													75
6–04													76
6–05													77
6–06													78
6–07													79
6–08	170												80
6–09	167	169	170										81
6–10	165	166	168	169	170								82
6–11	163	164	165	166	168	169	170						83
7–00	160	161	163	164	165	167	168	169	170				84
7–01	158	159	160	162	163	164	165	167	168	169	170		85
7–02	156	157	158	159	161	162	163	164	166	167	168	169	86
7–03	154	155	156	157	158	160	161	162	163	164	166	167	87
7–04	151	153	154	155	156	157	158	160	161	162	163	164	88
7–05	149	150	152	153	154	155	156	157	159	160	161	162	89
7–06	147	148	150	151	152	153	154	155	157	158	159	160	90
7–07	145	146	148	149	150	151	152	153	154	156	157	158	91
7–08	143	145	146	147	148	149	150	151	152	154	155	156	92
7–09	141	143	144	145	146	147	148	149	150	151	153	154	93
7–10	140	141	142	143	144	145	146	147	148	150	151	152	94
7–11	138	139	140	141	142	143	144	145	147	148	149	150	95
	132	133	134	135	136	137	138	139	140	141	142	143	TOTAL MONTHS

CHRONOLOGICAL AGE

YEARS / MONTHS	11 0	11 1	11 2	11 3	11 4	11 5	11 6	11 7	11 8	11 9	11 10	11 11	
8-00	136	137	138	139	140	141	143	144	145	146	147	148	96
8-01	135	136	137	138	139	140	141	142	143	144	145	146	97
8-02	133	134	135	136	137	138	139	140	141	142	143	144	98
8-03	131	132	133	135	136	137	138	139	140	141	142	143	99
8-04	130	131	132	133	134	135	136	137	138	139	140	141	100
8-05	129	130	131	132	132	133	134	135	136	137	138	139	101
8-06	127	128	129	130	131	132	133	134	135	136	137	138	102
8-07	126	127	128	129	130	131	132	133	133	134	135	136	103
8-08	124	125	126	127	128	129	130	131	132	133	134	135	104
8-09	123	124	125	126	127	128	129	130	131	132	132	133	105
8-10	122	123	124	125	125	126	127	128	129	130	131	132	106
8-11	120	121	122	123	124	125	126	127	128	129	130	131	107
9-00	119	120	121	122	123	124	125	126	126	127	128	129	108
9-01	118	119	120	121	122	123	123	124	125	126	127	128	109
9-02	117	118	119	119	120	121	122	123	124	125	126	127	110
9-03	116	117	117	118	119	120	121	122	123	124	124	125	111
9-04	115	116	116	117	118	119	120	121	122	122	123	124	112
9-05	114	114	115	116	117	118	119	120	120	121	122	123	113
9-06	113	113	114	115	116	117	118	118	119	120	121	122	114
9-07	111	112	113	114	115	116	116	117	118	119	120	121	115
9-08	110	111	112	113	114	115	115	116	117	118	119	120	116
9-09	110	110	111	112	113	114	114	115	116	117	118	118	117
9-10	108	109	110	111	112	113	113	114	115	116	117	117	118
9-11	108	108	109	110	111	112	112	113	114	115	116	116	119
10-00	107	107	108	109	110	111	111	112	113	114	115	115	120
10-01	106	107	107	108	109	110	111	111	112	113	114	114	121
10-02	105	106	107	107	108	109	110	110	111	112	113	113	122
10-03	104	105	106	107	107	108	109	110	110	111	112	113	123
10-04	104	104	105	106	107	107	108	109	110	110	111	112	124
10-05	103	103	104	105	106	106	107	108	109	109	110	111	125
10-06	102	103	104	104	105	106	106	107	108	109	109	110	126
10-07	101	102	103	104	104	105	106	106	107	108	109	109	127
10-08	101	101	102	103	103	104	105	106	106	107	108	109	128
10-09	100	101	101	102	103	104	104	105	106	106	107	108	129
10-10	99	100	101	101	102	103	104	104	105	106	106	107	130
10-11	99	99	100	101	101	102	103	104	104	105	106	106	131
	132	133	134	135	136	137	138	139	140	141	142	143	TOTAL MONTHS

CHRONOLOGICAL AGE

MA 11-0 / CA 8-0

YEARS → MONTHS ↓	11-0	11-1	11-2	11-3	11-4	11-5	11-6	11-7	11-8	11-9	11-10	11-11	TOTAL MONTHS
11-00	98	99	99	100	101	101	102	103	104	104	105	106	132
11-01	97	98	99	99	100	101	101	102	103	103	104	105	133
11-02	97	97	98	99	99	100	101	102	102	103	104	104	134
11-03	96	97	98	98	99	100	100	101	102	102	103	104	135
11-04	96	96	97	98	98	99	100	100	101	102	102	103	136
11-05	95	96	96	97	98	98	99	100	100	101	102	102	137
11-06	94	95	96	96	97	98	98	99	100	100	101	102	138
11-07	94	95	95	96	97	97	98	98	99	100	100	101	139
11-08	93	94	95	95	96	97	97	98	98	99	100	100	140
11-09	93	93	94	95	95	96	97	97	98	98	99	100	141
11-10	92	93	94	94	95	95	96	97	97	98	99	99	142
11-11	92	92	93	94	94	95	96	96	97	97	98	99	143
12-00	91	92	92	93	94	94	95	96	96	97	97	98	144
12-01	91	91	92	93	93	94	94	95	96	96	97	97	145
12-02	90	91	91	92	93	93	94	94	95	96	96	97	146
12-03	90	90	91	92	92	93	93	94	95	95	96	96	147
12-04	89	90	90	91	92	92	93	93	94	95	95	96	148
12-05	89	89	90	90	91	92	92	93	93	94	95	95	149
12-06	88	89	89	90	91	91	92	92	93	94	94	95	150
12-07	88	88	89	90	90	91	91	92	93	93	94	94	151
12-08	87	88	88	89	90	90	91	91	92	93	93	94	152
12-09	87	87	88	89	89	90	90	91	91	92	93	93	153
12-10	86	87	88	88	89	89	90	90	91	92	92	93	154
12-11	86	87	87	88	88	89	89	90	91	91	92	92	155
13-00	85	86	87	87	88	88	89	89	90	91	91	92	156
13-01	85	86	86	87	87	88	88	89	90	90	91	91	157
13-02	85	86	86	87	87	88	88	89	90	90	91	91	158
13-03	84	85	86	86	87	87	88	88	89	89	90	91	159
13-04	84	84	85	86	86	87	87	88	88	89	90	90	160
13-05	84	84	85	86	86	87	87	88	88	89	90	90	161
13-06	83	84	84	85	86	86	87	87	88	88	89	89	162
13-07	83	83	84	85	85	86	86	87	87	88	88	89	163
13-08	83	83	84	84	85	86	86	87	87	88	88	89	164
13-09	82	83	83	84	85	85	86	86	87	87	88	88	165
13-10	82	82	83	84	84	85	85	86	86	87	87	88	166
13-11	82	82	83	83	84	84	85	86	86	87	87	88	167
TOTAL MONTHS	132	133	134	135	136	137	138	139	140	141	142	143	

CHRONOLOGICAL AGE

MA 11-0 / CA 11-0

YEARS / MONTHS	11 0	11 1	11 2	11 3	11 4	11 5	11 6	11 7	11 8	11 9	11 10	11 11	
14–00	81	82	82	83	83	84	85	85	86	86	87	87	168
14–01	81	81	82	82	83	84	84	85	85	86	86	87	169
14–02	81	81	82	82	83	84	84	85	85	86	86	87	170
14–03	80	81	81	82	82	83	84	84	85	85	86	86	171
14–04	80	80	81	81	82	83	83	84	84	85	85	86	172
14–05	80	80	81	81	82	83	83	84	84	85	85	86	173
14–06	79	80	80	81	82	82	83	83	84	84	85	85	174
14–07	79	79	80	81	81	82	82	83	83	84	84	85	175
14–08	79	79	80	80	81	82	82	83	83	84	84	85	176
14–09	78	79	80	80	81	81	82	82	83	83	84	84	177
14–10	78	79	79	80	80	81	81	82	82	83	83	84	178
14–11	78	78	79	80	80	81	81	82	82	83	83	84	179
15–00	78	78	79	79	80	80	81	81	82	82	83	83	180
15–01	77	77	78	78	79	80	80	81	81	82	82	83	181
15–02	77	77	78	78	79	79	80	80	81	81	82	83	182
15–03	76	77	77	78	78	79	79	80	80	81	81	82	183
15–04	75	76	76	77	77	78	79	79	80	80	81	81	184
15–05	75	76	76	77	77	78	78	79	79	80	81	81	185
15–06	75	75	76	76	77	77	78	78	79	79	80	80	186
15–07	74	74	75	75	76	77	77	78	78	79	79	80	187
15–08	74	74	75	75	76	76	77	77	78	79	79	80	188
15–09	73	74	74	75	75	76	76	77	77	78	78	79	189
15–10	72	73	73	74	75	75	76	76	77	77	78	78	190
15–11	72	73	73	74	74	75	75	76	76	77	78	78	191
16–00 / 16–02	72	72	73	73	74	74	75	75	76	76	77	77	192 / 194
16–03 / 16–07	71	72	72	73	73	74	74	75	75	76	76	77	195 / 199
16–08 / 17–00	70	71	71	72	73	73	74	74	75	75	76	76	200 / 204
17–01 / 17–05	69	70	70	71	72	72	73	73	74	74	75	75	205 / 209
17–06 / 17–10	68	69	69	70	71	71	72	72	73	73	74	74	210 / 214
17–11 / 18–00	68	69	69	70	71	71	72	72	73	73	74	74	215 / 216
TOTAL MONTHS	132	133	134	135	136	137	138	139	140	141	142	143	

CHRONOLOGICAL AGE

MA 11–0 / CA 14–0

YEARS↲ MONTHS	12 0	12 1	12 2	12 3	12 4	12 5	12 6	12 7	12 8	12 9	12 10	12 11	
7–00													84
7–01													85
7–02	170												86
7–03	168	169	170										87
7–04	166	167	168	169	170								88
7–05	163	165	166	167	168	169	170						89
7–06	161	162	163	165	166	167	168	169	170				90
7–07	159	160	161	162	164	165	166	167	168	169	170		91
7–08	157	158	159	160	161	163	164	165	166	167	168	169	92
7–09	155	156	157	158	159	160	161	163	164	165	166	167	93
7–10	153	154	155	156	157	158	159	160	162	163	164	165	94
7–11	151	152	153	154	155	156	157	158	159	161	162	163	95
8–00	149	150	151	152	153	154	155	156	157	158	160	161	96
8–01	147	148	149	150	151	152	153	155	156	157	158	159	97
8–02	145	146	147	149	150	151	152	153	154	155	156	157	98
8–03	144	145	146	147	148	149	150	151	152	153	154	155	99
8–04	142	143	144	145	146	147	148	149	150	151	152	153	100
8–05	140	141	142	143	144	145	146	147	148	149	150	151	101
8–06	139	140	141	142	143	144	145	146	147	148	149	150	102
8–07	137	138	139	140	141	142	143	144	145	146	147	148	103
8–08	136	137	138	139	140	141	142	142	143	144	145	146	104
8–09	134	135	136	137	138	139	140	141	142	143	144	145	105
8–10	133	134	135	136	137	138	138	139	140	141	142	143	106
8–11	132	132	133	134	135	136	137	138	139	140	141	142	107
9–00	130	131	132	133	134	135	136	136	137	138	139	140	108
9–01	129	130	131	132	132	133	134	135	136	137	138	139	109
9–02	127	128	129	130	131	132	133	134	135	135	136	137	110
9–03	126	127	128	129	130	131	132	132	133	134	135	136	111
9–04	125	126	127	128	129	129	130	131	132	133	134	135	112
9–05	124	125	126	126	127	128	129	130	131	132	132	133	113
9–06	123	124	124	125	126	127	128	129	129	130	131	132	114
9–07	121	122	123	124	125	126	126	127	128	129	130	131	115
9–08	120	121	122	123	124	124	125	126	127	128	129	129	116
9–09	119	120	121	122	123	123	124	125	126	127	127	128	117
9–10	118	119	120	121	121	122	123	124	125	125	126	127	118
9–11	117	118	119	120	120	121	122	123	123	124	125	126	119
	144	145	146	147	148	149	150	151	152	153	154	155	TOTAL MONTHS

CHRONOLOGICAL AGE

CHRONOLOGICAL AGE

YEARS MONTHS	12 0	12 1	12 2	12 3	12 4	12 5	12 6	12 7	12 8	12 9	12 10	12 11	
10–00	116	117	118	118	119	120	121	122	122	123	124	125	120
10–01	115	116	117	118	118	119	120	121	121	122	123	124	121
10–02	114	115	116	117	117	118	119	120	120	121	122	123	122
10–03	113	114	115	116	116	117	118	119	119	120	121	122	123
10–04	113	113	114	115	116	116	117	118	119	119	120	121	124
10–05	112	112	113	114	115	115	116	117	118	118	119	120	125
10–06	111	112	112	113	114	115	115	116	117	117	118	119	126
10–07	110	111	112	112	113	114	114	115	116	117	117	118	127
10–08	109	110	111	111	112	113	114	114	115	116	116	117	128
10–09	108	109	110	111	111	112	113	113	114	115	116	116	129
10–10	108	108	109	110	111	111	112	113	113	114	115	115	130
10–11	107	108	108	109	110	110	111	112	113	113	114	115	131
11–00	106	107	108	108	109	110	110	111	112	112	113	114	132
11–01	106	106	107	108	108	109	110	110	111	112	112	113	133
11–02	105	106	106	107	108	108	109	110	110	111	112	112	134
11–03	104	105	106	106	107	108	108	109	110	110	111	112	135
11–04	104	104	105	106	106	107	108	108	109	109	110	111	136
11–05	103	103	104	105	105	106	107	107	108	109	109	110	137
11–06	102	103	104	104	105	105	106	107	107	108	109	109	138
11–07	102	102	103	104	104	105	106	106	107	107	108	109	139
11–08	101	102	102	103	104	104	105	105	106	107	107	108	140
11–09	100	101	102	102	103	103	104	105	105	106	107	107	141
11–10	100	100	101	102	102	103	104	104	105	105	106	107	142
11–11	99	100	100	101	102	102	103	104	104	105	105	106	143
12–00	99	99	100	100	101	102	102	103	104	104	105	105	144
12–01	98	99	99	100	100	101	102	102	103	104	104	105	145
12–02	98	98	99	99	100	101	101	102	102	103	104	104	146
12–03	97	98	98	99	99	100	101	101	102	102	103	104	147
12–04	96	97	98	98	99	99	100	101	101	102	102	103	148
12–05	96	96	97	98	98	99	99	100	101	101	102	102	149
12–06	95	96	97	97	98	98	99	99	100	101	101	102	150
12–07	95	95	96	97	97	98	98	99	100	100	101	101	151
12–08	94	95	95	96	97	97	98	98	99	100	100	101	152
12–09	94	94	95	95	96	97	97	98	98	99	100	100	153
12–10	93	94	94	95	96	96	97	97	98	98	99	100	154
12–11	93	93	94	95	95	96	96	97	97	98	99	99	155
	144	145	146	147	148	149	150	151	152	153	154	155	TOTAL MONTHS

MA 12–0 / CA 10–0

CHRONOLOGICAL AGE YEARS–MONTHS	12-0	12-1	12-2	12-3	12-4	12-5	12-6	12-7	12-8	12-9	12-10	12-11	TOTAL MONTHS
13–00	92	93	93	94	95	95	96	96	97	97	98	99	156
13–01	92	92	93	93	94	95	95	96	96	97	97	98	157
13–02	92	92	93	93	94	95	95	96	96	97	97	98	158
13–03	91	92	92	93	93	94	95	95	96	96	97	97	159
13–04	91	91	92	92	93	93	94	95	95	96	96	97	160
13–05	91	91	92	92	93	93	94	95	95	96	96	97	161
13–06	90	91	91	92	92	93	93	94	95	95	96	96	162
13–07	90	90	91	91	92	92	93	93	94	95	95	96	163
13–08	90	90	91	91	92	92	93	93	94	95	95	96	164
13–09	89	90	90	91	91	92	92	93	93	94	95	95	165
13–10	88	89	90	90	91	91	92	92	93	93	94	95	166
13–11	88	89	89	90	91	91	92	92	93	93	94	94	167
14–00	88	88	89	90	90	91	91	92	92	93	93	94	168
14–01	87	88	88	89	90	90	91	91	92	92	93	93	169
14–02	87	88	88	89	90	90	91	91	92	92	93	93	170
14–03	87	87	88	88	89	90	90	91	91	92	92	93	171
14–04	86	87	87	88	89	89	90	90	91	91	92	92	172
14–05	86	87	87	88	89	89	90	90	91	91	92	92	173
14–06	86	86	87	87	88	89	89	90	90	91	91	92	174
14–07	85	86	86	87	88	88	89	89	90	90	91	91	175
14–08	85	86	86	87	88	88	89	89	90	90	91	91	176
14–09	85	85	86	86	87	88	88	89	89	90	90	91	177
14–10	84	85	85	86	87	87	88	88	89	89	90	90	178
14–11	84	85	85	86	87	87	88	88	89	89	90	90	179
15–00	84	84	85	86	86	87	87	88	88	89	89	90	180
15–01	83	84	84	85	85	86	86	87	87	88	89	89	181
15–02	83	84	84	85	85	86	86	87	87	88	88	89	182
15–03	82	83	83	84	85	85	86	86	87	87	88	88	183
15–04	82	82	83	83	84	84	85	85	86	87	87	88	184
15–05	82	82	83	83	84	84	85	85	86	86	87	87	185
15–06	81	81	82	83	83	84	84	85	85	86	86	87	186
15–07	80	81	81	82	82	83	83	84	84	85	86	86	187
15–08	80	81	81	82	82	83	83	84	84	85	85	86	188
15–09	79	80	80	81	82	82	83	83	84	84	85	85	189
15–10	79	79	80	80	81	81	82	82	83	83	84	85	190
15–11	79	79	80	80	81	81	82	82	83	83	84	84	191
TOTAL MONTHS	144	145	146	147	148	149	150	151	152	153	154	155	

MA 12–0 / CA 13–0

YEARS MONTHS	12 0	12 1	12 2	12 3	12 4	12 5	12 6	12 7	12 8	12 9	12 10	12 11	TOTAL MONTHS
16–00 / 16–02	78	78	79	79	80	81	81	82	82	83	83	84	192 / 194
16–03 / 16–07	77	78	78	79	79	80	80	81	81	82	83	83	195 / 199
16–08 / 17–00	77	78	78	79	79	80	80	81	81	82	83	83	200 / 204
17–01 / 17–05	76	77	77	78	78	79	79	80	80	81	82	82	205 / 209
17–06 / 17–10	75	76	76	77	77	78	78	79	79	80	81	81	210 / 214
17–11 / 18–00	75	76	76	77	77	78	78	79	79	80	81	81	215 / 216
TOTAL MONTHS	144	145	146	147	148	149	150	151	152	153	154	155	

CHRONOLOGICAL AGE

MA 12–0 / CA 16–0

YEARS / MONTHS	13 0	13 1	13 2	13 3	13 4	13 5	13 6	13 7	13 8	13 9	13 10	13 11	TOTAL MONTHS
7-00													84
7-01													85
7-02													86
7-03													87
7-04													88
7-05													89
7-06													90
7-07													91
7-08	170												92
7-09	168	169	170										93
7-10	166	167	168	169	170								94
7-11	164	165	166	167	168	169	170						95
8-00	162	163	164	165	166	167	168	169	170				96
8-01	160	161	162	163	164	165	166	167	168	169	170		97
8-02	158	159	160	161	162	163	164	165	166	167	168	169	98
8-03	156	157	158	159	160	161	162	163	164	165	166	167	99
8-04	154	155	156	157	158	159	160	161	162	163	164	165	100
8-05	152	153	154	155	156	157	158	159	160	161	162	163	101
8-06	151	152	153	154	155	156	157	158	159	160	160	161	102
8-07	149	150	151	152	153	154	155	156	157	158	159	160	103
8-08	147	148	149	150	151	152	153	154	155	156	157	158	104
8-09	146	147	148	149	149	150	151	152	153	154	155	156	105
8-10	144	145	146	147	148	149	150	151	152	152	153	154	106
8-11	143	144	144	145	146	147	148	149	150	151	152	153	107
9-00	141	142	143	144	145	146	146	147	148	149	150	151	108
9-01	140	141	141	142	143	144	145	146	147	148	149	149	109
9-02	138	139	140	141	142	143	143	144	145	146	147	148	110
9-03	137	138	139	139	140	141	142	143	144	145	146	146	111
9-04	135	136	137	138	139	140	141	141	142	143	144	145	112
9-05	134	135	136	137	138	138	139	140	141	142	143	144	113
9-06	133	134	135	135	136	137	138	139	140	140	141	142	114
9-07	131	132	133	134	135	136	136	137	138	139	140	141	115
9-08	130	131	132	133	134	134	135	136	137	138	139	139	116
9-09	129	130	131	132	132	133	134	135	136	136	137	138	117
9-10	128	129	129	130	131	132	133	133	134	135	136	137	118
9-11	127	127	128	129	130	131	131	132	133	134	135	135	119
TOTAL MONTHS	156	157	158	159	160	161	162	163	164	165	166	167	

CHRONOLOGICAL AGE

MA 13-0 / CA 7-0

YEARS → MONTHS ↓	13 0	13 1	13 2	13 3	13 4	13 5	13 6	13 7	13 8	13 9	13 10	13 11	TOTAL MONTHS
10–00	126	126	127	128	129	129	130	131	132	133	133	134	120
10–01	125	125	126	127	128	128	129	130	131	132	132	133	121
10–02	123	124	125	126	127	127	128	129	130	130	131	132	122
10–03	123	123	124	125	126	126	127	128	129	129	130	131	123
10–04	122	122	123	124	125	125	126	127	128	128	129	130	124
10–05	121	121	122	123	124	124	125	126	127	127	128	129	125
10–06	120	120	121	122	123	123	124	125	126	126	127	128	126
10–07	119	120	120	121	122	122	123	124	125	125	126	127	127
10–08	118	119	119	120	121	121	122	123	124	124	125	126	128
10–09	117	118	118	119	120	121	121	122	123	123	124	125	129
10–10	116	117	118	118	119	120	120	121	122	123	123	124	130
10–11	115	116	117	117	118	119	119	120	121	122	122	123	131
11–00	115	115	116	117	117	118	119	119	120	121	121	122	132
11–01	114	114	115	116	116	117	118	118	119	120	120	121	133
11–02	113	114	114	115	116	116	117	118	118	119	120	120	134
11–03	112	113	114	114	115	116	116	117	118	118	119	120	135
11–04	111	112	113	113	114	115	115	116	117	117	118	119	136
11–05	111	111	112	113	113	114	115	115	116	117	117	118	137
11–06	110	111	111	112	113	113	114	115	115	116	117	117	138
11–07	109	110	111	111	112	113	113	114	114	115	116	116	139
11–08	109	109	110	111	111	112	112	113	114	114	115	116	140
11–09	108	109	109	110	110	111	112	112	113	114	114	115	141
11–10	107	108	109	109	110	110	111	112	112	113	114	114	142
11–11	107	107	108	109	109	110	110	111	112	112	113	113	143
12–00	106	107	107	108	108	109	110	110	111	112	112	113	144
12–01	105	106	107	107	108	108	109	110	110	111	111	112	145
12–02	105	105	106	107	107	108	108	109	110	110	111	111	146
12–03	104	105	105	106	107	107	108	108	109	110	110	111	147
12–04	104	104	105	105	106	107	107	108	108	109	110	110	148
12–05	103	104	104	105	105	106	107	107	108	108	109	110	149
12–06	102	103	104	104	105	105	106	107	107	108	108	109	150
12–07	102	103	103	104	104	105	105	106	107	107	108	108	151
12–08	101	102	102	103	104	104	105	105	106	107	107	108	152
12–09	101	101	102	102	103	104	104	105	105	106	107	107	153
12–10	100	101	101	102	103	103	104	104	105	105	106	107	154
12–11	100	100	101	101	102	103	103	104	104	105	105	106	155
TOTAL MONTHS	156	157	158	159	160	161	162	163	164	165	166	167	

CHRONOLOGICAL AGE

MA 13–0 / CA 10–0

YEARS MONTHS	13 0	13 1	13 2	13 3	13 4	13 5	13 6	13 7	13 8	13 9	13 10	13 11	
13–00	99	100	100	101	101	102	103	103	104	104	105	105	156
13–01	99	99	100	100	101	101	102	103	103	104	104	105	157
13–02	99	99	100	100	101	101	102	103	103	104	104	105	158
13–03	98	98	99	100	100	101	101	102	102	103	104	104	159
13–04	97	98	99	99	100	100	101	101	102	102	103	104	160
13–05	97	98	99	99	100	100	101	101	102	102	103	104	161
13–06	97	97	98	98	99	100	100	101	101	102	102	103	162
13–07	96	97	97	98	98	99	100	100	101	101	102	102	163
13–08	96	97	97	98	98	99	100	100	101	101	102	102	164
13–09	96	96	97	97	98	98	99	100	100	101	101	102	165
13–10	95	96	96	97	97	98	98	99	100	100	101	101	166
13–11	95	96	96	97	97	98	98	99	99	100	101	101	167
14–00	94	95	96	96	97	97	98	98	99	99	100	101	168
14–01	94	94	95	96	96	97	97	98	98	99	99	100	169
14–02	94	94	95	96	96	97	97	98	98	99	99	100	170
14–03	93	94	95	95	96	96	97	97	98	98	99	99	171
14–04	93	93	94	95	95	96	96	97	97	98	98	99	172
14–05	93	93	94	95	95	96	96	97	97	98	98	99	173
14–06	92	93	93	94	95	95	96	96	97	97	98	98	174
14–07	92	92	93	93	94	95	95	96	96	97	97	98	175
14–08	92	92	93	93	94	95	95	96	96	97	97	98	176
14–09	91	92	92	93	93	94	95	95	96	96	97	97	177
14–10	91	91	92	92	93	94	94	95	95	96	96	97	178
14–11	91	91	92	92	93	93	94	95	95	96	96	97	179
15–00	90	91	91	92	92	93	94	94	95	95	96	96	180
15–01	90	90	91	91	92	92	93	93	94	94	95	95	181
15–02	90	90	91	91	92	92	93	93	94	94	95	95	182
15–03	89	89	90	90	91	91	92	93	93	94	94	95	183
15–04	88	89	89	90	90	91	91	92	92	93	93	94	184
15–05	88	89	89	90	90	91	91	92	92	93	93	94	185
15–06	87	88	88	89	89	90	90	91	92	92	93	93	186
15–07	87	87	88	88	89	89	90	90	91	91	92	92	187
15–08	86	87	88	88	89	89	90	90	91	91	92	92	188
15–09	86	86	87	87	88	88	89	89	90	91	91	92	189
15–10	85	86	86	87	87	88	88	89	89	90	90	91	190
15–11	85	85	86	87	87	88	88	89	89	90	90	91	191
	156	157	158	159	160	161	162	163	164	165	166	167	TOTAL MONTHS

CHRONOLOGICAL AGE

	13 0	13 1	13 2	13 3	13 4	13 5	13 6	13 7	13 8	13 9	13 10	13 11	
YEARS MONTHS													
16–00 16–02	84	85	85	86	86	87	87	88	88	89	90	90	192 194
16–03 16–07	84	84	85	85	86	86	87	88	88	89	89	90	195 199
16–08 17–00	84	84	85	85	86	86	87	88	88	89	89	90	200 204
17–01 17–05	83	83	84	84	85	85	86	87	87	88	88	89	205 209
17–06 17–10	82	82	83	83	84	84	85	86	86	87	87	88	210 214
17–11 18–00	82	82	83	83	84	84	85	86	86	87	87	88	215 216
	156	157	158	159	160	161	162	163	164	165	166	167	TOTAL MONTHS

CHRONOLOGICAL AGE

311

MA 13–0 / CA 16–0

MENTAL AGE

YEARS ⟶ MONTHS	14 0	14 1	14 2	14 3	14 4	14 5	14 6	14 7	14 8	14 9	14 10	14 11	
8–00													96
8–01													97
8–02	170												98
8–03	168	169	170										99
8–04	166	167	168	169	170								100
8–05	164	165	166	167	168	169	170						101
8–06	162	163	164	165	166	167	168	169	170				102
8–07	161	162	163	163	164	165	166	167	168	169	170		103
8–08	159	160	161	162	163	164	164	165	166	167	168	169	104
8–09	157	158	159	160	161	162	163	164	165	166	166	167	105
8–10	155	156	157	158	159	160	161	162	163	164	165	166	106
8–11	154	155	155	156	157	158	159	160	161	162	163	164	107
9–00	152	153	154	155	156	156	157	158	159	160	161	162	108
9–01	150	151	152	153	154	155	156	157	158	158	159	160	109
9–02	149	150	151	151	152	153	154	155	156	157	158	159	110
9–03	147	148	149	150	151	152	153	153	154	155	156	157	111
9–04	146	147	148	148	149	150	151	152	153	154	154	155	112
9–05	144	145	146	147	148	149	149	150	151	152	153	154	113
9–06	143	144	145	146	146	147	148	149	150	151	151	152	114
9–07	142	142	143	144	145	146	147	147	148	149	150	151	115
9–08	140	141	142	143	143	144	145	146	147	148	148	149	116
9–09	139	140	140	141	142	143	144	145	145	146	147	148	117
9–10	137	138	139	140	141	142	142	143	144	145	146	146	118
9–11	136	137	138	139	139	140	141	142	143	143	144	145	119
10–00	135	136	137	137	138	139	140	141	141	142	143	144	120
10–01	134	135	135	136	137	138	139	139	140	141	142	142	121
10–02	133	133	134	135	136	137	137	138	139	140	140	141	122
10–03	132	132	133	134	135	135	136	137	138	138	139	140	123
10–04	131	131	132	133	134	134	135	136	137	137	138	139	124
10–05	129	130	131	132	132	133	134	135	135	136	137	138	125
10–06	129	129	130	131	131	132	133	134	134	135	136	137	126
10–07	128	128	129	130	130	131	132	133	133	134	135	135	127
10–08	126	127	128	129	129	130	131	131	132	133	134	134	128
10–09	126	126	127	128	128	129	130	131	131	132	133	133	129
10–10	125	125	126	127	127	128	129	130	130	131	132	132	130
10–11	124	124	125	126	126	127	128	128	129	130	131	131	131
TOTAL MONTHS	168	169	170	171	172	173	174	175	176	177	178	179	

CHRONOLOGICAL AGE

YEARS / MONTHS	14 0	14 1	14 2	14 3	14 4	14 5	14 6	14 7	14 8	14 9	14 10	14 11	
11–00	123	123	124	125	126	126	127	128	128	129	130	130	132
11–01	122	123	123	124	125	125	126	127	127	128	129	129	133
11–02	121	122	122	123	124	124	125	126	126	127	128	128	134
11–03	120	121	122	122	123	124	124	125	126	126	127	128	135
11–04	119	120	121	121	122	123	123	124	125	125	126	127	136
11–05	119	119	120	121	121	122	122	123	124	124	125	126	137
11–06	118	118	119	120	120	121	122	122	123	124	124	125	138
11–07	117	118	118	119	120	120	121	122	122	123	123	124	139
11–08	116	117	118	118	119	119	120	121	121	122	123	123	140
11–09	115	116	117	117	118	119	119	120	121	121	122	122	141
11–10	115	115	116	117	117	118	119	119	120	120	121	122	142
11–11	114	115	115	116	117	117	118	118	119	120	120	121	143
12–00	113	114	115	115	116	116	117	118	118	119	120	120	144
12–01	113	113	114	114	115	116	116	117	118	118	119	119	145
12–02	112	113	113	114	114	115	116	116	117	118	118	119	146
12–03	111	112	113	113	114	114	115	116	116	117	117	118	147
12–04	111	111	112	113	113	114	114	115	116	116	117	117	148
12–05	110	111	111	112	112	113	114	114	115	115	116	117	149
12–06	110	110	111	111	112	112	113	114	114	115	115	116	150
12–07	109	110	110	111	111	112	112	113	114	114	115	115	151
12–08	108	109	109	110	111	111	112	112	113	114	114	115	152
12–09	108	108	109	109	110	111	111	112	112	113	113	114	153
12–10	107	108	108	109	109	110	111	111	112	112	113	113	154
12–11	107	107	108	108	109	109	110	111	111	112	112	113	155
13–00	106	107	107	108	108	109	109	110	111	111	112	112	156
13–01	105	106	107	107	108	108	109	109	110	110	111	112	157
13–02	105	106	107	107	108	108	109	109	110	110	111	112	158
13–03	105	105	106	106	107	108	108	109	109	110	110	111	159
13–04	104	105	105	106	106	107	107	108	109	109	110	110	160
13–05	104	105	105	106	106	107	107	108	109	109	110	110	161
13–06	103	104	105	105	106	106	107	107	108	108	109	110	162
13–07	103	103	104	105	105	106	106	107	107	108	108	109	163
13–08	103	103	104	105	105	106	106	107	107	108	108	109	164
13–09	102	103	103	104	105	105	106	106	107	107	108	108	165
13–10	102	102	103	103	104	104	105	106	106	107	107	108	166
13–11	102	102	103	103	104	104	105	106	106	107	107	108	167
TOTAL MONTHS	168	169	170	171	172	173	174	175	176	177	178	179	

CHRONOLOGICAL AGE

MA 14–0 / CA 11–0

YEARS → MONTHS ↓	14 0	14 1	14 2	14 3	14 4	14 5	14 6	14 7	14 8	14 9	14 10	14 11	
14–00	101	102	102	103	103	104	104	105	105	106	107	107	168
14–01	101	101	102	102	103	103	104	104	105	105	106	107	169
14–02	101	101	102	102	103	103	104	104	105	105	106	107	170
14–03	100	101	101	102	102	103	103	104	104	105	105	106	171
14–04	99	100	100	101	102	102	103	103	104	104	105	105	172
14–05	99	100	100	101	102	102	103	103	104	104	105	105	173
14–06	99	99	100	100	101	102	102	103	103	104	104	105	174
14–07	98	99	99	100	100	101	102	102	103	103	104	104	175
14–08	98	99	99	100	100	101	102	102	103	103	104	104	176
14–09	98	98	99	99	100	100	101	102	102	103	103	104	177
14–10	97	98	98	99	99	100	100	101	102	102	103	103	178
14–11	97	98	98	99	99	100	100	101	102	102	103	103	179
15–00	97	97	98	98	99	99	100	100	101	102	102	103	180
15–01	96	97	97	98	98	99	99	100	100	101	101	102	181
15–02	96	96	97	98	98	99	99	100	100	101	101	102	182
15–03	95	96	96	97	97	98	98	99	99	100	101	101	183
15–04	94	95	96	96	97	97	98	98	99	99	100	100	184
15–05	94	95	95	96	96	97	98	98	99	99	100	100	185
15–06	94	94	95	95	96	96	97	97	98	98	99	99	186
15–07	93	93	94	95	95	96	96	97	97	98	98	99	187
15–08	93	93	94	94	95	95	96	97	97	98	98	99	188
15–09	92	93	93	94	94	95	95	96	96	97	97	98	189
15–10	91	92	92	93	94	94	95	95	96	96	97	97	190
15–11	91	92	92	93	93	94	94	95	96	96	97	97	191
16–00 } 16–02	91	91	92	92	93	93	94	94	95	95	96	96	{ 192 194
16–03 } 16–07	90	91	91	92	93	93	94	94	95	95	96	96	{ 195 199
16–08 } 17–00	90	91	91	92	92	93	93	94	94	95	95	96	{ 200 204
17–01 } 17–05	89	90	90	91	92	92	93	93	94	94	95	95	{ 205 209
17–06 } 17–10	88	89	89	90	91	91	92	92	93	93	94	94	{ 210 214
17–11 } 18–00	88	89	89	90	91	91	92	92	93	93	94	94	{ 215 216
	168	169	170	171	172	173	174	175	176	177	178	179	TOTAL MONTHS

CHRONOLOGICAL AGE

MA 14–0 / CA 14–0

YEARS / MONTHS	15 0	15 1	15 2	15 3	15 4	15 5	15 6	15 7	15 8	15 9	15 10	15 11	
8–00													96
8–01													97
8–02													98
8–03													99
8–04													100
8–05													101
8–06													102
8–07													103
8–08	170												104
8–09	168	169	170										105
8–10	166	167	168	169	170								106
8–11	165	166	167	167	168	169	170						107
9–00	163	164	165	166	167	167	168	169	170				108
9–01	161	162	163	164	165	166	167	167	168	169	170		109
9–02	159	160	161	162	163	164	165	166	167	167	168	169	110
9–03	158	159	160	160	161	162	163	164	165	166	167	167	111
9–04	156	157	158	159	160	161	161	162	163	164	165	166	112
9–05	155	155	156	157	158	159	160	161	161	162	163	164	113
9–06	153	154	155	156	156	157	158	159	160	161	162	162	114
9–07	152	152	153	154	155	156	157	157	158	159	160	161	115
9–08	150	151	152	153	153	154	155	156	157	157	158	159	116
9–09	149	149	150	151	152	153	154	154	155	156	157	158	117
9–10	147	148	149	150	150	151	152	153	154	154	155	156	118
9–11	146	147	147	148	149	150	151	151	152	153	154	155	119
10–00	144	145	146	147	148	148	149	150	151	152	152	153	120
10–01	143	144	145	146	146	147	148	149	149	150	151	152	121
10–02	142	143	143	144	145	146	147	147	148	149	150	150	122
10–03	141	142	142	143	144	145	145	146	147	148	148	149	123
10–04	140	140	141	142	143	143	144	145	146	146	147	148	124
10–05	138	139	140	141	141	142	143	144	144	145	146	147	125
10–06	137	138	139	140	140	141	142	142	143	144	145	145	126
10–07	136	137	138	138	139	140	141	141	142	143	143	144	127
10–08	135	136	137	137	138	139	139	140	141	142	142	143	128
10–09	134	135	135	136	137	138	138	139	140	140	141	142	129
10–10	133	134	134	135	136	137	137	138	139	139	140	141	130
10–11	132	133	133	134	135	135	136	137	138	138	139	140	131
	180	181	182	183	184	185	186	187	188	189	190	191	TOTAL MONTHS

CHRONOLOGICAL AGE

315

MA 15–0 / CA 8–0

MENTAL AGE

YEARS → MONTHS ↓	15 0	15 1	15 2	15 3	15 4	15 5	15 6	15 7	15 8	15 9	15 10	15 11	
11–00	131	132	132	133	134	134	135	136	136	137	138	139	132
11–01	130	131	131	132	133	133	134	135	135	136	137	137	133
11–02	129	130	130	131	132	132	133	134	134	135	136	137	134
11–03	128	129	130	130	131	132	132	133	134	134	135	136	135
11–04	127	128	129	129	130	131	131	132	133	133	134	135	136
11–05	126	127	128	128	129	130	130	131	132	132	133	134	137
11–06	126	126	127	128	128	129	129	130	131	131	132	133	138
11–07	125	125	126	127	127	128	129	129	130	131	131	132	139
11–08	124	125	125	126	126	127	128	128	129	130	130	131	140
11–09	123	124	124	125	126	126	127	127	128	129	129	130	141
11–10	122	123	124	124	125	125	126	127	127	128	129	129	142
11–11	122	122	123	123	124	125	125	126	127	127	128	128	143
12–00	121	121	122	123	123	124	124	125	126	126	127	127	144
12–01	120	121	121	122	122	123	124	124	125	125	126	127	145
12–02	119	120	121	121	122	122	123	124	124	125	125	126	146
12–03	119	119	120	120	121	122	122	123	123	124	125	125	147
12–04	118	119	119	120	120	121	122	122	123	123	124	125	148
12–05	117	118	118	119	120	120	121	121	122	123	123	124	149
12–06	117	117	118	118	119	120	120	121	121	122	123	123	150
12–07	116	117	117	118	118	119	120	120	121	121	122	122	151
12–08	115	116	116	117	118	118	119	119	120	121	121	122	152
12–09	115	115	116	116	117	118	118	119	119	120	120	121	153
12–10	114	115	115	116	116	117	117	118	119	119	120	120	154
12–11	113	114	115	115	116	116	117	117	118	119	119	120	155
13–00	113	113	114	115	115	116	116	117	117	118	119	119	156
13–01	112	113	113	114	114	115	116	116	117	117	118	118	157
13–02	112	113	113	114	114	115	116	116	117	117	118	118	158
13–03	111	112	113	113	114	114	115	115	116	117	117	118	159
13–04	111	111	112	113	113	114	114	115	115	116	116	117	160
13–05	111	111	112	113	113	114	114	115	115	116	116	117	161
13–06	110	111	111	112	112	113	114	114	115	115	116	116	162
13–07	110	110	111	111	112	112	113	113	114	115	115	116	163
13–08	110	110	111	111	112	112	113	113	114	115	115	116	164
13–09	109	109	110	111	111	112	112	113	113	114	114	115	165
13–10	108	109	109	110	111	111	112	112	113	113	114	114	166
13–11	108	109	109	110	110	111	112	112	113	113	114	114	167
	180	181	182	183	184	185	186	187	188	189	190	191	TOTAL MONTHS

CHRONOLOGICAL AGE

YEARS MONTHS	15 0	15 1	15 2	15 3	15 4	15 5	15 6	15 7	15 8	15 9	15 10	15 11	
14–00	108	108	109	109	110	110	111	112	112	113	113	114	168
14–01	107	108	108	109	109	110	110	111	111	112	113	113	169
14–02	107	108	108	109	109	110	110	111	111	112	113	113	170
14–03	107	107	108	108	109	109	110	110	111	111	112	113	171
14–04	106	106	107	108	108	109	109	110	110	111	111	112	172
14–05	106	106	107	108	108	109	109	110	110	111	111	112	173
14–06	105	106	106	107	108	108	109	109	110	110	111	111	174
14–07	105	105	106	106	107	107	108	109	109	110	110	111	175
14–08	105	105	106	106	107	108	108	109	109	110	110	111	176
14–09	104	105	105	106	106	107	107	108	109	109	110	110	177
14–10	104	104	105	105	106	106	107	107	108	108	109	110	178
14–11	104	104	105	105	106	106	107	107	108	109	109	110	179
15–00	103	104	104	105	105	106	106	107	107	108	108	109	180
15–01	102	103	103	104	105	105	106	106	107	107	108	108	181
15–02	102	103	103	104	104	105	106	106	107	107	108	108	182
15–03	102	102	103	103	104	104	105	105	106	106	107	107	183
15–04	101	101	102	102	103	103	104	105	105	106	106	107	184
15–05	101	101	102	102	103	103	104	104	105	106	106	107	185
15–06	100	101	101	102	102	103	103	104	104	105	105	106	186
15–07	99	100	100	101	101	102	102	103	104	104	105	105	187
15–08	99	100	100	101	101	102	102	103	103	104	105	105	188
15–09	98	99	100	100	101	101	102	102	103	103	104	104	189
15–10	98	98	99	99	100	100	101	101	102	102	103	104	190
15–11	98	98	99	99	100	100	101	101	102	102	103	103	191
16–00 } 16–02	97	97	98	98	99	100	100	101	101	102	102	103	192 194
16–03 } 16–07	97	97	98	98	99	99	100	100	101	101	102	102	195 199
16–08 } 17–00	96	97	97	98	98	99	99	100	100	101	102	102	200 204
17–01 } 17–05	96	97	97	98	98	99	99	100	100	101	102	102	205 209
17–06 } 17–10	95	96	96	97	97	98	98	99	99	100	101	101	210 214
17–11 } 18–00	95	96	96	97	97	98	98	99	99	100	101	101	215 216
	180	181	182	183	184	185	186	187	188	189	190	191	TOTAL MONTHS

MA 15–0 / CA 14–0

MENTAL AGE

YEARS MONTHS	16 0	16 1	16 2	16 3	16 4	16 5	16 6	16 7	16 8	16 9	16 10	16 11	TOTAL MONTHS
8–00													96
8–01													97
8–02													98
8–03													99
8–04													100
8–05													101
8–06													102
8–07													103
8–08													104
8–09													105
8–10													106
8–11													107
9–00													108
9–01													109
9–02	170												110
9–03	168	169	170										111
9–04	167	167	168	169	170								112
9–05	165	166	167	167	168	169	170						113
9–06	163	164	165	166	167	167	168	169	170				114
9–07	162	162	163	164	165	166	167	167	168	169	170		115
9–08	160	161	162	162	163	164	165	166	167	167	168	169	116
9–09	158	159	160	161	162	163	163	164	165	166	167	167	117
9–10	157	158	158	159	160	161	162	162	163	164	165	166	118
9–11	155	156	157	158	159	159	160	161	162	163	163	164	119
10–00	154	155	155	156	157	158	159	159	160	161	162	163	120
10–01	153	153	154	155	156	156	157	158	159	160	160	161	121
10–02	151	152	153	153	154	155	156	157	157	158	159	160	122
10–03	150	151	151	152	153	154	154	155	156	157	157	158	123
10–04	149	149	150	151	152	152	153	154	155	155	156	157	124
10–05	147	148	149	150	150	151	152	153	153	154	155	156	125
10–06	146	147	148	148	149	150	151	151	152	153	153	154	126
10–07	145	146	146	147	148	149	149	150	151	151	152	153	127
10–08	144	144	145	146	147	147	148	149	149	150	151	152	128
10–09	143	143	144	145	145	146	147	148	148	149	150	150	129
10–10	141	142	143	144	144	145	146	146	147	148	148	149	130
10–11	140	141	142	142	143	144	144	145	146	147	147	148	131
TOTAL MONTHS	192	193	194	195	196	197	198	199	200	201	202	203	

CHRONOLOGICAL AGE

MA 16–0 / CA 8–0

318

| YEARS | 16 | 16 | 16 | 16 | 16 | 16 | 16 | 16 | 16 | 16 | 16 | 16 | |
MONTHS	0	1	2	3	4	5	6	7	8	9	10	11	
11–00	139	140	141	141	142	143	143	144	145	145	146	147	132
11–01	138	139	140	140	141	142	142	143	144	144	145	146	133
11–02	137	138	139	139	140	141	141	142	143	143	144	145	134
11–03	136	137	138	138	139	140	140	141	142	142	143	144	135
11–04	135	136	137	137	138	139	139	140	141	141	142	143	136
11–05	134	135	136	136	137	138	138	139	140	140	141	141	137
11–06	133	134	135	135	136	137	137	138	139	139	140	141	138
11–07	132	133	134	134	135	136	136	137	138	138	139	140	139
11–08	132	132	133	133	134	135	135	136	137	137	138	139	140
11–09	131	131	132	132	133	134	134	135	136	136	137	138	141
11–10	130	130	131	132	132	133	134	134	135	135	136	137	142
11–11	129	130	130	131	131	132	133	133	134	135	135	136	143
12–00	128	129	129	130	131	131	132	132	133	134	134	135	144
12–01	127	128	129	129	130	130	131	132	132	133	133	134	145
12–02	127	127	128	128	129	130	130	131	131	132	133	133	146
12–03	126	127	127	128	128	129	130	130	131	131	132	133	147
12–04	125	126	126	127	128	128	129	129	130	131	131	132	148
12–05	124	125	126	126	127	127	128	129	129	130	130	131	149
12–06	124	124	125	125	126	127	127	128	128	129	130	130	150
12–07	123	124	124	125	125	126	127	127	128	128	129	129	151
12–08	122	123	123	124	125	125	126	126	127	128	128	129	152
12–09	122	122	123	123	124	124	125	126	126	127	127	128	153
12–10	121	122	122	123	123	124	124	125	126	126	127	127	154
12–11	120	121	122	122	123	123	124	124	125	126	126	127	155
13–00	120	120	121	121	122	122	123	124	124	125	125	126	156
13–01	119	120	120	121	121	122	122	123	124	124	125	125	157
13–02	119	120	120	121	121	122	122	123	124	124	125	125	158
13–03	118	119	119	120	121	121	122	122	123	123	124	124	159
13–04	118	118	119	119	120	120	121	122	122	123	123	124	160
13–05	118	118	119	119	120	120	121	122	122	123	123	124	161
13–06	117	117	118	119	119	120	120	121	121	122	122	123	162
13–07	116	117	117	118	118	119	120	120	121	121	122	122	163
13–08	116	117	117	118	118	119	120	120	121	121	122	122	164
13–09	116	116	117	117	118	118	119	119	120	121	121	122	165
13–10	115	116	116	117	117	118	118	119	119	120	120	121	166
13–11	115	115	116	117	117	118	118	119	119	120	120	121	167
	192	193	194	195	196	197	198	199	200	201	202	203	TOTAL MONTHS

CHRONOLOGICAL AGE

319

MA 16–0 / CA 11–0

YEARS MONTHS	16 0	16 1	16 2	16 3	16 4	16 5	16 6	16 7	16 8	16 9	16 10	16 11	
14–00	114	115	115	116	116	117	118	118	119	119	120	120	168
14–01	114	114	115	115	116	116	117	118	118	119	119	120	169
14–02	114	114	115	115	116	116	117	118	118	119	119	120	170
14–03	113	114	114	115	115	116	116	117	117	118	119	119	171
14–04	112	113	114	114	115	115	116	116	117	117	118	118	172
14–05	112	113	114	114	115	115	116	116	117	117	118	118	173
14–06	112	112	113	113	114	115	115	116	116	117	117	118	174
14–07	111	112	112	113	113	114	115	115	116	116	117	117	175
14–08	111	112	112	113	113	114	115	115	116	116	117	117	176
14–09	111	111	112	112	113	113	114	114	115	116	116	117	177
14–10	110	111	111	112	112	113	113	114	114	115	115	116	178
14–11	110	111	111	112	112	113	113	114	114	115	115	116	179
15–00	110	110	111	111	112	112	113	113	114	114	115	115	180
15–01	109	109	110	110	111	111	112	113	113	114	114	115	181
15–02	109	109	110	110	111	111	112	112	113	114	114	115	182
15–03	108	108	109	110	110	111	111	112	112	113	113	114	183
15–04	107	108	108	109	109	110	110	111	111	112	113	113	184
15–05	107	108	108	109	109	110	110	111	111	112	112	113	185
15–06	106	107	107	108	109	109	110	110	111	111	112	112	186
15–07	106	106	107	107	108	108	109	109	110	110	111	111	187
15–08	106	106	107	107	108	108	109	109	110	110	111	111	188
15–09	105	105	106	106	107	107	108	109	109	110	110	111	189
15–10	104	105	105	106	106	107	107	108	108	109	109	110	190
15–11	104	105	105	106	106	107	107	108	108	109	109	110	191
16–00 / 16–02	103	104	104	105	105	106	106	107	107	108	109	109	192 / 194
16–03 / 16–07	103	103	104	104	105	105	106	107	107	108	108	109	195 / 199
16–08 / 17–00	103	103	104	104	105	105	106	107	107	108	108	109	200 / 204
17–01 / 17–05	103	103	104	104	105	105	106	107	107	108	108	109	205 / 209
17–06 / 17–10	102	102	103	103	104	104	105	106	106	107	107	108	210 / 214
17–11 / 18–00	102	102	103	103	104	104	105	106	106	107	107	108	215 / 216
TOTAL MONTHS	192	193	194	195	196	197	198	199	200	201	202	203	

CHRONOLOGICAL AGE

MA 16–0 / CA 14–0

320

YEARS MONTHS	17 0	17 1	17 2	17 3	17 4	17 5	17 6	17 7	17 8	17 9	17 10	17 11	
8–00													96
8–01													97
8–02													98
8–03													99
8–04													100
8–05													101
8–06													102
8–07													103
8–08													104
8–09													105
8–10													106
8–11													107
9–00													108
9–01													109
9–02													110
9–03													111
9–04													112
9–05													113
9–06													114
9–07													115
9–08	170												116
9–09	168	169	170										117
9–10	167	167	168	169	170								118
9–11	165	166	167	167	168	169	170						119
10–00	163	164	165	166	167	167	168	169	170				120
10–01	162	163	163	164	165	166	167	167	168	169	170		121
10–02	160	161	162	163	163	164	165	166	167	167	168	169	122
10–03	159	160	161	161	162	163	164	164	165	166	167	167	123
10–04	158	158	159	160	161	161	162	163	164	164	165	166	124
10–05	156	157	158	158	159	160	161	161	162	163	164	164	125
10–06	155	156	156	157	158	159	159	160	161	162	162	163	126
10–07	154	154	155	156	157	157	158	159	159	160	161	162	127
10–08	152	153	154	154	155	156	157	157	158	159	159	160	128
10–09	151	152	153	153	154	155	155	156	157	157	158	159	129
10–10	150	151	151	152	153	153	154	155	155	156	157	158	130
10–11	149	149	150	151	151	152	153	153	154	155	156	156	131
	204	205	206	207	208	209	210	211	212	213	214	215	TOTAL MONTHS

CHRONOLOGICAL AGE

MA 17–0 / CA 8–0

MENTAL AGE

YEARS MONTHS	17 0	17 1	17 2	17 3	17 4	17 5	17 6	17 7	17 8	17 9	17 10	17 11	
11–00	147	148	149	150	150	151	152	152	153	154	154	155	132
11–01	146	147	148	148	149	150	150	151	152	152	153	154	133
11–02	145	146	147	147	148	149	149	150	151	151	152	153	134
11–03	144	145	146	146	147	148	148	149	150	150	151	152	135
11–04	143	144	145	145	146	147	147	148	148	149	150	150	136
11–05	142	143	143	144	145	145	146	147	147	148	149	149	137
11–06	141	142	142	143	144	144	145	146	146	147	148	148	138
11–07	140	141	141	142	143	143	144	145	145	146	147	147	139
11–08	139	140	140	141	142	142	143	144	144	145	146	146	140
11–09	138	139	139	140	141	141	142	143	143	144	144	145	141
11–10	137	138	139	139	140	140	141	142	142	143	144	144	142
11–11	136	137	138	138	139	140	140	141	141	142	143	143	143
12–00	135	136	137	137	138	139	139	140	140	141	142	142	144
12–01	135	135	136	136	137	138	138	139	139	140	141	141	145
12–02	134	134	135	136	136	137	138	138	139	139	140	141	146
12–03	133	134	134	135	136	136	137	137	138	139	139	140	147
12–04	132	133	133	134	135	135	136	136	137	138	138	139	148
12–05	132	132	133	133	134	134	135	136	136	137	137	138	149
12–06	131	131	132	133	133	134	134	135	136	136	137	137	150
12–07	130	131	131	132	132	133	134	134	135	135	136	137	151
12–08	129	130	130	131	132	132	133	133	134	135	135	136	152
12–09	129	129	130	130	131	131	132	133	133	134	134	135	153
12–10	128	128	129	130	130	131	131	132	132	133	134	134	154
12–11	127	128	128	129	130	130	131	131	132	132	133	134	155
13–00	126	127	128	128	129	129	130	130	131	132	132	133	156
13–01	126	126	127	127	128	129	129	130	130	131	131	132	157
13–02	126	126	127	127	128	129	129	130	130	131	131	132	158
13–03	125	126	126	127	127	128	128	129	130	130	131	131	159
13–04	124	125	125	126	127	127	128	128	129	129	130	131	160
13–05	124	125	125	126	127	127	128	128	129	129	130	131	161
13–06	124	124	125	125	126	126	127	127	128	129	129	130	162
13–07	123	123	124	125	125	126	126	127	127	128	128	129	163
13–08	123	123	124	125	125	126	126	127	127	128	128	129	164
13–09	122	123	123	124	124	125	126	126	127	127	128	128	165
13–10	122	122	123	123	124	124	125	125	126	127	127	128	166
13–11	122	122	123	123	124	124	125	125	126	127	127	128	167
	204	205	206	207	208	209	210	211	212	213	214	215	TOTAL MONTHS

CHRONOLOGICAL AGE

YEARS MONTHS	17 0	17 1	17 2	17 3	17 4	17 5	17 6	17 7	17 8	17 9	17 10	17 11	
14–00	121	121	122	123	123	124	124	125	125	126	126	127	168
14–01	120	121	121	122	122	123	124	124	125	125	126	126	169
14–02	120	121	121	122	122	123	124	124	125	125	126	126	170
14–03	120	120	121	121	122	122	123	123	124	125	125	126	171
14–04	119	120	120	121	121	122	122	123	123	124	124	125	172
14–05	119	120	120	121	121	122	122	123	123	124	124	125	173
14–06	118	119	119	120	121	121	122	122	123	123	124	124	174
14–07	118	118	119	119	120	120	121	122	122	123	123	124	175
14–08	118	118	119	119	120	120	121	122	122	123	123	124	176
14–09	117	118	118	119	119	120	120	121	121	122	123	123	177
14–10	117	117	118	118	119	119	120	120	121	121	122	122	178
14–11	117	117	118	118	119	119	120	120	121	121	122	122	179
15–00	116	116	117	118	118	119	119	120	120	121	121	122	180
15–01	115	116	116	117	117	118	118	119	119	120	120	121	181
15–02	115	116	116	117	117	118	118	119	119	120	120	121	182
15–03	114	115	115	116	116	117	118	118	119	119	120	120	183
15–04	114	114	115	115	116	116	117	117	118	118	119	119	184
15–05	114	114	115	115	116	116	117	117	118	118	119	119	185
15–06	113	113	114	114	115	115	116	116	117	118	118	119	186
15–07	112	113	113	114	114	115	115	116	116	117	117	118	187
15–08	112	112	113	114	114	115	115	116	116	117	117	118	188
15–09	111	112	112	113	113	114	114	115	115	116	116	117	189
15–10	110	111	111	112	113	113	114	114	115	115	116	116	190
15–11	110	111	111	112	112	113	114	114	115	115	116	116	191
16–00 } 16–02 }	110	110	111	111	112	112	113	113	114	114	115	115	{ 192 { 194
16–03 } 16–07 }	109	110	110	111	112	112	113	113	114	114	115	115	{ 195 { 199
16–08 } 17–00 }	109	110	110	111	112	112	113	113	114	114	115	115	{ 200 { 204
17–01 } 17–05 }	109	110	110	111	112	112	113	113	114	114	115	115	{ 205 { 209
17–06 } 17–10 }	108	109	109	110	111	111	112	112	113	113	114	114	{ 210 { 214
17–11 } 18–00 }	108	109	109	110	111	111	112	112	113	113	114	114	{ 215 { 216
	204	205	206	207	208	209	210	211	212	213	214	215	TOTAL MONTHS

CHRONOLOGICAL AGE

MA 17–0 / CA 14–0

CHRONOLOGICAL AGE — YEARS MONTHS	18 0	18 1	18 2	18 3	18 4	18 5	18 6	18 7	18 8	18 9	18 10	18 11	TOTAL MONTHS
10–00													120
10–01													121
10–02	170												122
10–03	168	169	170										123
10–04	167	167	168	169	170								124
10–05	165	166	167	167	168	169	170						125
10–06	164	165	165	166	167	167	168	169	170				126
10–07	162	163	164	165	165	166	167	167	168	169	170		127
10–08	161	162	162	163	164	165	165	166	167	167	168	169	128
10–09	160	160	161	162	162	163	164	165	165	166	167	167	129
10–10	158	159	160	160	161	162	162	163	164	165	165	166	130
10–11	157	158	158	159	160	160	161	162	162	163	164	165	131
11–00	156	156	157	158	158	159	160	161	161	162	163	163	132
11–01	154	155	156	157	157	158	159	159	160	161	161	162	133
11–02	153	154	155	155	156	157	157	158	159	159	160	161	134
11–03	152	153	154	154	155	156	156	157	158	158	159	160	135
11–04	151	152	152	153	154	154	155	156	156	157	158	158	136
11–05	150	151	151	152	153	153	154	155	155	156	157	157	137
11–06	149	150	150	151	152	152	153	153	154	155	155	156	138
11–07	148	149	149	150	150	151	152	152	153	154	154	155	139
11–08	147	147	148	149	149	150	151	151	152	153	153	154	140
11–09	146	146	147	148	148	149	150	150	151	151	152	153	141
11–10	145	145	146	147	147	148	149	149	150	150	151	152	142
11–11	144	144	145	146	146	147	148	148	149	149	150	151	143
12–00	143	143	144	145	145	146	147	147	148	148	149	150	144
12–01	142	143	143	144	144	145	146	146	147	147	148	149	145
12–02	141	142	142	143	144	144	145	145	146	147	147	148	146
12–03	140	141	142	142	143	143	144	145	145	146	146	147	147
12–04	139	140	141	141	142	142	143	144	144	145	145	146	148
12–05	139	139	140	140	141	142	142	143	143	144	145	145	149
12–06	138	138	139	140	140	141	141	142	143	143	144	144	150
12–07	137	138	138	139	139	140	141	141	142	142	143	144	151
12–08	136	137	137	138	139	139	140	140	141	142	142	143	152
12–09	136	136	137	137	138	138	139	140	140	141	141	142	153
12–10	135	135	136	137	137	138	138	139	139	140	141	141	154
12–11	134	135	135	136	136	137	138	138	139	139	140	140	155
TOTAL MONTHS	216	217	218	219	220	221	222	223	224	225	226	227	

MA 18–0 / CA 10–0

324

YEARS MONTHS	18 0	18 1	18 2	18 3	18 4	18 5	18 6	18 7	18 8	18 9	18 10	18 11	
13–00	133	134	134	135	136	136	137	137	138	138	139	140	156
13–01	133	133	134	134	135	135	136	137	137	138	138	139	157
13–02	133	133	134	134	135	135	136	137	137	138	138	139	158
13–03	132	132	133	134	134	135	135	136	136	137	137	138	159
13–04	131	132	132	133	133	134	134	135	136	136	137	137	160
13–05	131	132	132	133	133	134	134	135	136	136	137	137	161
13–06	130	131	131	132	133	133	134	134	135	135	136	136	162
13–07	130	130	131	131	132	132	133	134	134	135	135	136	163
13–08	130	130	131	131	132	132	133	134	134	135	135	136	164
13–09	129	129	130	131	131	132	132	133	133	134	134	135	165
13–10	128	129	129	130	130	131	132	132	133	133	134	134	166
13–11	128	129	129	130	130	131	131	132	133	133	134	134	167
14–00	127	128	129	129	130	130	131	131	132	132	133	134	168
14–01	127	127	128	128	129	130	130	131	131	132	132	133	169
14–02	127	127	128	128	129	130	130	131	131	132	132	133	170
14–03	126	127	127	128	128	129	129	130	131	131	132	132	171
14–04	125	126	127	127	128	128	129	129	130	130	131	132	172
14–05	125	126	127	127	128	128	129	129	130	130	131	132	173
14–06	125	125	126	126	127	128	128	129	129	130	130	131	174
14–07	124	125	125	126	126	127	127	128	129	129	130	130	175
14–03	124	125	125	126	126	127	127	128	129	129	130	130	176
14–09	124	124	125	125	126	126	127	127	128	128	129	129	177
14–10	123	124	124	125	125	126	126	127	127	128	128	129	178
14–11	123	124	124	125	125	126	126	127	127	128	128	129	179
15–00	122	123	123	124	124	125	126	126	127	127	128	128	180
15–01	122	122	123	123	124	124	125	125	126	126	127	127	181
15–02	122	122	123	123	124	124	125	125	126	126	127	127	182
15–03	121	121	122	122	123	123	124	124	125	126	126	127	183
15–04	120	120	121	122	122	123	123	124	124	125	125	126	184
15–05	120	120	121	122	122	123	123	124	124	125	125	126	185
15–06	119	120	120	121	121	122	122	123	123	124	124	125	186
15–07	118	119	119	120	120	121	122	122	123	123	124	124	187
15–08	118	119	119	120	120	121	121	122	123	123	124	124	188
15–09	118	118	119	119	120	120	121	121	122	122	123	123	189
15–10	117	117	118	118	119	119	120	120	121	121	122	123	190
15–11	117	117	118	118	119	119	120	120	121	121	122	123	191
	216	217	218	219	220	221	222	223	224	225	226	227	TOTAL MONTHS

CHRONOLOGICAL AGE

MA 18–0 / CA 13–0

YEARS MONTHS	18 0	18 1	18 2	18 3	18 4	18 5	18 6	18 7	18 8	18 9	18 10	18 11	
16–00 } 16–02 }	116	116	117	117	118	119	119	120	120	121	121	122	{ 192 { 194
16–03 } 16–07 }	116	116	117	117	118	119	119	120	120	121	121	122	{ 195 { 199
16–08 } 17–00 }	116	116	117	117	118	119	119	120	120	121	121	121	{ 200 { 204
17–01 } 17–05 }	116	116	117	117	118	119	119	120	120	120	121	121	{ 205 { 209
17–06 } 17–10 }	115	116	116	117	117	118	118	119	119	120	121	121	{ 210 { 214
17–11 } 18–00 }	115	116	116	117	117	118	118	119	119	120	121	121	{ 215 { 216
	216	217	218	219	220	221	222	223	224	225	226	227	TOTAL MONTHS

CHRONOLOGICAL AGE

CHRONOLOGICAL AGE YEARS / MONTHS	19 0	19 1	19 2	19 3	19 4	19 5	19 6	19 7	19 8	19 9	19 10	19 11	
10–00													120
10–01													121
10–02													122
10–03													123
10–04													124
10–05													125
10–06													126
10–07													127
10–08	170	170											128
10–09	168	169	170	170									129
10–10	167	167	168	169	170	170							130
10–11	165	166	167	167	168	169	169	170					131
11–00	164	165	165	166	167	167	168	169	169	170			132
11–01	163	163	164	165	165	166	167	167	168	169	169	170	133
11–02	161	162	163	163	164	165	165	166	167	167	168	169	134
11–03	160	161	162	162	163	164	164	165	166	166	167	168	135
11–04	159	160	160	161	162	162	163	164	164	165	166	166	136
11–05	158	158	159	160	160	161	162	162	163	164	164	165	137
11–06	157	157	158	159	159	160	161	161	162	163	163	164	138
11–07	156	156	157	158	158	159	159	160	161	161	162	163	139
11–08	154	155	156	156	157	158	158	159	160	160	161	161	140
11–09	153	154	155	155	156	156	157	158	158	159	160	160	141
11–10	152	153	154	154	155	155	156	157	157	158	159	159	142
11–11	151	152	153	153	154	154	155	156	156	157	157	158	143
12–00	150	151	151	152	153	153	154	154	155	156	156	157	144
12–01	149	150	150	151	152	152	153	153	154	155	155	156	145
12–02	148	149	150	150	151	151	152	153	153	154	154	155	146
12–03	148	148	149	149	150	151	151	152	152	153	154	154	147
12–04	147	147	148	148	149	150	150	151	151	152	153	153	148
12–05	146	146	147	148	148	149	149	150	151	151	152	152	149
12–06	145	146	146	147	147	148	149	149	150	150	151	151	150
12–07	144	145	145	146	147	147	148	148	149	149	150	151	151
12–08	143	144	144	145	146	146	147	147	148	149	149	150	152
12–09	142	143	144	144	145	145	146	147	147	148	148	149	153
12–10	142	142	143	143	144	145	145	146	146	147	147	148	154
12–11	141	142	142	143	143	144	144	145	146	146	147	147	155
	228	229	230	231	232	233	234	235	236	237	238	239	TOTAL MONTHS

MA 19–0 / CA 10–0

YEARS / MONTHS	19 0	19 1	19 2	19 3	19 4	19 5	19 6	19 7	19 8	19 9	19 10	19 11	
13–00	140	141	141	142	142	143	144	144	145	145	146	146	156
13–01	139	140	140	141	142	142	143	143	144	145	145	146	157
13–02	139	140	140	141	142	142	143	143	144	145	145	146	158
13–03	139	139	140	140	141	141	142	143	143	144	144	145	159
13–04	138	138	139	140	140	141	141	142	142	143	143	144	160
13–05	138	138	139	140	140	141	141	142	142	143	143	144	161
13–06	137	138	138	139	139	140	140	141	141	142	143	143	162
13–07	136	137	137	138	139	139	140	140	141	141	142	142	163
13–08	136	137	137	138	139	139	140	140	141	141	142	142	164
13–09	136	136	137	137	138	138	139	139	140	141	141	142	165
13–10	135	135	136	137	137	138	138	139	139	140	140	141	166
13–11	135	135	136	136	137	138	138	139	139	140	140	141	167
14–00	134	135	135	136	136	137	137	138	138	139	140	140	168
14–01	133	134	134	135	136	136	137	137	138	138	139	139	169
14–02	133	134	134	135	136	136	137	137	138	138	139	139	170
14–03	133	133	134	134	135	135	136	137	137	138	138	139	171
14–04	132	133	133	134	134	135	135	136	136	137	138	138	172
14–05	132	133	133	134	134	135	135	136	136	137	138	138	173
14–06	131	132	132	133	134	134	135	135	136	136	137	137	174
14–07	131	131	132	132	133	133	134	135	135	136	136	137	175
14–08	131	131	132	132	133	133	134	135	135	136	136	137	176
14–09	130	131	131	132	132	133	133	134	134	135	135	136	177
14–10	129	130	130	131	132	132	133	133	134	134	135	135	178
14–11	129	130	130	131	132	132	133	133	134	134	135	135	179
15–00	129	129	130	130	131	131	132	132	133	134	134	135	180
15–01	128	128	129	130	130	131	131	132	132	133	133	134	181
15–02	128	128	129	130	130	131	131	132	132	133	133	134	182
15–03	127	128	128	129	129	130	130	131	131	132	132	133	183
15–04	126	127	127	128	128	129	130	130	131	131	132	132	184
15–05	126	127	127	128	128	129	129	130	131	131	132	132	185
15–06	125	126	127	127	128	128	129	129	130	130	131	131	186
15–07	125	125	126	126	127	127	128	128	129	129	130	131	187
15–08	125	125	126	126	127	127	128	128	129	129	130	130	188
15–09	124	124	125	125	126	127	127	128	128	129	129	130	189
15–10	123	124	124	125	125	126	126	127	127	128	128	129	190
15–11	123	124	124	125	125	126	126	127	127	128	128	129	191
TOTAL MONTHS	228	229	230	231	232	233	234	235	236	237	238	239	TOTAL MONTHS

CHRONOLOGICAL AGE

YEARS MONTHS	19 0	19 1	19 2	19 3	19 4	19 5	19 6	19 7	19 8	19 9	19 10	19 11	
16–00 } 16–02 }	122	123	123	124	124	125	125	126	126	127	128	128	{ 192 { 194
16–03 } 16–07 }	122	123	123	124	124	125	125	126	126	127	128	128	{ 195 { 199
16–08 } 17–00 }	122	122	123	123	124	124	125	126	126	127	127	128	{ 200 { 204
17–01 } 17–05 }	122	122	123	123	124	124	125	126	126	127	127	128	{ 205 { 209
17–06 } 17–10 }	122	122	123	123	124	124	125	126	126	127	127	128	{ 210 { 214
17–11 } 18–00 }	122	122	123	123	124	124	125	126	126	127	127	128	{ 215 { 216
	228	229	230	231	232	233	234	235	236	237	238	239	TOTAL MONTHS

CHRONOLOGICAL AGE

YEARS MONTHS	20 0	20 1	20 2	20 3	20 4	20 5	20 6	20 7	20 8	20 9	20 10	20 11	
11–00													132
11–01													133
11–02	170												134
11–03	168	169	170										135
11–04	167	168	168	169	170	170							136
11–05	166	166	167	168	168	169	170	170					137
11–06	164	165	166	166	167	168	168	169	170				138
11–07	163	164	165	165	166	167	167	168	168	169	170		139
11–08	162	163	163	164	165	165	166	167	167	168	168	169	140
11–09	161	161	162	163	163	164	165	165	166	167	167	168	141
11–10	160	160	161	162	162	163	164	164	165	165	166	167	142
11–11	159	159	160	161	161	162	162	163	164	164	165	166	143
12–00	158	158	159	159	160	161	161	162	162	163	164	164	144
12–01	157	157	158	158	159	160	160	161	161	162	163	163	145
12–02	156	156	157	158	158	159	159	160	161	161	162	162	146
12–03	155	155	156	157	157	158	158	159	160	160	161	161	147
12–04	154	154	155	156	156	157	157	158	159	159	160	160	148
12–05	153	154	154	155	155	156	156	157	158	158	159	159	149
12–06	152	153	153	154	154	155	156	156	157	157	158	159	150
12–07	151	152	152	153	154	154	155	155	156	156	157	158	151
12–08	150	151	152	152	153	153	154	154	155	156	156	157	152
12–09	149	150	151	151	152	152	153	153	154	155	155	156	153
12–10	149	149	150	150	151	151	152	153	153	154	154	155	154
12–11	148	148	149	150	150	151	151	152	152	153	154	154	155
13–00	147	148	148	149	149	150	150	151	152	152	153	153	156
13–01	146	147	147	148	148	149	150	150	151	151	152	152	157
13–02	146	147	147	148	148	149	150	150	151	151	152	152	158
13–03	145	146	146	147	148	148	149	149	150	150	151	152	159
13–04	145	145	146	146	147	147	148	148	149	150	150	151	160
13–05	145	145	146	146	147	147	148	148	149	150	150	151	161
13–06	144	145	145	145	146	147	147	148	148	149	149	150	162
13–07	143	144	144	145	145	146	146	147	147	148	149	149	163
13–08	143	144	144	145	145	146	146	147	147	148	149	149	164
13–09	142	143	143	144	144	145	146	146	147	147	148	148	165
13–10	141	142	143	143	144	144	145	145	146	146	147	148	166
13–11	141	142	143	143	144	144	145	145	146	146	147	148	167
	240	241	242	243	244	245	246	247	248	249	250	251	TOTAL MONTHS

CHRONOLOGICAL AGE

MA 20–0 / CA 11–0

330

YEARS MONTHS	20 0	20 1	20 2	20 3	20 4	20 5	20 6	20 7	20 8	20 9	20 10	20 11	
14–00	141	141	142	142	143	143	144	145	145	146	146	147	168
14–01	140	140	141	142	142	143	143	144	144	145	145	146	169
14–02	140	140	141	142	142	143	143	144	144	145	145	146	170
14–03	139	140	140	141	141	142	143	143	144	144	145	145	171
14–04	139	139	140	140	141	141	142	142	143	144	144	144	172
14–05	139	139	140	140	141	141	142	142	143	144	144	144	173
14–06	138	138	139	139	140	141	141	142	142	143	143	144	174
14–07	137	138	138	139	139	140	140	141	142	142	143	143	175
14–08	137	138	138	139	139	140	140	141	142	142	143	143	176
14–09	136	137	138	138	139	139	140	140	141	141	142	142	177
14–10	136	136	137	137	138	139	139	140	140	141	141	142	178
14–11	136	136	137	137	138	139	139	140	140	141	141	142	179
15–00	135	136	136	137	137	138	138	139	139	140	140	141	180
15–01	134	135	135	136	136	137	138	138	139	139	140	140	181
15–02	134	135	135	136	136	137	138	138	139	139	140	140	182
15–03	134	134	135	135	136	136	137	137	138	138	139	139	183
15–04	133	133	134	134	135	135	136	136	137	137	138	139	184
15–05	133	133	134	134	135	135	136	136	137	137	138	139	185
15–06	132	132	133	133	134	135	135	136	136	137	137	138	186
15–07	131	132	132	133	133	134	134	135	135	136	136	137	187
15–08	131	132	132	133	133	134	134	135	135	136	136	137	188
15–09	130	131	131	132	132	133	133	134	134	135	136	136	189
15–10	129	130	130	131	132	132	133	133	134	134	135	135	190
15–11	129	130	130	131	131	132	133	133	134	134	135	135	191
16–00 / 16–02	129	129	130	130	131	131	132	132	133	133	134	134	192 / 194
16–03 / 16–07	129	129	130	130	131	131	132	132	133	133	134	134	195 / 199
16–08 / 17–00	128	129	129	130	131	131	132	132	133	133	134	134	200 / 204
17–01 / 17–05	128	129	129	130	131	131	132	132	133	133	134	134	205 / 209
17–06 / 17–10	128	129	129	130	131	131	132	132	133	133	134	134	210 / 214
17–11 / 18–00	128	129	129	130	131	131	132	132	133	133	134	134	215 / 216
TOTAL MONTHS	240	241	242	243	244	245	246	247	248	249	250	251	

CHRONOLOGICAL AGE

331

MA 20–0 / CA 14–0

YEARS → MONTHS ↓	21 0	21 1	21 2	21 3	20 4	21 5	21 6	21 7	21 8	21 9	21 10	21 11	TOTAL MONTHS
11–00													132
11–01													133
11–02													134
11–03													135
11–04													136
11–05													137
11–06													138
11–07													139
11–08	170												140
11–09	168	169	170										141
11–10	167	168	169	169	170								142
11–11	166	167	167	168	169	169	170						143
12–00	165	166	166	167	167	168	169	169	170				144
12–01	164	164	165	166	166	167	168	168	169	169	170		145
12–02	163	164	164	165	165	166	167	167	168	168	169	170	146
12–03	162	163	163	164	164	165	166	166	167	167	168	169	147
12–04	161	162	162	163	163	164	165	165	166	166	167	168	148
12–05	160	161	161	162	162	163	164	164	165	165	166	167	149
12–06	159	160	160	161	162	162	163	163	164	164	165	166	150
12–07	158	159	159	160	161	161	162	162	163	164	164	165	151
12–08	157	158	159	159	160	160	161	161	162	163	163	164	152
12–09	156	157	158	158	159	159	160	160	161	162	162	163	153
12–10	156	156	157	157	158	158	159	160	160	161	161	162	154
12–11	155	155	156	156	157	158	158	159	159	160	160	161	155
13–00	154	154	155	156	156	157	157	158	158	159	159	160	156
13–01	153	154	154	155	155	156	156	157	158	158	159	159	157
13–02	153	154	154	155	155	156	156	157	158	158	159	159	158
13–03	152	153	153	154	154	155	156	156	157	157	158	158	159
13–04	151	152	152	153	154	154	155	155	156	156	157	157	160
13–05	151	152	152	153	154	154	155	155	156	156	157	157	161
13–06	150	151	152	152	153	153	154	154	155	155	156	157	162
13–07	150	150	151	151	152	152	153	154	154	155	155	156	163
13–08	150	150	151	151	152	152	153	154	154	155	155	156	164
13–09	149	149	150	151	151	152	152	153	153	154	154	155	165
13–10	148	149	149	150	150	151	151	152	153	153	154	154	166
13–11	148	149	149	150	150	151	151	152	152	153	154	154	167
TOTAL MONTHS	252	253	254	255	256	257	258	259	260	261	262	263	

CHRONOLOGICAL AGE

MA 21–0 / CA 11–0

YEARS MONTHS	21 0	21 1	21 2	21 3	21 4	21 5	21 6	21 7	21 8	21 9	21 10	21 11	
14–00	148	148	148	149	149	150	151	151	152	152	153	153	168
14–01	147	147	148	148	149	149	150	150	151	151	152	153	169
14–02	147	147	148	148	149	149	150	150	151	151	152	153	170
14–03	146	146	147	147	148	149	149	150	150	151	151	152	171
14–04	145	146	146	147	147	148	148	149	149	150	150	151	172
14–05	145	146	146	147	147	148	148	149	149	150	150	151	173
14–06	144	145	145	146	147	147	148	148	149	149	150	150	174
14–07	144	144	145	145	146	146	147	147	148	148	149	150	175
14–08	144	144	145	145	146	146	147	147	148	148	149	150	176
14–09	143	143	144	145	145	146	146	147	147	148	148	149	177
14–10	142	143	143	144	144	145	146	146	147	147	148	148	178
14–11	142	143	143	144	144	145	146	146	147	147	148	148	179
15–00	142	142	143	143	144	144	145	145	146	146	147	147	180
15–01	141	141	142	142	143	143	144	144	145	146	146	147	181
15–02	141	141	142	142	143	143	144	144	145	146	146	147	182
15–03	140	140	141	141	142	143	143	144	144	145	145	146	183
15–04	139	140	140	141	141	142	142	143	143	144	144	145	184
15–05	139	140	140	141	141	142	142	143	143	144	144	145	185
15–06	138	139	139	140	140	141	141	142	142	143	144	144	186
15–07	137	138	138	139	140	140	141	141	142	142	143	143	187
15–08	137	138	138	139	140	140	141	141	142	142	143	143	188
15–09	137	137	138	138	139	139	140	140	141	141	142	142	189
15–10	136	136	137	137	138	138	139	139	140	141	141	142	190
15–11	136	136	137	137	138	138	139	139	140	140	141	142	191
16–00 / 16–02	135	135	136	136	137	138	138	139	139	140	140	141	192 / 194
16–03 / 16–07	135	135	136	136	137	138	138	139	139	140	140	141	195 / 199
16–08 / 17–00	135	135	136	136	137	138	138	139	139	140	140	141	200 / 204
17–01 / 17–05	135	135	136	136	137	138	138	139	139	140	140	141	205 / 209
17–06 / 17–10	135	135	136	136	137	138	138	139	139	140	140	141	210 / 214
17–11 / 18–00	135	135	136	136	137	138	138	139	139	140	140	141	215 / 216
	252	253	254	255	256	257	258	259	260	261	262	263	TOTAL MONTHS

CHRONOLOGICAL AGE

MA 21–0 / CA 14–0

CHRONOLOGICAL AGE YEARS MONTHS	22 0	22 1	22 2	22 3	22 4	22 5	22 6	22 7	22 8	22 9	22 10	22 11	
11–00													132
11–01													133
11–02													134
11–03													135
11–04													136
11–05													137
11–06													138
11–07													139
11–08													140
11–09													141
11–10													142
11–11													143
12–00													144
12–01													145
12–02	170												146
12–03	169	170											147
12–04	168	169	169	170									148
12–05	167	168	168	169	170	170							149
12–06	166	167	167	168	169	169	170						150
12–07	165	166	166	167	168	168	169	169	170				151
12–08	164	165	166	166	167	167	168	168	169	170	170		152
12–09	163	164	164	165	166	166	167	167	168	169	169		153
12–10	162	163	164	164	165	165	166	166	167	168	168		154
12–11	162	162	163	163	164	164	165	166	166	167	167		155
13–00	161	161	162	162	163	163	164	165	165	166	166		156
13–01	160	160	161	161	162	163	163	164	164	165	165		157
13–02	160	160	161	161	162	163	163	164	164	165	165		158
13–03	159	159	160	161	161	162	162	163	163	164	165		159
13–04	158	159	159	160	160	161	161	162	163	163	164		160
13–05	158	159	159	160	160	161	161	162	163	163	164		161
13–06	157	158	158	159	159	160	161	161	162	162	163		162
13–07	156	157	157	158	159	159	160	160	161	161	162		163
13–08	156	157	157	158	159	159	160	160	161	161	162		164
13–09	156	156	157	157	158	158	159	159	160	160	161		165
13–10	155	155	156	156	157	157	158	159	159	160	160		166
13–11	155	155	156	156	157	157	158	159	159	160	160		167
TOTAL MONTHS	264	265	266	267	268	269	270	271	272	273	274		

CHRONOLOGICAL AGE

YEARS MONTHS	22 0	22 1	22 2	22 3	22 4	22 5	22 6	22 7	22 8	22 9	22 10	22 11	
14–00	154	154	155	156	156	157	157	158	158	159	159		168
14–01	153	154	154	155	155	156	156	157	158	158	159		169
14–02	153	154	154	155	155	156	156	157	158	158	159		170
14–03	152	153	153	154	155	155	156	156	157	157	158		171
14–04	152	152	153	153	154	154	155	155	156	156	157		172
14–05	152	152	153	153	154	154	155	155	156	156	157		173
14–06	151	151	152	152	153	154	154	155	155	156	156		174
14–07	150	151	151	152	152	153	153	154	155	155	155		175
14–08	150	151	151	152	152	153	153	154	155	155	155		176
14–09	149	150	150	151	152	152	153	153	154	155	155		177
14–10	149	149	150	150	151	151	152	152	153	154	154		178
14–11	149	149	150	150	151	151	152	152	153	154	154		179
15–00	148	148	149	150	150	151	151	152	152	153	153		180
15–01	147	148	148	149	149	150	150	151	151	152	152		181
15–02	147	148	148	149	149	150	150	151	151	152	152		182
15–03	146	147	147	148	148	149	149	150	151	151	152		183
15–04	145	146	147	147	148	148	149	149	150	150	151		184
15–05	145	146	147	147	148	148	149	149	150	150	151		185
15–06	145	145	146	146	147	147	148	148	149	149	150		186
15–07	144	144	145	145	146	146	147	147	148	149	149		187
15–08	144	144	145	145	146	146	147	147	148	149	149		188
15–09	143	143	144	145	145	146	146	147	147	148	148		189
15–10	142	143	143	144	144	145	145	146	146	147	147		190
15–11	142	143	143	144	144	145	145	146	146	147	147		191
16–00 } 16–02 }	141	142	142	143	143	144	144	145	145	146	147		{ 192 { 194
16–03 } 16–07 }	141	142	142	143	143	144	144	145	145	146	147		{ 195 { 199
16–08 } 17–00 }	141	142	142	143	143	144	144	145	145	146	147		{ 200 { 204
17–01 } 17–05 }	141	142	142	143	143	144	144	145	145	146	147		{ 205 { 209
17–06 } 17–10 }	141	142	142	143	143	144	144	145	145	146	147		{ 210 { 214
17–11 } 18–00 }	141	142	142	143	143	144	144	145	145	146	147		{ 215 { 216
	264	265	266	267	268	269	270	271	272	273	274		TOTAL MONTHS

MA 22–0 / CA 14–0

Appendixes

Appendixes

APPENDIX A

CONVERSION TABLES

The following table of means and K values, used in establishing the tables for the various chronological ages in Part Three, will facilitate the transformation of conventional IQ scores which have already been obtained into the revised IQs.

To obtain a subject's deviation IQ from his conventional IQ, subtract the mean for his age group (given in the table) from his conventional ratio IQ score, multiply by the accompanying constant (K), and add 100.

$$\text{Revised IQ} = (\text{conventional IQ} - \text{mean})\,K^* + 100.$$

$$*K \text{ in the table is } \frac{16}{\text{SD}}.$$

Constants for Transforming Conventional IQs into Deviation IQs [1]

CA	Mean	K	CA	Mean	K	CA	Mean	K
2–00	102	.99	3–00	104	.88	4–00	102	.98
2–01	102	.97	3–01	104	.89	4–01	102	.99
2–02	103	.95	3–02	104	.89	4–02	101	1.00
2–03	103	.93	3–03	103	.90	4–03	101	1.01
2–04	103	.91	3–04	103	.91	4–04	101	1.02
2–05	103	.89	3–05	102	.92	4–05	101	1.03
2–06	103	.87	3–06	102	.92	4–06	101	1.04
2–07	103	.87	3–07	102	.93	4–07	101	1.04
2–08	104	.87	3–08	102	.94	4–08	101	1.05
2–09	104	.87	3–09	102	.95	4–09	101	1.06
2–10	104	.88	3–10	102	.96	4–10	100	1.07
2–11	104	.88	3–11	102	.97	4–11	100	1.08

[1] The constants in this table have been rounded off to two places. Hence IQs computed from them will differ occasionally by one point from those presented in Part Three.

Constants for Transforming Conventional IQs into Deviation IQs

CA	Mean	K	CA	Mean	K	CA	Mean	K
5–00	100	1.09	8–00	102	1.02	11–00	102	.91
5–01	100	1.09	8–01	102	1.02	11–01	102	.90
5–02	100	1.10	8–02	102	1.01	11–02	102	.90
5–03	100	1.11	8–03	102	1.01	11–03	102	.90
5–04	100	1.11	8–04	102	1.01	11–04	102	.90
5–05	100	1.12	8–05	102	1.00	11–05	102	.90
5–06	100	1.12	8–06	102	1.00	11–06	102	.90
5–07	100	1.12	8–07	102	.99	11–07	102	.89
5–08	100	1.12	8–08	102	.99	11–08	102	.89
5–09	100	1.12	8–09	102	.99	11–09	102	.89
5–10	100	1.12	8–10	103	.99	11–10	102	.89
5–11	100	1.12	8–11	103	.98	11–11	102	.89
6–00	100	1.11	9–00	103	.98	12–00	102	.88
6–01	100	1.11	9–01	103	.98	12–01	102	.88
6–02	100	1.11	9–02	103	.98	12–02	102	.88
6–03	100	1.10	9–03	103	.97	12–03	101	.88
6–04	100	1.10	9–04	103	.97	12–04	101	.88
6–05	100	1.10	9–05	103	.97	12–05	101	.89
6–06	100	1.09	9–06	103	.96	12–06	101	.89
6–07	100	1.09	9–07	103	.96	12–07	101	.89
6–08	100	1.08	9–08	103	.96	12–08	101	.89
6–09	100	1.08	9–09	103	.95	12–09	101	.89
6–10	101	1.08	9–10	103	.95	12–10	101	.89
6–11	101	1.07	9–11	103	.95	12–11	101	.89
7–00	101	1.07	10–00	103	.94	13–00	101	.89
7–01	101	1.06	10–01	103	.94	13–01	101	.89
7–02	101	1.06	10–02	103	.94	13–02	101	.89
7–03	101	1.06	10–03	103	.94	13–03	101	.89
7–04	101	1.05	10–04	103	.93	13–04	101	.89
7–05	101	1.05	10–05	103	.93	13–05	101	.89
7–06	101	1.04	10–06	103	.93	13–06	101	.90
7–07	102	1.04	10–07	102	.92	13–07	101	.90
7–08	102	1.04	10–08	102	.92	13–08	101	.90
7–09	102	1.03	10–09	102	.92	13–09	101	.90
7–10	102	1.03	10–10	102	.91	13–10	101	.90
7–11	102	1.02	10–11	102	.91	13–11	101	.90

Constants for Transforming Conventional IQs into Deviation IQs

CA	Mean	K	CA	Mean	K
14–00	101	.90	16–00	103	.95
14–01	101	.90	16–01	103	.95
14–02	101	.90	16–02	103	.95
14–03	101	.91	16–03	104	.96
14–04	101	.91	16–04	104	.96
14–05	101	.91	16–05	104	.96
14–06	101	.91	16–06	104	.96
14–07	101	.91	16–07	104	.96
14–08	101	.91	16–08	104	.98
14–09	101	.91	16–09	104	.98
14–10	101	.92	16–10	104	.98
14–11	101	.92	16–11	104	.98
15–00	102	.92	17–00	104	.98
15–01	102	.92	17–01	104	.98
15–02	102	.92	17–02	104	.98
15–03	102	.93	17–03	104	.98
15–04	102	.93	17–04	104	.98
15–05	102	.93	17–05	104	.98
15–06	102	.93	17–06	105	1.00
15–07	102	.94	17–07	105	1.00
15–08	103	.94	17–08	105	1.00
15–09	103	.94	17–09	105	1.00
15–10	103	.94	17–10	105	1.00
15–11	103	.95	17–11	105	1.00
			18–00	105	1.00

The following examples illustrate how to transform conventional IQ scores which have already been obtained into revised (deviation) IQs:

Example 1: CA 8–0, MA 8–0,
IQ 100
Revised IQ = (100–102) 1.02 + 100
= 98

Example 3: CA 12–0, MA 16–6,
IQ 138
Revised IQ = (138–102) .88 + 100
= 132

Example 2: CA 6–1, MA 4–0,
IQ 66
Revised IQ = (66–100) 1.11 + 100
= 62

Example 4: CA 12–0, MA 6–4,
IQ 53
Revised IQ = (53–102) .88 + 100
= 57

See also APPENDIX C, page 348.

Tests of the L–M Scale in 1937 and in 1960

		1960 Scoring Standard	1937 % +	1960 % +	Biserial Correlation 1937	Biserial Correlation 1960	Former Location
II,	1. Three-hole Form Board	1 +	79		.67		L, II, 1 M, II, 4
	2. Delayed Response	2 +	80		.43		M, II, 1
	3. Identifying Parts of Body	4 +	74	71	.74		L, II, 3 M, II, 3
	4. Block Building: Tower	4 +	67		.43		L, II, 4
	5. Picture Vocabulary	3 +	79	75	.69		L, II, 5 M, II, 5
	6. Word Combinations	±	77		.71		L, II, 6 M, II, 6
	A. Identifying Objects by Name	5 +	81	81	.70		M, II, 2
	Aver. of 6 Tests		76		.61		
II–6,	1. Identifying Objects by Use	3 +	72	71	.69	.55	L, II–6, 1
	2. Identifying Parts of Body	6 +	82	78	43	.63	L, II–6, 2
	3. Naming Objects	5 +	76		.41	.70	L, II–6, 3 M, II–6, 3
	4. Picture Vocabulary	8 +	76	79	.77	.61	L, II–6, 4 M, II–6, 4
	5. Repeating 2 digits	1 +	74	56	.62	.63	L, II–6, 5
	6. Obeying Simple Commands	2 +	68	79	.59	.56	M, II–6, 6
	A. Three-hole Form Board: rotated	2 +	72		.46	.51	L, II–6, 6
	Aver. of 6 Tests		75	73	.58	.61	
III,	1. Stringing Beads	4 +	73	76	.41	.47	L, III, 1
	2. Picture Vocabulary	10 +	69	67	.77	.64	L, III, 2 M, III, 2
	3. Block Building: Bridge	±	73	67	.53	.62	L, III, 3 M, III, 1
	4. Picture Memories	1 +	65	56	.61	.53	L, III, 4
	5. Copying a Circle	1 +	62	53	.35	.45	L, III, 5
	6. Drawing a Vertical Line	±	87	80	.46	.45	M, III, 4
	A. Repeating 3 digits	1 +	76	45	.72	.62	L, III, 6
	Aver. of 6 Tests		71	67	.52	.53	

Tests of the L–M Scale in 1937 and in 1960

		1960 Scoring Standard	1937 % +	1960 % +	Biserial Correlation 1937	Biserial Correlation 1960	Former Location	
III–6,	1. Comparison of Balls	3 +						
		5 +	79	79	.82	.62	M, III–6, 1	
	2. Patience: Pictures	1 +	66	63	.54	.55	M, III–6, 2	
	3. Discrimination: Animal							
	Pictures	4 +	69	59	.66	.66	M, III–6, 3	
	4. Response to Pictures:							
	Level I	2 +	75	65	.60	.50	M, III–6, 4	
	5. Sorting Buttons	±	81	79	.66	.65	M, III–6, 5	
	6. Comprehension I	1 +	72	60	.70	.62	L, III–6, 6	
	A. Comparison of Sticks	3 +						
		5 +	67	52	.81	.43	L, III–6, 3	
	Aver. of 6 Tests		74	69	.66	.60		
IV,	1. Picture Vocabulary	14 +	71	71	.68	.79	L, IV, 1	M, IV, 1
	2. Naming Objects from							
	Memory	2 +	79	51	.64	.53	L, IV, 2	
	3. Opposite Analogies I	2 +	62	67	.62	.56		M, IV, 3
	4. Pictorial Identification	3 +	77	79	.56	.88	L, IV, 4	
	5. Discrimination of Forms	8 +	64	79	.72	.75	L, IV, 5	
	6. Comprehension II	2 +	62	64	.78	.70	L, IV, 6	
	A. Memory for Sentences I	1 +					L, IV, A	
	Aver. of 6 Tests		69	68	.72	.75		
IV–6,	1. Aesthetic Comparison	3 +	76	63	.64	.44	L, IV–6, 1	
	2. Opposite Analogies I	3 +		70	.62	.83		M, IV, 3.
	3. Pictorial Similarities and							
	Differences I	3 +	71	78	.51	.69	L, IV–6, 3	
	4. Materials	2 +	79	65	.62	.56		M, IV–6, 5
	5. Three Commissions	3 +	71	53	.69	.65	L, IV–6, 5	
	6. Comprehension III	1 +	77	69	.63	.60		M, IV–6, 6
	A. Pictorial Identification	4 +	66		.66		L, IV–6, A	
	Aver. of 6 Tests		73	66	.62	.63		
V,	1. Picture Completion: Man	2 +	66	71	.48	.46	L, V, 1	
	2. Paper Folding: Triangle	±	82	81	.43	.54	L, V, 2	
	3. Definitions	2 +	86	79	.75	.57	L, V, 3	
	4. Copying a Square	1 +	67	62	.46	.62	L, V, 4	
	5. Pictorial Similarities and							
	Differences II	9 +	70	72	.64	.73		M, V, 3
	6. Patience: Rectangles	2 +	63	52	.49	.57		M, V, 4
	A. Knot	±	69		.49		L, V, A	M, V, A
	Aver. of 6 Tests		72	69	.54	.58		

		1960 Scoring Standard	1937 % +	1960 % +	Biserial Correlation 1937	Biserial Correlation 1960	Former Location	
VI,	1. Vocabulary	6 +	67	66	.65	.67	L, VI, 1	
	2. Differences	2 +	57	61	.52	.71		M, VI, 3
	3. Mutilated Pictures	4 +	67	76	.46	.65	L, VI, 3	
	4. Number Concepts	4 +	71	71	.56	.77	L, VI, 4	M, VI, 1
	5. Opposite Analogies II	3 +		60	.78	.67	L, IV–6, 6	
	6. Maze Tracing	2 +	81	82	.60	.69	L, VI, 6	
	A. Response to Pictures: Level II	2 +						M, VI, 4
	Aver. of 6 Tests		69	69	.59	.69		
VII,	1. Picture Absurdities I	4 +	59	58	.49	.64	L, VII, 1	M, VII, 3
	2. Similarities: Two Things	2 +	51	51	.71	.65	L, VII, 2	
	3. Copying a Diamond	1 +	69	68	.65	.62	L, VII, 3	
	4. Comprehension IV	3 +	59	73	.69	.48	L, VII, 4	
	5. Opposite Analogies III	2 +		62	.72	.62		M, VIII, 6
	6. Repeating 5 Digits	1 +	70	53	.60	.59	L, VII, 6	
	A. Repeating 3 Digits: Reversed	1 +						M, VII, 4
	Aver. of 6 Tests		62	61	.64	.60		
VIII,	1. Vocabulary	8 +	66	62	.75	.75	L, VIII, 1	
	2. Memory for Stories: The Wet Fall	5 +	67	62	.70	.64	L, VIII, 2	
	3. Verbal Absurdities I	3 +	58	49	.74	.75		M, VIII, 3
	4. Similarities and Differences	3 +	57	54	.75	.83	L, VIII, 4	
	5. Comprehension IV	4 +		65	.66	.69	L, VII–VIII, 5	
	6. Naming the Days of the Week	±	70	58	.61	.67		M, VIII, 4
	A. Problem Situations I	2 +	62	69	.50	.64		M, VIII, 5
	Aver. of 6 Tests		63	58	.70	.72		
IX,	1. Paper Cutting	1 +	64	57	.71	.62	L, IX, 1	
	2. Verbal Absurdities II	3 +	48	50	.73	.83	L, IX, 2	
	3. Memory for Designs I	1 +	50	44	.28	.60	L, IX, 3	
	4. Rhymes: New Form	3 +	56	65	.52	.62	L, IX, 4	
	5. Making Change	2 +	70	58	.62	.62	L, IX, 5	
	6. Repeating 4 Digits: Reversed	1 +	61	48	.58	.52	L, IX, 6	
	A. Rhymes: Old Form	2 +	59	51	.64	.69		M, IX, 5
	Aver. of 6 Tests		58	54	.58	.64		

Tests of the L–M Scale in 1937 and in 1960

		1960 Scoring Standard	1937 % +	1960 % +	Biserial Correlation 1937	Biserial Correlation 1960	Former Location	
X,	1. Vocabulary	11 +	59	54	.84	.77	L, X, 1	
	2. Block Counting	8 +	54	51	.34	.49		M, X, 1
	3. Abstract Words I	2 +	60	57	.60	.59		M, X, 4
	4. Finding Reasons I	2 +	63	67	.53	.59	L, X, 4	
	5. Word Naming	28	55	59	.46	.63	L, X, 5	
	6. Repeating 6 Digits	1 +	67	49	.45	.47	L, X, 6	
	A. Verbal Absurdities III	2 +	54	41	.77	.68		M, X, 3
	Aver. of 6 Tests		60	56	.53	.63		
XI,	1. Memory for Designs I	1½	43	42	.46	.61	L, XI, 1	
	2. Verbal Absurdities IV	2 +	65	50	.73	.73	L, XI, 2	
	3. Abstract Words II	3 +	58	63	.89	.84	L, XI, 3	
	4. Memory for Sentences II	1 +	50	55	.53	.67	L, XI, 4	
	5. Problem Situation II	±	65	69	.50	.44	L XI, 5	
	6. Similarities: Three Things	3 +	59	50	.61	.70	L, XI, 6	
	A. Finding Reasons II	2 +	54	58	.51	.64		M, XI, 1
	Aver. of 6 Tests		57	55	.62	.67		
XII,	1. Vocabulary	15 +	64	65	.79	.79	L, XII, 1	
	2. Verbal Absurdities II	4 +	62	76	.64	.77	L, XII, 2	
	3. Picture Absurdity II: The Shadow	±		58	.60	.51	L, XIV, 3	M, XIV, 2
	4. Repeating 5 Digits: Reversed	1 +	61	49	.48	.64	L, XII, 4	M, XII, 6
	5. Abstract Words I	3 +	68	54	.81	.85		M, XII, 4
	6. Minkus Completion I	3 +	61	67	.55	.72	L, XII, 6	M, XII, 3
	A. Memory for Designs II	±	65	67	.56	.46		M, XII, 1
	Aver. of 6 Tests		63	61	.64	.71		
XIII,	1. Plan of Search	±	54	55	.46	.47		M, XIII, 1
	2. Abstract Words II	4 +	68	65	.91	.72		M, XIII, 4
	3. Memory for Sentences III	1 +	67	63	.48	.65		M, XIII, 6
	4. Problems of Fact	2 +	69	60	.33	.53	L, XIII, 4	M, XIII, 5
	5. Dissected Sentences	2 +	66	57	.66	.79	L, XIII, 5	M, XIII, 3
	6. Copying a Bead Chain from Memory	±	64	63	.59	.70	L, XIII, 6	
	A. Paper Cutting	2 +	60	47	.56	.72	L, XIII, 3	
	Aver. of 6 Tests		65	60	.57	.64		

Tests of the L–M Scale in 1937 and in 1960

		1960 Scoring Standard	+ 1937 %	+ 1960 %	Biserial Correlation 1937	Biserial Correlation 1960	Former Location	
XIV,	1. Vocabulary	17 +	70	77	.89	.71	L, XIV, 1	
	2. Induction	±	53	58	.75	.76	L, XIV, 2	
	3. Reasoning I	±	51	44	.54	.70		M, XIV, 1
	4. Ingenuity I	1 +	62	58	.56	.74		M, XIV, 5
	5. Orientation: Direction I	3 +	65	65	.57	.57	L, XIV, 5	
	6. Reconciliation of Opposites	2 +	56	67	.61	.71		M, XIV, 6
	A. Ingenuity II	1 +	59	56	.57	.64	L, XIV, 4	
	Aver. of 6 Tests		60	61	.65	.70		
AA,	1. Vocabulary	20 +	50	55	.78	.86	L, AA, 1	
	2. Ingenuity I	2 +	47	45	.74	.70		M, AA, 2
	3. Differences between Abstract Words	2 +	54	44	.80	.80	L, AA, 3	
	4. Arithmetical Reasoning	2 +	55	48	.64	.61	L, AA, 4	
	5. Proverbs I	2 +	45	32	.75	.73		M, AA, 5
	6. Orientation: Direction II	4 +	53	57	.75	.82		M, AA, 6
	7. Essential Differences	2 +	42	48	.84	.82		M, AA, 7
	8. Abstract Words III	4 +	53	48	.90	.86		M, AA, 1
	A. Binet Paper Cutting	±	38	53	.53	.60		M, AA, 8
	Aver. of 8 Tests		50	47	.77	.77		
SAI,	1. Vocabulary	23 +	30	20	.76	.96	L, SAI, 1	
	2. Enclosed Boxes	4 +	39	37	.42	.61	L, SAI, 2	
	3. Minkus Completion II	2 +	39	19	.53	.58	L, SAI, 3	M, SAI, 1
	4. Repeating 6 Digits: • Reversed	1 +	39	43	.55	.55	L, SAI, 4	
	.5. Sentence Building	2 +	35	41	.86	.74		M, SAI, 5
	6. Essential Similarities	3 +	39	27	.66	.75	L, SAI, 6	
	A. Reconciliation of Opposites	4 +	30	51	.60	.60		M, SAI, 6
	Aver. of 6 Tests		37	31	.63	.70		
SAII,	1. Vocabulary	26 +	22	13	.68	.91	L, SAII, 1	
	2. Finding Reasons III	2 +	34	27	.37	.72	L, SAII, 2	
	3. Proverbs II	1 +	33	48	.61	.83		M, SAII, 1
	4. Ingenuity I	3 +	34	24	.43	.73		M, SAII, 2
	5. Essential Differences	3 +	28	24	.56	.81		M, SAII, 3
	6. Repeating Thought of Passage I	±	26	37	.71	.82	L, SAII, 6	M, SAII, 6
	A. Codes	1 +	38	41	.55	.82		M, SAII, 5
	Aver. of 6 Tests		29	29	.56	.80		

Tests of the L–M Scale in 1937 and in 1960

		1960 Scoring Standard	+ 1937 %	+ 1960 %	Biserial Correlation 1937	1960	Former Location
SAIII,	1. Vocabulary	30 +	13	8	.71	.90	L, SAIII, 1
	2. Proverbs III	2 +	22	12	.66	.42	M, SAIII, 1
	3. Opposite Analogies IV	2 +	20	26	.71	.84	L, SAIII, 3
	4. Orientation: Direction III	2 +	24	33	.57	.80	M, SAIII, 3
	5. Reasoning II	±	8	30	.62	.48	L, SAIII, 5
	6. Repeating Thought of Passage II	±	16	27	.77	.44	M, SAIII, 6
	A. Opposite Analogies V	2 +	9	6	.69	.63	M, SAIII, 5
Aver. of 6 Tests			17	23	.67	.64	

Quotient

APPENDIX C

Corrected CA Divisors for Ages beyond 13–00*

CA	Corrected CA Divisor (months)	CA	Corrected CA Divisor (months)	CA	Corrected CA Divisor (months)
13–00	156	14–00	164	15–00	172
13–01	157	14–01	165	15–01	173
13–02	157	14–02	165	15–02	173
13–03	158	14–03	166	15–03	174
13–04	159	14–04	167	15–04	175
13–05	159	14–05	167	15–05	175
13–06	160	14–06	168	15–06	176
13–07	161	14–07	169	15–07	177
13–08	161	14–08	169	15–08	177
13–09	162	14–09	170	15–09	178
13–10	163	14–10	171	15–10	179
13–11	163	14–11	171	15–11	179

For CAs 16–00 to 18–00 and all adult CAs, corrected CA divisor is 180 months.

* This table of corrected CA divisors for ages beyond 13–00 is adapted from one that appeared in *Measuring Intelligence*, the manual which accompanied the 1937 revision of the Stanford-Binet scales (page 31).

The corrected CA Divisors should be used in determining conventional and deviation IQs of subjects beyond age 13–00 and of adults whose MA scores yield IQs not included in the Pinneau tables. The Pinneau Revised IQ Tables include mental age scores in the range from 2–00 to 22–10 inclusive, and the chronological age range extends from age 2–00 to age 18–00 inclusive. Within the limits of these ages IQs between 30 and 170 have been included. To estimate IQs *not* included in the tables, a conventional or ratio IQ is first obtained, using the appropriate CA divisor, then the DIQ is computed by use of the formula on page 339.[1]

[1] For a further discussion of the conversion of Stanford-Binet conventional IQs into Stanford-Binet deviation IQs see Pinneau, Samuel R., *Changes in Intelligence Quotient, Infancy to Maturity,* Boston: Houghton Mifflin, 1961, especially Appendix C and Appendix D.

In order to point out a difficulty inherent in the deviation IQ technique which affects such extreme deviations at the lower end of the scale, examples have been chosen which illustrate the method of computing DIQs of adolescent and adult subjects of extremely low mental ability — IQs below minus four standard deviations.

The deviation IQ is a more accurate measure of relative standing than was the ratio IQ of the earlier revisions. If, however, for individuals of extremely low intelligence level mental growth ceases at an earlier age than for the average and the superior person, such a measure will not adequately reflect consistency in rate of mental growth. There is some evidence, based on retests of institutionalized mental defectives over a period of years, that this is the case. A decrease in IQ on retest after mental growth has ceased would not indicate a corresponding loss of ability, or loss in number of items passed. Pending further analysis of mental growth patterns of individuals of such low ability levels, scores on the test, in this case mental age scores, may be of greater value for practical purposes than a measure of standing relative to the general population of comparable age.

EXAMPLES

1. Subject at CA 15–00 (MA 2–06) obtained ratio IQ of 17. What is his deviation IQ?
   MEAN at CA 15–00 is 102, K is .92.
   $DIQ = [(17 - 102) \times .92] + 100$
   $= (-85 \times .92) + 100$
   $= -78.2 + 100$
   $DIQ = 22$

2. Subject at CA 16–00 (MA 2–06) obtained ratio IQ of 17. What is his deviation IQ?
   MEAN at CA 16–00 is 103, K is .95.
   $DIQ = [(17 - 103) \times .95] + 100$
   $= (-86 \times .95) + 100$
   $= -81.7 + 100$
   $DIQ = 18$

3. Subject at CA 18–00 (MA 2–06) obtained ratio IQ of 17. What is his deviation IQ?
   MEAN at CA 18–00 is 105, K is 1.00.
   $DIQ = [(17 - 105) \times 1.00] + 100$
   $= (-88 \times 1.00) + 100$
   $= -88 + 100$
   $DIQ = 12$

4. Subject at CA 28–00 (MA 2–06) obtained ratio IQ of 17. What is his deviation IQ?
   MEAN at CA 28–00 is 105, K is 1.00.
   $DIQ = [(17 - 105) \times 1.00] + 100$
   $= (-88 \times 1.00) + 100$
   $= -88 + 100$
   $DIQ = 12$

References

1. Anastasi, A. *Psychological Testing.* New York: Macmillan, 1954.
2. Bayley, N. "Consistency and Variability in the Growth of Intelligence from Birth to Eighteen Years," *J. Genet. Psychol.*, 1949, 75, 165–196.
3. Bayley, N. "On the Growth of Intelligence," *Amer. Psychologist*, 1955, 10, 805–818.
4. Bradway, K. P. "IQ Constancy on the Revised Stanford-Binet from the Preschool to the Junior High School Level," *J. Genet. Psychol.*, 1944, 65, 197–217.
5. Bradway, K. P. "Predictive Value of Stanford-Binet Preschool Items," *J. Educ. Psychol.*, 1945, 36, 1–16.
6. Bradway, K. P., Thompson, C. W., and Cravens, R. B. "Preschool IQs after Twenty-five Years," *J. Educ. Psychol.*, 1958, 49, 278–281.
7. Cole, R., "An Item Analysis of the Terman-Merrill Revision of the Binet Tests," *Brit. J. Psychol., Statist. Sect.*, 1948, 1, 137–151.
8. Cronbach, L. J. *Essentials of Psychological Testing.* New York: Harper, 1949.
9. Department of Commerce, Bureau of the Census, *1950 United States Census of Population*, Bulletin P-C-1. Washington: U. S. Gov. Printing Office.
10. Frandsen, A. N., McCullough, B. R., and Stone, D. R. "Serial versus Consecutive Order Administration of the Stanford-Binet Intelligence Scales," *J. Consult. Psychol.*, 1950, 14, 316–320.

11. Hebb, D. O. *Organization of Behavior*. New York: Wiley, 1949.
12. Hofstaetter, P. R. "The Changing Composition of 'Intelligence': A Study of the t-Technique," *J. Genet. Psychol.*, 1954, 85, 159–164.
13. Honzik, M. P., Macfarlane, J. W., and Allen, L. "The Stability of Mental Test Performance Between Two and Eighteen Years," *J. Exper. Educ.*, 1948, 17, 309–324.
14. Hutt, M. L. "A Clinical Study of 'Consecutive' and 'Adaptive' Testing with the Revised Stanford-Binet," *J. Consult. Psychol.*, 1947, 11, 93–103.
15. Jones, L. V. "A Factor Analysis of the Stanford-Binet at Four Age Levels," *Psychometrika*, 1949, 14, 299–331.
16. McNemar, Q. *The Revision of the Stanford-Binet Scale*. Boston: Houghton Mifflin, 1942.
17. Merrill, M. A. "The Significance of IQs on the Revised Stanford-Binet Scales," *J. Educ. Psychol.*, 1938, 29, 641–651.
18. Pintner, R., Dragositz, A., and Kushner, R. "Supplementary Guide for the Revised Stanford-Binet Scale" (Form L), *Appl. Psychol. Monogr.*, 1944, No. 3. p. 135.
19. Sontag, L. W., Baker, C. T., and Nelson, V. L. "Mental Growth and Personality Development: A Longitudinal Study," *Monogr. Soc. Res. in Child Developm.*, 23, 68, No. 2, 1958. p. 143.
20. Terman, L. M. *The Measurement of Intelligence*. Boston: Houghton Mifflin, 1916.
21. Terman, L. M. and Merrill, M. A. *Measuring Intelligence*. Boston: Houghton Mifflin, 1937.
22. Watson, R. I. *The Clinical Method in Psychology*. New York: Harper, 1951.
23. Wright, C. "A Modified Procedure for the Abbreviated Stanford-Binet in Determining the Intelligence of Mental Defectives," *Amer. J. Ment. Def.*, 1942, 47, 178–184.

·HIJ−R−73210/698765

Index

Abbreviated tests, 61–62
Abstract Words I (X, 3), 95–96; scoring, 181–183; (XII, 5), 101; scoring, 197; II (XI, 3), 98; scoring, 189–192; (XIII, 2), 102–103; scoring, 201; III (AA, 8), 112; scoring, 215–218; tests of, 345, 346
Abstract Words, Differences between (AA, 3), 110; scoring, 208–210; tests of, 346
Absurdities, Picture, I (VII, 1), 86; scoring, 151–153; II (XII, 3), 100; scoring, 196–197; tests of, 344, 345
Absurdities, Verbal, I (VIII, 3), 90; scoring, 162–164; II (IX, 2), 92–93; scoring, 169–174; (XII, 2), 100; scoring, 196; III (X, A), 97; scoring, 185–187; IV (XI, 2), 97–98; scoring, 188–189; tests of, 344–346
Accelerated performance, 5
Adaptive testing, 48
Administration of tests, 6, 22, 25; general directions, 45–62; order of giving tests, 48–49; specific instructions, 67–121

Aesthetic Comparison (IV–6, 1), 79; scoring, 138; tests of, 343
Age, basal, 60–61
Age norms, 8
Age scales, 13, 25, 26
Alternative tests, 62
Ambiguous responses, 49–50, 55
Analogies, Opposite, I (IV, 3), 77; scoring, 136; (IV–6, 2), 79; scoring, 138; II (VI, 5), 85; scoring, 148–149; III (VII, 5), 87–88; scoring, 159–160; IV (SA III, 3), 119–120; scoring, 229–230; V (SA III, A), 121; scoring, 232; tests of, 343–347
Anastasi, Anne, 19, 35
Animal Pictures, Discrimination of (III–6, 3), 74; scoring, 133; tests of, 343
Appraisal of responses, 55–56
Arithmetical Reasoning (AA, 4), 110–111; scoring, 210; tests of, 346
Assessment groups, 1950s, 21
Attention, necessity of obtaining, 54
Average ability, 17

Balls, Comparison of (III–6, 1), 74; *scoring*, 132; *tests of*, 343

Basal age, 60–61

Bayley, Nancy, vi, 22 n., 27, 35

Bead Chain, Copying (XIII, 6), 104; *scoring*, 204; *tests of*, 345

Beginning the testing, 59

Benvenista, Frances, 23

Berkeley Growth studies, 17, 20, 27

Binet, A., 6, 8, 12

Binet Paper Cutting (AA, A), 112–113; *scoring*, 218; *tests of*, 346

Biserial correlations, 33–34, 35, 342–347

Block Building: Tower (II, 4), 68; *scoring*, 126; Bridge (III, 3), 72; *scoring*, 130; *tests of*, 342

Block Counting (X, 2), 95; *scoring*, 181; *tests of*, 345

Box, Enclosed, problem of (SA I, 2), 113–114; *scoring*, 218; *tests of*, 346

Bradway, K. P., 17, 27

Bridge, building with blocks (III, 3), 72; *scoring*, 130; *tests of*, 342

Buttons, Sorting (III–6, 5), 75; *scoring*, 134; *tests of*, 343

California Institute of Child Welfare, 22

Ceiling (maximal) level, 60–61

Change, Making (IX, 5), 94; *scoring*, 179; *tests of*, 344

Chi square probabilities, 24

Chronological age and mental age, 8, 11, 14, 25

Circle, Copying (III, 5), 73; *scoring*, 130–131; *tests of*, 342

Clinician, competent, 52, 54; validity of, 13

Codes (SA II, A), 118; *scoring*, 227; *tests of*, 346

Cole, R., 34

Commands, Simple, Obeying (II–6, 6), 71; *scoring*, 130; *tests of*, 342

Commissions, Three (IV–6, 5), 80; *scoring*, 139; *tests of*, 343

Comparison, Aesthetic (IV–6, 1), 79; *scoring*, 138; *tests of*, 343

Comparison of Balls (III–6, 1), 74; *scoring*, 132; *tests of*, 343

Comparison of Sticks (III–6, A), 76; *scoring*, 135; *tests of*, 343

Completion, Minkus, I (XII, 6), 101; *scoring*, 197–198; II (SA I, 3), 114; *scoring*, 218–219; *tests of*, 345, 346

Completion, Picture of Man (V, 1), 81; *scoring*, 140–141; *tests of*, 343

Comprehension items, 24–25

Comprehension I (III–6, 6), 75; *scoring*, 135; II (IV, 6), 78; *scoring*, 137; III (IV–6, 6), 80; *scoring*, 139–140; IV (VII, 4), 87; *scoring* 157–159; (VIII, 5), 90–91; *scoring*, 167; *tests of*, 343, 344

Connotations of words, new, 50

Conventional IQ, 6

Copying a Bead Chain from Memory (XIII, 6), 104; *scoring*, 204; *tests of*, 345

Copying a Circle (III, 5), 73; *scoring*, 130–131; *tests of*, 342

Copying a Diamond (VII, 3), 87; *scoring*, 155–157; *tests of*, 344

Copying a Square (V, 4), 82; *scoring*, 143–144; *tests of*, 343

Counting Blocks (X, 2), 95; *scoring*, 181; *tests of*, 345

Cravens, R. B., 17, 27

Cronbach, Lee J., 13

Crozier, Louise, 23 n.

Curves showing per cents passing, 29–32

Cutting Paper (IX, 1), 92; *scoring*,

168–169; (XIII, A), 104–105; scoring, 204; tests of, 344, 345

Cutting Paper, Binet (AA, A), 112–113; scoring, 218; tests of, 346

Days of the Week, Naming (VIII, 6), 91; scoring, 167; tests of, 344

Definitions (V, 3), 81–82; scoring, 142–143; tests of, 343

Delayed Response (II, 2), 67–68; scoring, 126; tests of, 342

Designs, Memory for, I (IX, 3), 93; scoring, 174–177; (XI, 1), 97; scoring, 187; II (XII, A), 102; scoring, 198–199; tests of, 344, 345

Deviation IQ, 27, 28; method of computing, 28, 339

Diamond, Copying (VII, 3), 87; scoring, 155–157; tests of, 344

Differences (VI, 2), 84; scoring, 145–146; tests of, 344

Differences, Essential (AA, 7), 112; scoring, 213–215; (SA II, 5), 117; scoring, 226; tests of, 346

Differences, Similarities and (VIII, 4), 90; scoring, 164–167; Pictorial, I (IV–6, 3), 79; scoring, 138; II (V, 5), 82; scoring, 144; tests of, 343–344

Differences between Abstract Words (AA, 3), 110; scoring, 208–210; tests of, 346

Digits, Repeating of: 2 (II–6, 5), 70–71; scoring, 130; 3 (III, A), 73; scoring, 131; 5 (VII, 6), 88; scoring, 160; 6 (X, 6), 96–97; scoring, 185; tests of, 342, 344–345

Digits, Reversed, Repeating of: 3 (VII, A), 88; scoring, 160; 4 (IX, 6), 94; scoring, 179; 5 (XII, 4), 101; scoring, 197; 6 (SA I, 4),

114; scoring, 219; tests of, 344–346

Direction, Orientation: I (XIV, 5), 107–108; scoring, 206; II (AA, 6), 111; scoring, 213; III (SA III, 4), 120; scoring, 230; tests of, 346, 347

Discrimination of Animal Pictures (III–6, 3), 74; scoring, 133; tests of, 343

Discrimination of Forms (IV, 5), 78; scoring, 137; tests of, 343

Dissected Sentences (XIII, 5), 103–104; scoring, 203–204; tests of, 345

Distribution, of per cents passing, 29–32; of successes, 59–60

Drawing tests, 54

Drawing a Vertical Line (III, 6), 73; scoring, 131; tests of, 342

Duration of test, 58

Economic status of subjects. See Socioeconomic status

"Eight Best Tests" (English children), 34

Enclosed Box Problem (SA I, 2), 113–114; scoring, 218; tests of, 346

Environment, test, 56–57

Essential Differences (AA, 7), 112; scoring, 213–215; (SA II, 5), 117; scoring, 226; tests of, 346

Essential Similarities (SA I, 6), 115; scoring, 221–222; tests of, 346

Examiner, competent, 52, 54; validity of, 13

Factor analyses, 34–35

Fatigue, 58

Fels Research Institute studies, 16, 17, 20

Finding Reasons I (X, 4), 96; *scoring*, 183–185; II (XI, A.), 99; *scoring*, 195–196; III (SA II, 2), 116; *scoring*, 222–224; *tests of*, 345, 346

Folding Paper, Triangle (V, 2), 81; *scoring*, 142; *tests of*, 343

Form Board, Three-Hole (II, 1), 67; *scoring*, 126; Rotated (II–6, A), 71; *scoring*, 130; *tests of*, 342

Forms, Discrimination of (IV, 5), 78; *scoring*, 137; *tests of*, 343

Frame of reference, for classifying IQ, 17–19; working within, 47

Galton, F., 25
Grade placement, 23, 36, 37
Group factors, 35
Groups, Assessment, 1950s, 21

"Halo" effect, 55
Harris, D. 22 n.
Hebb, D. O., 19
Hofstaetter, P., 35
Hutt, M. L., 48

Identification, Pictorial (IV, 4), 77; *scoring*, 136; (IV–6, A), 80–81; *scoring*, 140; *tests of*, 343

Identifying Objects by Name (II, A), 69; *scoring*, 129; *tests of*, 342

Identifying Objects by Use (II–6, 1), 69–70; *scoring*, 129; *tests of*, 342

Identifying Parts of the Body (II, 3), 68; *scoring*, 126; (II–6, 2), 70; *scoring*, 129; *tests of*, 342

Induction (XIV, 2), 106; *scoring*, 204–205; *tests of*, 346

Ingenuity I (XIV, 4), 107; *scoring*, 206; (AA, 2), 109–110; *scoring*, 208; (SA II, 4), 117; *scoring*, 226;

II (XIV, A), 108–109; *scoring*, 208; *tests of*, 346

Intelligence, in action, 6; general, 8, 12; unevenness of, 60. *See also* IQ

Internal consistency, 24, 25, 33

Iowa Child Welfare Research Station, 22

IQ, first use of, 6; frame of reference for classifying, 17–19; reliability in 1937 standardization sample, 10; revised tables of, 27–28, 64, 257–335; variability in, 14–15, 26–27, 38–39.
See also Conventional IQ *and* Deviation IQ

Item selection, 1937 revision, 9; 1960 revision, 21

Jones, L., 35

K values for converting IQs, 339–341
Knot (V, A), 83; *scoring*, 144; *tests of*, 343

L and M Forms, 1937 revision, 7–12, 14, 16, 20, 21, 28, 32, 33–34, 37

L–M Form, 1960 revision, 12–39; *tests of*, 342–347

Macfarlane Guidance study, 17
Making Change (IX, 5), 94; *scoring*, 179; *tests of*, 344
Man, Picture Completion: (V, 1), 81; *scoring*, 140–141, *tests of*, 343
"Manipulation of Symbols", 35
Manipulative tests, 34
Materials (IV–6, 4), 79; *scoring*, 138–139; *tests of*, 343
Materials, test, 54, 57–58
Maximal (ceiling) level, 60–61
Maze Tracing (VI, 6), 85–86; *scoring*, 149; *tests of*, 344

McCandless, Boyd, 22 n.
McNemar, Quinn, vi, 10, 15, 19, 26, 34, 35, 38
Meaning of words, standard, Vocabulary Test, 50
Mecia, Elizabeth, 23
Merrill, Maud, 17, 22, 34 n.
Memories, Picture (III, 4), 72–73; scoring, 130; tests of, 342
Memory, Copying a Bead Chain from (XIII, 6), 104; scoring, 204; tests of, 345
Memory, Naming Objects from (IV, 2), 76–77; scoring, 135; tests of, 343
Memory for Designs I (IX, 3), 93; scoring, 174–179; (XI, 1), 97; scoring, 187; II (XII, A), 102; scoring, 198–199; tests of, 344, 345
Memory for Sentences I (IV, A), 78; scoring, 137; II (XI, 4), 98; scoring, 192; III (XIII, 3), 103; scoring, 201; tests of, 343, 345
Memory for Stories: The Wet Fall (VII, 2), 89; scoring, 160–162; tests of, 344
Memory tests, 34, 35, 49
Mental age and chronological age, 8, 11, 14, 25
Mental age scores, 5, 6; computation of, 62–64; fluctuation in, 10–11
Mental deficiency, 17
Mental faculties theory, 6
Mental growth beyond age sixteen, 26, 27
Minkus Completion I (XII, 6), 101; scoring, 197–198; II (SA I, 3), 114; scoring, 218–219; tests of, 345, 346
Minnesota Institute of Child Welfare, 22

Motivation, 53–54
Mutilated Pictures (VI, 3), 84; scoring, 146–148; tests of, 344

Naming the Days of the Week (VIII, 6), 91; scoring, 167; tests of, 344
Naming Objects (II–6, 3), 70; scoring, 129; tests of, 342
Naming Objects from Memory (IV, 2), 76–77; scoring, 135; tests of, 343
Naming Words (X, 5), 96; scoring, 185; tests of, 345
Negativism, 54
Non-verbal tests, 34
Normal (average) ability, 5, 17
Number Concepts (VI, 4), 84–85; scoring, 148; tests of, 344

Obeying Simple Commands (II–6, 6), 71; scoring, 130; tests of, 342
Observers, exclusion of, 53, 57
Occupational groups, 23, 36, 37
Opposite Analogies I (IV, 3), 77; scoring, 136; (IV–6, 2), 79; scoring, 138; II (VI, 5), 85; scoring, 148–149; III (VII, 5), 87–88; scoring, 159–160; IV (SA, III, 3), 119–120; scoring, 229–230; V (SA III, A), 121; scoring, 232; tests of, 343, 344, 347
Opposites, Reconciliation of (XIV, 6), 108; scoring, 206–208; (SA I, A), 115; scoring, 222; tests of, 346
Order of giving tests, 48–49
Orientation: Direction I (XIV, 5), 107–108; scoring, 206; Direction II (AA, 6), 111; scoring, 213; Direction III (SA III, 4), 120; scoring, 230; tests of, 346, 347

Paper Cutting (IX, 1), 92; *scoring,* 168–169; (XIII, A), 104–105; *scoring,* 204; *tests of,* 344, 345

Paper Cutting, Binet (AA, A), 112–113; *scoring,* 218; *tests of,* 346

Paper Folding: Triangle (V, 2), 81; *scoring,* 142; *tests of,* 343

Parents, presence of, during testing, 53, 57

Patience: Pictures (III–6, 2), 74; *scoring,* 132–133; Rectangles (V, 6), 82–83; *scoring,* 144; *tests of,* 343

Performance tests, 8, 34

"Persistence", 35

Pictorial Identification (IV, 4), 77; *scoring,* 136; (IV–6, A), 80–81; *scoring,* 140; *tests of,* 343

Pictorial Similarities and Differences I (IV–6, 3), 79; *scoring,* 138; II (V, 5), 82; *scoring,* 144; *tests of,* 343

Pictorial tests, 34

Picture Absurdities I (VII, 1), 86; *scoring,* 151–153; II (XII, 3), 100; *scoring,* 196–197; *tests of,* 344, 345

Picture Completion: Man (V, 1), 81; *scoring,* 140–141; *tests of,* 343

Picture Memories (III, 4), 72–73; *scoring,* 130; *tests of,* 342

Picture Vocabulary (II, 5), 68; *scoring,* 126–128; (II–6, 4), 70; *scoring,* 130; (III, 2), 72; *scoring,* 130; (IV, 1), 76; *scoring,* 135; *tests of,* 342, 343

Pictures, Animal, Discrimination of (III–6, 3), 74–75; *scoring,* 133; *tests of,* 343

Pictures, Patience: (III–6, 2), 74; *scoring,* 132–133; *tests of,* 343

Pictures, Mutilated (VI, 3), 84; *scoring,* 146–148; *tests of,* 344

Pictures, Response to, Level I (III–6, 4), 75; *scoring,* 133–134; Level II (VI, A), 86; *scoring,* 149–151; *tests of,* 343, 344

Pinneau Revised IQ Tables, 64, 257–335

Pintner, R., 46 n.

Plan of Search (XIII, 1), 102; *scoring,* 200–201; *tests of,* 345

Preschool testing, 22–23, 53–54

Problem, Enclosed Box (SA I, 2), 113–114; *scoring,* 218; *tests of,* 346

Problem Situations I (VIII, A), 91; *scoring,* 167–168; II (XI, 5), 98–99; *scoring,* 192; *tests of,* 344, 345

Problems of Fact (XIII, 4), 103; *scoring,* 201–203; *tests of,* 345

Profile analysis, 13

Promotions, social, 36

Proverbs I (AA, 5), 111; *scoring,* 211–213; II (SA II, 3), 116; *scoring,* 224–225; III (SA III, 2), 119; *scoring,* 227–229; *tests of,* 346, 347

Questions, repetition of, 49; of success or failure, 52; unnecessary, 50; varying form of, 45

Rapport, importance of, 50–52

Reasoning I (XIV, 3), 106–107; *scoring,* 205–206; II (SA III, 5), 120; *scoring,* 230; *tests of,* 346, 347

Reasoning, Arithmetical (AA, 4), 110–111; *scoring,* 210; *tests of,* 346

Reasons, Finding, I (X, 4), 96; *scoring,* 183–185; II (XI, A), 99; *scoring,* 195–196; III (SA II, 2), 116; *scoring,* 222–224; *tests of,* 345, 346

Reconciliation of Opposites (XIV, 6), 108; *scoring,* 206–208; (SA

I, A), 115; *scoring, 222; tests of,* 346

Rectangles, Patience: (V, 6), 82–83; *scoring,* 144; *tests of,* 343

Regional differences, 24

Reliability, 1937 Revision, 10–11; 1960 Revision, 30, 342–347

Repeating 2 Digits (II–6, 5), 70–71; *scoring,* 130; *tests of,* 342

Repeating 3 Digits (III, A), 73; *scoring,* 131; *tests of,* 342

Repeating 3 Digits Reversed (VII, A), 88; *scoring,* 160; *tests of,* 344

Repeating 4 Digits Reversed (IX, 6), 94; *scoring,* 179; *tests of,* 344

Repeating 5 Digits (VII, 6), 88; *scoring,* 160; *tests of,* 344

Repeating 5 Digits Reversed (XII, 4), 101; *scoring,* 197; *tests of,* 345

Repeating 6 Digits (X, 6), 96–97; *scoring,* 185; *tests of,* 345

Repeating 6 Digits Reversed (SA I, 4), 114; *scoring,* 219; *tests of,* 346

Repeating Thought of Passage I: Value of Life (SA II, 6), 117–118; *scoring,* 226–227; II: Tests (SA III, 6), 120–121; *scoring,* 231–232; *tests of,* 346, 347

Repetition of questions, 49

Re-scoring, 58

Responses to Pictures: Level I (III–6, 4), 75; *scoring,* 133–134; Level II (VI, A), 86; *scoring,* 149–151; *tests of,* 343–344

Retarded performance, 5

Retests, correlations between, 16–17

Reversed Digits, Repeating: 3 (VII, A), 88; *scoring,* 160; 4 (IX, 6), 94; *scoring,* 179; 5 (XII, 4), 101; *scoring,* 197; 6 (SA I, 4), 114; *scoring,* 219; *tests of,* 344, 345, 346

Rhymes: New Form (IX, 4), 93; *scoring,* 178–179; Old Form (IX, A), 94; *scoring,* 180–181; *tests of,* 344

Roberts, Katherine, 22 n.

Robinson, H., vi

Robinson, Nancy, vi

Sampling, 6, 8, 9–10, 17, 21–22

Scattering of successes, 59–60, 61

School, grade placement in, 23, 36, 37

School testing, 21–22

Schummers, John, 23

Scoring of tests, 6, 55, 56, 58, 62–64, 125–253; clarification of principles of, 25; standards for, 125, 342–347

Search, Plan of (XIII, 1), 102; *scoring,* 200–201; *tests of,* 345

"Sensori-motor Alertness", 35

Sentence Building (SA I, 5), 114–115; *scoring,* 219–220; *tests of,* 346

Sentences, Dissected (XIII, 5), 103–104; *scoring,* 203–204; *tests of,* 345

Sentences, Memory for, I (IV, A), 78; *scoring,* 137; II (XI, 4), 98; *scoring,* 192; III (XIII, 3), 103; *scoring,* 201; *tests of,* 343, 345

Serial testing, 48

Sex differences in IQs, 38

Similarities, Essential (SA I, 6), 115; *scoring,* 221–222; *tests of,* 346

Similarities: Two Things (VII, 2), 86–87; *scoring,* 154–155; *tests of,* 344

Similarities: Three Things (XI, 6), 99; *scoring,* 192–194; *tests of,* 345

Similarities and Differences (VIII, 4), 90; *scoring,* 164–167; *tests of,* 344

Similarities and Differences, Pictorial, I (IV–6, 3), 79; *scoring,* 138; II (V, 5), 82; *scoring,* 144; *tests of,* 343

Simple Commands, Obeying (II–6, 6), 71; *scoring,* 130; *tests of,* 342

Sisk, Augusta, 23 n.

Social promotions, 36

Socioeconomic status, 24

Sorting Buttons (III–6, 5), 75; *scoring,* 134; *tests of,* 343

Square, Copying (V, 4), 82; *scoring,* 143–144; *tests of,* 343

Standard deviations, 26–27, 28, 38

Standard meaning of words, Vocabulary Test, 50

Standard procedure, necessity for, 47–49, 54, 58–59

Standardization, 6, 7, 9–10, 17, 18, 19, 28

Stanford-Binet revisions: 1916 revision, 5–6; 1937 revision, 7–12; 1960 revision, 12–40; abilities sampled by, 33–34; changes in, 25–28; essential features of, 20–25; factor analyses of items in, 34–35; preliminary considerations, 12–20; shifts in item difficulty in, 28–32; stratified samples in, 35–39; validity and reliability of, 32–33. *See also* Administration of tests, Pinneau Revised IQ Tables, *and* Scoring of tests

Starred tests, 61

Sticks, Comparison of (III–6, A), 76; *scoring,* 135; *tests of,* 343

Stories, Memory for: The Wet Fall (VIII, 2), 89; *scoring,* 160–162; *tests of,* 344

Stratified samples, 23, 24, 28, 32, 35–39

Stringing Beads (III, 1), 71–72; *scoring,* 130; *tests of,* 342

Subjects, selection of, 1937 revision, 9–10; selection of, 1960 revision, 21–22; unselected, 29

Subtests, description of, 67–121; determining difficulty of, 31–32; limiting of, 20; retained in 1937 revision, 8; scoring of, *see* Scoring of tests; selection of for L-M scale, 21, 40

Successes, questions about, 52; scattering of, 59–60, 61

Superior ability, 19

Surroundings during testing, 56–57

Terman, Lewis M., v, vi

Terman-Merrill method of abbreviating tests, 61, 62

Testing-room, 56–57

Thomas, Shirley, 23 n.

Thompson, C. W., 17, 27

Thought of Passage, Repeating, I: Value of Life (SA II, 6), 117–118; *scoring,* 226–227; II: Tests (SA III, 6), 120–121; *scoring,* 231–232; *tests of,* 346, 347

Three Commissions (IV–6, 5), 80; *scoring,* 139; *tests of,* 343

Three-Hole Form Board (II, 1), 67; *scoring,* 126; *tests of,* 342

Three-Hole Form Board: Rotated (II–6, A), 71; *scoring,* 130; *tests of,* 342

Time requirements, 58

Tower, building with blocks (II, 4), 68; *scoring,* 126; *tests of,* 342

Triangle, paper folding: (V, 2), 81; *scoring,* 142; *tests of,* 343

Validity, of the clinician, 13; factorial, 35; test, 6, 9, 11–12, 13, 32–33

Validity coefficient for English children, Form L, 34

Variability, IQ, 14–15, 26–27, 38–39; in mental age group, 10–11

Verbal Absurdities I (VIII, 3), 90; *scoring,* 162–164; II (IX, 2), 92–93; *scoring,* 171–174; (XII, 2), 100; *scoring,* 196; III (X, A), 97; *scoring,* 185–187; IV (XI, 2), 97–98; *scoring,* 188–189; *tests of,* 344, 345

Verbal tests, 33–34

Verbatim recording, 58

Vertical Line, Drawing (III, 6), 73; *scoring,* 131–132; *tests of,* 342

Vocabulary, *scoring,* 232–253; (VI, 1), 83–84; *scoring,* 145; (VIII, 1) 88–89; *scoring,* 160; (X, 1), 94–95; *scoring,* 181; (XII, 1), 99–100; *scoring,* 196; (XIV, 1), 105; *scoring,* 204; (AA, 1), 109; *scoring,* 208; (SA I, 1), 113; *scoring,* 218; (SA II, 1), 115–116; *scoring,* 222; (SA III, 1), 119; *scoring,* 227; *tests of,* 344–347

Vocabulary, Picture, *scoring,* 126–128; (II, 5), 68; *scoring,* 128; (II–6, 4), 70; *scoring,* 130; (III, 2),

72; *scoring,* 130; (IV, 1), 76; *scoring,* 135; *tests of,* 342, 343

Watson, R. I., 62

Week, Naming the Days of (VIII, 6), 91; *scoring,* 167; *tests of,* 343

Winder, C. L., vi

Word Combinations (II, 6), 69; *scoring,* 129; *tests of,* 342

Word Naming (X, 5), 96; *scoring,* 185; *tests of,* 345

Words, Abstract, I (X, 3), 95–96; *scoring,* 181–183; (XII, 5), 101; *scoring,* 197; II (XI, 3), 98; *scoring,* 189–192; (XIII, 2), 102–103; *scoring,* 201; III (AA, 8), 112; *scoring,* 215–218; *tests of,* 345, 346

Words, Abstract, Differences between (AA, 3), 110; *scoring,* 208–210; *tests of,* 346

Words, Naming (X, 5), 96; *scoring,* 185; *tests of,* 345

Wright, C., 61, 62

NOTES

NOTES